Psychological Evaluation in Psychotherapy

Psychological Evaluation in Psychotherapy

Ten Case Histories

Leonard Blank

AldineTransaction
A Division of Transaction Publishers
New Brunswick (U.S.A.) and London (U.K.)

First paperback printing 2009

This book is printed on acid-free paper that meets the American National Standard for Permanence of Paper for Printed Library Materials.

Library of Congress Catalog Number: 2009025664
ISBN: 978-0-202-36321-9
Printed in the United States of America

Library of Congress Cataloging-in-Publication Data

Blank, Leonard.
Psychological evaluation in psychotherapy : ten case histories / Leonard Blank.
p. cm.
Originally published: London : Allen and Unwin, 1966.
Includes bibliographical references.
ISBN 978-0-202-36321-9
1. Psychotherapy--Evaluation--Case studies. 2. Personality tests. I. Title.

RC465.B59 2009
616.89'14--dc22

2009025664

To

BERNICE, JORDAN, RONA

and LYDA

CONTENTS

FOREWORD

In his more meditative moments, when he has the time for them, the psychodiagnostician is sometimes assailed by the feeling that he is a member of a vanishing species, a relic from the days when psychological testing served as the hallmark of the clinical psychologist. During the palmy days following the development of projective techniques and their eager utilization by the clinical psychologist it was tacitly assumed that a breakthrough had been achieved, that the dream alone was no longer the royal road to the unconscious. The examiner now believed that he could evaluate the patient's personality in depth, delineate and order its components at many levels, expose its psychodynamics and psychoeconomics, and make predictions that would forewarn and arm the therapist for his struggles with the patient's conflicts.* This hope was reinforced by accounts of remarkable agreement between "blind" Rorschach evaluations and the clinical picture, the detection of significant hidden aspects of the patient's life and problems, and the fulfillment of predictions of things to come in the therapy.

Projective techniques were to psychology what the "wonder drugs" were to psychiatry, and in the first flush of success no thought was given to the possibility of disconcerting side-effects. The side-effects came from research studies that soon offered evidence refuting the widely promulgated claims for the efficacy of projective techniques and that led a respected figure in the field to state that "there is nothing in the literature to encourage reliance on Rorschach interpretations."† Meehl's cogent advocacy of a cookbook approach to diagnosis and personality delineation aroused resentment, anxiety and uncertainty among adherents to the ideographic approach who, by their very nature, regarded actuarially derived methods with skepticism.

Those who regard the projectively oriented clinician as a prime example of egregious intransigence might suspect that he has sus-

---

* Brown, F. Contribution of the psychodiagnostician to problems of therapy. *Amer. J. Orthopsych.*, 1960, 30, 811-818.

† Cronbach, L. J. Assessment of Individual Differences. *Annual Review of Psychology*, 7:173, 1956.

pended his thinking functions and joined Tertullian in the conclusion "credo quia absurdum." They could not be more mistaken. The psychodiagnostician's evaluations and conclusions are constantly subjected to the harsh light of psychological reality in hospital, clinic and private practice. If they consistently diverged from external criteria, at the time of testing and later in therapy, the usefulness of the psychodiagnostician would have been questioned long since, and his functions as a professional would by now be only an incident in the history of psychology. The fact that the demand for competent examiners is far greater than the supply suggests that they have demonstrated their worth and have something of value to offer.

The psychodiagnostician is not immune to the need for systematic and rigorous validation, but he tends to be more receptive to clinical validation on a case-by-case basis for practical purposes than he is to experimental validation. Unfortunately, he thus becomes dependent upon the referring therapist for validative feedback and lacks sufficient data for the construction of a reliable concordance.

Dr. Blank is a unique and harmonious blend of therapist and psychodiagnostician, doubling in brass so to speak and demonstrating an enthusiasm for both disciplines that enables him to make a significant contribution. So far as I know, there has been no comprehensive and detailed presentation of treatment sessions with correspondingly supportive test data. What is most gratifying in Dr. Blank's work and what sets it apart from other approaches is the emphasis he places upon the living treatment session rather than upon case history material abstracted from the therapy. One sees the gradual unfolding of the patient's conflicts as these, in turn, are related to test data. It is a rare privilege for the psychodiagnostician to witness this unrolling scroll of the patient's personality. In most instances statements in the psychological report pertain to information about the patient that is not yet available to the therapist and concerning which no conclusions relevant to agreement or disagreement can be reached.

The difficulties encountered in the pursuit of supportive validation for projective test findings can be traced to various sources. Among these may be listed the therapist's sole interest in nosological information, his wish to obtain confirmation of his clinical impression, or the desire to know whether the patient is a suitable prospect for treatment. It is seldom that the therapist is taught to regard the psychological report as a road map or itinerary of the terrain he is to traverse with the patient. It is also unfortunately true that many psychologists trained in the use of psychodiagnostic techniques and engaged in the practice of psychotherapy abandon the use of tests for diagnostic and psychodynamic evaluation; they fail to formulate a therapeutic plan, and often embark upon "blind" therapy without psychological charts, compass or sextant.

Dr. Blank's comprehensive approach establishes a model that is not only ideal from the standpoint of the conscientious clinician, but lends itself admirably to the practical needs of diagnostician and therapist. In this book he takes the reader step-by-step from sophisticated inferences derived from the patient's history, to testable hypotheses and postulates distilled from his tests, and from there to confirmation in successive treatment sessions. Sometimes puzzling and even anxiety-provoking (for the therapist as well as for the patient) occurrences in the treatment session become meaningful in the light of test data, as Dr. Blank so cogently demonstrates, and facilitate a therapeutic process that might otherwise bog down and be dismissed as "resistance" without an understanding of causation.

The demonstration of valid correspondences between test and treatment data, as exemplified in this work, provides the psychodiagnostician with a firmer foundation for the formulation of immediate and long-range predictive statements about the patient. These can be spelled out in more specific terms and with maximum relevance to the therapeutic process.

The reader will find in this book not only information but clinical wisdom as well. It will be invaluable for training advanced students in clinical psychology programs and for psychology interns, and it should occupy a prominent place among the workbooks of the practicing psychodiagnostician and therapist.

Fred Brown

Mount Sinai Hospital
New York

PREFACE

When I was a clinical psychology trainee in hospital settings, I was so dedicated to psychological testing that I was convinced that any therapist who considered doing psychotherapy without test data was ignorant or even unethical. When next I found myself in a mental hygiene clinic doing primarily psychotherapy and with ample resources for psychological reports, I had little inclination to call for them; and this turnabout was experienced by many of my colleagues. Another phase was introduced with the advent of my private practice. Many referrals were made to me for diagnostic evaluation and, subsequently, were seen by me in psychotherapy. Here, then, was a psychotherapist trained to make deductions from test data, possessing such data, and faced frequently with the quandaries presented by psychotherapy. So, whenever I was puzzled by the therapeutic process, I reread my report and ploughed through the raw test material.

To my edification, the psychological evaluation often clarified the events that transpired in therapy and frequently provided cues for therapeutic intervention. Again, I became, and am, dedicated to the value of reports for therapy, this time not from slavish devotion but because of practical application.

The purpose of this text is to enable the reader to judge whether psychological evaluations elucidate the material presented by patients in psychotherapy. The reader may determine what implications are conveyed when test items and constellations are related to the thinking, fantasy, and behavior expressed by the patient in the therapeutic context. Ten cases are presented. Although many character disorders are included rather than "classical" neuroses, by virtue of their varying psychodynamic orientations, the cases illustrate the more frequently encountered clinical problems. At every point, the writer attempts to relate the therapeutic process, in detail, to the psychological evaluation and to its constituent test elements.

For several years, I have wrestled with the ideas and material presented in this book. Often they appeared unamanageable like an unruly group of children. Perhaps that is why my wife, Bernice, with her nursery school experience and a couple of enthusiastic children of her own, has been so helpful in suggesting the necessary discipline and structure. Of course, she also served in every other conceivable capacity, from revising contents to retrieving lost data.

Nick Nichols and Virginia Erdman also served as baby sitters for this text. They read, reread, and then read again great stacks of material. With infinite patience, they teased out pertinent ideas, scolded distortions in the manuscript and generally nursed along a rather colicky report.

Readers courageous, and all with valuable recommendations for a meaningful format, were Samuel Kutash, Gordon Derner, Lou Levine, and Molly Harrower.

Then came the undaunted proofers with quick eyes and ready pencils: Cyril and Violet Franks, Harry and Shirley Stein, and Mary Bigelow.

Finally, my thanks to Donna Wilkinson, who typed the bulk of the manuscript with an enthusiasm beyond the call of duty.

LEONARD BLANK

Introduction:

PROCEDURES AND PREMISES

The ten patients presented in this book were referred to the author for psychological evaluation and each of them subsequently was seen by him in individual psychotherapy. The cases, mostly personality disorders, are felt to be representative of the problems encountered by the practitioner. Cases were selected on the basis of diagnostic representation and available data—psychological reports and psychotherapy notes both made by the author, who then evaluated the interrelationship between testing and therapy. The success of the case and the ideal quality of the report were not considerations for inclusion. In fact, the preponderant number of referrals were primarily for diagnostic evaluation, and the reports were not geared towards prognosis in psychotherapy. The advantage of such case selection is that it offers an opportunity to determine generally the relatedness of diagnostic reports to psychotherapy. If cases had been selected because they represented either ideal reports or model therapy, the generality of the results would have been seriously impaired.

REPORTS & PSYCHOTHERAPY

A report serves the function of communicating information—the evaluation of personality features. The reason for referral dictates the report's format, that of answering the immediate questions that prompted the report. The report also serves as a record for future unspecified readers. The communicative function demands a meaningful interaction between the writer and the particular reader in terms of language as well as message.

A psychological report has value only if it contributes to an appraisal something additional, more comprehensive, with greater clarity, or more quickly than would be possible in the absence of test data. The application of a psychological evaluation to psychotherapy is meaningful if it leads to conclusions that otherwise could be derived only after many hours of therapeutic contact.

The valid utilization of a report is not necessarily predicated on direct prediction of behavior. Rather it serves to measure, describe, and analyze psychological processes with *explanation* as its primary goal. Prediction of behavior, even when probabilistic, is determined by a far wider scope of data than is encompassed by a psychological evaluation; it is heavily influenced by fortuitous circumstances. Cogent explanation provided in a meaningful report does facilitate generalization and hypotheses. Knowledge of what, how, and why a person thinks and feels the way he does—at least a sampling of such knowledge as presented in an evaluation—provides inferences relevant to how this person has behaved in the past and may act in the future. The issue of validity, however, rests on the calibre of information communicated, whereas the accuracy of inferences, deductions, and predictions are dependent on the ability of the users of this information. If the psychological report aids in clarifying the patient's behavior in psychotherapy, or provides cues for intervention on the therapist's part, then the report has valid use. The latter instance approximates prediction. For example, if the therapist asks certain questions, the patient may uncover particular material which may remove emotional blocks and ultimately lead to different behavior. What makes this fall short of prediction is the therapist's hypothesizing attitude and his readiness to shift ground and approach from another direction.

The data upon which an evaluation is based is only a limited sampling of the patient's thinking and behavior. The test battery, therefore, must be constructed to produce a comprehensive, multidimensional, and multilevel appraisal of his psychodynamics [4, p. 263]. By *multidimensional* is meant the various phases of a person's life or expressions of his personality: personal, interpersonal, emotional, intellectual, physical, vocational, social, and so forth. By *multilevel* we mean the levels or layers of personality functioning denoting such concepts as the superficial or the persona; the more intimate, less exposed facets; and the deepest, most basic, primitive, ingrained personality features. The Freudian position would express these levels in "topographical" terms as conscious, pre-conscious, and unconscious [10]. Leary conceptualizes *multilevel* in terms of public, personal, and private communication [15].

Whatever battery of techniques is employed ought to be geared to these three perspectives of comprehensive, multidimensional, and multilevel data gathering. Each technique, indeed every test item, is to be viewed as material that generates as many hypothetical threads as possible. When a hypothesis is isolated, not corroborated by other evidence, it may be considered a loose thread to be discarded, at least temporarily. Only when there is substantiation and corroboration from other tests or data, is it felt permissible to weave these threads into the fabric of a report.

The importance of hypothesizing and speculating cannot be overly stressed. Although one must contend with the peril of projecting oneself into the material and finding what one is looking for, the alternate hazard of inability to tolerate ambiguity, of waiting for ironclad proof leads to a sterile report. The clinician must use himself as an instrument by responding to his reactions to the patient and test material as diagnostic clues. He must use his stockpile of empirical knowledge, and his capacity to do what no computer or mathematical formula can do—and that is the resolution of contradictory evidence and postulation of *new* behavior. Evidence converging from several sources suggests to the clinician substantiation of hypotheses; conflicting data suggest to him either incorrect assumptions or the reflection of the patient's conflicts.

So, any one test in isolation (or, for that matter, an entire battery) serves its function only to the degree that it generates hypotheses for a clinician as it interacts with his experience and talent. Therefore, one clinician may favor the Rorschach, another the MMPI. Without doubt the current "standard" battery eventually will be altered drastically.* As long as there is a clinician, however, rather than a diagnostic computer, the *techniques* of relating test data to a dynamic description of the patient's psychological processes will remain basically unchanged. The battery employed in this book is the Rorschach, Thematic Apperception Test (TAT), Draw-A-Person (DAP), Minnesota Multiphasic Personality Inventory (MMPI), Interpersonal Check-list (ICL), Wechsler Adult Intelligence Scale (WAIS), and a diagnostic interview. The rationale for inclusion of these techniques is presented below as well as brief descriptions and illustrations of how they are utilized in the cases included in this book. Other techniques, of course, could be substituted.

The language of the reports included in this volume as well as the particular information communicated were determined by the sources of referral. Eight of the ten reports were designed primarily

* New tests will be added: in this text ICL is relatively new. Old tests will be modified: recently the Holtzman [11] version of the Rorschach and chromatic adaptation of figure drawing have been introduced. [8]

for non-psychiatric physicians with lay knowledge of psychological principles. The other two were directed towards readers sophisticated in psychodynamics, and consequently contained more technical terms and depth interpretations.

Rorschach

This technique often provides the skeletal framework in a personality evaluation. Beck sees the Rorschach as gauging three dimensions of personality—intellectual activity, inner psychological functioning and fantasy living [2]. The Rorschach appears to be valuable in shedding light on unconscious and symbolic aspects of the personality. Often it spotlights creative abilities and the utilization of imagination. Emotional control, conceptual ability, and interpersonal percepts may be revealed by this test. Rorschach users too often have stressed pathology, but coping mechanisms and resiliency of mental functioning also may be indicated. In this text, its adaptive features will be underscored in the spirit of Shafer, Rapaport, and the later writings of Klopfer. [2, 4, 12 and 13, chs. 14, 18, 19, 20, 21, 22.]

The mechanics of scoring and interpreting the Rorschach may be found in the above sources. In the illustrations that follow and in the Rorschach protocols referred to in chapters 1-10 of this book, the location, determinant, content, and stylism employed in a response are welded into a hypothesis (in the form of a commentary) of the needs, motives, and conflicts that contributed to the response. The author's commentary is colored by his psychoanalytic orientation and his predilection for content association. Other workers, from varying orientations, place more stress on the formal Rorschach features, interpreting the psychogram (graph based on frequency of these formal features), and on analysis of the visual percepts (form, color, shading, movement, location, size, degree of correspondence between objective blot shape and subjective image) [17]. These latter approaches are not minimized in importance when the author presents his own view which, at any rate, is heavily influenced by similar considerations.

The following examples illustrate how test data and the author's comments appear in each of the cases presented in chapters 1 - 10.*

* For those unfamiliar with Rorschach symbols and terminology a simple explanation may be helpful.

The card designation is in Roman numerals and may follow the name of the test, or may appear anywhere in the test data. The arabic number in parentheses is the number of the response made to a given card. Examiner's questions appear in

Case of Amorality: Rorschach III, (1): Very much two ladies facing one another. Inquiry: Ladies with bosoms and high heels. Look wind-swept, therefore, spinning, hold purses, Look like blown from behind. (Why?) Direction of ink, smooth outer line, skirt blown forward.

Comment: Excellently conceived women (human movement) indicating creativity and sociability (color and form) but with much tension (inanimate movement, leaf in the wind). Woman nurturant (or wish for same). (Nurturant because emphasis on bosoms.)

Case of Orality, Rorschach III: Reminds me of a skeleton-like mask. Inquiry: ∨ Skeleton, blood on side, two eyes, frame of head, brains, blood on sides.

Comment: Hysterical (reaction to color and blood.) Judgment fails, impulsive (response not defined by form).

Thematic Apperception Test (TAT)

This technique often supplies the flesh and sinews of the personality picture. Where the Rorschach may illuminate the internal conflicts, the TAT can spotlight the projection of these conflicts externally. Here, the test taker reveals how he thinks in words and even in syntax. Moods, actual techniques of dealing with people, emotions, fantasies, familial and social relationships, and the like, are often delineated in this test. Bellak reviews various procedures in interpreting the TAT [1, 185-229]. These techniques vary from Murray's analysis of the Need-Press Method (where every sentence is analyzed as to the needs of the hero and the environmental forces or press he is exposed to) to Rapaport's analysis of the formal characteristics of the story structure and of the story content.

Bellak believed that since, ". . . the strength of the TAT lies in its ability to elicit the content and dynamics of interpersonal relationships and the psychodynamic patterns, my method of interpretation . . . is primarily concerned with these dimensions and only to a small extent with the formal characteristics. . . .

"The main thing to remember in the interpretation of the TAT is the following: the TAT pictures are best seen psychologically as a series of social situations and interpersonal relations. Instead of responding to real people in real situations, the subject is responding to people in the pictures, which he imagines in certain social situations. Since he is under less constraint of conventionality or reality,

---

parentheses. Comment: refers to interpretive comments by the author. ∧ ∨ > <: The points of these symbols indicate the position of the top of the card when the response was made by the patient. (Q): This symbol denotes a question asked by the examiner.

his responses are more likely to depict his inner feelings. By this means we get at the contemporary patterns of his social behavior and may be able to infer the genesis of these patterns. Interpretation is the process of finding a common denominator in the contemporary and genetic behavior patterns of a person. . . .

"Among other things, this definition of interpretation implies what cannot be emphasized too much, particularly for the beginner: hardly ever should a diagnostic statement be made on a datum revealed in only one story. Impressions gleaned in one instance can be considered a very tentative inference only, for which one must try to find corroboration in other stories or some source of information external to the TAT. *A repetitive pattern is the best assurance that one does not deal with an artifact. . . .*" (Emphasis is his.) [*Ibid*, pp. 195-196]

The writer follows Bellak's procedure closely as he did with Rorschach in not stressing formal analyses, with the added emphasis of liberal questioning of the story teller about the themes and motives of the story characters. The reader is referred to other sources [12, 13, 18] for more comprehensive treatment of the TAT.

EXAMPLES

Case of Orality: TAT 1*: Looks like a young kid like to go out and play. Mother makes him play or father. Looks disgusted—like me. Does not want to play but parents forcing. Mad they're forcing him, not going to play for meanness. Ends up in future years playing the violin.

Comment: Disgusted and angry over conforming to parental demands. Rebelliousness ends in conformity.

Case of Hypochondria: TAT 8BM: Looks like someone operating on someone. Must be during underground movement. Looks like gun down here. Underground movement. Can't figure this (figure in foreground). Must be thieves or someone shot in burglary and they're removing bullet and this other man looking on to see that they're not interrupted. Cannot tell what outcome with they're digging into abdomen but think he survives. [Technical explanation by her demonstrating why it is not a serious wound.] Such an odd face. (Q) Don't like face, like someone with abnormal glandular, out of proportion.

Comment: Wrongdoing leads to abnormal surgery. Patient complains of multitudinous physical symptoms in interview. This in turn leads to successful outcome but feeling of being wrong glandularly. Serious projective thinking (odd face and abnormal glands).

* Numbers and letters refer to TAT card numbers.

Draw-A-Person (DAP)

Human figure drawings can present a multilevel picture of self-concept in its relationship to sexual and social role. Its particular contribution to a battery is a non-verbal index of conceptualization, one which is especially sensitive to the presence of distorted judgment (or its reflection in motoric performance) that may not have permeated to the verbal level. DAP also can be useful in indicating the body image concept of the patient [2, 3, 8, 16, and 24].

Since the idiosyncratic representation of figures and their *qualitative* aspect play so prominent a part in the interpretations of drawings, formal considerations (such as size, ratio of size of body parts to each other, position on paper, line pressure, line consistency, features included or excluded) have largely been relegated to qualitative interpretations by examiners, and research has been most controversial with this technique. In a sense, the uniqueness of each drawing and its proclivity for symbolic representation make it one of the most projective of techniques. Therefore, while formalized scoring systems have been suggested [8], interpretations approaching associations to, or symbolic explanation of, drawings or to parts of drawings seem to be the method of choice for many workers. Nevertheless, the author has found that colleagues, some not particularly familiar with DAP, can easily understand and communicate with him in the terms found in the examples below and in the DAP protocols in chapters 1-10. It is most important in the interpretation of drawings to have a theoretical frame of reference and to relate the drawings to other test material and background information.

Here, patients were asked to draw a person and greatly encouraged to draw only a *whole* person, not to sketch. Then they were requested to draw a figure of the opposite sex. They were then asked to tell something about the figures. If they were not productive in the latter instance, such direct questions were asked as, "How old?" "What intelligence?" "What kind of looking person?" and so on.

EXAMPLES

Case of Sadomasochism: DAP.

Female indicates impaired judgment, perhaps primarily in relation to sex (transparency of skirt with hand showing through in proximity to genital area).

Case of Rebellion: DAP.

Although presents aggressive facade, demonstrates strong need to be protected (helmet on male).

Case of Dysphoria: DAP.

Marked sense of inability in coping with environment (no hands) or standing on own two feet (no feet).

Case of Shakes: DAP

Poor sexual differentiation (only gross distinction is hair on female, *both* have broad shoulders and flare hips).

Minnesota Multiphasic Personality Inventory (MMPI)

This procedure can present the defensive network of the personality and the characteristic techniques used by the person in handling affect and tension. It can also provide information with respect to adaptive ego resources. As a personality inventory, it is keenly sensitive to the social desirability implied to the patient by the various items and is very much structured by the situation and the examiner. (In the cases presented here, the situation was a diagnostic one stemming generally from a referral by a physician who implicitly or explicitly was suggesting psychological factors associated with somatic disorder. The examiner, a clinical psychologist, already had probed into life history, motives, and conflicts before the MMPI had been administered.) Accordingly, each patient has to assume a set or role so that a manifest level is tapped, probably associated with the patient's defensive maneuvers.

The empirical results and underlying determining tendencies in each patient throw light on adaptability, as well as deviant thinking (variations from the norm). Scales derived from the MMPI have proliferated and there are many scoring systems to differentiate diagnostic categories. Coding procedures, in which each clinical scale is assigned a numerical symbol, are also used to categorize [6, 7, 9].

In the ten cases to be presented and in the therapy notes associated with each case, references to MMPI scales and scale configurations are made not so much to suggest diagnostic categories as to indicate a personality description, ego defenses, and especially a presentation of an aspect of the patient's personality to others—often not conscious to the former. The comparison of MMPI, ICL, and DAP features in conjunction in these cases frequently presents an interesting multilevel picture. All the patients took the group form of the MMPI at home and were asked to work on it by themselves.

EXAMPLES*

Case of Fantasy: MMPI.

Despite a "floating profile," the psychotic features are not

* See MMPI profiles, pp. 361, 350, and 326.

gross, or they are well contained by defenses (Hs, Hy, and Ma within 50-70 boundaries).

Case of Hypochondria: MMPI.

Sourness (Hs), rebellion (F,Sc), and open hostility (Hs,Ma) all freely expressed or very near surface (relatively high peaks).

Case of Sadomasochism: MMPI.

Somatizes her anxiety (Hs,Hy) with depressive features (D), but little manifest anxiety (relatively lower Pt).

Interpersonal Checklist (ICL)

This measure indicates the conscious presentation of the self to others and also can be utilized to contrast this presentation with how one would like to be or with how one believes others see him. On a gross quadrant interpretive level, the ICL defines whether a person presents himself as basically dominant or submissive and affiliated or disaffiliated towards others. On a more fine octant level, the person is rated as to the relative stress he places on managerial-autocratic, competitive-exploitive, blunt-aggressive, skeptical-distrustful, modest-self-effacing, docile-dependent, cooperative-overconventional, and responsible-overgenerous attitudes. Thus, there is representation that ranges from adaptive to maladaptive attitudes. Research has related the latter to conventional psychiatric diagnosis (14, 15).

Self dissatisfaction, conflicts, alleged interactions with others, and blind spots in interpersonal dealings can be gleaned from the ICL. Not only does it offer important communicative leads in an interview and psychotherapy, but lends depth to personality appreciation when compared and contrasted to other techniques such as MMPI and DAP. Every patient filled out one set describing how they currently saw themselves. They then filled out another set indicating how they felt others saw them or a set indicating how they would like to be.

EXAMPLES*

Case of Fantasy: ICL.

She presents an exaggerated sense of helplessness and weakness (exaggerated lower hemisphere).

Case of Denial: ICL.

She admits to, but is highly conflicted over, distrustful, suspicious motives and would like to deny all of this (discrepancy between Self and Ideal for octant 4).

---

* See ICL profiles on pp. 360, 333, and 325.

Case of Sadomasochism: ICL.

She presents self as an extremely responsible and generous person (octant 8) who is quite cooperative and conventional (octant 7). In others terms, she has a "psychosomatic" orientation and is hysterical in her interactions.

Wechsler Adult Intelligence Scale (WAIS)

This test is one of the best measures of intelligence. Moreover, since it is a scale that includes eleven subtests measuring a variety of verbal and performance skills, it also serves as a diagnostic tool. Discrepancies among scores from one test to another, intratest scatter, configuration of test and qualitative aspects of answers shed light on personality dynamics. (References to the Wechsler-Bellevue are generally applicable to the WAIS.) [2, 5, 18]. Of the ten cases presented here, only three were administered the WAIS. All three were adolescents whose histories were not categorical in establishing their intellectual functioning and whose age and problems dictated an assessment of skills for vocational evaluation.

Diagnostic Interview

Depending on the technique, skill, and theoretical orientation of the examiner, the diagnostic interview can embody the three phases of comprehensiveness, multidimensionality, and multilevel approach. The interview not only serves to gather information, it establishes a relationship, fosters the evaluation climate, and can and ought to be a therapeutic contact in its own right. (That is, a depth interview explains as it learns, juxtaposes events and behavior, by its very investigation relates current modes of action with genetic material, and permits affect and self-evaluation to be expressed in an appropriate context.) Some workers prefer to interview after they have obtained leads from the test material. This writer usually begins with the interview for the reasons cited above and also to be in a more flexible position with respect to *administering* the tests in as clinical a fashion as possible. At times, when the patient's emotional tone indicates, or material germane to the tests occurs, interviewing may be conducted concurrently with test administration.

The diagnostic interviews were opened with a remark such as, "Dr. K. has told me only a little about your situation, why don't you fill me in?" Or, "We had an opportunity only to touch on your problems on the phone, why don't you tell me more about it?" The stream of conversation then was allowed to meander on its own course, although the flow had to be rechanneled, dammed, or the eddies quickened when necessary. The basic areas always investigated, however, were these: the nature, chronology, and context of the psychological or physical symptomatology; biography, initiated with some comment such as, "Tell me about yourself beginning with the beginning—where and when were you born?" relationship to family members; school history; social (including sexual) development; vocational background; marital history, if pertinent; hobbies; interests; medical history; idosyncrasies; dreams and fantasies; and the patient's own evaluation or impression of this material.

The diagnostic interviews are presented in the exact fashion in which they were originally written down. The original grammar and sequence have been retained (when this has not made reading too difficult). The wording of the patients has been maintained, but to stress the special significance or peculiarity of phrasing, certain of their comments have been included within question marks. Occasional comments of the author are placed in parentheses. Following each paragraph of the diagnostic interview notes in reduced type are explanations of the interview material. Next are examples of evidence converging from different tests and interviews and so reinforcing hypotheses initially based on results from any one of the tests alone.

EXAMPLES

Case of Hypochondria:

Many sources of evidence pointed to the extreme stress place on somatic expression of anxiety—the myriad physical complaints in the interview, peak Hs on the MMPI, stress on octant 8 in the ICL, and somatic theme on Card 8BM on the TAT.

Case of Rebellion:

The thin veneer of toughness covering hypersensitivity was indicated by the helmet in the DAP, the turtle shell on Card IV in the Rorschach, PdMf but low K and high Sc on the MMPI, and the obsessive, aggressive fantasies described in the interview.

THE TEN CASES

Of the ten cases, seven were referred by physicians in conjunction with medical treatment, one was referred jointly by a psychologist and an obstetrician, one was a clinic psychiatric ward patient, and one was a clinic psychiatric outpatient. The first eight cases were referred for psychological evaluation and subsequently entered therapy on a private basis with the author. The outpatient was evaluated psychologically by a fourth year doctoral student under the author's supervision and was then seen by the latter for therapy on an outpatient basis. The ward patient was referred to the writer for a screening psychological evaluation, was seen by him as a therapy inpatient, and then referred by him to another fourth year doctoral student for a full test battery evaluation under the writer's supervision. This patient subsequently entered therapy on a private basis with the author.

Diagnostically, the cases were divided as follows: (1) character disorder with masochistic features, therapy somewhat successful; (2) an anxiety reaction, therapy somewhat successful; (3) a schizoid personality with marked hypochondriacal features, patient not really able to enter into treatment; (4) hysterical personality, therapy somewhat successful; (5) a character disorder (adolescent reaction) with hysterical features, therapy somewhat successful; (6) a hysterical character disorder with acting out features, therapy successful; (7) a character disorder with underlying psychotic features, therapy unsuccessful; (8) a hysterical disorder with marked compulsive features, therapy successful; (9) a character disorder with marked hypochondriacal features, therapy unsuccessful; and (10) an emotionally unstable personality with psychotic potential, therapy successful.

Success or failure in psychotherapy has been considered in terms of the presenting complaints, stated goals of the patient, behavioral and psychodynamic expression, and the diagnostic picture. This, of course, is a relative determination, and lacks validating follow-up. Thus, the Unstable Personality was considered a successful case because for the first time she really looked at herself, was highly motivated to continue self-investigation, and made, *for her,* vast behavioral changes despite her continued marginal functioning. Conversely, the Character Disorder with hypochondriacal features was considered a failure in treatment despite a variety of social successes, leadership roles, and even her pronouncement of well-being to her physician subsequent to termination of therapy and *after* she had undergone a surgical procedure. To the therapist, it seemed that she was continuing her headlong flight from her internal conflicts and that any behavioral changes (including somatic experiences) would be transient.

The relationship of treatment to diagnostic considerations, to stated goals, to self-concept, and to clues provided in the test material will be considered in chapter 11, the concluding chapter of the book.

PSYCHOTHERAPY NOTES

The psychotherapy notes are those that were jotted down by the author immediately after each session. An effort was made in this note-taking to retain the flavor and sequence of the actual communication. Little, and primarily grammatical, editing was made for this presentation. The nature of the psychotherapy as well as the test interpretations reflect, of course, the orientation of the writer, which is psychoanalytic. That is, stress has been placed on internal conflicts and interpersonal interactions in their historical context. Support and encouragement to express pent-up affect were not absent from the author's approach (notably for the emotionally unstable patient with psychotic potential, discussed in chapter 10.) This was subordinated in importance, however, to the goal of educating the patient to assume responsibility for uncovering his underlying motivation for his behavior and symptoms, noting his own patterns and sequences of thinking and action, comprehending the present—particularly his relationship to the therapist and significant people in his life—in relation to his past history and especially to his family interaction. Very early in psychotherapy, and increasingly so as therapy progressed, the author suggested to patients that they experiment with behavior other than their customary rigid patterns and that they constantly evaluate their attitude.

In short, the approach was psychoanalytic, but active, with the responsibility for initiating change placed squarely upon the patient. Doubtlessly, observations made both in the testing and psychotherapy situations were heavily colored by the writer's orientation. The reader is asked, not to accept this orientation, but to follow the assumptions made in the psychological evaluation, the comments relevant to the psychotherapy notes, and the interrelations of both. If this is done, it is our contention that the reader will be in a position to evaluate the test formulations and can then determine what to keep, modify, or discard for himself in light of his own frame of reference.

FORMAT

Each of the ten cases is presented as a separate chapter (chapters 1-10). The chapter is introduced by the figure drawings. These provide the reader with literal illustrations of the patients' productions. The drawings are followed by the diagnostic overview in which the patient's diagnostic category is related to typical and salient features in the test data. The implication of these test patterns for behavior is related to the therapeutic process particularly with respect to suggested weaknesses and strengths in the patient. The reader is thus alerted beforehand to significant detail to which he can pay special attention. This is followed by the report of the psychological evaluation and the therapy notes (for the first 24 or so sessions, if the patient remained in treatment that long). Offset from the therapy notes, in smaller type, are paragraph-by-paragraph references to test and interview material that are relevant to the therapeutic events. The raw test data for each case, with comments pinpointed to specific test items or test configurations, are included in the appendix.

SUGGESTED USES OF THE BOOK

One objective for which this material is designed is to teach the relationship of a diagnostic category to test results and to behavior in psychotherapy. For this purpose, the reader first should select the Diagnostic Overview for the category in question. He then may compare the test patterns indicated in the overview to the actual test data in the appendix. He may also compare the test data with the offset test comments in the chapter. He may then verify his observations with the therapy notes in the chapter.

Thus, the reader interested in the category Hysterical Personality would read the Diagnostic Overview for this case in Chapter 4, note the indicated test patterns, and relate them to the test results in appendix 4. He would check these observations with the offset test comments, introduced by the appropriate test references in Chapter 4. As an additional step, the Diagnostic Overview and test data for another case might be contrasted with the data for the Hysterical Personality.

Test techniques may be studied singly or in combinations. For example, all the Rorschachs or, for a screening battery, the MMPI's, ICL's and DAP's may be compared to the offset test comments which are introduced by the appropriate test references. This material may then be related to behavior by reading the therapy notes in the paragraph above the test comments. Thus, at a glance the reader may contrast the ten DAP's and note the differences along a diagnostic continuum.

A dramatic means of appreciating the utilization of test results in psychotherapy is for the reader to try to reconstruct the test data from the therapy notes alone (disregarding the offset test comments). The reader is urged to surmise the test configurations from the therapeutic process. When this procedure is followed, the interrelatedness of the therapy and test material becomes clearer and the character of the therapy may seem more consistent and predictable. Conversely, the reader may predict the outcome of the therapy from the test material—a function partially served by the psychological evaluation. This permits the reader to participate in a validating procedure and provides a dramatic illustration of the value of test findings for psychotherapy.

CHAPTER ONE

MISS AMORALITY: CHARACTER DISORDER WITH MASOCHISTIC FEATURES

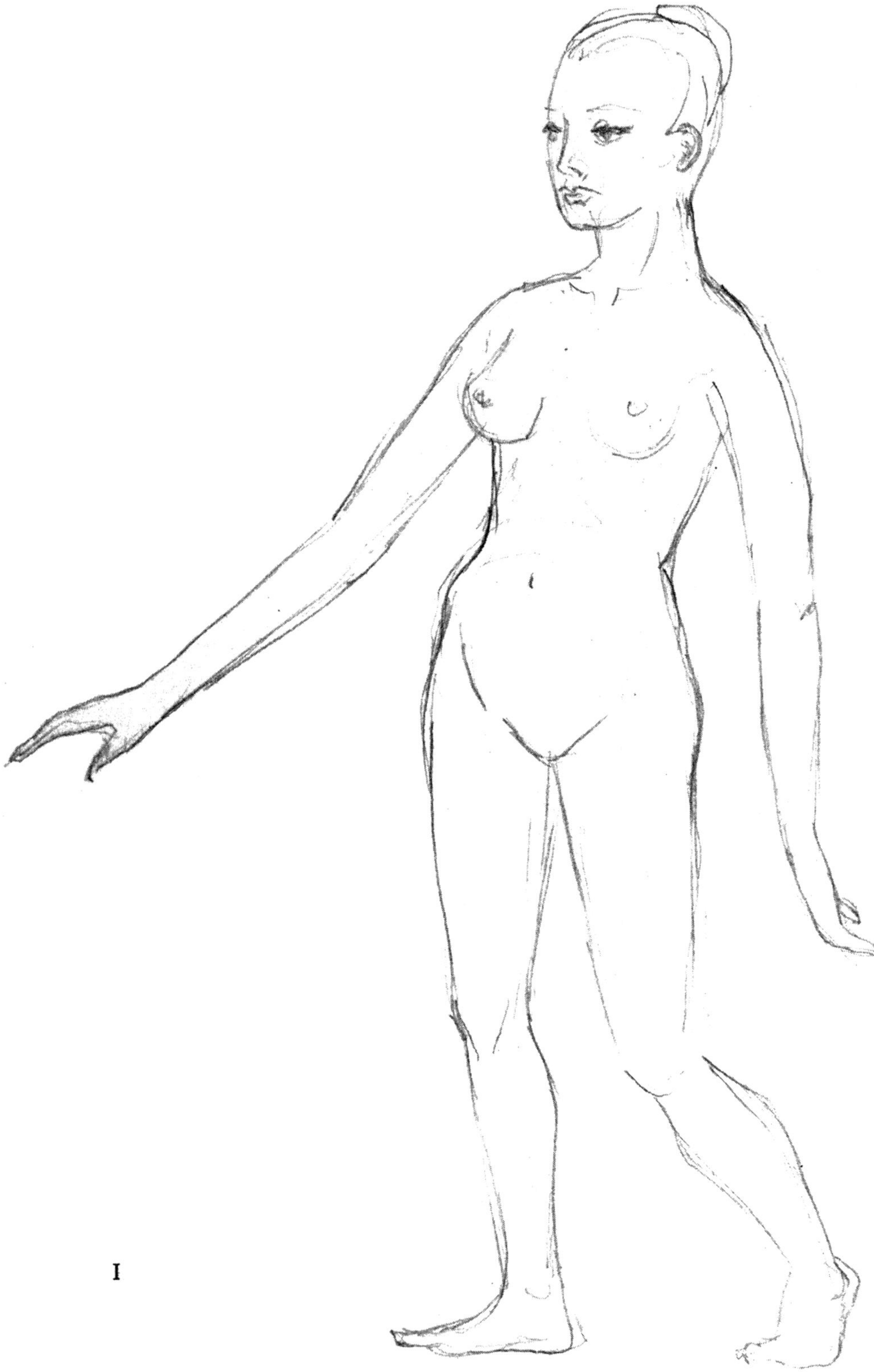

I

II

DIAGNOSTIC OVERVIEW:

A Character Disorder with Masochistic Features

The diagnostic category to which we may assign this patient (realizing that such categorization is narrow and artificial, but, nevertheless, necessary) is the character disorder. Shafer [23] and Rapaport [18] have described test patterns for various diagnostic categories. For this patient and the nine that follow, some of these patterns, as well as others with which the author has had experience, will be pointed out.

The character disorder is particularly noted for impulsive actions. In this case, the interview data is replete with such actions, which apparently have gotten the patient into trouble. The Rorschach demonstrates her poor control of affect (color) and loose evaluation of appropriate reasoning (almost bizarre quality of content). The TAT stories are also indicative of this impulsivity, while the MMPI pattern of profile peaks on F, Pd, Sc, Pa is another corroboration.

Associated with the above characteristics are rebellion, unconventionality, and amorality. Sexual diffusion, violence, and strange behavior in general are found in the interview and all the tests. Additional evidence in this respect are the nude exhibitionistic figures in the DAP; manipulations and upside-down view of cards, as well as sexual and anal content, on Rorschach; sex and violence in the TAT; and peaks on F, Pd, and Sc on the MMPI.

The masochistic features are very prominent in this patient. The violence is often shown in terms of self-destructive behavior. The most notable examples of this are her seemingly almost reasonless pregnancies and abortions, her marital fiasco, and her erratic sexual relationships, all discussed in the interview. TAT themes resemble the interview in this matter, while high Pd and low Ma and K on the MMPI, and anatomical emphasis on the Rorschach (emipirically related to somatic concern which seems to be a turning inward of hostility) are also suggestive of self-destructiveness.

Pushing beyond the narrow confines of diagnostic category and generalizations, we focus our attention on the hints provided in the test material as to the therapeutic prospects. The most notable negative feature to be found in this case is the sense of alienation and basic mistrust of others which is revealed in the interview description of little or no intimacy even with family; and in themes of mistrust on the TAT, stories of aloofness on the DAP, and high Pd, Sc and extremely low Pa on the MMPI. Related to this mistrust is the extremely valuable data concerning her relationships with authority and possibly with the therapist. The interview disclosed previous bouts of suspiciousness, seduction, and testing of therapists; also the suggestion of such attitudes towards authority as demonstrated on the TAT—card 12 particularly—forewarned the author. He also was provided with an explanation of her behavior in therapy and thereby probably avoided considerable stickiness in treatment. Additional negative features were her pot-boiling proclivity (i.e., tendency to move from one crisis to another) and lack of commitment, as indicated in the interview and TAT themes (especially her inability to give), and her disordered defenses, as suggested by the manner in which all sorts of usually repressed or at least suppressed material came out in both interview and the associations to Rorschach cards.

Conversely, there were a number of positive features and prospective toeholds for therapy. The interview disclosed stability and satisfaction in her work. It also disclosed her care and attention for her children while the TAT suggested that being a mother was important for her, and the DAP indicated her reaching out to the environment (long arms). A degree of depression and/or anxiety sufficient to motivate her for treatment was indicated on her MMPI (high D, Pt) and in her phobic responses to the Rorschach (monsters and weird figures). The Rorschach also suggested imagination (many well organized M's and originals) as did the organization of her TAT stories and her conceptualization of the DAP. The absence of distortion of the formal considerations on all her tests indicated her ability to evaluated the realities confronting her.

PSYCHOLOGICAL EVALUATION:

Miss Amorality

Patient: female, age, 30, divorced, two children	Education: college and Art School
	Occupation: artist

Referred by: A psychologist and an obstetrician, for personality evaluation to determine the advisability of a therapeutic abortion.

Tests Administered:

Rorschach, Thematic Apperception Test (TAT), Minnesota Multiphasic Inventory (MMPI), and Draw-A-Person (DAP).

Interview:

Mrs. A., attractive and smartly dressed, appeared completely at ease. She presented volubly an image of sophistication (*e.g.*, volunteering superficial insights and self-analyses), yet at the same time she naively, frankly, and compulsively poured out details of all manner of unconventional behavior—particularly of a sexual and mercenary nature. Indirectly, she revealed a paucity of meaningful relations and emotional warmth in her early life: her father had deserted the family when she was only an infant, and her mother was preoccupied with important and widely scattered jobs. Her adult life has been a confused, impulsive flight from one difficult situation to another and has been characterized by immaturity, amorality, rebelliousness, and self-destructive tendencies (*e.g.*, myriad affairs, failure in marriage and as a parent, rejection by people important to her, etc.). This hardly has been fun for her.

In addition to a keen and chronic sense of loneliness and frequent depression, she appears to have suffered at least two emotional collapses—one at age 17 and one at age 28—periods when her environmental props were kicked out from under her.

Evaluation:

The patient is seriously emotionally disturbed. She appears to suffer from a severe character disorder with a psychotic potential that is activated whenever her environmental pressures are more than usually aggravated. That is, she follows a lifelong pattern of handling her chronic sense of depression and loneliness by a constant headlong flight from any commitments. The result is that she is victimized by her own impulses. She demonstrates little ability to tolerate frustration or to delay immediate gratification—no matter how dire the consequences—in favor of more durable, long-term goals. When additional emotional stress causes crises for her, she is unable to deal adequately with them (although she seems to set them up). Her judgment, particularly related to people, becomes distorted and tenuous, and her testing of reality fails. Her already primitive defenses (*e.g.*, projecting her motives onto others, denial that anything is wrong, and first-line defense of anatomical preoccupation) crumble, and she either collapses emotionally or acts in a confused and destructive manner. Thus she has had at least two "breakdowns" —at 17 when squeezed out by, and separated from, her mother; and at 28 when involved in separation proceedings from her husband. Significantly, she reported never having experienced orgasm because she was unable to give and was fearful of being hurt and rejected. She guessed this was related to her father's leaving her and the family. There also is the case in point of her impulsive marriage, confused affairs and the several pregnancies that have meant near-catastrophe for her, all evidences of her confusion and self-destruction.

Mrs. A's interpersonal relations are notably poor. She relates only in the most superficial manner, feeling so different from others as to approach a sense of almost complete alienation. She cannot trust or even comprehend the motives of others. Desperately, she employs sexuality as a means of relating, but in her hands it becomes more of a weapon than a mode of effective communication. Likewise, her compulsive amorality and rebellion seem to be an attempt to establish her identity, if only by contrast. Actually, she is markedly phobic of people and even terrified of relationships with them. Consequently, she overreaches into her environment and, in her frantic efforts to make contact, pushes people away. Her appearance of being blasé is not feigned but rather counterphobic and, as in all counterphobias, contains self-destructive elements. For example, she sees all women as calculating, revengeful creatures seeking to destroy or emasculate males. Males also wish to destroy women (herself) because the women are no good. It may be speculated that the absence of a father in the home, save for reminders of his desertion and irresponsible philandering, and the presence of a mother who had to be both parents but who herself was callous and rejecting contributed to Mrs. A's confused sexual identity, predilection for effeminate males, and counterphobic sexual behavior in general.

Of greatest significance is the fact that the patient's confusion, impulsivity, bitterness, and guilt combine in extremely self-destructive behavior. For example, her current pregnancy threatens to spell catastrophe for her in terms of finances, career, custody of her children, current "love" relationship—in general to bring the roof down on her head. (Motives of revenge toward her lover, her husband, society in general, and her parents in particular also seem pertinent.) And her previous three pregnancies (at least), two terminating in births, seem to have been of similar nature. Despite her conscious attitude, she may derive gratification in carrying a child and thus temporarily finding identity as a woman.

There is serious doubt, however, whether Mrs. A. can emotionally tolerate becoming a mother again. The evidence suggests that she was unable to weather such a role in the past and that now she is even more besieged by her circumstances and weakening defenses. (It hardly seems necessary even to point out the extremely questionable environment in which a new child would be placed.)

A therapeutic abortion can be considered only as ameliorative and expedient. This patient needs intensive psychotherapy. She does have creative potential and a drive for self-realization. Whether she can muster sufficient motivation, stick to a commitment, and refrain from rash actions is questionable but well worth trying.

Therapy Notes

First Session (6/16): Mrs. A. phoned to say she would be ten minutes late because of babysitting problems. She began with a nightmare she had had, one she had described in the interview about a man in women's clothing, and spoke about incidents that had stimulated the dream. A fellow student when she was 19 was attracted to her because she came from a prominent family. After inviting her for a drink, he showed her a cartoon attacking her family. He accused her family of influencing the cartoonist to attack him; then he slugged her. She was very fearful of him thereafter (he was hospitalized), and she emphasized several times that he has been in therapy. Since the dream showed him in women's clothing, she feared "Lesbian" tendencies in herself. Her sister had learned this about her herself in treatment and had thought that her very close relationship with the patient explained it. Also, the patient's mother made advances to her sister. The patient was repelled by her own sister's crushes on girls; she could not tolerate the idea of close contact with women, especially her nearest sib, D., and her mother—or even with "any girl to the extent that she has developed breasts."

We looked at her fear that therapy would "slug" her with revelations that she had unacceptable impulses. She said that she feared learning that she should not be married or a parent, but insisted that she loves her children. She went on to explain her problems in loving, particularly with her son.

TAT—(12) Theme of evil hypnotist (or doctor) interested only in experimenting with her sexually; or fear of being slugged with interpretations of her impulses. (18) Homosexual theme of story correlates with her almost immediately expressed preoccupation with this subject.

Rorschach—I (1) As soon as she enters a situation, she wonders whether she can cope with her basic (unacceptable) impulses (biological urges on the Rorschach and Lesbian tendencies in therapy). (3) Response indicates her sexual preoccupation.

MMPI—Pd over 70 indicative of sense of alienation from family and despair of being loved by them and being able to love back.

Second Session (6/21): Mrs. A. questioned how the test results demonstrated that she had problems, implying that she did not have many. Also she asked me to list her problems. She indicated that the counselor she used to have was "dynamic" (and also attracted to her) so that she could with pleasure follow him docilely, but that she also resented him.

TAT—(12) Often suggests relationship to therapist. In her story, patient suggests therapist would use her for his own needs.

MMPI—MfPd often suggests the "masochistic attack." Low Mf signified how feminine and helpless the patient is. In association with high Pd, a sense of mistreatment and estrangement from people, this message appears to be sent: "People and the world give me a raw deal because I am so femininely helpless." (". . . and I'll make them feel guilty because of this—I'll use sex as a means of controlling men at least.")

Her problem, she said, is her inability to give up things. Thus, she is disturbed that her lover repels her friends, especially her brother-in-law. She is also bothered about his irresponsibility and sexual maladjustment, and the chance of his turning out like her husband. But she is attracted to him physically as well as by his sensitivity and creativity and his enormous consideration for her. She wants to be treated like a woman but also strongly needs to be "motherly" and dominating.

TAT—(4) Theme of woman being the more dominant.

DAP—Stories and hand posture: Aloofness in stories, pushing-away position of hands correlates with her inability to commit herself to relationships.

We considered her "but" relationship. She may consciously commit herself to relationships, but there is always an unconscious or preconscious "but" to let her off the hook.

MMPI—High F and Sc means "I'm different and can't get close to others"; high Pd means "I feel alienated from people especially my family"; High FPdSc suggests considerable difficulty in establishing durable relationships.

Third Session (6/22): She mildly expressed that she had felt criticized during the previous hour. Then she told of a dream: Gist of the dream was that she felt squeezed out by her ex-husband and his new wife. She also was apprehensive that her children would be won over by them. She felt that her husband was dominated by his mother. The patient had had to tolerate his mother's literally wanting to feed him. Other associations led to her feeling that she had to use people to win privileges; then she felt obligated. And other people did the same with her. Particularly, she felt this about men because the only men in her life as a child (two uncles) were cold, dominating men who extracted privileges in this manner.

TAT—(4) Theme of relationship tearing apart, woman not worth it. (18) Relationship with male conflicted and violent.

MMPI—High Pa associated with FPdSc (cf. previous session) adds distrust to that picture and a sense of being used.

TAT—(4, 18) Both themes disparage men.

Fourth Session (6/28): Mrs. A. was depressed and anxious about the possibility that the abortion would be rejected. The theme of the hour was her feeling that she could not be liked by her contemporaries unless she was "attractive." This, though, made her a "threat" and forced her never to be herself but only how they imagined they would like her to be. On the other hand, she feels more confident with older people (her mother's circle of friends). They view her more objectively (*e.g.*, a harmless kid, one who gets sympathy).

DAP—Emphasis on attractiveness and exhibitionism.

MMPI—MfPd "I'm no threat, I'm really helpless"; low Mf, high Pd signifies "How feminine, helpless, and weak I am" (masochistic).

When she was little she spoke guilelessly with a lisp and a winsome, almost boyish manner. (The Shirley Temple syndrome nauseates her because it is so cloyingly feminine and calculated.) This behavior got her the attention and affection of her elders, much to the resentment of her sisters. Then, like a dash of cold water, she found that this approach could no longer be used naturally.

TAT—(1, 4) Theme of being a gifted, charming child no longer and thus no longer securing the accompanying attention and gratification.

MMPI–Pd,Mf: low Mf, high Pd signifies "How feminine, helpless, and weak I am" (masochistic).

Fifth Session (6/29): Mrs. A.'s latest dream: A group is playing her piano composition but it is not full quality. A conductor tells her how to correct it. He has a deformed left hand, which runs in his family. She and the conductor are thinking of marrying, and he wants 80 children. She is fearful that they will inherit his defect.

Eight seemed to be determined in multiple ways, including the references to *piano* and *mother* (her mother often plays the piano and has arthritis). The patient volunteered memories of the last time she sat on her mother's lap, when she was *8* in 1938. Mother was maudlin. The patient was repelled by her mother's consoling her during prolonged labor. She felt that her mother would see her erotically as a man. She related several erotic memories with women. She described her mother as cold, phony, etc., but there were a few conflicting memories of her in rare affectionate expressions. (We made no reference to possible transference implications.)

TAT–(2) Mother central figure, father unimportant. (3) Suggestion mother both most loved and hated person in her life. (4) Woman calculating.

Rorschach–VII (1) Nightmare from childhood suggests phobic qualities and possible ambivalent attitudes to mother. (2) Woman disparaged in "mother" context.

Sixth Session (7/6): The board vetoed the request for therapeutic abortion. Mrs. A. was very depressed and considered resigning herself to the unhappy solution of marrying her lover, who continues to reveal to her unsettling immature characteristics. She faced squarely her pot boiling patterns and enumerated her helplessness in the face of "amoral" stimuli.

MMPI–Low K, MfPd connotes sense of helplessness and, with high F, weakness before one's own impulses–or amorality.

Rorschach content–Preoccupation with sexuality, anatomy, and hostility suggests immaturity and inadequacy of her defenses.

Seventh Session (7/14): She underwent the abortion arranged by friends, and afterwards she became hysterical, remorseful, and guilty. She is still very depressed.

Theme: She is very lonely and so looks for relationships with men, but somehow always ends up with the men expecting her to go to bed with them. Only on exploration did she reveal that she picks a situation where she can feel first grateful and obligated, and then victimized. In fact, they are usually older, married men. She is fearful of competing, and so picks men that other women might not be interested in (more precisely, those who are lonely, handicapped, weak, etc.). She related this somewhat to earlier experiences.

> MMPI–Low K, high Pd indicates sense of weakness and impulsivity and alienation, an orientation that with adversity easily converts to depression.
>
> MMPI–High F and Sc and low K signifies the sense of differentness and rebellion, and high Pd suggests that this is acted out against environment.

Eighth Session (7/19): Financial problems prevent further treatment. She said she felt all right although she knew she needed further therapy. Exploration revealed her concern about my "background." She wondered if I would be too academic, because last session I told her she dwelled too much on "shoulds" (an oversimplification). After discussing this, she rather too quickly decided to continue. However, I thought she ought to weigh the decision more, so that she could feel that this is what she wants to do, not something pressured by me or her sister, who is pushing her to continue. She said that the fees were so high and wished she could give me a trade. I questioned her meaning, which she explained via her work. I suggested that in any event, "taking it out in trade" would not be a very therapeutic process.

> MMPI–High Pa signifies basic mistrust which manifests itself.
>
> TAT–(12) Suspicion of motives of others, here doctors (therapist).
>
> MMPI–KMfPd: Superficial docility, readiness to be "pushed" by others (yet use of sexuality as a "weapon").
>
> TAT–(4) Woman calculating.
>
> DAP–Sexuality flaunted (suggested in "trade").

Ninth Session (7/21): Mrs. A. decided to remain in treatment, explaining that she had "no sales resistance." I picked this up in terms of necessary commitments, whereupon she claimed little gain from previous therapeutic situations–all of which were with people she knew, therapists in whom her confidence was shaky and who "were quite disturbed themselves." We explored the implications again in terms of her removing the focus from herself. "Why do I have to go through this?" led to her great sense of guilt and her interpretation of therapy as punishent, which she both wants and dreads.

> Rorschach—I (2) Judgment more reserved after initial impulsivity. IV (1) Phobic quality of response and viewing of authority figure as monster associated with seeing therapists as disturbed and with fear of punishment in therapy. IV Vague anatomical emphasis suggests weak defense against feelings of guilt and punishment.
>
> TAT—(1) Distorted notion of people, very pathological. (13) Diffuse and confused feelings of guilt and punishment.

Tenth Session (7/26): Mrs. A. called to say she would be late. She called again to say she had miscalculated and it was too late to come in. She mentioned that her mother had come in for a visit.

Eleventh Session (7/28): The patient was a half hour late because of excitement with mother, who had encouraged her to marry a fairly elderly gentleman or at least to be nice to him so as to get his money. Then the patient voiced her pride in her mother's career and striking appearance. She felt that her mother reflects on her; also, she likes to be considered a dutiful daughter.

> Rorschach—I (1) Rebels against but then conforms to authority. (II) (3) Childlike concept—wish for affection. VII Resentment and disparagement of mother.
>
> TAT—(3) Conflict between love and rage over someone (mother?) she loves.

Twelfth Session (8/2): Theme: The patient is not consciously aware, but dimly perceives that her mother never really approved of her in an unqualified fashion but was geared always towards her own interests. Consequently, the patient pulled for negative attention in the form of critical or scolding behavior from her mother (*i.e.*, competitiveness, arguments about morals, etc.). Even this interest on the mother's part was transient, and the expected hurt or anger was not expressed. It was either displaced towards her sister D., or bottled up, so that patient continued to need punishment, guilt, depression, etc.

> TAT—(3) Conflict between love and rage over someone (mother?) she loves. (6) Mother not interested in giving to child.

This theme developed out of two dreams: (1) The patient, with friends, had to enter some sort of mill where she would be crushed but come out alive. She didn't know which part of her to expose to be hurt least. She had to undergo this because all her friends did; they had "the guts to do it" (my expression *re* undergoing treatment). (2) She had to plunge herself in gas chamber for same reasons.

Rorschach–I, IV (I) Defecating and phobic quality of response as well as anality (seated), associated with fear of destruction and analyity of "guts" and "gas chamber" (Freudian theory of anal sadism and aggression).

Thirteenth Session (8/4): Theme: She never expressed direct anger because of her fear of being rejected, criticized, and retaliated against. This feeling was most prominent with her mother. She did strike back at her husband when she felt that he was weaker but stopped when he retaliated. The ones at whom she gets angry consistently are her children because they will continue to love her anyway.

MMPI–KMfPd: Superficial docility, readiness to be "pushed" by others (yet use of sexuality as a "weapon").

TAT–(1) Unhappy and victimized child theme. (3) Hurts persons she loves.

Rhetorically, she questioned why she sleeps with men when she hates to do so. She thought she was not able to "grow" with mother who, if she knew, would vastly disapprove—so she defies her. She could "evaluate" more with her sister, who would not disapprove.

MMPI–F is rebellion; associated with Pd it finds expression or is acted out.

Fourteenth Session (8/9): The patient was fifteen minutes late (she has been late for a number of sessions). Apparently because she felt ready to be criticized for her lateness, she took the offensive: Why was I not smoking a cigar today? Was I trying to impress her because previously she had mentioned my appearance and manners? However, she went on to say that she was not only late to my office, but to other appointments as well. This comment contained both defiance (idea of why-should-you-care-since-I-pay-you-anyhow) and a suggestion of her inability to be anything but an unreliable, bad little girl.

MMPI–F, Pd: She acts out her rebellion.

Rorschach–I (1) Aggressive and rebellious. II (1) Disparaging of older (authority) figure.

DAP–Defiance conveyed by frank sexual detail and forward thrust of bodies.

She went on to talk of both her husband and lover growing to resent her because she was cold and not understanding. She suggested that these reactions to her stemmed from her competing on masculine terms. She then described how unmannerly and "bitchy" her lover was.

> Interview—Early in interview she indicated both her need to "disparage" her lover and her need for a feminine or childlike mate, suggesting her confused sexual identity.
>
> Rorschach—IV Beak (phallic-like) response suggests aggressive sexuality.

I felt at this point that the patient could use support rather than exploration. I will try to look at, with her, good reasons for her annoyance with her husband, her lover, and myself.

Fifteenth Session (8/11): She is thinking of giving up her lover because her family disapproves of him. She must decide between the lover who offers gratification but little promise for future, and the sister whom she loves dearly. She always seems to pick such a male. To stimulate her sensually, he must be different, almost *exotic*. A male who would be integrated, stable, protective, and so on, would leave her cold. She suggested that such a man would outcompete her, find her wanting, and inevitably leave her.

> TAT—(3, 4, 13, 18) Themes of these stories suggest competition with males on many levels, including sexual.
>
> MMPI—KMfPd: Superficial docility, readiness to be "pushed" by others (yet use of sexuality as a "weapon").

Sixteenth Session (8/12): Mrs. A.'s former husband is not making payments to her. This raised all sorts of conflicts. She felt that she really did not deserve it on the basis of her conduct and that he could challenge her with being an improper mother. Yet she does not want to give up her lover. She was also undecided as to the implication for therapy. We dwelled on her feeling of being unable to give up anything, her frustration tolerance, experience of anxiety, and her despair of long-term satisfaction. She demonstrated her rationalizing by decrying the lack of any guarantee that therapy would help her, since she may be too old to change her ways—and, at the same time, hoping everything would work out, and the right man would come along and solve everything for her. This led to our talking about the desirability of making commitments and choices.

> MMPI—High Pt connotes obsessiveness (indecision).
>
> Rorschach—I (1) Defecating and (IV) sitting, suggests anality which dynamically is correlated with obsessiveness.

Seventeenth Session (8/16): Dream: She felt that she had no money and was in desperate straits. She asked friends but they could not help. Then she went into the next room and was "terrified" to see her mother's hairpiece fall off exposing a balding head; she was holding her hand to her head as if with a headache. An aunt with black hair was lying across the mother, saying into the phone to the aunt's husband, "I don't love you, I never have loved you, I'm through with you."

Associations: Husband has reneged on payments for some time. The friends in the dream had taken children to see him. They reported that he thinks the patient makes a great deal of money. Her mother's luxuriant white hair is thinning, and the patient is very bothered that people will see her mother as she really is, rather than as she presents herself to them. The patient was very angry and hurt by her mother telling her that she does not want to see her boyfriend, then tearfully adding that she does not want to hurt her. The dream seemed to suggest that the patient despairs of her mother loving her, so that she retaliates by telling her the phrase quoted in the dream. But she also craves close contact (love and affection as in childhood). The patient argued that since this incident with her mother, she is tremendously repelled in even touching her.

> Rorschach–II (3) Soft, childlike response indicates craving of close contact with mother. VII Anger at mother because hurt at lack of love from her.
>
> TAT–(1) Child left very much alone.

Eighteenth Session (8/17): The patient wondered about my writing a prescription for an ataratic. It seems she has used it off and on (100 tablets in a year). She feels anxious now and has taken two since her mother's arrival and an argument last night. I kept focus on her seeming wish to test me (because she knew I was not a physician and she still is in contact with referring doctor), wanting me to do something for her, all the while she was saying she could not tolerate anxiety. At the end of the hour, I suggested that, unless she could not get along without the drug, she consider doing without it for therapeutic reasons. The theme of the hour was that she could not make decisions. When she apparently did (*e.g.*, said "no" to visiting with mother without boyfriend, agreed to his proposal of marriage, etc.), she really wasn't committing herself. She felt that she could not tolerate frustration or give up anything.

MMPI—Low K says, "I'm helpless or at least cannot tolerate frustration." Both high Hy and high Pd especially in combination suggest over-reactivity to frustration or anxiety. Ego strength indicated by no formal distortions on TAT, DAP, or Rorschach.

Nineteenth Session (8/25): The patient felt anxiety as well as depression yesterday. The other day she told her boyfriend he could not spend nights with her because of the children. She was also depressed because she had had to draw on her savings. We considered how she had weathered the giving up of these things and the sense of loss—she even felt pretty good today. As for her finances, she felt that she could carry on for a while and rejected the notion of further reduced fees if her income would so warrant.

TAT—(8, 10) Can be conventional and deal effectively with environment.

Most of this hour was spent supporting her when she blamed herself for being critical of others even when it was appropriate. However, this resulted in my commenting (in context of her criticizing a dilettante for dragging out his culture to make her feel low) that she was a "notorious name-dropper" herself. This made her quite defensive. (Thus, she succeeded in feeling, if not in believing, that I was critical of her.)

TAT—(12) Feels therapist critical or sadistic towards her. Suspicion of motives of others, here doctors (therapist).

MMPI—KMfPd: Feeling too critical of others, yet also sense of being used, or disapproved of, by them. Superficial docility, readiness to be "pushed" by others (yet use of sexuality as a "weapon").

Twentieth Session (8/30): Dream: She cut up old people standing in way of her inheritance (husband's parents, etc.). She is to be sentenced to three years but let off in six months for good behavior. While waiting for her cell, she felt almost relieved that she would be fed, clothed, etc. A friend, J. Prop, (fictitious but similar name) and his friend try to take her away, give her army clothes and have her switch with a girl in kerchief and heavy make-up. She has to decide whether to sail away with her boyfriend or face the music. Problem of being branded for life and of losing children.

Associations: She originally tried and succeeded in getting my sympathy, but as I got to know her as she really was, I grew more aloof. Thus, during the previous hour she felt criticized by me when

I called her a name-dropper. I suggested that she also was apprehensive that I would be sympathetic, as when I suggested reduced fees.

Conflict: She wants to be liked and taken care of, but fears that she must give in return and that she really can't be liked. *Conflict:* To determine what is really making her feel guilty or to flee from this.

> TAT—(3, 12, 13) Theme of all three stories is conflict of wanting to be liked with fear she cannot give in return; nor can she be loved or respected for herself.
>
> DAP—Stories: Theme of aloofness.
>
> MMPI—Pa, Pd: Pa connotes distrust and Pd sense of alienation. Latter also suggests fleeing meaningful relationships by action.

Twenty-first Session (9/1): Revealed bizarre relationship with boyfriend in which he used her to score points against his homosexual friends (*e.g.*, encouraged her to cultivate a relationship with a man with whom he had had an unsuccessful affair; he then grew jealous when she did not talk about him to this man). She admitted that she hangs on to this boyfriend because she has to have an exclusive "child playmate." Moreover, she has tremendous inadequate feelings about sex, feels frigid, and is "satisfied" this way. She presented all sorts of rationalizations, such as the dire things her boyfriend would do if she terminated the affair, but she also conceded her fear of losing or surrendering something she has as well as her anxiety about making a wrong decision.

> DAP—Drawing II: Sexual relationship with man in DAP story interchangeably can be man and wife or sister and brother (sexual relations confused).
>
> MMPI—Mf, Pd, F: High F indicates differentness and is so high for this patient that it indicates antisocial and/or amoral behavior. With high Pd, she acts out, and very low Mf suggests this takes form of sexuality.
>
> TAT—(4) Woman calculating uses male "playmate." (18) Again hostility toward male, castrating him by charging him with homosexuality.

Twenty-second Session (9/3): The patient was early and on couch. She complained about being so bitchy to her boyfriend. It seems she displaced hostility from a female authority (a principal who rejected her son in school). Patient felt inferior because she was more attractive, younger, faster, etc., and yet the other woman was so morally right, without compassion, and in control.

She told of a memory of when she was 17 and consciously tried to behave so adult in comparison to all the other grandchildren of her famous grandaunt, to whom she looked up. Before going to bed, she was told by her mother that this aunt has said she was really immature. Patient then had nightmare she was riding a "cockhorse," most beautiful black *stallion* who would do anything for her and whom she loved more than anyone else. Someone stuck a needle in the horse, making it powerless or deflated, and then hands were reaching out to get her.

We considered the implications, including the horse as part of her ego and her idea of maleness (phallus, beautiful, powerful, respected—The only man she called "daddy" had black hair and was charmed by her). She resisted "such references to Freud" and volunteered that she did not want "to ride a cock" and never even thought of penises at that age. But she also worked with these notions.

> Rorschach—IV (1), VI (1, 2), VII (1, 2):—IV (1) Preoccupation with phallic beak. VI (1) Indian (aggressive figure). VI (2) Indian weapon or wand. VII (1) Nightmare in Rorschach response and reported dream, and VII (2) unfriendly mother representative suggests relation of anxiety to mother.
> DAP—Both drawings: Emphasis on sexuality.

Twenty-third Session (9/13): Immediately after their second child's birth (13 months after first child), her husband began bringing home friends in a drunken stupor. She was so exhausted and confused that she did not know whether her husband or one of his friends made love to her. Moreover, she vaguely remembered or imagined murdering some male who was placed in a chest (reported in a fantasy manner). Only J. Prop (fictitious name), then a mutual friend of her and the "victim," may have suspected. In her opening remarks, the "victim" was also the lover.

> Rorschach—II (1) Macabre, bizarre concepts. III (3) Weird, monstrous response. IV (2) Contaminated (diffuse) thinking. VII (1) Distorted, phobic response.

Her husband's behavior was so irresponsible and gruesome that I asked, "Why did you put up with it?" Her answer for this and for her pattern of behavior was that she makes any bargain for a measure of security—and that these bargains are notoriously poor, predicated on the idea that she can't expect better.

> MMPI—K, Mf, Pd: Superficial docility, readiness to be "pushed" by others (yet use of sexuality as a "weapon"). Feeling

too critical of others, yet also sense of being used, or disapproved of, by them.

Twenty-fourth Session (9/16): She was characteristically ten minutes late.

Rorschach—I (1) Hostility expressed in open talk of defecation (hostility indicated by lateness of hour and admission of being a bitch). IV (1) Phallic beak-like association also hostile, shredding fantasy. VI (2) Phallic (wand) and hostile (weapon). (Phallic is used synonomously with aggressive, pronounced assertive behavior.)

She told of making it clear to her boyfriend that she was unsure whether they could work out a marriage and also that he was not to remain in her home after dates. He asked her why she made him fall in love with her in the first place. She said that many men have called her a bitch and that she feels that she must be one because she hurts them and has to "be on top of a situation."

TAT—(4) Violence, hostile theme.

MMPI—Hy, Pd, Mf: HyPdMf triad is indicative of hysterical acting out—namely "bitchy" use of sex and having to "be on top" of situation even if must be frigid to do so.

This led to an exploration of her lateness and her reluctance to use couch: Does she have to be on top of therapy situation? As for this, she gave every conceivable explanation (except anxiety), stressing that her hair would be disarrayed, her clothes rumpled, and her make-up streaked—conceding that such an exaggeration sounded like the result of a sexual attack. She thought of other "irrelevant" things, such as how her mother talked of being interested in her but was really interested in her own needs. I wondered about the implication for me, the sexual connotation, and certainly about her need to be "in control" of the situation.

TAT—(3) Cannot trust one she loves. (12) Cannot trust doctor or therapist, he might have sexual designs on her.

MMPI—Pa: High Pa indicates basic suspicion of motives of others.

Subsequent Comments

She began to form more deep and positive transference, to investigate her relationships to people significant to her (*e.g.*, her children), and to make more contributions (giving) in this area, experimenting more freely with her interpersonal dealings and gaining a greater sense of confidence.

The psychological evaluation provided valuable clues for psychotherapy in at least four respects: It warned the therapist of the patient's morbid distrust; her tendency to test relationships with seduction; the need to focus on her sense of inability to give; and especially to underscore her need to make commitments—with respect to relationships in general and treatment in specific.

CHAPTER TWO

A CASE OF ORALITY: ANXIETY REACTION

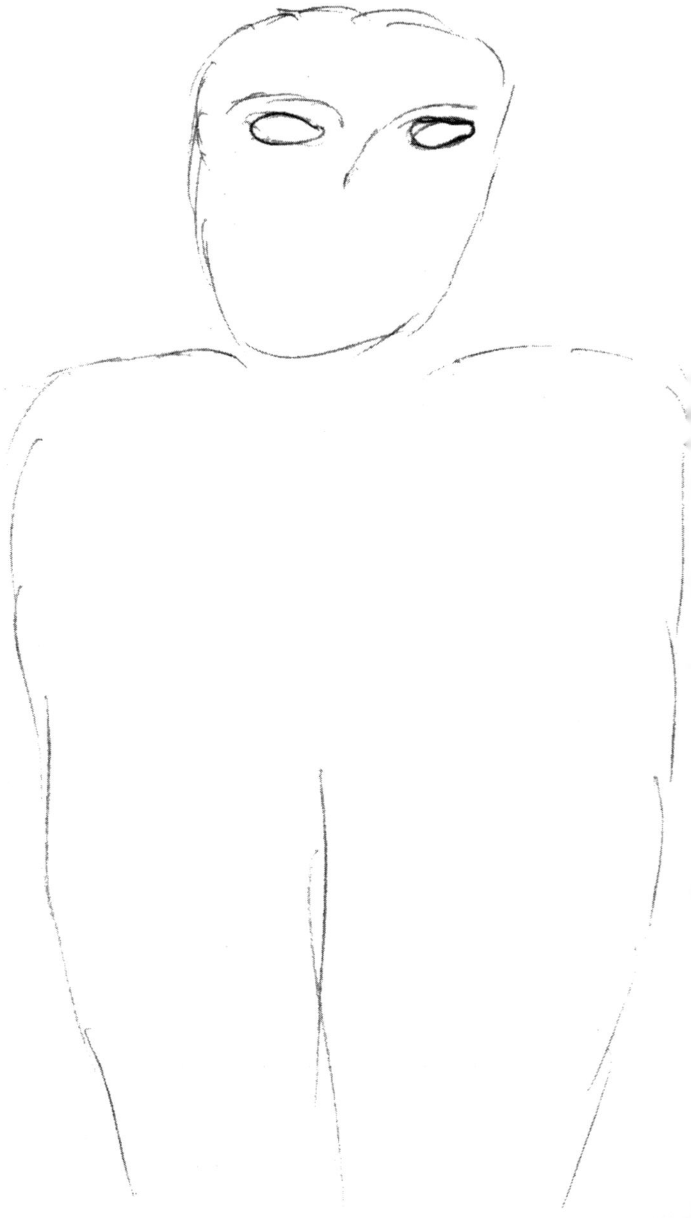

I

III

IV

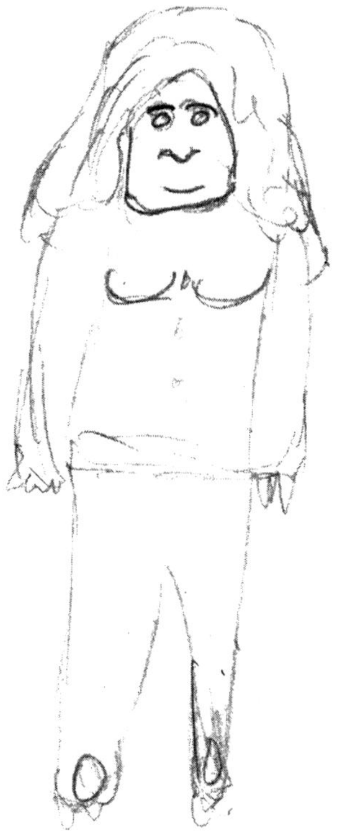

DIAGNOSTIC OVERVIEW:

An Anxiety Reaction

This diagnostic category implies marked anxiety of a diffuse nature. In the interview, the patient exhibited nervous mannerisms, and expressed anxious expectation when faced with new situations, when demands were placed upon him, and in his relationship to authority, females, and almost everyone in general. The exaggerated peaks of Pt (79) and D on the MMPI suggest both manifest anxiety and depressed feeling.

An anxiety reaction always has a large hysterical component. Again, phobic and dependent feelings indicated by exaggerated 6th and 7th ICL octants were suggestive, as were the many, only fair, Rorschach populars. The poor ability to cope with affect (color) on the Rorschach along with the naivete and massive denial demonstrated in the interview underscore the hysterical features. Differentiation from the more typical hysterical functioning is based on the grossly immature characteristics of the anxiety reaction (DAP childlike with little detail and anatomy responses on the Rorschach), and the extremely impaired self-image (TAT theme of being a big pig; the ugly, misshapen, pathetic quality of the drawings; and sexual confusion manifested in interview, TAT, and DAP). Further, with less well-developed neurotic defenses than the hysteric, the patient with an anxiety reaction often fails in judgment (distortion or close to it on Rorschach such as on Card III; and sketchiness, poor space orientation, and a somewhat bizarre quality in DAP).

With this patient, the psychological evaluation indicated that his anxiety could be, and frequently was, focused on particular problems such as his weight and relationships to people, that is, that he could be more hysterical, (conventionality in Rorschach populars, stress on ICL octant 7 and desire to be less alienated from people expressed on Ideal ICL, octant 4). In addition, a tendency to bounce back and master his circumstances was demonstrated by recovery on the Rorschach. The psychological evaluation suggested the patient's need to express his anger more meaningfully (the stopped-up rebelliousness portrayed in TAT themes; the self-directed fury related to derogatory self-image on TAT and DAP; self-effacing tendency implied by exaggerated ICL octant 5; and poorly defined hostility, even sadism, in Rorschach and TAT). The evaluation also predicted the problem of weaning the patient from his mother to more independent behavior (unusual stress by the patient on how dominated he was, and ought to be, by his mother; his wish to be even more dependent, in octant 7 Ideal ICL; and the sense of guilt and self-punishment expressed in TAT themes whenever he struck back at or away from parental figure).

PSYCHOLOGICAL EVALUATION:

A Case of Orality

Patient: male, age 18, only child of broken home, living with mother and stepfather	Education: high school junior Occupation: part-time Food line

Referred by: Dr. S. for personality evaluation and determination of possible emotional contribution to patient's obesity.

Tests Administered:

Rorschach, Thematic Apperception Test (TAT), Minnesota Multiphasic Inventory (MMPI), Draw-A-Person (DAP), Interpersonal Check-list (ICL), and 4 verbal subtests of the Wechsler Adult Intelligence Scale (WAIS).

Behavior and Background:

Mr. M, a huge young man, manifested a pronounced neck tic that took two forms: a compulsive negative head shake, and a restless movement of his head back and forth. He was eager to cooperate in any way to remove the only real problem he saw—his excessive weight. However, he did admit to "nervousness," from which his whole family suffers, and which in him is often accompanied by hand rashes. While always heavy, he reported putting on a burst of weight at the age of about thirteen or fourteen, which was approximately when his parents were divorced. He expressed unusual devotion to his mother, conceding her overprotectiveness, but defending this by saying that he was the most important "responsibility" in her life. Moreover, he demonstrated considerable docility in her presence. His mother not only hovered over him in the interview (until she was invited to leave), but demonstrated a keen interest in the materials that he took home to work on. She reported that her marriage at an early age had been unhappy from the start; her pregnancy with the patient had been difficult. Because of him, she put up with the marriage for so long. But she admits that from childhood he was sensitive to the strain between his parents and cried when they were separated. She has tried to be both a mother and father to him, and this has made for difficulties in the sexual area. For example, she has warned him that any kind of masturbation would result in illness.

Soft-spoken and shy, the patient said he had many friends of both sexes, but that he was acutely self-conscious in any situation where his weight was obvious, such as swimming. Driving, collecting guns, and hunting are his favorite forms of recreation. School holds little interest for him although he does not find it particularly difficult. He does put in long hours as part-time food worker in his grandfather's firm.

Evaluation

Despite the impression of slowness that he may give, Mr. M manifested average intelligence (Pro-rated Verbal I.Q. of 106) and particularly good common sense. He presents himself as hysterical in orientation: that is, stereotypic, naive, impulsive, depressed, and anxious. He is also bothered by many phobic and compulsive tendencies (*e.g.*, he avoids stepping on cracks in the sidewalk) as well as feelings of dependency. Although he is aware of powerful emotions, he turns them inward into ruminations. Bitter and uneasy with people, he is hypersensitive and feels that he is different and inadequate. Thus, he complains that no one understands him, that he is not so happy as others, and that his sex life is unsatisfactory.

The test material revealed a grossly immature and inhibited person. Actually, strong impulsive tendencies press counter to this inhibition and frequently result in poor judgment. It is difficult for him to relate to people because he fears them and is so unsure of himself. Thus, he sees males and himself as pathetic, dependent, and non-assertive. His own self-image is of someone ugly and misshapen. Females for him are quite masculine and to be feared and depreciated. Consequently, he has considerable sexual confusion and anxiety. One outlet for his anxieties in this area seems to be gratification of strong oral needs.

Apparently, the patient feels himself to be a pawn in an emotional war between his parents, with his needs relegated to the background. He becomes disgusted and angry over parental demands, but his rebellious ideas soon turn to conformity. A hint of how he feels about what has happened in his home and about his self-image is presented in the following TAT story: ". . . Looks like she has no parents. She is left alone and does not know what to do. She has no one to get advice from and becomes a tramp on the streets. She ends up a prostitute and doesn't care anymore, a big pig. She knows what she is doing is wrong, but she goes on doing it."

Many of the patient's other stories deal with a son killing one or the other of his parents, or the son as a victim of the father's hostility. Feelings of rejection and jealousy among the son and both parents are given as explanation for these murderous impulses. Actually, the patient has repressed these hostile impulses—so far. He turns them toward himself with consequent feelings of depression. He appears unconsciously to be punishing himself and making himself repulsive to women other than his mother. The very means with which he does this—eating—may also gratify his cravings for love. There is little doubt that Mr. M derives considerable gratification from his unusually close relationship with his mother, but his fantasies reveal resentment of the smothering aspects and guilt about the "closeness" of this relationship—hence the self-punishment. The mother genuinely wants her son to be happy but may, at some level, derive compensatory gratifications for her unhappy marriage in an emotional hold on him.

Therapeutic Implications

There are suggestions that the patient's obesity serves serveral needs of which he is unaware. In any event, he is very neurotic and unhappy. At present, his concern about his great weight and his feeling of being unloved are so intense that he is very motivated for help. His intelligence, cooperativeness, and ability to work hard are good prognosticators as well. Fairly intense uncovering procedures are recommended. Progress, after an initial spurt, may be slow and arduous; this, along with weaning from a mother-child relationship to a sense of independence, may prove upsetting to both the patient and his mother. Tactfully forewarned, however, they both appear sufficiently motivated in terms of desired long-term goals.

THERAPY NOTES

First Session (5/15): Mr. M arrived fifteen minutes late. He told how he remained out late even though he felt he shouldn't. He thought that he was "easily led" and bad because people might wonder what bad parents he had. This made him feel guilty because he loved his parents. He remembered how hurt he was at a fight between his parents when he was 13 or 14.

> TAT—(1) Anger and incipient rebellion against parental demand ends in conformity.
>
> MMPI—Pd: High Pd suggests resentment and feelings of rebellion towards environment (parents).
>
> Rorschach—(IV) Resentment—head cut or shot suggests anger and destructiveness, turning of card suggests that some aggression is directed towards environment. Position of frog has anal quality which gives aforementioned feelings a rebellious quality (Freudian theory of anality and sadism being correlated).
>
> TAT—(1) Resentment at parents. (2) Ashamed and rejected by mother. (7) Used as pawn by parents. (8) Treated meanly by father. (10) Parents callous and calculating. (12) Again son angry at parents and plans revenge.
>
> MMPI—Pd indicates sense of alienation from family.

The patient then said that he was just a kid and wanted some time to himself. Working six and sometimes seven days a week, along with going to school, was too much. However, he did not want to take advantage of his grandfather—he is always afraid of taking advantage of others.

> DAP—"Just a kid" All male drawings have a helpless, childlike quality. Association to male is that he is a "stupe."

Second Session (5/19): The patient overslept. We discussed possible reasons for this. He confided that he often was late, and told of being late for taking a girl out this past Sunday. He considered that he did not like her too much, did not want to show her that he's too anxious, and was concerned that she might just string him along to reject him (because he told her once that he didn't like her).

> TAT—(4) Rationalizes anticipated rejection, especially from family.

The patient spoke of his surprise at seeing his father after a long time (to discuss his coming to therapy). He was surprised to learn that his father wanted to see him. All his life, his father had not shown affection and had forgotten such things as presents, birthday cards, and calling or seeing him. The patient felt so miserable that he did not care what happened to his father. He also expressed resentment in sullen manner.

> TAT—(7, 8, 12) Ambivalent feelings toward father in all of these stories.
>
> MMPI—Pd: High Pd suggests resentment and feelings of rebellion towards environment (parents).

Third Session (5/22): After some difficulty getting started and requiring considerable support, he sought information about masturbation. He had heard that this made one weak, impaired vision, and did not make for a good marriage. This is what his mother had said when he asked her about it when he was 14. Nevertheless, he still masturbated, but felt guilty. He would like to have sexual experiences but worries about disease, impregnating girl, and taking advantage of nice girls. He does kiss girls on occasion. When he was 10, and with a boy of 12 or 13, he took a girl into garage and kissed her. He felt guilty but also good and wished that he was bigger.

> ICL—(6) Sixth quadrant exaggerated suggests phobic and anxious feelings.
>
> MMPI—Items listed on MMPI profile sheet (*e.g.*, sex life unsatisfactory).
>
> MMPI—Pt: Peak Pt suggests manifest anxiety and obsessive thinking.
>
> TAT—(13MF) Sex and violence, guilt and punishment, all associated.
>
> Rorschach—(VI) Phobic, depreciatory, and distorted concepts, possibly about sex.

When he was six, a much older boy tormented him. He wished that he were bigger so that he could vent his hate on his tormentor. Even now he exults in the strength of his bigness.

> TAT—(2) Self-concept of "big pig"—powerful but bad.
>
> DAP—First drawings: Expansive quality of first drawing.

The patient veered away from the implications of his bigness. Instead, he proudly told of eating little for the past three weeks, during which he has been taking Dr. S's pills. He generally gets hungry after 5 PM but has little desire for food in the morning.

> Rorschach—VIII (1) Emphasis on orality.

He said he felt something has been accomplished.

Fourth Session (5/26): The patient again expressed conflict about staying out late. It makes him feel independent but he also feels that he is not doing right in respect to his mother. He told of incident when he came home late Saturday night and his mother learned that he had eaten little that day. She encouraged him to eat despite her previous prohibitions.

Rorschach–VIII (1) Emphasis on orality.

He has decided to quit high school despite family advice to the contrary. He can see little advantage in continuing in school, since his vocation is food line and he is uninterested in school. He will think it over.

TAT–(1) He does not suppress awareness of his rebellion as in TAT story. Actually he represses it.

Rorschach–(IV) Resentment, anger, and destructiveness.

ICL–(4) Conflict about resentment and rebellion expressed by prominent representation in picture of self but de-emphasized in Ideal (4th quadrant).

The patient grew silent toward the end of hour. With much prodding, he thought of the following with some embarrassment and laughter: "Would it hurt a kid to have intercourse?" (Ambivalence and conflict about mother and oral and sexual needs.)

MMPI–Item stating sex life unsatisfactory.

TAT–(1) Anger and incipient rebellion against parental demand ends in conformancy.

TAT–(13MF) Sex and violence, guilt and punishment, all associated.

Rorschach–VI Phobic, depreciatory, and distorted concepts possibly about sex. VII Ambivalence, conflict and tension on "Mother" card.

Fifth Session (5/29): With difficulty and embarrassment, the patient tackled the problem of having intercourse. His judgment told him that there was nothing wrong with it, that it would make him less anxious and preoccupied with it, and that it was all right for people to do it now and then. On the other hand, he worried that other people would find out. We explored this, discovering that he really worried that his mother would find out. He felt that he and she would both feel that he was doing something bad.

Rorschach–VI Phobic, depreciatory, and distorted concepts possibly about sex. VII Ambivalence, conflict and tension on "Mother" card.

> DAP—Female: Both drawings and associations to female are fearful and depreciatory.
> TAT—(6BM) Mother rejects him if he "does something to her," he depreciates her.

He said that he really "isn't a man yet."

> DAP—Male: "Just a kid" All male drawings have a childlike, helpless quality. Association to male is that he is a "stupe."

He remembered that when he was about six, his mother told him not to play with his penis because he would hurt it and get sick.

> TAT—(6) Does mother reject him because of his sexual interests?
> Rorschach—VI Phobic, depreciatory, and distorted concepts possibly about sex.

Some discussion followed of how his mother considers him as just a child. He feels this way too, particularly with his mother.

Sixth Session (6/2): Dream: Girlfriend's mother invited him and another fellow to dinner. After dinner he watched TV with girl and he began to kiss her. She said, "There's a time and a place for such things." They watched TV again. *Associations:* Several months ago he helped this girl buy a jacket. He brought it to her home but she was not there. Instead, he had coffee with her mother, who told him that her other daughter, who had run away, had been seen and she was anxiously awaiting a call from her. The girl's mother was about 5′3″ tall, dark, heavy-set, and wore glasses, "maybe Spanish." (This description approximated that of his own mother.)

> TAT—(7, 8, 10, 12) Eternal triangle theme for all of these stories associated with Oedipal dream.

He discussed his feelings about mothers, including mothers who were sexual. He remembered, when about ten, he wanted very much to see how women are made. He spied his mother in the nude, with feelings of both guilt and pleasure. Once when he was playing ball in the garage, his mother told him, "There is a time and a place for everything." We related this to the other garage experience, which was sexual (he, a girl, and another fellow).

He told of how yesterday his mother's friend told of her son-in-law's stepfather dying. Patient felt very bad—just as if his stepfather had died. It would mean that he and his mother would be alone, but he never liked that, he always wanted a father.

TAT–(6, 7, 12) All three theme stress conflictual attachment to mother.

I suggested that some of the things that he had spoken of might occasion anxiety for him; if so, we'd try to understand what this meant.

Seventh Session (6/5): The patient had an argument with his mother and grandmother. He had agreed to pick up his aunt, even though he knew he couldn't because he was waiting for his friends. The gist of the situation was that he could not say no to anyone because he is afraid of angering them or losing their approval. He could find glimmers of fear of hostile intent behind this (including resentment at interference by grandmother).

ICL–(6) High sixth octant indicates manifest docility.
MMPI–Pd indicates sullenness and resentment.

Today he finally grabbed a schoolmate who called him an elephant. He was able to see that not only was he angry with this boy but that this was anger displaced from his family, including his grandfather. He felt that his grandfather takes advantage of him in many ways, but he could not say anything because he feels obligated to him. At this point, though, he was able to express resentment at his grandfather, and called him stupid, incapable, etc.

Rorschach–III, IV Destructive content in both responses indicates hostile potential.
TAT–Open hostility in many stories.

The patient was able to see that he stored up resentment until he exploded (*e.g.*, hitting schoolmate, walking out on grandfather, etc.) rather than expressing this feeling when it was appropriate. Further, he was confused at being able to resent people he also loved; he needed to feel pushed around.

ICL–(3) Although low third octant for Self, this increases appreciably for Ideal, suggesting suppressed hostility.
TAT–(7, 8, 13) Violence in all three themes.
DAP–Male: Male a rough character, a boxer or wrestler, thus potentially hostile.

Eighth Session (6/9): It was very difficult for the patient to get started. *Dissociated ideas:* He went with his grandfather on the bus yesterday, which was very boring and tiring; his mother suggested that he date a very cute thin girl, beside whom he would feel very self-conscious. These ideas were not productive in stimulating further associations.

> Rorschach—VII Conflict and tension related to mother
> TAT—(6) Theme of mother rejecting him.

I wondered why he was not discussing his problem of weight. This released a great deal of material. He felt very proud of himself for abstaining recently from food. He related this to his grandfather, who could control himself. Thus, he felt like a man for not eating and for besting his grandfather. Two weeks ago he had a brief relapse when he was tremendously hungry, but he could not remember the circumstances. When the patient was silent, he twitched his head markedly; sometimes he was conscious of this.

> MMPI—Pt: Manifest anxiety and compulsiveness related to head tic.
> ICL—(6) High sixth octant indicates manifest docility.
> Rorschach—VI Phobic quality of tarantula and his anxious behavior in therapy.

Ninth Session (6/12): The session began with ten minutes silence. Finally, I asked what he was thinking about—and, as he obviously did have something to say, I wondered why he wanted me to ask. He said that he was always like that. We explored this but were only able to get at the fact that he eventually would have spoken because he was paying for it and because he was getting anxious, and because I would be upset. I interpreted his need for permission to speak and his possible hostile feelings toward me.

> ICL—(3, 4) Low Self and higher Ideal for octant 3 suggests suppressed hostility while the converse picture for octant 4 suggests his craving for but fear of relations.

This brought out the following story: On the previous Friday (6/6), he had signed the withdrawal from school and then tried to get back in, but could not because of age. He had not spoken about it because it had not occurred to him. I questioned his fantasy about this—he imagined that I would disapprove of him, as his family did.

> Rorschach—II, III, VIII, IX, X Loose use of color on all color cards suggests his impulsivity as related in his impetuousness in leaving school.
> MMPI—Pd: High Pd suggests rash action.

He failed two courses and suggested an indirect need to fail (rebellion, feeling treated unfairly, etc.). He then confessed that he wanted to leave school because he was so much bigger than the others. He admitted that his family, particularly his mother, is very disturbed about this. We considered his need to express his anger in this way because he was very hurt and angry inside.

MMPI–Pd: Both rebellion and alienation from family.
ICL–(4) High 4th octant indicates alienation and rebellion.

Tenth Session (6/17): The patient asked a girl to go out, and felt good about this, but he had only asked after another boy pushed him to do so. Similarly, he asked his grandfather for regular hours and felt good when this was granted; but he did this only after his mother interceded for him.

ICL–(6) High sixth octant indicates manifest docility.
MMPI–Pt, K: Low K connotes sense of helplessness.

Exploration led to the idea that the patient was afraid of being rejected. Although he continually blamed this on his weight, we considered that this served only as a rationale for a more pervasive feeling of being unliked and unworthy.

TAT–(6) Mother rejects him.
MMPI–Sc, K: Low K high Sc indicates low sense of worth, differentness, and rejection.

The patient thought of his father's not loving him and leaving him without talking to him. He alternately worked with and resisted the idea that overweight covered up this basic feeling of inadequacy.

TAT–(7, 8, 12M) All three themes describe open anger or violence.

Eleventh Session (6/19): The patient was silent for 15 minutes. I inquired what he was thinking about. He said absolutely nothing. I asked whether there was something about our relationship. He said no. He then told of how angry he got at his stepmother and her mother because they picked on him and clearly showed that they did not like him. He expressed anger towards them. On questioning, he conceded that his grandmother was also picky, and that his mother used to be; although he got mad at them too, it was different because they loved him.

TAT—(6, 7, 10, 13MF) All themes describe open anger or violence.

DAP—Female: Harsh, forbidding-looking female.

I interpreted that he was pretty angry about being unloved and left out of things, and that apparently this emotion went back a long way and may somehow be represented in his feelings towards me.

MMPI—Pd: Sense of alienation from family.

Twelfth Session (6/23): He had an enjoyable date with a girl who voiced willingness to see him again at a picnic. Yet when he offered her a lift today, she preferred taking a bus. Although she has accepted lifts from him in the past and although there are other reasons possible, he was bothered by the possibility that she rejected him because of his bigness. We worked with this, getting at the rationalizations of his inner feelings. For example, he actually felt "in the way" with his family, picked on by them, etc. We attempted to relate this to historical material.

TAT—All stories: Pervasive theme of rejection and mistreatment by family.

The patient was very unproductive; there were long silences without his discussing feelings or ideas. We could not shake this, but on prompting he did volunteer early memories of being fearful of his father when doing things he shouldn't (riding bike, etc., and more recently denting his car). His father was critical on former occasions.

TAT—(7, 8, 12) Themes of rejecting, punitive father.

Thirteenth Session (6/26): He called girlfriend to apologize for embarrassing her. She assured him that he hadn't. Exploration revealed that he was just fishing for reassurance because of a readiness to feel rejected.

On questioning, he began to speak with considerable anger about his grandfather. The patient felt his grandfather took advantage of him and treated him like a stupid child. Because the patient was obligated to his family and looked to such advantages as eventually taking over the business, he put up with this. But we soon saw that this was only a rationalization for his need to have a grievance and feel pushed around because he himself felt that he was a stupid child. His protests in contrast to his behavior fool no one.

ICL—(3) Low Self and higher Ideal for octant 3 suggests suppressed hostility while the converse picture for octant 4 suggests his craving but fear of relations.

TAT—(7) Son fights back and here patient expresses his anger.

MMPI—Pd: Sense of grievance.

ICL—(4) Conflict about resentment and rebellion expressed by prominent representation in picture of self but de-emphasized in Ideal (4th quadrant).

Apparently such grievances serve to expiate his keen sense of guilt.

ICL—(5) High 5th octant indicates guilt and self-punishment.

TAT—(2) Identification with heroine which suggests self-depreciation.

Fourteenth Session (6/30): "Goof" incident: Last night at 3:30 AM he and his friend on impulse went upstate to his aunt. They were to go early Sunday but thought about lack of sleep and "were not worried about getting into trouble." He evinced pleasure in thus rebelling against and defying his parents.

TAT—(6) Theme of rebellious defiance towards mother.

The patient even answered his mother's scolding with the retort that she had not let him go on trip to Los Angeles last year. He felt more adult and in control.

Another "goofy" incident: The patient's uncle pointed out a woman of bad reputation, "old, about 40-45 with a child my age." And he fantasied going to bed with her, since a woman like that would consider even him. We explored this idea, opening up his impaired self-image and self-depreciation. "Goofy ideas" are apologies for his impulsive behavior or the impulses themselves.

TAT—(10, 12) Oedipal theme of both stories.

We worked past his complaint about his weight as a cause for his sense of inferiority. I worked hard on the inner core of this, referring to such other anxiety symptoms as tics, nail biting, biting skin off hands, etc.

MMPI—D, K, Pt: Low K and high D and Pt pattern demonstrates dysphoria and anxiety.

ICL—(6) High 6th octant suggests manifest anxiety.

Fifteenth Session (7/7): Last session the patient phoned two hours before appointment and said he would not make it and asked whether he would be charged anyway. He was informed the matter would be discussed when he came in.

> Rorschach–II Defiance indicated via rejection of card and expletives; also by broken appointment.
> MMPI–Pd: High Pd suggests rebelliousness.

As soon as the patient came in he wanted to know about charge. Discussion revealed that the day before, a holiday, he was busy at work. He was told that hereafter he would be held responsible. Exploration revealed that he was ready to be angry with me and was utilizing the charge for an excuse. Similarly, he took food from his grandfather without his permission and came in to work very late this morning. While discussing this, he could not control his mouth from twitching. It soon became apparent to him that he wanted to cross his grandfather in this indirect way and also wanted attention from him—even if unfavorable.

> TAT–(7) Looking for a fight with authority figures.
> ICL–(3) Low Self and higher Ideal for octant 3 suggests suppressed hostility while the converse picture for octant 4 suggests his craving but fear of relations.

It also developed that, in a very indirect way, the patient had managed on a preconscious level to have his grandfather see him with a date in a shiny new convertible at a baseball game; his grandfather was in a food wagon with his friends. The patient could not conceal his delight at thus lording it over his grandfather.

> ICL–(Self 2, 3) Octant representing competitiveness and octant 3 representing aggression de-emphasized yet increased in Ideal, suggesting their repression or only indirect expression.

Sixteenth Session (7/10): The patient was fifteen minutes late. He appeared vastly amused during the hour, although he could not or would not explain why. Exploration revealed that he was delighted that he could show authority figures like his grandfather that he was at least as important as they (newer car, etc.): He defies them to prove that he is not a helpless child (takes food, defies gym teacher, etc.); and something of that same sort goes on between us. Thus, missing an hour and being frequently late demonstrated control and hostility to him. And his car is newer than mine. (Just prior to the hour, we passed each other in our cars—he did not remember this but laughed heartily.) We discussed these considerations.

TAT—(7, 8, 12) Highly hostile fantasies towards father (authority).

ICL—(Therapist 2, 3) Octant 2 representing competitiveness and octant 3 representing aggression de-emphasized yet increased in Ideal, suggesting their repression or only indirect expression.

Seventeenth Session (7/14): The patient was 45 minutes late. He apologized and explained that a last-minute delivery was responsible. Exploration revealed that he had imagined I would be angry. Discussion with him presented very definite possibility that this is exactly what he unconsciously hoped for, that this was also testing behavior, and that possibly a revenge motive (towards adults and father figures) might lie beneath this. I stressed tremendous importance of understanding this behavior.

Rorschach—II Defiant behavior both in speech and in rejection of card.

MMPI—Pd: High Pd suggests impulsive or rebellious actions.

Eighteenth Session (7/16): The patient was about ten minutes late, and had a considerable block in talking. With prodding he mentioned that newspaper headlines made him very anxious about his getting drafted or a bomb being dropped on the city. Nothing succeeded in breaking through his resistance. We tried free association; it dried up after only the following hint, "knives-people." We talked about this blockage and his probable anger and defiance, again stressing such indications as lateness and missed hour. We considered frankly how this was shutting out therapeutic intervention and might even end in termination.

Rorschach—III, IV Morbid and phobic preoccupations.

MMPI—D, Pt: High D, Pt pattern is one of felt and expressed anxiety.

ICL—(6) High 6th octant indicates manifest anxiousness.

Nineteenth Session (7/21): Missed.

Twentieth Session (7/24): The patient told of getting sick eating mushrooms the day before the last appointment. He slept late and thus called shortly before the hour began. He stayed out of work a day and a half. He then told of how he was going to take a vacation at his uncle's home whether the latter said yes or no. He hadn't told his grandfather and was waiting until the last moment to do so because then he could not turn back. We related this to the therapy sessions and the fact that he was telling me, in effect, that he was taking a vacation on 8/2 for two weeks—more or less an ultimatum.

TAT—All stories: Pervasive themes of passive rebelliousness.

The patient discussed his inability to say what he felt in such situations. He revealed that he was glad that his father's marriage was not working out—even glad that his father's second wife had recently had a miscarriage. He resented this woman and felt revengeful towards his father. Secretly, he wished that his father had never left; he would always remember father and mother together. He hoped that his father would never have another child. He then touched on his inability to ask for anything because he felt obligated, giving examples of such situations with his father; so that he usually waited until he had to or the circumstances compelled him, as in the case of his vacation.

TAT—(7, 8, 12) Themes of preoccupation with family breakup.

MMPI—Pd: Sense of being alienated from family.

At the very end of the hour, he brought up question of sessions once a week. When I suggested that we talk about it next hour, he made it clear he was going on vacation immediately because he had decided to visit his grandmother first. I said that we would discuss it next visit.

Twenty-first Session (8/25): Patient twenty minutes late. We discussed his absence the last week of July and last week (four weeks in all rather than the expected two, with insufficient notice in respect to the first and the last week). He gave some explanations about getting an early start in deer season and the inconvenience of coming last week. I told him that he was held responsible for these hours.

Rorschach—III, IV, and most TAT stories: Morbid and phobic preoccupations.

MMPI—D, Pt: High D, Pt pattern is one of felt and expressed anxiety.

ICL—(6) High 6th octant indicates manifest anxiousness.

This brought up the whole issue of therapy. He wondered about its efficacy, but also added that he had gained 10 pounds since he had been away and has "lost will power." He also wanted to know about the implications of acting impulsively or not acting at all. We discussed frankly the question of commitment to therapy. In this context he again brought up the idea of sessions once a week. I told him this would present a special problem with him because of his massive resistance to working at therapy. I would not recommend it but if he felt he could commit himself on this basis, we could try.

> TAT—(2) "Doesn't care anymore, a big pig."
> Rorschach—VIII Emphasis on orality.

In any event, it was *his* decision whether to continue therapy and choice of hours per week, with my opinion being heavily expressed, it is true. There was some discussion about his feeling of being rejected, punished, and distrustful, and how he pulled for this, including with me.

> ICL—(4) High 4th octant (completely omitted in Ideal) connotes distrustfulness.
>
> Rorschach—III Morbid, mask-like skeleton head responses suggests pathological distrust (masking of real feelings.)

Twenty-second Session (8/28): After the last hour, the patient's mother called and said that she did not think her son could continue treatment because of money and difficulty with job and getting to therapy. I suggested that I discuss this with the patient.

He arrived a half hour late. We discussed his problem of focusing primarily on his weight problem as well as equivocal motivation from start. In his interpretation his mother pushed him in and mother took him out. We considered some of the things that might be churning beneath the surface. He spontaneously brought up his sense of inferiority and hypersensitivity, the relationship to his broken home, his feelings about himself, and his dependence on his mother. I briefly and not deeply spoke about his relationship with his mother and the implications of his weight problem. We went into feelings about leaving therapy and the possibility of return or a referral. He said he thought he would be seeing me again.

The psychological evaluation predicted that the "weaning" process occasioned for the patient by therapy might prove a stumbling block. The test material related to the unfolding therapeutic material was very suggestive of the need to encourage expression of his anger and to foster independent, autonomous behavior on his part.

CHAPTER THREE

POLLYANNA: SCHIZOID WITH MARKED HYPOCHONDRIACAL FEATURES

I

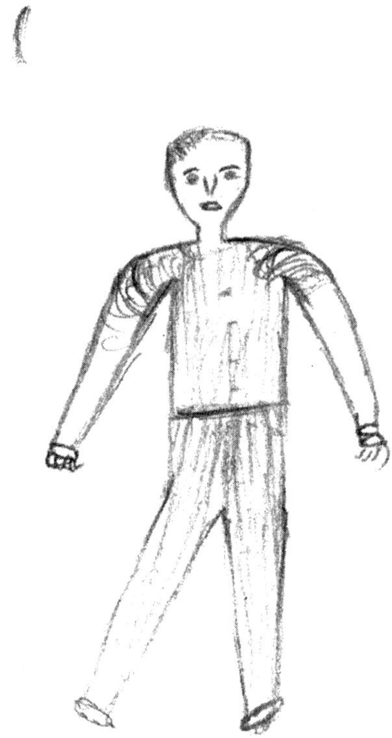

II

DIAGNOSTIC OVERVIEW:

Schizoid Personality with Hypochondriacal Features

This is an example of a case with a poor prognosis. Almost all motivation was from without; the patient very ambivalently dabbled a toe into treatment when, as she put it, all her physicians "insisted" she do so.

This is a case of Schizoid character. Character disorders have as their hallmark a lifelong pattern of maladjustment characterized by lack of closeness in interpersonal relationships. The schizoid personality, in particular, is impoverished in his dealings with other persons, preoccupied with a world of fantasy, and often either idiosyncratic in outlook and or morbidly introspective. The last may be centered around his own soma so that there are manifested bodily concern, hypochondriacal complaints, and, in extreme instances, somatic delusions (at this point the schizoid personality merges into a schizophrenic process).

The schizoid features of this patient were notable in all these respects. The interview material emphasized a lifelong history of impoverished interpersonal relationships, including familial—no friends, no dates, and a sense of alienation so keen that at times she wondered if she were losing her mind. In the ICL, this was indicated by the low representation in the fourth octant with a desire to be even less affiliated (Ideal ICL). Her isolation from human affairs was suggested on the Rorschach by a plethora of dehumanized responses such as people without heads, Santa Claus and so on. The hypochondriacal character was morbidly expressed in the interview by the myriad somatic complaints, medical terminology, and stable of physicians which began with her very late menarche; on the MMPI by the exaggerated "psychosomatic inverted V" (extremely high Hs and Hy and relatively lower D) and little manifest anxiety (relatively low Pt as well as D); and, again on the ICL, high representation in the psychosomatic of eighth octant. The exaggeration of these features and her odd interview statement of wishing she had a new body suggested a tinge, at least, of somatic delusion. Other idiosyncratic thinking was conveyed by blurred (contaminated and F "minus") concepts on the Rorschach, where she also demonstrated a fairly rich fantasy life (not an unpositive feature).

This case has been labeled a case of Pollyanna because of the patient's very narcissistic involvement (the bodily preoccupation, sensual rubbing and wriggling in interview; the tactual responses on the Rorschach; and loving attention to detail and cosmetic features in DAP) and her bland, denying, and presumably anxiety-free attitudes. (Thus, her repeated assertions in the interview that everything was wonderful except illnesses, despite a markedly pathogenic childhood, paucity of relationships, and admitted phobic and listless experiences). The DAP emphasized smiling, colorless people, as did her TAT themes; and the MMPI presented her as low in anxiety as represented by low D and Pt. On the Rorschach however, considerable inner tension was conveyed by the relatively large number of inanimate motion determinants, fluid reaction to emotional stimuli (color), and content such as tug of war and explosions.

PSYCHOLOGICAL EVALUATION:

A Case of Pollyanna

Patient: female, age 28, single living with parents and sister
Education: high school graduate
Occupation: clerical worker
Referred by doctor for personality evaluation in light of a multiplicity of longstanding somatic complaints.

Tests Administered

Rorschach, Thematic Apperception Test (TAT), Minnesota Multiphasic Personality Inventory (MMPI), Draw-A-Person (DAP), and Interpersonal Checklist (ICL).

Behavior

Miss P was a slim attractive girl who spoke in a low voice with a mild German accent, so that it was frequently necessary to have her repeat what she said. She gave the impression of being introverted and was evasive about details of her interaction with people. This impression was substantiated by the history she gave of a minimal social life. However, this was an area about which she was quite sensitive; she took many opportunities to decry the "false impression" she gave of being "shy" although she really was "popular and extroverted." She appeared unconscious of her seductive and narcissistic mannerisms such as rubbing her arms and chest, wriggling sinuously in her chair, fingering her hair sensually, etc.

She presented a long and involved medical history, complete with technical diagnoses and studded with a galaxy of physicians. She commented wryly that she thought she had a "doctor complex." Some of these problems had begun coincident with a late menarche at 15; they became exacerbated six months after she graduated from high school and began to work. With considerable feeling she said "Nobody, not even my own parents, has hurt me or interfered with my life or babied me as much as Dr. R, even though he preached my achieving independence." Nevertheless, despite a pathogenic history (broken home, separation from mother, etc.), generalized fearfulness, and hints of keen loneliness, she adamantly maintained she had no psychological problems. Her overprotestations in this direction were significant in their own right.

Evaluation

The patient presents herself as a responsible, self-sustaining person who is overly anxious to please others and thus in the process is self-effacing and ingratiating. She has little insight into the exaggerated and symptomatic aspects of this orientation—particularly her basic distrust of people, which she cannot admit even to herself. Consequently, she is eager to please people even more than she thinks she does now; outwardly she does manage to deal with them openly and to cope with her environment. However, her ability to relate and her sociability are achieved with considerable effort. Similarly, she presents an extremely feminine facade which cloaks, even from own awareness, marked masculine strivings.

Although Miss P is not very manifestly anxious and, indeed, attempts to convey a Pollyanna impression, this seems to be counterreactive. That is, she appears to be smiling on the outside and crying on the inside. She is extremely defensive and even tries to deny her marked dysphoria. Nevertheless, there is no doubt about the considerable tension and emotionality going on within her. Using compulsive defenses, denial, and reaction formations, she is able to channelize most of this anxiety. There are many indications that she also resorts to conversion processes. But despite all these neurotic defenses (or perhaps because of them), she feels listless and increasingly phobic.

Dependency on an extensive fantasy life and intense preoccupation with physical symptoms are proving less successful for her. She derives "satisfaction" from the masochistic way she uses such symptoms, such as what a burden she is to her family, how sacrificing women must be, etc., but she is unaware of their hostile purpose as well (i.e., "Aren't you guilty to see how I suffer? Be ashamed of your responsibility in making me so unhappy").

The patient has many strengths. She is intelligent and creative (when she can overcome her inhibitions), and demonstrates a degree of resiliency. At present she fritters away her energy via neurotic defenses and conversion into physical complaints. She is capable of being assisted to utilize more direct, rather than her current hysterical, approaches to life. However, at present her denial is so operant that motivation is lacking.

THERAPY NOTES

First Session (4/22): (almost a year after initial testing): Miss P placed tremendous emphasis on physical symptoms, although she was very anxious in her mannerisms. Although she averred her desperateness in ridding herself of these symptoms, she also suggested a need to cling to them.

> MMPI–Hs: Peak on Hs indicates her preoccupation with physical symptoms.
>
> ICL–(8) Exaggerated 8th octant describes psychosomatic personality ("I'm so good, so generous, so efficient–the only thing wrong with me could be physical").

She came to see me at the insistence of "all my doctors." She presented all sorts of reasons why she has no emotional problems and how happy her past has been (while revealing considerable data to the contrary). She did admit to shyness but thought that this was only an initial impression she made.

> MMPI–Hy, K, L: Peaks on all 3 scales suggest rigid denial.
>
> ICL–(7, 8) Exaggeration in 7th and 8th octants suggest denial.
>
> TAT–General tone: Superconventional and denial themes.

She has contacted an introduction agency in order to meet a man. Now, however, she is too sick to follow through. Recently, she voluntarily kept herself in bed for six weeks. She would like to try staying in bed for a much longer time and thus finally rule out organic conditions. Then she would consider her emotional problems.

Again, her dress and movements appeared seductive.

> MMPI–Hy, Mf: High Hy low Mf says "See how feminine I am."
> DAP–Female: Oh-so-femininely drawn female.
> Rorschach–VII (3) Response indicates performing and exhibiting for others.

I attempted to sidestep delicately her physical symptomatology without attacking the symptoms, since she apparently *must cling* to this defensive structure. It seems very problematical whether she will be able to work with psychological matters, even though she did come in to talk about her problems and also committed herself to two more visits.

Second Session (4/24): Although she still showed enormous concentration on somatic complaints, more psychological factors emerged. The latter were always presented as the opinions of doctors or friends, not as her own. Mother was seen as overprotective, very domineering, and a hypochondriac in her own right, as well as preoccupied with her daughter's symptoms.

> Rorschach–VII (1, 3) In possible mother context, performing and aggression (lions) rather than peacefulness or playfulness (*e.g.*, lambs or little girls).

The patient said that others might think that illnesses get her attention, but she doesn't. When she feels ill, she is shy, unsure, compulsive, etc., but that is because of physical factors.

> DAP–Manner of handling: Extremely compulsive execution of drawings.

She started to talk about early memories. She made some mention of her natural father being in a fight and being a "bad daddy."

> TAT–(9GF) Male insecure and unfaithful. (13MF) Female victimized by male.
> DAP–Male: Weak, childlike male.

She showed pictures of herself from childhood to adulthood, trying to demonstrate how happy and secure she was (as well as an apparent narcissistic pleasure in exhibiting herself).

> MMPI–K: High K says "everything is Pollyanna."

Miss P's 25-year old sister is sick and so now "sleeps with *her* father." When Miss P is sick herself, she sleeps *"with my sister's father."* She corrected this to say "both our father." It developed that their mother also happens to be in the same bed. Miss P said that others might think she feels inferior to her sister—this is not so, she merely admires her sister's ambition. (However, she frequently compared herself to the sister, stressing that she, the patient, received more attention from their mother and that when she felt well, she was "even more ambitious than my sister.")

TAT—(1) Wish for father, since unacceptable, inevitable conflict.

TAT—(9GF) Competitiveness between sisters.

Third Session (4/25): The patient seemed somewhat more psychologically oriented. She told me how she felt that I helped her make decisions (*e.g.*, more confidence in herself, not so much fear of offending Dr. R by switching to Dr. E—who will give her more medicine).

She did admit to lack of confidence and fear of others. She always imagined that others did not like her because she really did not think too much of herself. I worked on the historic factors involved. When I gave support to the realness of her somatic complaints, she was more able to relate them to her emotional problems. But she had very little insight into the angry feelings underlying them, and only a little bit more into the gnawing hurt and sense of rejection (although she searched for examples of this).

ICL—(4) Fourth octant only one barely represented in Self and not at all in Ideal—suggests conflict about trust in others.

MMPI—Pa: Fairly high Pa (high peak on right side, over 65), notwithstanding rigid denial (high K, L, and Hy), indicates basic mistrust of others.

She expended prodigious effort in trying to convince me that her mother was not overprotective; and worked hard to prevent my getting the "wrong impression" of the latter. This effort was pointed out to her.

MMPI—Hy, Pt: Hy, the denial, and Pt, the compulsive efforts to avoid anxiety.

Rorschach—II (a), IV (3), X (1): II (a) Denial so sharp, it's counterphobic. Thus, aggression or impulsivity (firecrackers) break through but she must counter this (only sparklers). IV (3)

In same way, explosion becomes passive flower. X (1) potentially fearful beetles are made nice-looking.

I was supportive but frank in expressing my opinion of the emotional aspects for her symptoms. She said she was very motivated for psychotherapy but could not afford it. She would like to enter treatment when she *felt better* and got a job!!!

The psychological tests indicated her massive denial and channeling of anxiety via somatic avenues. They also indicated her basic mistrust and fear of self-examination. The suggestion for psychotherapeutic intervention appeared to have been an attempt at sidestepping the inevitable flood of somatic complaints and focusing on psychological factors that she could accept. Even this approach was not sufficient to overcome the primary and secondary gains of her hypochondriacal orientation.

CHAPTER FOUR

A CASE OF SHAKES: HYSTERICAL PERSONALITY

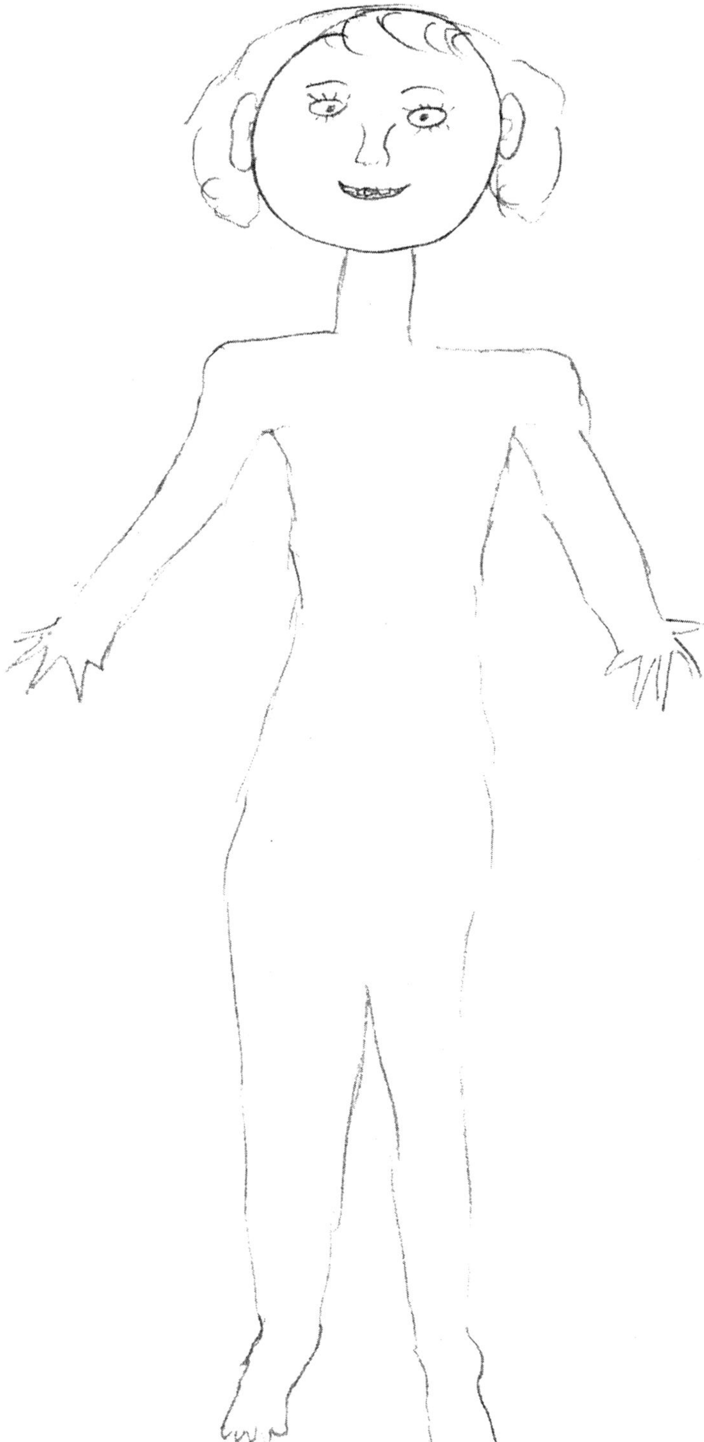

I

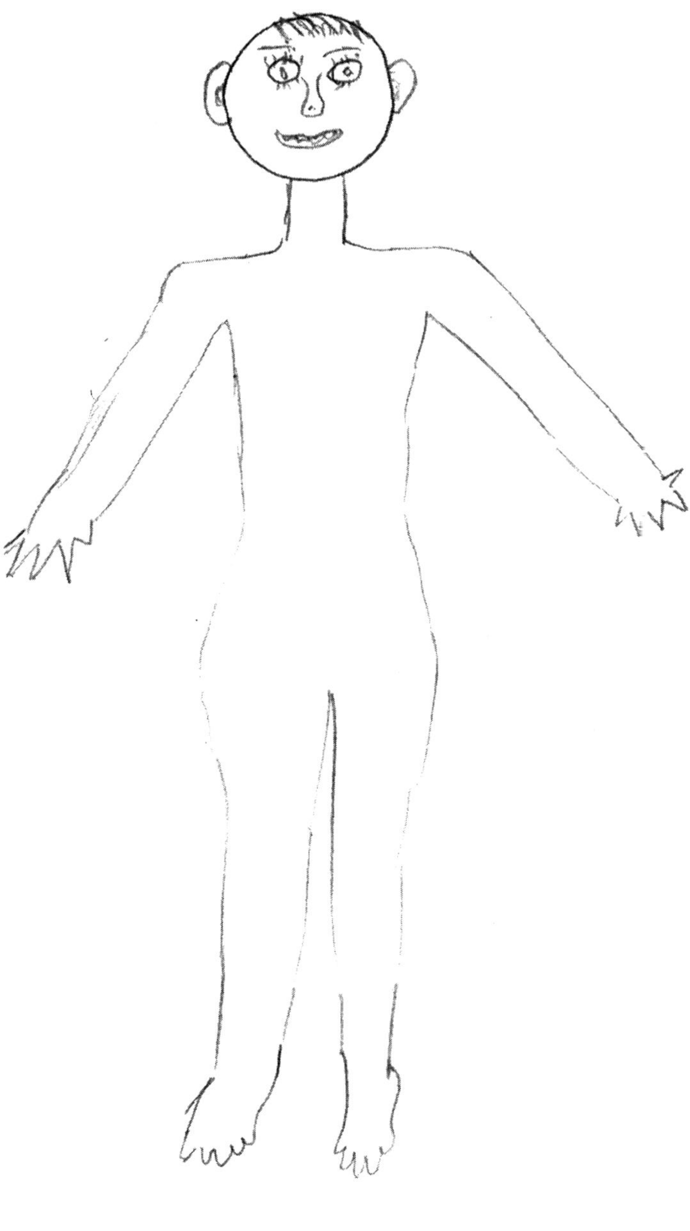

DIAGNOSTIC OVERVIEW:

Hysterical Personality

The hysterical orientation may be described primarily in terms of fluidity of affect–running emotionally hot or cold (and usually hot). Associated with this is a characteristic massive denial or general repression of motives and conflicts, particularly those of a sexual or hostile nature. Instead, there is a somatic conversion of emotional tension and anxiety. Although there is relatedness to people, sometimes even intense in nature, the veneer of warmth masks hostility. A childlike quality is revealed in inordinate demands for love and attention, which are sought in the guileless and primitive manner of a five-year-old. This case has been categorized as a Hysterical Personality rather than Hysteria alone. The implication is that the former categorization is a more ingrained character orientation that has evolved gradually; the more insulated Hysteria reaction has a more sudden onset, usually in late childhood or early adolescence. Thus, in this case, the patient has complained of her symptoms all her life; her masochistic orientation is embedded in her character structure.

The emotionality was connoted in this case on the Rorschach by the relatively large number of color responses, usually poorly defined by form and including such content as blood; the dramatic and histrionic material presented in the interview, TAT, and Rorschach; and anxiety and tenseness suggested on the MMPI by the pattern of HsDHy and Pt all above 60. The relations to people were ostensibly cooperative and dependent, denoted both by representation in the 7th ICL octant which was even more exaggerated in the Ideal, and by the naive, conventional attitudes expressed in the interview and TAT as well as by the large number of Rorschach populars. Nevertheless, the denial of hostile intentions was indicated by absence of aggression even where expected (*e.g.*, Cow where aggressive content is often seen on Rorschach, blandness on TAT card 13MF, yet teeth and spread fingers on DAP suggested repressed hostility). Not only was the present complaint the physical expression of shakes, but the patient began her interview with her somatic symptoms and retreated back to this whenever she waded too far into psychological explanations. The childlike quality of this patient was conveyed by the aforementioned naivete and histrionics, the immature DAP with little detail and poor sexual differentiation, a resentful exaggerated focus on her parents, and a phobic emphasis in the interview and Rorschach (bugs, tarantula, witches, etc.).

There were positive features indicated in the Rorschach by productive, well-formed concepts, and utilization of form with color and tactual determinants; the MMPI profile showed no peak above 70, and there was no serious distortion in any of the material. The evaluation forewarned that the patient would engage in somatic bouts whenever faced with conflictual material, and that rage beneath the surface, confused with sexual concepts, had to be uncovered. The evaluation also indicated that the patient derived neurotic gratification from her relationship with her mother; she repressed, but was ready to examine, her relationships to her father; and she was relating many of these feelings to her husband and children.

PSYCHOLOGICAL EVALUATION:

A Case of Shakes

Patient: female, age 36, married, two daughters (ages six years, 22 months)

Education: some postgraduate study

Occupation: housewife

Referred by: Dr. N. for personality evaluation; complains of "shakes," low back pain, and "nervousness."

Tests Administered

Rorschach, Thematic Apperception Test (TAT), Draw-A-Person (DAP), Minnesota Multiphasic Personality Inventory (MMPI), and Interpersonal Checklist (ICL).

Behavior and Background

Mrs. S was a tall, thin, well-groomed woman who appeared quite poised. However, she confessed that she was very nervous and fearful that the tests would reveal how inadequate she was. Nevertheless, she was quite frank, both in the interview and in her answers to the test material. Indeed, in the latter she was characterized by self-reference, relating many of her responses to her family, but particularly to the interaction between her mother and herself. After initially discussing various illnesses she has had, including rheumatic fever, a recent attack of bursitis, and periodic low back pain, she described two sets of nervous conditions: one is a "physiological" state resulting in shakes which is alleviated by eating chocolate; the other is "nervousness," characterized by shakes and feelings of helplessness. These states are usually triggered by confrontation with authority figures, such as her husband's boss, a policeman citing her for traffic violation, and so on. She soon threw caution to the winds and vividly and persistently described a selfish, controlling mother to whom she cannot stand up. Much to her dismay, Mrs. S finds that she re-enacts these feelings with her own daughter. The latter has become a "behavior problem" and upsets the patient with her contrariness. The patient's marriage, she reported, is a happy one, but then she admitted disinterest in sex on her part and frustration on her husband's part. He pushes his feelings inside and drives himself, while she is a "very compulsive housewife."

Frequently, she turned her right ear toward the examiner and asked that statements be repeated. When questioned about this, she said she had often wondered whether her hearing was defective, but no organic damage has been found.

Evaluation

Mrs. S presents herself as an extremely passive and self-punishing individual. She pictures herself as helpless and ultra feminine with accompanying severe anxiety, phobias, and indecisiveness. She does admit to verbal aggression such as sarcasm, but is unaware of considerable repressed hostility. She would like to be more forceful, dominant, and assertive and hopes to achieve this by being extra cooperative, friendly, and so colorless than she will offend no one. Although superficially she is outgoing and frank, basically she is rather suspicious and fearful of people.

The psychological examination revealed the patient to be pronouncedly hysterical: she is anxious, tense, phobic and compulsive. She manifests childish thinking, is highly impulsive, tends to be exhibitionistic, and massively represses her sexual and aggressive impulses. Masochistic features are also prominent: by means of her passive and self-punishing orientation she can express resentment toward people important to her by making them feel guilty. When her other defenses fail, she resorts to somatization. Despite a good degree of warmth, tact, and sociability, she tends to be so egocentric that at times her judgment suffers in her tremendous effort to relate everything to her experiences and problems.

The patient is particularly obsessed with her relationship to her mother. She takes every opportunity to describe her as controlling, childish and unreasonable. She is aware of her identification with her mother but not with her father, whom she describes as a poor victim. And while she proclaims her desperate need, but inability, to win independence from her mother, she is unaware of the considerable neurotic gratification that she derives from this kind of interaction, because it at least represents *some relationship* with her mother.

Therapeutic Implications

Despite her impulsivity and self-punishing tendencies, Mrs. S also manifests considerable strengths. She relates well to people, and is intelligent, adaptable, and eager to understand herself (particularly since this falls in wth her narcissistic needs). Her tendency to somaticize suggests that when her anxiety increases, as whenever she approaches conflictual material, the patient may succumb to one physical illness after another. Nevertheless, psychotherapeutic prognosis is good for a hysterical patient with such strengths.

THERAPY NOTES

First Session (6/4): Mrs. S arrived fifteen minutes late. She had been upset over the weekend because her mother obviously favored Mrs. S's brother and his children. She described the following incident: The family was watching a physicians' television conference on sex education. The mother was quite upset about this telecast; she childishly attempted to direct the family's attention away from the program and finally severely criticized the program. The patient was quite irritated and said, "Mother, sex is here to stay." The mother answered angrily, "No, it isn't." Mrs. S laughed while telling this.

> Interview—At very end of diagnostic interview, patient hints of conflict about mother—wants to be close yet resents her bitterly.

The patient remembered that her mother had been opposed to the first pregnancy of her daughter-in-law (the brother's wife). Therefore, the daughter-in-law was fearful of telling her of her second pregnancy. So the patient tried to "prepare her." Both the mother and brother are Catholics, and the patient stressed this as an issue. The mother was angered at the "facts of life" and "scandal" the patient was suggesting. Clarified theme: The patient resented yet was delighted at her mother's hysterical denial of sex; she took fairly evident pleasure in confronting her mother with this fact—and it always worked.

> TAT—(2, 7, 13, 18) Stress mother's "s-mothering." 13MF indicates patient's weak attempts to deny sexual and aggressive impulses.

Mrs. S agreed and added that her mother is this way about other areas also. At the age of 14, the patient was horrified at the idea of sex between parents. Yesterday was "true to form, should outlaw looking at dead bodies." (sic) She apologized for being late and promised punctuality in the future.

> TAT—(13MF) Weak attempts at denying aggression (*i.e.*, very superficially concealed).

Second Session (6/5): The patient called to say that her babysitter had not arrived. She came in 25 minutes late talking of the sitter's delinquency without apparent anger. She laughed instead which appeared characteristic, particularly when she was angry with her mother.

> MMPI—Pd, Mf: Instead of anger at others, directs to self. (PdMf—"See how helpless I am.")
>
> ICL—(5) Stress on 5th octant indicates masochism.
>
> ICL—(Self 3) Exaggerated 3rd octant indicates verbal aggression which, so far, is contradicted by patient's reports of not getting angry.

Yesterday the patient's baby had an accident while the patient was at a baseball game with her husband (the game ran into extra innings). The sitter (a different one) told a confusing story. Subsequently, the patient learned the true story from neighbors, which demonstrated the negligence of the sitter. Although she admitted brief feelings of anger because the sitter, whom she had known for a year, lied, she spent more time excusing human feelings and being forgiving. Exploration revealed that Mrs. S has been away most of the week and that her mother castigates her for having so many sitter hours. Further it occurred to her that the sitter might tell or at least think the patient was bad for talking about her mother to her, coming to therapy, etc. She quickly denied that such feelings were more than transient. We considered the possibility that the patient feels somewhat guilty about these things and about the accident to her daughter. She is quick to excuse others because she needs to excuse guilt in herself. It is important to investigate what happens to anger in her.

> MMPI–PdMf: Instead of anger at others, directs to self. PdMf–"See how helpless I am."
>
> ICL–(6) Exaggerated 6th octant suggests anxiousness and guilt.
>
> TAT–(2) Would like to stand on own two feet and make decisions rather than be criticized and "doubts put into her."

Third Session (6/13): Patient cancelled previous session because her baby was ill. (The baby has developed a fever apparently unrelated to last week's accident.) The patient told of a series of events surrounding the accident and accused herself of blundering, etc. This is what her family characteristically does to her and she admitted she likes to feel dependent. Trying to find why, she came up with two theories: (1) She had done something (or a series of things) so reprehensible that she feels guilty and unconfident—she can't imagine what; or (2) her parents are at fault.

> TAT–(7) Mother critical and makes her feel guilty.
>
> MMPI–PdMf: Instead of anger at others, directs to self. (PdMf–"See how helpless I am.")
>
> ICL–(5, 6, and lower half in general) Emphasis on octants 5 and 6 and lower half in general points to her submissive orientation.

I wondered about the hostile implications associated with her suggestions. She laughed as if to deny aggression. Soon after, she mentioned how I helped her and laughed again. I directed her attention to this laughter. She said she was fearful of me and guarded lest I pick up every gesture or word and use it against her. Discussion led to her fear of being hostile.

> TAT–(13MF) Weak attempts at denying aggression (*e.g.*, very superficially concealed.)
>
> ICL–(3) Exaggerated 3rd octant indicates verbal aggression.

The patient told of being inhibited and gauche at a party. She was angry at herself but actually uncovered her anger at others for putting her on the spot when she yearned to be more relaxed and less inhibited. At the end of the hour, she asked for advice about whether to tell her mother of coming to therapy. I suggested she brings this up next time. Then she asked my help in obtaining sitters.

> MMPI–PdMf: Instead of anger at others, directs to self. (PdMf–"See how helpless I am.")
> Rorschach–III (2) Sense of impotency and guilt.

Fourth Session (6/20): On 6/17 Mrs. S phoned to cancel her 6/18 appointment because both children were sick and had to be taken to the doctor. On 6/18 she called because she thought she might have to miss 6/20 for the same reason. Finally she left a message on 6/19 saying that she could make the appointment. We discussed these events. Although there were fairly objective reasons (such as leaving sick children with sitters), we considered also the question of her resistance, particularly in light of her lateness (again 5 minutes late this hour.) The patient emphasized her joy in coming–she has even told the referring physician of this. We considered denial aspects here as well.

> MMPI–Hy: Peak of Hy suggests denial tendencies.
> Rorschach–II, VIII, IX, X: The impulsive or hysterical handling of color on these cards would also suggest hysterical denial.
> ICL–(Ideal 7) Not only is the 7th octant well represented in the Self but is even more so, and the most exaggerated, in Ideal–again hysterical (denial).

We discussed the implications of the patient's requesting my aid in obtaining sitters and of her telling her mother about coming to therapy. In both cases, responsibility for missing hours could be put on me. Moreover, exploration revealed that the patient's fear that her mother would ridicule her about therapy because of stupidity and weakness coincided with her own feelings, which were largely unconscious.

> ICL–(bottom half) Lower hemisphere more represented connotes submissiveness.
> TAT–(1, 2, 7) Feelings of conformancy to, and domination by, mother.

The patient asked several times whether I had children.

Fifth Session (6/25): The patient said that she had been very anxious just before coming but did not know why; she added that she feels that way in "any authoritarian situation."

ICL–(6) Exaggerated 6th octant suggests anxiousness and guilt.

MMPI–D, Hy, K, Pt: High D and Pt signifies depression and tension, low K self-criticism, and high Hy exaggerated emotionality—or overall pattern of manifest anxiety.

Rorschach–II, VIII, IX, X: "Hysterical" use of color or hypersensitivity to emotional (really internal) stimulation.

Rorschach–VI (1) Bug suggests phobic feelings.

TAT–(2) Daughter "worried" in presence of mother.

Mrs. S spent most of the hour describing her unreasonable rage and anxiety when her 6-year-old daughter has "accidents." She had tried to toilet-train this daughter even before she was two despite her judgment in the situation. Feelings of dirtiness, shame, defiance, and stupidity are associated with toilet and reflect on her. (She accuses daughter of all this.) She feels particularly vulnerable to criticism from her mother and mother-in-law on these accounts. The patient said that her mother told her that *she* used to have accidents as well. We worked somewhat on the historic aspects to explain some of her "unreasonable emotions" in this situation.

DAP–Both drawings: Exaggerated 3 octant indicates verbal aggression.

MMPI–Pd: High Pd indicates resentment towards family members.

ICL–(5) High 5th octant represents shame, guilt, feelings of unworthiness.

Rorschach–III (4), VIII (6, 7): III (4) Masochistic response. VIII (6) Lava or hot destructive viscous material suggests anality. VIII (7) Spine—again suggests anal aggression.

Sixth Session (6/26): Mrs. S had considered going to a convention rather than coming to this session. She then told of her earlier intention to quit, which she had decided against because of the following circumstances (which completely slipped her mind last visit): She and her husband were to look for a house on Sunday. Instead of "nagging" him as she usually has to, she waited to see what he would do.

ICL–(3) Exaggerated 3rd octant indicates verbal aggressiveness.

Rorschach–VIII (1) Lion climbing–active, aggressive creature.

Rorschach–III (5) Bones connote morbidity and possibly destructiveness.

Late on Sunday afternoon she said, "We really have looked at a lot of homes today." He did not answer then, but later in the evening he threatened to go out and get drunk; she did not say anything because "that only makes it worse." He came back with a bottle, called her stupid and helpless, and criticized her for coming to therapy.

MMPI–PdMf: Instead of anger at others, directs to self. (PdMf–"See how helpless I am.")

ICL–(5) High 5th octant represents shame, guilt, feelings of unworthiness.

Then he had a few drinks. She became very frightened when he acted intoxicated and attempted to make love to her. She was repelled but after a while she submitted, to quiet him down. He has been nice ever since, but she has been repelled by him.

MMPI–Mf: Extremely low Mf indicates overprotestation or conflict about femininity.

ICL–(6) High 6th octant indicates docility and submissiveness.

On questioning, the patient told of unhappy sexual relationships since the beginning of their marriage. On their honeymoon, she was too frightened; even now, she is ashamed to undress before him. Although at first she could not reach orgasm, she does now; still, she often does not attain one because he reaches climax first. Questioned about this, she asked whether she should try to reach a climax anyway.

TAT–(13MF) Denial of sexuality.

ICL–(6) Stress in 6th octant presents phobic thinking.

MMPI–PdMf: Instead of anger at others, directs to self (PdMf–"See how helpless I am.")

Mrs. S offered fear of pregnancy as an explanation, but neither of them uses contraceptives–not specifically because of religion, even though her Catholicism does raise conflicts here. We considered the possibility of a sadomasochistic relationship (phrased in her terminology), relevant to their sexual maladjustment and carried over from childhood and family.

MMPI–PdMf: Instead of anger at others, directs to self. (PdMf–"See how helpless I am.")

ICL–(5, 6) Fifth octant suggests masochism, the 6th docility.

At the end of the hour, the patient asked advice about the psychological exhibits at the convention. Referred back and, because of end of hour, wondered whether she wasn't asking something of me. She laughed and wondered about those pills they were giving out for mental problems.

Seventh Session (6/29): The patient presented two conflict situations:

(1) She and her husband are invited to his boss's home, but they cannot go because one daughter's ear is inflamed and they have no competent baby sitter. To have her parents check in would involve dependence on them as well as criticism. If they don't go her husband loses out on important business relationship. Basically, she admits she hates to go because she feels out of place with these people; she has not discussed this with husband.

(2) They shopped for and found some homes, but they are not her *dream* house. That is, none of the houses conform to her mother's standards. In addition, she raised the question of her husband's ability to afford a house and his desires about the matter in general. (She dreamed about her mother saying that there was no such address, that there were no trees there, and that the home was in "the flats," a bad place to be.)

> ICL—(Self vs. Ideal 4, 6, 7) Stress (in Self) on octants 4, 5, & 6 describes submissive orientation which she alters in Ideal (indicating the conflict). Seventh octant even more stressed in Ideal indicates "need" to keep defense of Denial.
>
> TAT—(1) Conformancy to mother. (7B, 7MF, 18) criticism of mother.

The theme clarified was that the patient seemed to get caught in crossfires whenever what she did ran counter to somebody important to her. She was unimportant and helpless. Why was this and why did it have to be so?

> MMPI—PdMf: Instead of anger at others, directs to self. (PdMf—"See how helpless I am.")
>
> ICL—(5, 6) Fifth octant suggests masochism, the 6th docility.

Eighth Session (7/3): Mrs. S asked me to explain to her husband how upset she was, because she felt unable to do this for herself. We put this aside for a while. She then enumerated several situations in which she had decided to assert herself despite her fears of making other people angry or demolishing them with her anger: (1) going to boss's ranch and doing what she wanted there; (2) dismissing sitter; (3) playing the piano, returning a spotted chicken, etc. She felt proud of herself and surprised at the "*little* shakes" that followed. She ascribed such an improvement to therapy.

DAP—Both drawings: relative lack of distortion, front view, and hand extending toward environment suggests potential for coping with circumstances.

ICL—(Ideal 1, 2) Much stronger representation for octants 1 and 2 in Ideal indicates striving for more assertiveness.

Rorschach—IV (3, 4) Good use of shading for these responses in both warm and playful contexts indicates ability to be tactful and even somewhat forceful.

We referred these feelings back to her initial request; the patient herself suggested that she was casting me in a parental role and thought it would be valuable for her to try by herself, despite the anxieties. On leaving, she wished me a good Fourth and, when I returned the sentiment, she said determinedly, "I'll do all right."

TAT—Parental theme throughout.

Ninth Session (7/7): The patient described her weekend. It was generally very satisfying because she did what she wanted—which meant sleeping most of the time. However, on Sunday she had the shakes at breakfast. Exploration revealed the following: (1) After feeling out of place and ignored, she suddenly had the attention of everybody; (2) she made everyone else uncomfortable. The patient felt fearful of such tendencies on her part although she could see the need of being angry and noticed on this occasion; she could see, as well, how desperate, indirect, and crushing to her esteem this way of handling her feelings was. She could also see a withdrawal aspect to her sleeping and her busying herself with any activity that took her away from the other guests.

DAP—Both drawings: Exhibitionism (no clothes, large figures).

Rorschach—III (associations) Self-referent remarks associated to responses.

MMPI—Pd: Pd fairly high in her profile suggests aggressiveness.

ICL—(3) Exaggerated 3rd octant indicates verbal aggression which, so far, is contradicted by patient's report of not getting angry.

TAT–(13MF) Weak attempts at denying aggression (*i.e.*, very superficially controlled).

At the end of the hour, the patient was beginning to relate such behavior to having her teeth pulled and to her mother.

Tenth Session (7/10): Mrs. S has suffered several anxiety attacks, mostly when visiting doctors' offices, characterized by severe shakes, dizziness, and a sense of almost passing out.

ICL–(6) React to color. Stress in 6th octant presents phobic thinking.

Rorschach–Overreacting to color and impulsive responses such as blood suggest phobic anxious responses at times.

Exploration revealed that the effect of such attacks is to demonstrate her helplessness and secure her sympathetic help.

MMPI–Hy, Pt: Peak Hy in association with subpeak on Pt indicates hysterical and manifest anxious reactions.

Rorschach–III (4) Has to draw attention to herself.

She made an association to feelings of rejection and abandonment in childhood (*e.g.*, being left with neighbors when she was five, "before brother was born"; her parents fighting and mother threatening to leave; missing a period at 17 and her mother accusing her of being a "dirty slut," etc.) She first manifested these symptoms after she had some teeth pulled and her mother made her feel ashamed at gaps in her mouth.

Rorschach–VIII (6, 7) Anal responses may be correlated with shame and being dirty.

Rorschach–III (4), VIII (6, 7): III (4) Masochistic response. VIII (6, 7) Lava or hot destructive viscous material and spine suggests anality.

We got at her hostile feelings towards her children—for instance, she is hurting them if she should drop them while she is having an attack. She is afraid that her anxiety in general will hurt them psychologically. She is jealous of the sitter's relationship with the children. The patient is fearful of losing her mind (an uncle is in a mental institution and an aunt committed suicide). The meaning and genetic (psychological) implications of these apprehensions were discussed.

MMPI–Hy: All of these "irrational" fears describe an hysterical reaction. Basic conflict about one's own hostility often the source of these fears.

> ICL–(7) High 7th octant in Self and even higher (the most represented) octant in Ideal connotes hysterical orientation.
>
> Rorschach–Color reactions, stress on II (1): Overreactivity to color and such responses as "blood" are hysterical reactions.

Eleventh Session (7/14): The patient experienced anxiety twice this morning–once when she had to telephone to cancel order of Christmas cards, and again outside my office. The first attack related to her notion that asserting herself would anger another and incur loss of approval. The patient was eager to ascribe this attack to an effort to get sympathy and attention. She was able to see, however, that in addition to this she was afraid of being abandoned and rejected (as her memories of last hour indicated).

This brought up a stream of associations: (1) Her only childhood memory of her mother involved the latter chastizing her; (2) being molested by older boys and terrified that mother would find out; (3) mother telling her what pain and illness her birth had caused, compared with the birth of her brother.

> TAT–(2, 7GF) All themes of selfish, critical mother and resentful, victimized daughter.

We interpreted the idea that her mother had conveyed to her what a bad "horrible" little girl she was–something associated with being sexual. Just being born, much less asserting herself, was evidence of this.

> DAP–Childlike quality of drawings–just a child.

The patient told of being unable to tolerate her daughters' getting dirty, that she was unable to "enjoy" this. So she was a "dirty" as well as a "horrible" child herself.

> Rorschach–VIII (6, 7): Anal responses may be correlated with shame and being dirty. VIII (6) Lava or hot destructive viscous material and spine suggests anality, and spine on VIII (7) back part of anatomy.

Twelfth Session (7/19): Mrs. S came in with the "shakes"; she had them yesterday too. We went back over the events: The patient, who generally calls her mother every day, had not called for a week. Her mother reminded her pointedly of this and hinted broadly that she would like to be driven on various errands. The patient was infuriated at her mother's taking advantage of her, and anxious about this fury.

> Rorschach–I (2), II (3), III (2): Fearfulness of "witch" response, spider ("smothering" mother), and shaven, performing poodle link fear-anger conflict and anxiety to mother.
>
> TAT–(13MF) The weak attempt to deny hostility "leaves me cold."

The patient's mother had a toothache whenever she indicated resentment at her daughter for taking care of "the other children" rather than her. Moreover, the mother indicated that she *needed* to have her, the patient, take care of her (not her son or her husband). This gave the patient pleasure, and she got in a few digs about how poorly her mother had treated her when she had dental trouble. The patient terribly resented mother giving more love to her brother and *depriving* her of it, although she deserves at least as much. She almost believes she *needs* it.

> TAT–(7GF) Lonely child who desperately needs mother's love.

The patient's mother, in apparent gratitude for the patient's acceptance of her demands, invited her and her family to dinner; but she specified particular dates and times, and at first suggested that the dinner would be left-overs. Although the patient could see the neurotic action of her mother, she nevertheless felt forced to rebel.

> MMPI–Pd: Subpeak suggests moderate attempts (fantasy of rebellion.
>
> ICL–(Self and Ideal very low): Relatively low 4th octant, for her, in Self and barely represented in Ideal suggests conflict about rebellion (more like suppressed revolt).

Thirteenth Session (7/21): Mrs. S felt nervous before coming in. She related this to her guilt about keeping the negotiations for a house from her mother. In the past, the mother has interfered, causing considerable upset in addition to changing their minds. The patient remembered that in college (at age 19-20), she smoked "behind parents' backs." Her mother finally accused her of this, saying she knew all about it.

> ICL–(5) Her pronounced guilt feelings are indicated by extremely exaggerated fifth octant. In fact, this most represents her orientation–a masochistic facade.

We discussed this guilt over presumable acts of independence. Apparently they seem to her like rebellion rather than action on own evaluations.

> MMPI–Pd: Subpeak suggests moderate attempts at (fantasy of) rebellion.

I wondered whether she wasn't nervous when coming to see me because she felt guilty about her mother's disapproval (she said at first she felt I might "disapprove of something").

> ICL–(2) Again her denial defenses result in her understressing on the ICL certain of her tendencies; in this instance, octant 2 and her exploitiveness.

She agreed and then said her husband had a problem about therapy, and that she protected herself by not disclosing either the purchasing of a home *or* her coming to therapy. I wondered whether he did not share her apprehensions with respect to her family.

> ICL–(2) Again her denial defenses result in her understressing on the ICL certain of her tendencies; in this instance, octant 2 and her exploitiveness.

Fourteenth Session (7/24): Mrs. S wondered whether she could refer someone to me or whether referrals must come from a physician. Then she described the situation when she advised parents of her buying a home. (She indicated that she had contrived the situation to obviate discussion by her husband and to test her reactions to her parents' response.) Although her mother made some criticism, the patient did not get angry or have the shakes—just a "contained nervousness." Similarly, on the next day, she held her ground against her mother's criticism; she was also surprised when her mother confessed she was excited about house buying.

> Rorschach–Management of card X: Despite impulsivity, can handle herself reasonably well, and demonstrates "recovery" power so that she eventually can manage her affect appropriately.

The patient's focus on her mother's self-involvement prevented her from seeing her own feelings and needs. The mother's problems are a relatively comfortable explanation of why the patient is the way she is; this does not dissipate her resentment.

Fifteenth Session (7/28): They bought the house. The patient spent the entire hour telling how disapproving her mother was of the transaction (as well as of other things). The theme was that her mother approved of nothing unqualifiedly; she always had to demonstrate what a silly, litle girl with poor judgment the patient was. Since so much of this criticism was evidently irrational, my question to patient was "Why does this bother her so much"? It seemed to be more than a question of disapproval and a wish for approval. Why did she get so involved with this? What was the "*perverse satisfaction*" in addition to anxiety?

> TAT—(7) Enormous concentration on "negative" interaction with mother. In this story the sexual overtone hints at the almost physical or contact gratification involved.

Sixteenth Session (7/31): Most of the hour was devoted to the patient's description of her mother's unceasing criticism of her. Last evening, she responded angrily for a change but was "not proud of my disrespect." Patient could see the sadomasochistic relationship between parents where even criticism provokes pleasure, as in her relationship with her mother. She wants above all "constructive criticism," which seems to imply love from her mother for being herself—even if that was not so good. With affect, the patient suddenly said she could see that that's what her own daughter did with her—anything, even punishment, for attention.

> TAT—(7) Mother constantly critical and makes her feel guilty.
> MMPI—PdMf: Instead of anger at others, directs to self. (PdMf—"see how helpless I am.")
> Rorschach—III (2) Sense of impotency and guilt.

Seventeenth Session (8/4): This morning the patient again had a "woozy" feeling in a doctor's office. This time she did not feel that she would pass out, but it was nonetheless an anxiety attack. She felt that the reasons we discussed before were relevant but then she came to a dead end. Other than discussing various environmental difficulties, she had no other associations. When free association was encouraged, she gave the following dream:

Dream last night: Her husband bought a vicuna sportscoat. He burned a hole in the coat but could not afford another. Associations led to recent political scandal; the name of the man involved was the same as her father's. Yesterday she ran into several people with this surname who told her what a great man her father was. Then her mother insisted that her father buy a sportscoat. He did not need one and could not afford it.

This is the one thing she criticizes her father for—his passive surrender to her mother. The patient's husband does not do this. He is jealous of her admiration for her father and has wished that he were in a profession too so that she would admire him. The patient was angry with her husband over the weekend. We worked on her admiration and criticism of her father, her anger at her husband, her mother's hostility toward her own husband, and the patient's idea of being like her mother. The patient added that her husband is parsimonious; also, he fears taking advice from others.

TAT—(10) Wish for greater love between parents. (6GF, 4) Mother more aggressive, father more passive and victimized.

DAP—Male: Male drawn smaller and more childlike than female.

Eighteenth Session (8/7): Mrs. S had been in a department store with her two daughters, holding the younger one. She got dizzy looking down escalator, and associated her fear of falling down with hurting the baby. She then told of her difficulty in labor with oldest daughter. The baby had been conceived when the patient was angry with her husband, and she did not want him to even touch her. She showed a hint of shame at becoming pregnant (reflection of her mother's attitude.) Both children made considerable trouble this weekend—the baby got locked in the dryer, the older child's ear had to be lanced, etc. We considered the patient's symptom as denial of her hostile impulses.

MMPI—Hy: All of these "irrational" fears describe a hysterical reaction. Basic conflict about one's own hostility often the source of these fears.

TAT—(13MF) Weak attempts at denying aggression (*i.e.*, very superficially controlled).

Rorschach—II (1) and all color cards: Overreactivity to color and such responses as "blood" are hysterical reactions.

Rorschach—IV (2) Denial of aggression hinted at in her phlegmatic response where aggression is usually elicited.

Later on, a dog in the store bit the baby daughter's hand. The woman with the two dogs said that the child should not approach them, that they detested children. Mrs. S got the shakes when she was taking the woman's name and calling a physician. She wondered if she was being a fool and overconcerned, even though she cited the rationality of her action. We considered her fear of her own anger even when it was justified, and her readiness to displace this anger to symptoms of fear of something else.

ICL—(5, 6, 7) Overloading in these 3 octants presents submissive orientation.

Nineteenth Session (8/11): The patient had an argument with her mother over the rebellious behavior of her younger daughter. The patient does not want to discuss this in front of the child because it means giving into the daughter's desire for negative attention. Her mother persisted anyhow. The patient became very angry and spoke sharply to her mother, but held herself in. Later she suddenly realized she was afraid to speak to her mother because her father was there, and would have sided with her mother. The patient was really *afraid of him;* she feared she would hurt him and that he would not speak to her anymore.

She remembered a time when she was about six and alone with her father. Her mother was away, and the patient was to go to a ball game with father; instead she wandered away with a boyfriend to whom her parents objected. This was the only time she could remember his being angry with her as a child. The patient then said that all his employees are afraid of her father, who never gives praise. When women really feel sorry for themselves, he describes what a difficult time her mother had in delivering her. We found in the patient a sense of debt for even being born, along with tremendous resentment and guilt at being reminded of it—at having her nose rubbed in it continually.

> TAT—(7, 18GF) All themes of selfish, critical mother and resentful victimized daughter.
>
> MMPI—PdMf: Instead of anger at others, directs to self. (PdMf—"See how helpless I am.")
>
> ICL—(5) Stress on 5th octant indicates masochism.

Twentieth Session (8/14): Mrs. S spent most of the hour uninterruptedly telling with considerable affect about her handling of her youngest daughter. The child has been getting into a lot of trouble and growing very rebellious. All though the week, the patient has been dealing with everyone assertively, expressing anger when it was called for, even toward her mother. She even told the latter she was seeing a psychologist.

> TAT—(1, 7, 18GF) All themes problem of daughter relating to mother and conflict about rebellion and aggression.

Mrs. S has handled her daughter directly although she is not sure whether her way was correct. She was able to realize that her daughter has felt guilty about rebelling and has needed punishment to assuage this guilt. She also saw that this was due partly to the little attention she had paid the children. As a result, she has taken them to the zoo, and they and she have felt immensely better.

At the end of the hour she mentioned her anxiety before coming in; she felt that I would disapprove of her idea of coming in once a week, but if she had to she would anyway. I referred these attitudes to the feelings about her father that she mentioned last hour. She said that she had something to tell me about him.

MMPI–PdMf: Instead of anger at others, directs to self. (PdMf–"See how helpless I am.")

ICL–(5) Stress on 5th octant indicates masochism.

Twenty-First Session (8/18): Mrs. S devoted the hour to telling of her increased awareness of her "distorted feelings" of approval or rejection, and how she has acted accordingly (*e.g.*, submissively, shakes, and so on). She connected this with her feeling that her parents, particularly her father, are always implicitly or explicitly critical of her. Then she recounted incidents with a neighbor where she put up with all sorts of inconveniences rather than antagonize the neighbor or arouse her disapproval. The patient became speechless with anger when it built up to a head.

TAT–(13MF) Weak attempts at denying aggression (*i.e.*, very superficially controlled.)

ICL–Self, high lower half. Ideal, high upper–change bottom half of ICL from Self to Ideal. Although she presents submissive facade (low represented upper half and high lower for Self), she aspires to be, and suggests ability to see self as, more assertive and competent (the reverse pattern in Ideal).

Twenty-Second Session (8/21): The patient told of her apprehension about letting her younger daughter out of her sight because she feels she will be molested. She has heard reports of little boys playing with little girls; besides this, a man in her building was told to move because he was a pedophile.

MMPI–Hy: Here denial and conflict about sexuality. Peak on Hy suggests denial tendencies.

Rorschach–Color cards II, VIII, IX: The impulsive or hysterical handling of color on these cards would also suggest hysterical denial.

ICL–(7) Not only is the 7th octant well represented in the Self but is even more, and the most, exaggerated in Ideal–again hysterical (denial).

From this association to memories as child: in the baseball incident previously recounted, possibly her father felt that she was playing sexually with the little boy. When she was about 6, older boys got "fresh" with her. She was terrified that her parents might find out and punish her. She remembered seeing with her father the motion pictures "The Three Little Pigs" and "Rasputin." She was terrified by a close-up of Rasputin's eyes and dreamed about it. When 12, she slept with her father, and he got terribly angry when she wet the bed. She never did this before or after.

The patient was incredulous and shocked at the "Oedipal" implications. However, she said that the other night her daughter, who has the habit of slipping into bed with her father (he is sleeping alone in the living room ostensibly for some reason of illness), said, "Daddy, please lie on top of me." The patient was shocked, and wondered about her *six-year-old* daughter's bedwetting.

Twenty-Third Session (8/25): The patient reported conversations with her father—he said, for example, that there would be adolescent delinquents in the county to which the patient planned to move, that alcoholics do not have will power, and similar remarks. Behind content, father and daughter were conveying some message. He was criticizing her for moving, being weak, or in general inferior to him. Another message was each blaming the other for the patient's psychological development. Patient finally suggested that her father ought to get a "gold soapbox" for Christmas, and that she would buy it for him.

> ICL—Change of bottom half of ICL from Self to Ideal. Although she presents a submissive facade (low represented upper half and high lower for Self), she aspires to be, and suggests ability to see self as, more assertive and competent (the reverse pattern in Ideal).

The patient went on to describe her relationship with her husband. He implied that she was irrational about buying things—she was stupid. Wanting to indicate that she wished responsibility for such actions, she actually revealed that she shared her husband's attitudes about herself. In frustration, he slammed a glass against a wall and cut himself. We considered what her feelings might be about this, as well as the way they got messages fouled up.

MMPI–K: Relatively low K testifies to her seeing herself as not strong or as stupid and irrational (so too her hysterical reaction).

Twenty-Fourth Session (8/27): Mrs. S began the hour telling about how the nursery teacher was shocked when patient's youngest daughter told her that a four-year-old boy had induced another girl to take her clothes off in a closet and then had attempted to do same with her. The patient said she wasn't shocked because of our previous talk, but she quickly skipped to another subject.

She remembered that the first time she really had the shakes was when her husband stressed the importance of meeting a general at a "command performance." She felt small and laughed inappropriately. We discussed her feelings before authority. When in the discussion, I asked how she would have felt if the general was only in his underwear, these two memories emerged spontaneously: (1) When the patient was a little girl, before her brother was born, her father came home with a black eye from an associate. Her mother was furious and the patient was disillusioned (a giant fell). (2) Her mother handled a friend, purportedly a Lesbian, poorly—the patient, although a small child, had to deal with her. We considered her feelings of awe for parents followed by disillusionment. The patient then told of an incident when a salesman was disparaging her father. She was in conflict between sympathy for his point of view and a need to defend father's character—she got the shakes.

TAT—All stories.

DAP—Female: Conflict about exhibitionism—thus, nude but rather sexless female.

Interpreted conflict: Whether to maintain fear and awe of father with some security engendered therein; or to give up this illusion (disillusioned deep down anyway) and attack and rebel; or to compromise, expressed symptomatically in the shakes.

MMPI—K, D, Hy, Pt: High D and Pt signifies depression and tension, low K self-critical, and high Hy exaggerated emotionality —or an overall pattern of manifest anxiety.

Succeeding Hours

Mrs. S expressed more and more anger at her parents; at the same time she openly re-enacted earlier conflicts with her own children. She became more cognizant of her competition with her husband and faced the conflict between seeing her husband as a dependent child and wanting him to be a "man." At the same time, she paid more attention to her appearance. But in facing these conflicts, she also grew anxious and found all sorts of rationalizations and somatic complications to miss treatment. Finally, she complained that her husband was resenting her therapy, becoming depressed and withdrawn, and that in addition their finances were becoming a problem. She had to terminate but said she would definitely resume.

The psychological examination provided cues to the therapist, suggesting the patient's need (and near-readiness) to examine her relationship to her father; the neurotic gratification derived from her relationship with her mother; how both of these features were relevant to her interaction with her husband and children; and her need to tap the rage fulminating just below the surface (confused with her sexual concepts). It also forewarned him about her bouts with somaticization and her tendency to withdraw from confrontation of her conflicts.

CHAPTER FIVE

DYSPHORIA: CHARACTER DISORDER (ADOLESCENT REACTION) WITH HYSTERICAL FEATURES

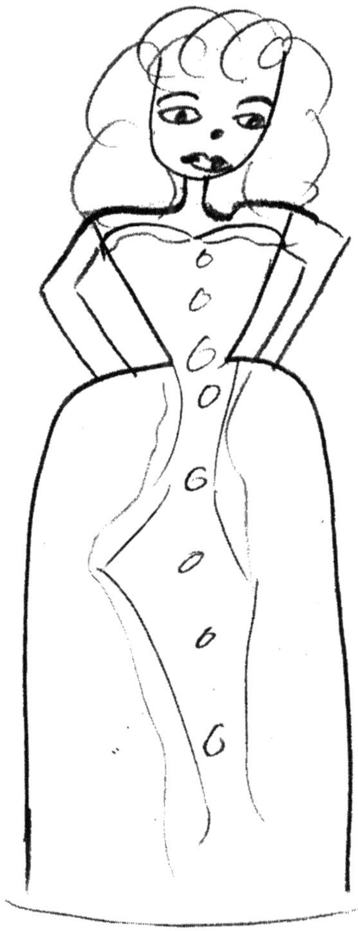

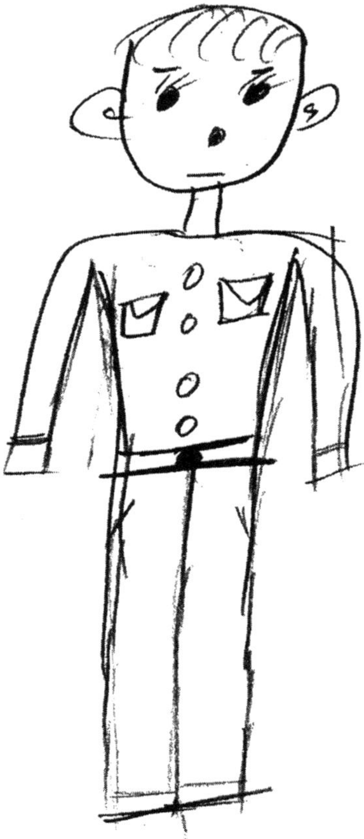

DIAGNOSTIC OVERVIEW:

A Character Disorder

(Adolescent Reaction)

with Hysterical Features

In previous chapters, the overviews have discussed character disorders (chs. 1 and 3) and hysterical orientations (chs. 2 and 4). The degree of alienation, unreliability, and acting out (rash, unheeding behavior) of this patient spells out her character deformation. Immaturity, emotionality, somatization, exaggerated dependence on others, and naivete describe her hysterical features. The additional issue of adolescent reaction is raised by her morbid vacillation between rebellious and dependent behavior, and sharp mood shifts, restlessness, and clumsy groping for identity. This behavior, moreover, has become noticeable or exacerbated since her middle teens. True, she demonstrated adjustment difficulties and such symptoms as stuttering in childhood. Were these features more crystallized and prominent in her behavior, she would have been and still might well be, considered essentially hysterical in orientation. True, her rebelliousness, asocial acts, and shallow interpersonal relationships have been pronounced. Were these features to assume centrality in her relationship to her environment, then a true Personality Disorder (with perhaps Schizoid aspects) might more accurately categorize her orientation. So far, however, there is not sufficient evidence to assume that the stresses and strains of adolescence do not account for this relatively transient reaction. Certain of her strengths, which will be pointed out, suggest that she may resolve her conflicts more adequately—*provided propitious and fortuitous factors are encountered in her environment.*

As for the character disorder elements in the test material, there were first of all (in addition to marginal vocational adjustment), the asocial and rash behavior indicated in the interview by an unprompted and exceedingly frank description of sexual behavior; on the MMPI, the extremely high Pd and high Ma, the latter suggesting restlessness, aggressivity, and irritability while the constellation of high Pd, Ma, Sc indicated poorly internalized modes of handling frustration.

There were also balking and irritability in completing the DAP; high representation on the 3rd octant of the ICL; turning Rorschach cards upside down and aggressive content (stern faces, angry insects, etc.); and TAT themes that were frankly sexual and inappropriately facetious.

The keen sense of alienation was portrayed in the interview by her bitter relationship with her family and by her shallow relationships in general—again the extremely high Pd on MMPI; poorly conceived human responses on Rorschach and lack of feeling or distance associated with them; and less than meaningful relationships expressed in TAT. (People always seemed to hurt or quarrel with each other in these themes.) In fact, the quality of relationships seemed so poor at times as to suggest a schizoid factor. Further suggestion of this was found in her interview statement about being a "split personality" (one part mean and moody, the other happy and goodlooking); in her dream of doing "crazy things"; and in her preoccupation on the Rorschach with disease and death.

The hysterical component was suggested by her marked naivete about many things, as well as by the variety of somatic complaints in the interview; by her erratic response on the WAIS to information with a Verbal IQ of 95 in contrast to her relatively better performance in abstract reasoning (similarities) and her well-conceived responses on Rorchach and TAT; on DAP, the larger, childlike, and Victorian female (narcissistically adorned); on the Rorschach, the over-responsiveness to emotion in a fairly uncontrolled manner (color responses tending towards CF's) and phobic emphasis on monsters and disease; and the stress on the 7th octant of the ICL.

Pointing to the adolescent reaction were the following factors: The bowtype profile on the ICL suggested sharp conflict of identity, with rebellion against or dependence on others (as in her complaint about being two kinds of people); on the MMPI, high Pd suggested rashness and impulsiveness and, in conjunction with a high Ma, indicated immaturity, as well as the latter's indication of mood shifts and irritability; the rebelliousness has already been described. Although the patient complained about mood shifts, the test material conveyed more strongly a basic and massive depressive element which has been labelled *dysphoric* here, because apparently it has not always been accessible to the patient's consciousness or extreme enough to be considered a frank depression. Thus, on the Rorschach, there were her gloomy responses to achromatic cards as well as morbid responses to color, dwelling on disease and soma, and the sad mood expressed again and again on the TAT.

Some strengths were indicated by her staying on the same job for several years, her reaching out—albeit clumsily—for interpersonal relationships, her well-conceived responses on Rorschach and TAT, her relatively good performance on the test of abstract reasoning (similarities), and her desire to change her life situation.

The psychological evaluation stressed the tendency of the patient to be both evasive and resistive as well as to be overly frank only to draw back in suspicion. It pointed up such poor prognosticators as her low sense of worth (low K on MMPI) combined with her tendency to act out (high Pd on MMPI) as well as her marginal social and vocational accomplishments. Forewarned of all this and of her basic mistrust (themes on TAT, balking on DAP and large ears on this test, high MMPI Pd, and no close relationships), the therapist was not able to establish a warm relationship with her but was able to nudge her in the direction of more critical self-evaluation.

PSYCHOLOGICAL EVALUATION: A Case of Dysphoria

Patient: female, age 20, unmarried, living with mother and sister
Education: high school graduate
Occupation: clerical worker
Referred by: Dr. P. for personality evaluation in light of problems of overweight and of adjustment in school and at home.

Tests Administered:

Rorschach, Thematic Apperception Test (TAT), Minnesota Multiphasic Personality Inventory (MMPI), Draw-A-Person (DAP), Interpersonal Checklist (ICL), and WAIS information and similarities intelligence subtests.

Interview Behavior:

Miss D, a tall, heavy, attractive young woman, occasionally displayed a ptosis of the left eyelid. However, she said she had no trouble with her eyes other than an occasional twitching and a need for glasses for reading. At first she was concerned with whether her words were being written down. But as she became more comfortable, she volunteered, unsolicited, exceedingly frank information; she grew rather coquettish, crossing and recrossing her legs while adjusting her skirt and speaking in a husky, "Miss Monitor" tone. In her second interview, she became very resistive when asked to draw human figures and even more defensive when administered intelligence tests because she felt she would be considered stupid. A lifelong problem for her has been her difficulty in understanding both in school (where she has been teased for this) and on the job. She has held a job at the same insurance company for three years, but opportunities for advancement have been upset by her inability to learn or adjust to the new tasks set her. She expressed considerable enmity toward her sister, who she felt was brighter and favored by her mother. Her feelings were ambivalent with respect to her parents who were divorced when she was nine (her father being an alcoholic). She has had several boy friends and has been "hurt" by at least one of them. A number of accidents (e.g., straining her back) have prevented her from attending such events as her senior prom and high school graduation. She has had a weight problem since she was 13, but has put on 18 pounds in the last three months after being on a diet for an ulcer (which has "cleared up"). Constipation also has been a problem for her. Whenever she feels upset, she admitted, she eats heavily.

Evaluation:

Miss D scored in the low average range of intelligence (Prorated Verbal IQ of 95). Her fund of information was poor and spotty. She did not know even one President of the United States since 1900, but did know that Shakespeare wrote *Hamlet* and, although a Catholic, she did not know what the capital of Italy or the Vatican was. However, on a test of abstract reasoning, less influenced by academic training, she performed much better. Similarly, on the projective tests, she demonstrated good conceptual ability as well as creative imagination. In short, her intellectual resources appear good, but her functioning is depressed by academic and emotional factors (the latter probably influencing the former).

The patient is a very alienated, immature, impulsive, unreliable, and restless young woman who experiences frequent mood shifts characterized by irritatibility, hypersensitivity, depression, and an "I-don't-give-a-damn" attitude. The personality picture she portrays is adolescent or even more childish. Burdened with a low sense of worth, she feels unable to cope satisfactorily with her environment or to stand on her own two feet. She is conflicted between an exaggerated dependence on others and a rebellious need to do things her own way (which she feels is always the wrong way). Characteristically, she is initially resistive and evasive, will suddenly revert to frankness, and then become suspicious again.

Superficially, Miss D makes a good discrimination between the sexes and yearns to be sexually attractive, popular, and chaste (although she feels she presents the contrary picture in all respects). More fundamentally, she sees women as more dominant and, particularly maternal figures, as stern and punitive. Men are pictured by her as almost completely irresponsible and callous. The world is a mess consisting of people who dash about frantically, getting into each other's way, constantly competing and arguing. She feels herself taken advantage of, rejected, and deserted. She, like other women, serves only as a passing fancy of any man who comes along. (It appears that she continually tries to recreate and make sense out of her relationship to her father but always ends on a despairing note). Few, if any, meaningful interpersonal relationships are presented by her. Instead, she expends her energies in a world of fantasy and morbid preoccupations, or impulsively acts out her tensions and needs by eating, drinking, or rash sexual behavior. Somatic channels are also used by her to allay her anxiety.

Miss D's psychopathy seems more ingrained and pervasive than merely a delayed adolescent reaction. The patient has demonstrated favorable prognostications in her continued employment and shows family loyalties despite her smoulderings in these quarters. Time itself may be helpful. But psychotherapy, although stormy and probably fated to be short-lived, may provide her with greater self-understanding and more efficient and gratifying ways of dealing with people and her emotions.

THERAPY NOTES

First Session (5/28): Miss D arrived twenty minutes late. She has lost her job, so lateness was due to miscalculations. Yesterday morning her employer told her she was not cut out to be an office girl and had not lived up to the chance given her. It developed that she also was frequently late. She was very hurt and disappointed but has already taken the test for a phone job.

> MMPI–K: Very low K indicates her self-presentation (and probable attempts to prove that she is inadequate).

Yesterday she also did not go to a shower for her girlfriend because of the $15.00 present involved. After work, she went with a friend as usual to typing class and then to a bar. She drank until 10:30 P.M. Her mother confronted her with drinking, accused her of pandering for money, and slapped her. Patient experienced no feeling although she is usually hurt by mother, who is seldom at home.

> MMPI–Pd: Very high (and her peak) Pd connote marked sense of alienation from family as well as a strong tendency to act out impulsively.

This led to feelings of defiance against her mother, who was never around because of jobs or, when not working, was out on her own dates. Further, her mother worried only about her own reputation and about her daughters supporting her. The patient feels that her mother ought to try to understand what she is looking for in bars —something she did not find at home.

> TAT–(2, 18) Themes of these stories are of hurt and rejection from loved ones and/or rash sexual and aggressive actions.

At the end of the hour, she asked if I thought girls who go to bars get bad reputations.

Second Session (5/30): Miss D phoned to say she would be twenty minutes late. She was actually thirty minutes late for which she apologized. This opened up implications of her lateness not only in coming to therapy but also on the job. She assured me she liked coming to treatment. I agreed with her motivation but considered it with her other possible feelings. She said that when she was a child, she was always late to dinner and for school, for which she was punished.

> DAP–Behavior: Balking, passively hostile behavior.
>
> TAT–(12) Theme of father killing little girl suggests she may view therapist as dangerous and necessary to resist in all possible ways.

She told of her mother's being hurt by her "rebellion." The patient seemed contrite about this, but also gratified by this recognition from her mother. She has taken an apartment by herself; her mother, although wanting to assist her, deplored her rashness. This led to our consideration of discussing decisions before actions.

MMPI–PdMa: Since her extremely high Pd already suggests resentment and aggression, her very high (secondary peak) Ma suggests that the aggression is directed outwardly toward her environment—or open rebellion.

TAT–(18) Daughter must find out for herself in context of rebelling against mother.

Third Session (6/4): With a rather passive expression and some sarcasm, the patient commented that she was early. With encouragement, she began to talk. Her boyfriend had proposed marriage in September; she had accepted, and he had not even written her since. This was said in a matter-of-fact tone with absolutely no feeling. When I pointed this out, she agreed but came to a grinding halt.

DAP–Behavior: Balking, passively hostile behavior.

TAT–(3, 4, 6, 8, 10) In all of these stories, central figure hurt and rejected by loved ones does not respond with notable (or even appropriate) affect.

Miss D then remarked about my books, wondered what kind of cigar I had, and so on. Exploration revealed difficulty in talking to *me,* but she would not explain. Finally, she said that I reminded her of a man she knew with the same chin. This man apparently depreciated her in various ways but "wasn't so brilliant." She seems to feel that this man's wife was responsible for her break-up with her first fiance. She told this man she went out with other fellows (such as her current fiance). She felt that whenever she trusted anyone, she got hurt. Moreover, it's hard to say things "to a man, a feller, and you're one."

MMPI–F, Sc, Pd: High F and Sc is declaration of feeling different and hypersensitive.

ICL–Contrast between Self and Ideal: Upper half of Self mostly low or moderately represented (weak, sensitive) whereas upper half of Ideal is exaggerated, particularly first octant (strong and dominant), suggesting her conflict in these areas.

Rorschach–III (1) Despite protestations of no feelings, acute sensitivity to literal aspects of people or their persons. IV (1) Actual phobic response to people (i.e., represented by monsters).

Fourth Session (6/6): The patient told of making up with her friend, but really only to get to the wedding. She resents this friend because she got her man and the patient did not. She felt you really cannot trust people, that they deceive you.

ICL–(4) To have the 4th octant filled to the second circumference, especially where there is little amelioration in Ideal, indicates a relatively high degree of resentment and aloofness.

> MMPI–Pd: Very high, and her peak Pd denotes marked sense of alienation from family as well as strong tendency to act out impulsively.
>
> TAT–(3, 8, 13, 18) In all of these TAT themes transactions between two people always end in hurt and separation rather than in closeness.

When an attempt was made to explore this feeling in relation to her life experiences, she asked the time. She admitted she was changing the subject but would not disclose why. Finally she said that her aunt had been a therapist's secretary and had told her that the psychiatrist had affairs with two of his patients. Also the secretary typed the sessions and then "blabbed" about them. We discussed the implications for her trust and confidence in me.

She then expressed guilt in getting a job although her sister did not, despite that fact that this job was her sister's idea and she (the sister) needed the job more. Further, her sister was more conscientious. We got at the patient's secret satisfaction in besting her sister in this way. This permitted the patient to talk about her family pushing her to be on time, responsible on the job, etc. Although it was for her own good, it made her feel either like a submissive, resentful child, or definitely guilty. Then she described how good she felt when making an evaluative choice (e.g., she could have had a drink but had an orange instead; she could have gotten involved with "fellers" but went home instead).

> Rorschach–VII Friendly, but distance between two women. possible ambivalence for mother displaced onto sister.
>
> ICL–Shift of bottom half from Self to Ideal: Despite her overt presentation of being weak and gauche, there is her desire to be strong and to exploit others indicated in the increased representation in the upper half of Ideal.
>
> MMPI–The "masochistic attack": High Pd (alienation and victimization) and low MF (weak and helpless). Thus, she talks of guilt and submissiveness but also demonstrates covert satisfaction in manipulating or feeling superior to others (by virtue of having a grievance against them).

Fifth Session (6/11): The patient announced that her fiance did not answer her phone calls or letters. She thinks it is all over. Also she was laid off from the new job she secured. She described this as a mess but with apparent satisfaction. We explored latter and discovered her pattern of setting things up (e.g., dating other men, flirting, and so on, while "interested" in marrying fiance). She was able to see some relationships to her feelings about her father.

Rorschach–X Relationships and life in general are a frenetic "mess."

TAT–(6, 8, 10) Tension in interpersonal relationships characterized by distance and fraught with hostility.

Similarly, on the job she feels "I do not give of myself" and thus loses job. She wondered if she were stupid; when the emotional aspect of this was clarified, she said that despite her desire to be attractive, she is cold and ungiving.

ICL–Self (8): Lesser representation in octant 8 than 6 or 7 for Self, and octant 8 even less represented in Ideal suggests conflict about giving and responsibility.

TAT–(6) Even two people very close in relationship do not give to each other.

There were many transference manifestations, including her asking whether she could phone me like other patients did (phone rang twice during the hour). I agreed to her request to defer payment several weeks until she obtained another job.

TAT–(12) Although fear of father (or authority or therapist) at first, craving to be taken care of (fed) emerges.

Sixth Session (6/13): The patient told, with characteristic denial of feelings, how after she won out over sister in getting a job, the sister attacked her for lying to their mother. Her absence of feelings was clarified, and she expressed her considerable resentment of both her sister and mother.

TAT–(2, 7) Absence of feelings save general dysphoria.

Rorschach–III (3) Oppositional, upside-down approach.

MMPI–PdMa: Since her extremely high Pd already suggests resentment and aggression, her very high (secondary peak) Ma suggests that the aggression is directed outward toward her environment–or open rebellion.

We worked on the fact that her mother, sister, and aunt treated her like a child–and she went along with them even when it seemed otherwise (defiance and rebellion signifying negative acceptance). She saw clearly how she set such situations up. She got a glimmer of satisfaction in fighting with and defying mother, because this got at least some feeling from her mother.

DAP–Female: Rebellious aspects indicated in test item comments (by author).

TAT–General theme of rebelliousness.

MMPI–F, Pd: F and Pd (estrangement from family and

friends) in combination suggests an orientation described by fleeing and fighting rather than approach relationships.

MMPI–F, Sc: High F and Sc is declaration of feeling different and hypersensitive.

Then very astutely the patient guessed that her *mother got pleasure vicariously from patient acting up*, and thus was so critical of her late hours and drinking, and so suspicious of her sexual activity. (Rather amazing insight for such an unsophisticated patient, with no spadework by the therapist.) We barely touched on *her* unconscious need to secure mother's approval.

Rorschach–III (1) Can be insightful into relationships but this soon gets distorted by vast craving for mother's (or her surrogate's) love. IX (1) Same.

Seventh Session (6/18): We discussed how her mother gives her no encouragement and, indeed, actively discourages her (e.g., frowning on patient using mother's friends as patrons for her cosmetic sales). Very indirectly, the patient was able to get at deep resentment about this, but the hurt was more accessible. She "let the cat out of the bag" by telling of spending $23 for cosmetics while not paying her therapy bill. She expected her mother as well as me to be on her neck for this. Instead, we considered the implications. She said that perhaps she was careless about money but that bills did not bother her. However, we focused on this as a problem.

MMPI–PdMa: Since her extremely high Pd already suggests resentment and aggression, her very high (secondary peak) Ma suggests that the aggression is directed outward toward her environment—or open rebellion.

TAT–(18) Daughter must find out for herself in context of rebelling against mother.

She reported that since beginning therapy she has felt more happy and independent than ever before. She then confided that she was terribly lonely and despaired of finding a friend, although she needed one desperately. She did not even wish to consider love now. Commenting upon how men looked at her appreciatively, she went on to say that she could not believe that she was attractive and that she knew that she was stupid.

MMPI–Sc: High Sc indicates marked sensitivity, sense of differentness, and loneliness.

ICL–(6) High 6th octant suggests docile acceptance and readiness to be self critical.

TAT–Mood, especially 12: Melancholy themes reach acme in death of daughter in story 12.

MMPI–K, Pd, MF: Low K and high Pd, low MF describe aggression turned toward self or at least orientation of "See how helpless I am." Very low K indicates her self-presentation (and probable attempts to prove) that she is inadequate.

At the very end of the hour she remembered a dream. We considered the implication of such timing.

Rorschach–II (1, 2) Morbid and gloomy associations.

ICL–Lower half: High representation of lower half in Self indicates depression and sense of weakness.

Eighth Session (6/20): No show, no call.

MMPI–Pd: Very high and her peak Pd denote marked sense of alienation from family as well as strong tendency to act out impulsively.

TAT–Mood: General themes of rebelliousness.

Ninth Session (6/25): She has been very depressed since last week. The "fellers" whom she danced with at a party she disliked, the others were not interested in her. She wondered what was wrong with her, why she was so unlovable. Considerable time was spent with the problem of overcoming her resistance to therapy. When this was related to her missing the last hour, she said she had overslept. She was still held responsible, a possibility which she had foreseen and which perhaps contributed to her depression.

Rorschach–VIII: Has "unpleasant" and "dreadful" context. II (1, 2) Morbid and gloomy associations.

TAT–(3, 4, 10, 12) In all of these stories, central figure hurt and rejected by loved ones does not respond with notable (or even appropriate) affect.

Tenth Session (6/27): Because she is still out of work and the therapy bill is accumulating, she has decided to postpone treatment until she could catch up with the bill. Yet she suggested the possibility of her resistance to therapeutic procedure and her desire to avoid it. However, she emphasized the influence of her inescapable financial realities.

MMPI–K, Pd: Low K and very high Pd, in describing weak ego resources and tendency to act out rashly, prognosticates poorly. (Compare MMPI note on poor prognosis).

Note that the last explanatory note fortuitously flows into this addendum, namely the poor prognosis which was unfortunately borne out. The psychological report stressed her tendency to resist initially and to be evasive, to overreact frankly, and then to grow suspicious again. Although forewarned, the therapist was not able to establish trust in the patient. Her tendency to act out was also known but inaccessible at this point of treatment. Although she did appear to derive some self-understanding, the therapist, despite more than adequate warnings from the psychologicals, probably did not promote skillfully enough a secure and sufficiently warm interpersonal therapeutic context.

CHAPTER SIX

THE RENEGADE— A CASE OF REBELLION: HYSTERICAL NEUROSIS WITH ACTING OUT FEATURES

DIAGNOSTIC OVERVIEW:

Hysterical Neurosis with Acting Out Tendencies

This case of a hysterical neurosis is distinguished from the previous case of an hysterical personality (ch. 5) by the prominence of acting-out features and by emotional storms. This case, nevertheless, is also differentiated from the character disorders (chs. 1, 3, 5, 7, 9, and 10) in that the patient suffered from a marked sense of guilt (unlike the character disorder, he blocked on Rorschach card VI where sexual responses are often given, was confused about females and was embarrassed in talking about them). He was relatively aware of his "transgressions" and was eagerly seeking to integrate a value system. He might well be considered in terms of an adolescent reaction because of the acuteness of his condition and his marked ambivalence towards parental figures. The extremely pronounced hysterical and compulsive features, however, as well as the extent and quality of his interpersonal relations suggested, at least more descriptively, the categorization in the title above.

The hysterical aspects were exaggerated. This patient may be likened to an emotional teakettle in a low atmosphere, resulting in a low boiling point with affect frequently steaming out. Thus, the tantrums and possibly the seizure-like states; the C's and CF's and blood on Rorschach; the uproarious and inappropriate laughter on the TAT; and the impaired judgment with respect to females on the DAP (transparencies). Often, conversion is a factor in hysterical reactions, serving to channelize anxiety. The patient also enthusiastically described physical complaints, and the epileptoid symptoms might have approximated a somatic conversion, if not a psychophysiologic reaction. The somatizations for this patient, however, served more as a safety valve, and their secondary gains were relatively apparent to him. Their defensive function was poorly integrated so that he still suffered from anxiety: on the MMPI, peaks on D, Pt; on the Rorschach, the response of a snail quivering under its shell for fear of being stepped on; in the DAP, the helmet for protection; and nervous behavior with the examiner on TAT and generally during the evaluation, manifested particularly by forced facetiousness.

His compulsive defenses also were elaborate and equally ineffective. Thus, the inordinately long and intense attention to detail on all tests; Pt peak on the MMPI; and compulsive behavior associated with fantasies before sleep. Associated with compulsivity was his preoccupation with matters that one might classify as anal: fascination and enthusiasm in describing infections and blemishes; "messed-up" frog concept, throwing of ink, and blasting responses on the Rorschach, the messed-up frog and crushed snail responses.

Rage and rebellion were notably present in all that the patient said and produced. Almost every TAT theme stressed these feelings; the constellation of HyPdMa indicated impulsive (Hy) acting out (Pd) of anger (Ma); the aforementioned destructiveness on the Rorschach; and his belief, stated on the ICL, that others view him as a brash, bitter, angry rebel. He appeared actually to strain to keep this image up, using derogatory terms for minorities on the Rorschach, then apologizing, just as he frequently felt it necessary to retract hostile remarks in interview.

The ICL and MMPI shed light on this patient's need to rebel and its meaning for him. Particularly, TAT stories 1 and 2 explained the implication of his behavior towards authority and predicted the maneuvers he would attempt in psychotherapy. His humor and ability to laugh at himself, his yearning for limits, expressed in the interview and TAT, the degree of integration denoted by mostly inner circle representation on ICL and a profile near to normal range on MMPI (for a teenager), his degree of anxiety previously cited, and his sensitivity (Low K, D, Sc on MMPI) all offered encouraging prognostication in light of his fight (and struggle to cope) with the world —a prognostication borne out in psychotherapy.

PSYCHOLOGICAL EVALUATION:

A Case of Rebellion

Patient: male, age 19, unmarried, living with parents

Education: one term of junior college

Occupation: unemployed

Referred by: Dr. O for personality evaluation in light of educational maladjustment and idiopathic epilepsy.

Tests Administered

Rorschach, Thematic Apperception Test (TAT), Minnesota Multiphasic Personality Inventory (MMPI), Bender-Gestalt, and Bender Recall. Wechsler-Bellevue Intelligence Scale and academic aptitude tests administered by a rehabilitation service 2½ years earlier.

Behavior and Background

Although Mr. R was friendly, he appeared tense and on edge. He handled this tension with compulsive facetiousness and inappropriate laughter. He would laugh particularly hard when describing some sadistic or self-punishing experience. Despite himself, words would tumble out that he would immediately regret and want to retract. These were always hostile or disparaging thoughts. He handled the test material very obsessively, while in conversation he got mired down in circumstantial detail with tenacious enthusiasm. He gave the impression of superior intelligence, but chose to play this down and even to express contempt at his ability and irresponsibility. Mr. R was bland about his *grand mal* seizures. With pleasure and disdain he commented how surprising it was that his parents thought seriously of these attacks. Moreover, the two seizures and the premonition he experienced appeared to serve the combined purpose of avoiding stress, expressing hostility, and getting attention. Althought he bantered and wisecracked, he manifested bitterness at feelings of emotional deprivation despite material indulgence. As a consequence, he himself suggested that his mischievous behavior and inadequate adjustment in school and vocation were both a revenge and a bid for attention from his parents. He could see that he felt ambivalent about them. Indeed, he demonstrated insight into his parents' intense but inadequate relationship to him, as well as some of his own contribution to the situation. As the interviewing wore on, he became increasingly frank and revealed extremely obsessive thoughts (*e.g.*, repeated, formalized, aggressive fantasies before he can fall asleep).

Evaluation

The patient attempts to present himself as an essentially integrated individual although he concedes that he is cold, selfish, and often unfriendly. He is aware that others see him as a brash, boastful, angry rebel, but is unaware that he creates an impression of marked lack of confidence. Actually, he is quite self-depreciatory, labeling himself as an "illiterate bum." Behind a facade of bravado, he trembles like a snail ensconced in its shell for fear of being squashed. Thus, he reveals himself as extremely anxious, insecure, hypersensitive, and alienated (for which he compensates with autistic and grandiose fantasies).

At a deeper level, the patient is preoccupied with sadistic and morbid fantasies. Extreme hostile feelings are directed toward his parents. He believes they exploit him for their own needs and expect things of him of which he is incapable. Although he severely disparages people, he cannot bring himself to express open hostility to his parents without excessive guilt. He has marked conflicts between feelings of love and hate, moral and amoral impulses. Rage and rebellion seem to have the upper hand temporarily. He tries to control these impulses by obsessive thinking and as a result, is full of doubts and concerned about his sanity. Turning his aggression inward results in suicidal ideas. Even so, these defenses do not sufficiently bind his anxiety so that at times he impulsively, even hysterically, acts out. It is possible that his seizures are a form of temper tantrum as well as a way of securing such secondary advantages as avoiding stressful situations and getting attention. Moreover, he is somatically preoccupied; he "resolves" one of his TAT stories by having the hero develop a brain tumor.

When tested two years ago, the patient scored within the Bright Normal range of intelligence (Wechsler IQ 112, 75th percentile). However, his verbal ability was superior, while his performance was only average. Other test results, then and now, suggest both anxiety as a depressing feature and a need to minimize what he can do; his potential overall ability is probably superior. But in his previous testing he also revealed academic skills far below average; at present he demonstrates poor performance and judgment, absolutely as well as relative to his intelligence. In conjunction with emotional conflict about vocational choice, such performance would undermine academic and occupational adjustment until such time as he gained greater security. Whether intracranial pathology is a contributing agent, or these features are solely idiopathic, is indeterminate. In any event, the patient's psychopathology is an acute and primary factor. Treatment, for which he is motivated, is recommended strongly before his psychopathology becomes rigidly integrated into his character structure. He would make a good candidate for intensive psychotherapy.

THERAPY NOTES

First Session (1/27): Mr. R stated his appreciation of my accepting his standards and not giving him advice, but then he sought advice in every way. He wanted me to give him a story to fool his parents about his going to traffic school (for violations).

> MMPI–Pd: Very high Hy or overemotional, histrionic behavior associated with high Pd or rashness and fluid morality describes tendency to manipulate others, usually via emotional fireworks and/or charm ("cute child" syndrome).
>
> TAT–(1) and general asocial themes: Story theme closely correlated with impression he attempts to make of an amoral, devil-take-you attitude.

When I would not, he said that he would tell his parents that he spent many hours with me today and asked, "I guess you must think I'm crazy."

> TAT–(4) Theme of being sick in the brain, "brain tumor."

Second Session (1/28): After only a slight trouble at beginning, the patient rambled on. Indeed, his problem was to focus his attention. However, he did more or less focus on his relationship to his father. He spoke of this pattern: Grandfather, 74, senile and babyish, expects everyone to take care of him, threatens suicide, and bathes in orgy of self-pity, extorting attention from others; father also very dependent on others. The patient is afraid that he will turn out this way too because the grandfather was hypercritical of the father just as the father is to the patient. Then he was able to say very positive things about grandfather and father.

> Rorschach–III Uses racial term in disparaging manner and immediately feels guilty. Disparaging also on DAP and TAT.

The patient was able to see that no matter what his father said, he expected the patient to be incapable and a baby, and that the patient shares this illusion, although infuriated about it. Moreover, his father does not know how to get close and chooses criticism as one way. His son, the patient, reacts in kind.

> Rorschach–III (2) Patient's fantasy of infancy suggests that although he resents being treated like a baby, he also craves it.
>
> TAT–(1, 2) Even titles story "Very confused kid."
>
> MMPI–K: Very low K indicates intense self-criticism.

Third Session (2/2): Mr. R arrived about ten minutes late, complaining about parking space. He said that he was burned up and was surprised to consider that he was burned up at me for this. He told about parking illegally, and laughed when we discussed his expectation that I would "bawl him out" for such "crimes" or get a kick out of it myself or both. He said that was exactly how he experiences reactions from his father.

> MMPI—Pd, rebelliousness on TAT: High Pd suggests rebellion.
> TAT—(1) and general Pd themes: Story theme closely correlated with impression he attemts to make of an amoral, devil-take-you attitude.
> ICL—(4) High representation in 4th octant suggests rebelliousness.

During the rest of the hour he told of how he habitually lied to parents, but did not know why. Particularly, he never told his parents when he went on a date, yet he was bothered when they got the idea that he had no love life and tried to fix him up. He considered the facts that he was ashamed of having his parents know this and that he also got some gratification from his parents' ordering his life in this way.

We considered his ploy, "Now don't tell anyone, especially my parents about this." Apparently on some level, this is just what he wanted me to do. He still shakes hands before leaving.

Fourth Session (2/4): No show. Mother phoned later to ascertain that there were two appointments a week (later three a week) and apologized profusely for son.

> MMPI—Pd, rebelliousness on TAT: High Pd suggests rebellion.
> TAT—(1) and general Pd themes: Story theme closely correlated with impression he attempts to make of an amoral, devil-take-you attitude.
> ICL—(4) High representation in 4th octant suggests rebelliousness.

Fifth Session (2/9): With respect to missing the last hour, he said that it completely slipped his mind. However, he revealed that he had his mother call and thought that his parents and I would be very put out. This led to his talk of seeing how far he could go with people. Once he really knew where he stood, he really applied himself.

He then went on to describe several incidents (gang beefs, hitting a child, etc.) where he revealed pleasure yet guilt at his irresponsible and sadistic behavior. He particularly felt guilty about hitting the child even though he felt he was not responsible. He then told with considerable remorse of shooting a child with a BB-gun when he was about 9. He has never told this to anyone else.

> MMPI–PdMa: Actively aggressive towards environment. (Pd connotes resentment and Ma connotes action and hostility.) Very high Hy or overemotional, histrionic behavior associated with high Pd or rashness and fluid morality describes tendency to manipulate others, usually via emotional fireworks and/or charm ("cute child" syndrome).
>
> Rorschach–I, II, III, IV, V, X, and TAT general themes of hostility: Destruction, sadism, or hostility expressed in these responses.

Sixth Session (2/11): The patient recounted many incidents describing mischief, sadism, and pleasure. He was able to see the possibility of feeling hurt himself and needing to strike back. But he also insisted on the prankishness of youth. We worked on idea that he apparently still considers himself just a bad little boy, with perhaps more subtle ways of expressing this.

> Rorschach–III (2) Patient's fantasy of infancy suggests that although he resents being treated like a baby, he also craves it.

When he told of these incidents with marked pleasure and amusement, he definitely triggered interest and laughter in me—he probably does same with most people, particularly his parents.

> TAT–(1, 2) Countertransference: Facetiousness, sarcasm, and histrionics presented in obvious attempt to win examiner's (therapist's) interest.

The patient then told of his interests. He feels that he is misfit and that there is something wrong with him for not being more decisive in school and vocationally. Yet he railed at parents' expectations for him to be a "genius" when he feels far from that. But sometimes he does get a "strong feeling that I'm something special."

> Rorschach–IV Self-contempt of a "snail." VII Concerned about his "craziness."
>
> DAP, TAT–(4) DAP associations of gross disparagement and overly self-referred.
>
> MMPI–Sc: High Sc, feeling of being different and even strange.

Rorschach—I Opposite side of the coin—the grandiosity suggested by Cadillac prestige, power emblem.

Seventh Session (2/16): The patient apologized for being so late and ascribed it to traffic. We considered other possibilities and he conceded a sense of stigma in coming to therapy—people would know that he has a screw loose.

Rorschach—IV Self-concept of a "snail." VII Concerned about his "craziness."

TAT—(4) Destruction, sadism, or hostility expressed in these responses.

DAP—DAP associations of gross disparagement and overly self-referred.

He remembered that he thought I was 28 and just out of college. Then he lauded my profession, wishing that he could emulate it and mentioning that he wanted "just to be a chemist." I picked this up.

Eighth Session (2/18): The patient was about fifteen minutes late, again, with a story of parking. He asked how late it was and then looked at his watch. We discussed this maneuver and he volunteered that he was probably drawing attention to his lateness. I wondered what reaction he expected from me, to which he responded with TV story of students pushing teacher out of window. He ran out of conversation except for occasional remarks that there was something wrong with him. A number of times he tried to ascertain whether I had seen a show that he had. We discussed meaning of this and got to his need to shake hands with me. He said that he had this habit with *older friends,* stressing both words. Then he wondered whether I thought he was "egocentric." At times, he thought he was "special," bigger, smarter, etc. When he ran into a child with his car, he did not have feelings and wondered about this.

TAT—(1, 2, 12, 13) All stories deal with expressed hostility, often towards authority figures.

When he left, he tried not to shake hands but it was almost as if he could not control his hand (thrust into his pocket). Finally, he stuck out his hand and I shook it. Laughing and embarrassed, he said sarcastically, "There's nothing wrong with me."

TAT, DAP—Obsessiveness on both.

Ninth Session (2/23): He was on time and proud of it, but then had difficulty in talking and concentrated on firing questions at me. When he saw that I would not answer, he grew increasingly uncomfortable but he denied, although very clearly revealed, increased hostility towards me. At one point, he blurted out that I wanted him to talk about his life but I could not make him, he would not "spill the beans." Then he took this back as a big joke.

> TAT—(12) Authority figure (uncle) threatens harm to boy —therapist a threat.
>
> MMPI—Hy (denial): High Hy suggests strong denial tendencies.

Tenth Session (2/25): He was twenty-five minutes late but insisted that he would not feel compelled to tell why (later on he had to weave it in and could see that he felt guilty because he determined his lateness and had to *confess* it to me).

> TAT—(8) Superego wins out—gives in to conscience.

I was supportive and leading since he felt so anxious about talking. Helping him focus on his current problems (no school, no work), he said that he failed because he had no interest and could not remember things and blamed this all on laziness. I got him to see his massive denial and his projection onto me. He revealed that he was afraid to "grow up," that he "had it made" with his family, and was fearful of separating from them. Thus, we related failure in biology as a requirement for a career in chemistry, suggesting to him he would have to leave and be on his own.

> Rorschach—III (2) Patient's fantasy of infancy suggests that although he resents being treated like a baby, he also craves it.
>
> TAT—(1) Even titles story "Very confused kid." (2) Child treated poorly by parents.

Again he attempted to deny, very unsuccessfully this time. He projected the discussed ideas onto me and insisted that I should not kid myself, that he did not have to be dependent on his family. I thought it was the opposite—I believed that he could fend for himself and assume adult responsibilities, but *he* kidded himself into feeling the contrary.

> MMPI—Hy (denial): High Hy suggests strong denial tendencies.

Eleventh Session (3/2): He told about his father taking him to a show. Although this made him happy, he had to deny this because it meant so much to him. Also he was disillusioned, as well as pleased, that father acted somewhat childishly away from home, ogled girls with him, and drank with him.

> MMPI–Hy: High Hy suggests strong denial tendencies.
> Rorschach–Color cards: Strong reactions to color (e.g., blood, fire, art, blob, etc.) indicate his hysterical orientation which almost always implies marked denial trends.

With feeling, he told of how his father insisted that he drive and then criticized his driving. We related that to my requesting that he talk in treatment and bring out his feelings while he expected me to criticize him and think that he was stupid and crazy.

> TAT–(12M) Authority figure (uncle) threatens harm to boy –therapist a threat.

We considered the patient's tremendous use of denial. I was considerably supportive, and he was able to admit that he was extremely sensitive and concerned about how others felt towards him –that he acted hard-boiled and a wiseguy to cover this up. I thought that he must have been hurt terribly and repeatedly and so expected everyone to hurt him again.

> MMPI–D, Hy, K, Sc: Neurotic pattern. D points up both dysphoria and sensitivity, Hy a sense of being buffeted by one's impulses, low K feeling weak and criticized, and Sc being different and hypersensitive.
> Rorschach–IV Self-concept of being a mess and stepped on.

The hour was up but he wanted to prolong it. Unsuccessful, he said, "Yeah, you want to get rid of me." But he tapped me affectionately on the arm (hostile too?).

> TAT–(12M) Authority figure (uncle) threatens harm to boy–therapist a threat.

Twelfth Session (3/4): Mr. R was about twenty-five minutes late, and rushed in out of breath. He complained about his watch, questioned what time it was, and then after complaining what a valuable but treacherous watch he had, he deprecated it and pounded hell out of it, ostensibly to fix it. An attempt was made to convey the displacement maneuver which he saw yet resisted. We worked diligently, although still very supportively, on his resistance. I appreciated how difficult it was for him to talk but how necessary it was for him to overcome this. We discussed his statement last hour of being gotten rid of–at this point he blurted that he "beat around the bush" for most of the hour and then when he did talk of something, the time was up. He commended me for my wonderful memory since I saw "so many other screwballs." He conceded that maybe he was hurt and mad but then said this was only a joke. We considered this denial.

I tried to pave the way for his lifting up his shell, indicating that he would not be hurt and rejected (because he spoke earnestly of how he could not talk to parents).

> Rorschach—IV Underneath his shell, he quivers helplessly, fearful of being stepped on.
>
> DAP—Drawing II: Helmets and pads signify his armor protecting his real sense of helplessness.

Thirteenth Session (3/9): Arriving ten minutes late, he asked the time of me. We again discussed the meaning of this, and again his feeling was that I would hurt him or get angry and he had needed to test me.

> TAT—(12) Authority figure (uncle) threatens harm to boy —therapist a threat.

Last Friday and Saturday nights, he came home about 4 A.M. He told lies to his parents because otherwise they would imagine all sorts of things that he did. He was not ashamed of what he did do; nevertheless, he would not discuss what this was, although he thought I imagined certain things which he would not talk about. He insisted that they were irrelevant but was uncomfortable and said that his mind kept coming back to this subject and he could not be silent.

> MMPI—Pd, Sc: Pd combined with Sc suggests keen sense of resentment as well as acting out these feelings.
>
> DAP, TAT—Obsessiveness of themes.
>
> Rorschach—II, Anality—splattering and blasting suggest anal sadistic tendencies. Dynamically, obsessive symptoms are utilized to control such anal tendencies.

Fourteenth Session (3/11): He was thirty minutes late. He showed considerable ambivalence about telling me why he came home late last weekend, even though there was no intervention on my part. Finally, he blurted that it was his girlfriend's birthday and he was at a party with her. He insisted that I would think various things, just like his parents, and that I knew what he meant. I said that I had no idea what he meant. Things became rather sticky and we talked about this.

Rorschach—VI Avoidance of sex—partially blocks on card often stimulating sex responses.

TAT—(13MF) Very easily interpreted sexual theme but he deals with violence.

Very animated, he told how his father insisted on getting his way, achieving this by spending lots of money on the patient as well as acting arbitrarily (*e.g.*, buying patient four new tires for $125 if patient would take off the old tires, raising the low slung body of patient's car when patient was away, etc.). He was irate but could not cope with these "kindnesses." He told of how he had filched the above old tires last year, presumably for spending money but rather obviously because he wanted to be a big shot at school. With little demonstrable guilt, he said, "I know it's wrong."

MMPI—Pd and TAT themes: (Emotional, rash, rebellious, and, in general, hysterical tendencies).

TAT—(especially 10) Even glorifies role of the thief.

Fifteenth Session (3/16): The patient was several minutes late. He expressed marked anger at his girlfriend's father whom he described as a tyrant and exploiter—like his own father but worse. Moreover, he was angry because he felt that the girlfriend's father thought he was a bad influence on his daughter. Yet he admitted that the father invited him to his ranch and wasn't such a bad guy.

MMPI—Pd: Very high Pd or rashness and fluid morality describes tendency to manipulate others, usually via emotional fireworks and/or charm ("cute child" syndrome).

He then talked of how he "had it made" now, very much taken care of by his parents. However, there were strings attached and he could not do what he wanted. When he was 21, all of this would change. Also he would like to be a chemist if he could magically stuff his head wtih knowledge, but working for it was another matter. We discussed his feelings as to how tyrannical his parents were and how they were exploiting "cruds"; they owed him things because he was a result of their "pleasure." Moreover, he seemed to feel he was at a crossroads: (1) Stay in a "childish rut" with many pleasures but feeling pushed around and small; or (2) Work to get what he wanted along with independence, despite the anxiety.

Rorschach—III (2) The string attached in the umbilical cord; *i.e.*, being dependent on his parents for having it made and being just a child.

Sixteenth Session (3/25): No show.

Seventeenth Session (3/18): The patient was forty-five minutes late. When he mentioned lateness, we discussed it in generally the same terms that we had before. In addition, I wondered if he was attempting to determine whether I was just interested in getting paid. He conceded that, after all, why should I care since I did get paid. We discussed this and I told him that I *was* very interested in working with him, as well as in getting paid, but that for me to do this he would have to be there. I related this to the fact that his parents paid the bill. He said that if he were paying, he would be waiting outside my office before the hour began. We considered his savings of $100 and his getting a job. He said that would really hurt. I agreed but wondered whether it might not be worth it. He insisted that he would come early, mentioning how he felt an *incompleteness* about our talks, and that he saw my point about his responsibility for his bills. He added that his birthday was in two days; I wished him a happy birthday.

TAT–(1) Even titles story "Very confused kid." (2) Child treated poorly by parents.

Eighteenth Session (3/23): He was fifteen minutes late. He said that he could not possibly work and pay his own bill. He had found out what the bill was because he let his mother take care of it. Discussing this, we saw that he did not want to work and pay so much for treatment, which he felt was my expectation.

He spent the remainder of hour attacking his girlfriend's father, who is extremely possessive and unreasonable about his daughter, forbidding the patient to see her. After stating very realistically how he had insisted she stand up to her father (which is really not very realistic) rather than their sneaking around or calling off the relationship, he wondered what I thought and told of all sorts of childish pranks he ought to pull on this father. We considered this regression from adult actions to childishness, but he was now so hepped up with his fantasies that he hardly listened.

TAT–(1) Even titles story "Very confused kid." (2) Child treated poorly by his parents.

Nineteenth Session (3/30): Last week he had two flat tires coming here—he had started late anyway. He did call later (verified).

Then he told of how rotten he felt about what he did last Saturday night. With several other fellows, all of them quite drunk, he harassed couples parked on lovers' lane, particularly Negro men with white women.

> Rorschach–III, TAT–General Pd flavor: Must let out his hostility on someone in even weaker position (disparages Negroes here and women and homosexuals in TAT stories).

Coming here last hour he was speeding with defective tires, and realized how dangerous this was. I questioned why he was so angry and destructive with everyone, including himself and me (he hardly disguised his mockery, with sarcasm in his tone and ideas). He admitted he felt very unhappy, and that things were not so happy at home.

> MMPI–D, Pd, Sc: This pattern is one of keen loneliness and misery (Depression D, alienation Pd, differentness Sc).
>
> Rorschach–IV Underneath his bravado and destructive facade, he himself feels a mess and vulnerable to attack.

Twentieth Session (4/1): The patient was about twenty minutes late. He evinced interest in me indirectly—for instance, he asked whether I was attending a publicized professional meeting, looked at my pen, etc. But looking at this interest was quite anxiety-provoking for him.

We discussed his need to resist, flee, fight, and so on until very near the end of the hour (or to cut time from hour by his lateness), when he then felt I kicked him out.

> ICL–(4) High representation in 4th octant suggests rebelliousness.
>
> MMPI–Hy, Pd, Ma: Hy indicates denial, Pd displacement onto environment or into action, and Ma extroverted (often hostile) expression of anxiety—or a pattern of fleeing and/or fighting.

He was very ambivalent about going to school because he feared he would flunk, and Dr. O's tutor could not help him anyway. It seems that this is related to his feeling of why he should do this anyway—why study years to be a chemist when he does all these things in a chemical company already? His parents would really react if he flunked out.

> TAT–(1, 2, 6) In all 3 stories, he shows parents that he does not have to be what they expect of him, even if he hurts himself in the process.

Twenty-first Session (4/6): He arrived about twenty minutes late, very facetious, sarcastic, and definitely on edge. He wanted me to advise him whether or not to consult a tutor. At the same time, he clearly indicated that he would defeat any such suggestion because he felt that parents (and I) expected him to do such things for their own needs—not his. We touched on this matter of rebellion and submission.

> TAT (1, 2, 6) In all 3 stories, he shows parents that he does not have to be what they expect of him, even if he hurts himself in the process.

Twenty-second Session (4/13): He was only five minutes late and very proud of it. But he did not know what to talk about. Threatened by the silence, he grew facetious (not very) and threatened to leave. He began to tell bad jokes and tried to get me either to laugh or to be angry. He felt he had succeeded in the latter because I told him to cut the baloney when he began to ask the root derivatives of word derivations and so on. (Incidentally, he was obsessed with curiosity as to the meaning of *psychopath.*)

Again he asked me to advise him about a tutor. He thinks it is best; it would please his parents, Dr. O and me. However, it would be expensive and he would feel guilty about this added burden for his parents. Moreover, they would then be in a position to complain about his doing nothing. It is not worth it for him to work; he feels too "chicken" and he's afraid of "goofing up" in school.

> MMPI—K: Very low K indicates intense self-criticism.
> ICL—(5) This octant, when high, suggests guilt and self-depreciation.
> TAT—(4) Theme of being sick in the brain, "brain tumor."
> Rorschach—IV Self-concept of being a mess and stepped on.
> DAP—Male: DAP associations of gross disparagement and overtly self-referred.

Twenty-third Session (4/14): The patient arrived thirty-five minutes late, wearing dark prescription glasses. He spoke of being sensitive about wearing ordinary glasses and also tackled the idea of people not seeing his expression. In the few minutes left, he told of how he and a friend had planned to roll a homosexual. After they flirted with him, he took them to his apartment, whereupon they grew frightened of his advances, and the patient smashed a radio over his head.

The patient rationalized a great deal about this incident. There was little time for me to point out (1) apparently he was looking for trouble; and (2) what was the meaning of his desire to smash or rob such an individual?

> MMPI—Pd: Must let out his hostility on someone in even weaker position (disparages Negroes here and women and homosexuals in TAT stories).
>
> TAT—(12, 13) Hostility and violence pour through his defenses.

Twenty-fourth Session (4/15): At thirty minutes past the hour, he called from bridge to report car trouble and asked whether he should come in. I advised him he had twenty minutes left. He said he would try to make it, but never arrived.

Twenty-fifth Session (4/20): He was twenty-five minutes late; his apologies about missing last hour were confused. He asked how long I see other patients, etc. Finally I asked him for a straight story and he said he had lied. We discussed this as well as the implications of the previous hour's discussion. He felt that I disapproved of him and expressed a wish to punch his fist through my wall. But he did admit that he would like to see himself accurately and that he feels relaxed when he leaves therapy sessions.

> MMPI—PdMa: Actively aggressive towards environment. (Pd connotes resentment and Ma action and hostility.)
>
> DAP—Male: Male all decked out in armor (football) ready for combat.
>
> TAT—(7, 12) Violence in both themes.
>
> Rorschach—I, II Highly destructive quality of responses.

Twenty-sixth Session (4/22:) He arrived forty minutes late, rushing in very anxiously, directing questions about what I was reading, and bantering in various other ways. He was able to see that he was both being aggressive towards me and directing fire away from himself. He did ask whether I thought there was something wrong with him because he used an alias with girls. This led to an investigation of what he felt about himself; he looked at this for a moment and then attempted to direct conversation to me. He was reluctant to leave.

> MMPI—K: Very low K indicates intense self-criticism.
>
> ICL—(5) This octant, when high, suggests guilt and self-depreciation.

Rorschach—IV Self-concept of being a mess and stepped on.
TAT—(4) Theme of being sick in the brain, "brain tumor."

Twenty-seventh Session (4/27): The patient was on time and very proud of it, but then became very facetious, personal, and irrelevant. Characteristically he then dropped the fact that he was sick last Saturday, but determinedly avoided going into it. At my persistence, he started talking about himself, rapidly and without feeling, telling of double date: they drank two bottles of wine, got sick, and fell asleep in car until very late. He refused to investigate meaning here.

I attempted firmly and yet supportively to structure our roles in treatment. He remained silent for a long time. Finally, he said that his father was going on a fishing trip. With exploration, he revealed (and denied) that he was hurt by his father not inviting him and trying to get closer to him. On the other hand he is afraid that in this case his father would want to know more about him.

It was very important for him to say that the hour was up (when it wasn't) because it hurt to think that I'd "kick him out." Then he demanded to know why he did not get a full sixty minutes.

TAT—(1, 8) Fairly clear that unconscious wish behind both of these themes is for the parents really to love him and each other rather than be wrapped up in their own interests.

Subsequent Treatment

Mr. R was in treatment eight more months, the preponderant part at three sessions per week. He worked prodigiously for the longest time to get me to react to him as either a benevolent or tyrannical parent. He compulsively and tenaciously clung to his concept of himself as a kid depending on his parents, making no decisions, and having it made—for the time being at least. This was accompanied by self-depreciation, unhappiness, and self-destructive behavior. At first, *he* could not believe that I was interested in what he wanted for himself but, despite my words, was only furthering my own designs and ambitions, just like his parents. Then he formed a strong positive transference and stated explicitly that he wished to change his ways in order to get *my* approval.

He entered a junior college program and, after some initial floundering and weeding-out of courses to build a more realistic course load, he worked satisfactorily in school. By the last month of treatment he was going steady, manifesting positive attitudes towards his parents, and working part-time in addition to going to school.

To give an example of his increased insight, he verbalized the following in the last month. His pattern of getting approval from others, which he needs all the time because he feels that he does not fit in and is unworthy, is to get *everybody* to accept him or at least to react to him. Often the only way he feels he can do this is by shocking them or getting criticized—this is the only way that his parents *sincerely* relate to him. He started to think of more efficient ways of attaining gratification and enumerated his successes in this respect.

He is still prone to be rash but also explained that this behavior obviated his growing too dependent on treatment (and me and, by extrapolation, on his parents). Despite a continued tendency to be defensive and impish, he was warmer and more serious. Other than some mention of feeling faint at periods during the first few weeks of treatment, he reported no further convulsive or even dizzy attacks. Treatment was presumably terminated because school, work, and family finances indicated this at least temporarily. (However, there was indication that the parents were threatened by his increasing signs of maturity and independence.) Certainly, his rebelliousness, particularly as enacted with automobiles, was not worked through.

Post hoc Comments

The first paragraph under "Subsequent Treatment" might well have been written on the basis of the psychological test material, rather than on the basis of the actual therapy. And the report did allude to these aspects of the patient's dynamic make-up. Particularly, the ICL and MMPI shed light on the need to rebel and its meaning, while TAT stories such as 1 and 2 explained his behavior towards authority and predicted the maneuvers he would attempt in psychotherapy.

CHAPTER SEVEN

SADOMASOCHISM: CHARACTER DISORDER WITH UNDERLYING PSYCHOTIC FEATURES

I

II

DIAGNOSTIC OVERVIEW:

A Character Disorder

with Underlying Psychotic Features

Character disorders typically are oriented to their world by fighting or fleeing. To the degree that they are successful in combatting anxiety in this way, to that extent they do not develop neurotic defenses. Consequently, with intensified stress and/or weakened ability to fight or flee (as with age, illness, incarceration, etc.), the character disorder has only one direction in which to go—a regression into even more severe psychopathology. For this reason, serious character disorders often are not easily distinguished from psychotics (e.g., "stir crazy" behavior when incarcerated, frenzied acting out behavior under the influence of alcohol, the readiness to be provoked into tantrums, etc.)

This particular patient is characterized by an extremely severe character disorder with psychotic features including paranoid ideation. (On the MMPI, extreme stress on the lefthand scales of Hs and Hy as high as D but relatively low Pt indicates depressive features but little manifest anxiety. Peaks in Pd and Pa suggest acting out of her distrust of others by pushing them away or fleeing from them). Suspicion and distrust of others, or at least inability to relate meaningfully, were indicated in the ICL by the representation in the 4th octant completely missing in Ideal (expressing conflict here); the dehumanized responses on Rorschach ('M,' 'H'); and her description of people and described means of relating on DAP and TAT and in the interview, were almost exclusively in terms of hostility. In fact, a sadomasochistic orientation was most pronounced. This form of relation was expressed by the patient in the interview, particularly towards her husband; shown repeatedly in stories on the TAT; and markedly portrayed in her picture of her husband on the ICL as a ruthless, exploitive, sadistic person.

Her interpersonal relations were so weak that the patient appeared to rely heavily on very primitive somatic defenses. Marked hypochondria was indicated by her long, varied, and vague somatic complaints (with considerable secondary gain) listed in the interview; very high Hs on MMPI: pronounced representation on the ICL of the 8th octant (presentation of self as overly responsible and generous, or a "psychomatic" orientation); and TAT story of a grave illness as the only factor holding a married couple together. The soma, it would seem, represented a last-ditch means of fleeing inner and outer pressures by obviating recognition of psychological conflicts.

The inadequacy of the patient's defenses resulted in, besides the extreme distrust previously mentioned, morbid preoccupations (subliminal awareness of ego deterioration) and distorted judgment. The former was suggested on the Rorschach content, skeleton, on card VIII, on card IV, rotting and decay, and gruesomeness on card IX. Confused and distorted judgment was displayed by transparency on the DAP; contaminated (fused) concepts on Rorschach card VIII; and confusion of identity indicated by sexual confusion on TAT stories 12M and 18GF and Rorschach card III. A sense of her desperate state was hinted at by the bare "hanging on" content on Rorschach cards I and II; and by MMPI items as "urge to do something harmful or shocking," "memory not all right," "no one understands me," and "I have been in trouble because of sex."

The psychological evaluation presented a poor prognosis especially underscored by the patient's weakly integrated defenses against anxiety, her poor ability to relate to anyone other than with hostility, and her equivocal motivation—entering treatment only on urging of her physician. It was felt, however, that clarification of her motives to the patient would enable her to capitalize on whatever propitious circumstances arose during therapy.

PSYCHOLOGICAL EVALUATION:

A Case of Sadomasochism

Patient: female, age 36, married, four children — Occupation: housewife, former medical technician

Education: technical school

Referred by: Dr. L. for personality evaluation with particular reference to current marital difficulties.

Tests Administered

Rorschach, Thematic Apperception Test (TAT), Minnesota Multiphasic Inventory (MMPI), Draw-A-Person (DAP), and Interpersonal Checklist (ICL).

Test Behavior

The patient was generally cooperative and pleasant. However, at times she attempted to be evasive. For example, she laughingly asked whether she could draw stick figures for people, but when told to draw the whole person, she suddenly became dizzy. She became most enthusiastic and detailed when describing her physical symptoms or the unbearable behavior of her husband. She threatens divorce in order to calm the turmoil in the household. As for her hospitalization, "My husband now has to take care of the kids—it will do him good and he will learn how hard it is."

Test Evaluation

Mrs. S presents herself as an extremely responsible and generous person who is cooperative and conventional to a compulsive degree. However, she also admits to considerable distrust and suspicion of others, but would like to expunge the slightest trace of such feelings of disaffiliation toward people. This is an area of raging conflict for her, suggesting that such primitive defenses as projecting and displacing her own emotional disturbance outward are becoming more and more necessary and disturbing to her. She would like to assume an exaggerated "milk and honey" attitude toward others, but instead, her distrust of others makes for a sour outlook and a cynical viewpoint of being used and pushed around (I get a raw deal out of life—no one understands me). She emphasizes her femininity in demonstrating her helplessness and ill treatment. There are indications that often she impulsively acts out and/or somaticizes anxiety.

The husband is seen by the patient as a ruthless and exploitive person who is even more suspicious of others than she is, and whose sole purpose in dealing with other people (and herself in particular, no doubt) is to manage and manipulate them. In short, she sees him as a sadistic and narcissistic personality.

Beneath a compulsive and somewhat hysterical facade, the patient reveals even more serious psychopathology. She is preoccupied with morbid fantasies of rotting and decay underscored by a marked masochism. These feelings are linked to her conceptions of what a female is and what she may feel she is, now, at 36. She manifests considerable sexual confusion and has made only a superficial identification with the feminine role. Therefore, she sees sex as a tool or weapon rather than as an integral part of a loving relationship. As a consequence, she assumes a submissive, masochistic orientation as a wife and pulls for sadistic treatment in return. This presents a miserable state of affairs leading to extreme desperation at times, for she has marked cravings for affection and love, which she does not know how to handle. Consequently, her very neurotic and unhappy solution is to assume a sadomasochistic relationship with the males significant in her life.

People are threatening to her. Females, although immature and narcissistic, are powerful; in one TAT story the wife literally "pins down her smaller husband" who has made her unhappy. (Nevertheless, the woman goes on in the same disconsolate rut). Men are even more immature and severely disparaged, but they are very dangerous. Marital discord is a prevailing theme running through her projective material. She suggests that illness is one way of making a couple hold onto one another. Her tendency to somaticize anxiety thus finds added gain in any illness that might be seized upon to serve these purposes and, in turn, the emotional factor might well aggravate the illness. The revenge motive directed against the husband (he has "made her sick and has to care for the children") should not be discounted either.

The picture she presents, in summary, is of a frightened and confused woman who resorts to primitive and ineffectual measures in coping with her anxiety. These defenses have become integrated into her characterological make-up. Under chronic stress, as well as in unusual stressful situations, she may well regress to even more serious psychopathology; her test material warns of this. A schizophrenic reaction in such situations, and involutional melancholia succeeding the menopause, are possibilities.

Therapeutic intervention aimed at permitting her to gain a sense of worth and to integrate a meaningful identification as a woman is recommended. Extensive uncovering techniques are indicated for such pervasive psychopathology. Her basic distrust and equivocal motivation prognosticate poorly, but are mitigated by her desperate need for help. She sees (and his test material corroborates) her husband as a contributing influence. Successful therapy, other than eventual environmental manipulation, would require the husband to enter therapy as well.

Diagnostic Impression:
(1) Character disorder with compulsive features; and (2) Paranoid ideation.

THERAPY NOTES

First Session (4/23): Mrs. S started the hour by saying that the referring physician had told her that three times a week (an arrangement she had considered) would be too difficult with the considerable travel necessary. This brought up her feelings about therapy and her equivocal motivation. However, after discussing how she met her husband, she entered more into the therapeutic situation.

> MMPI–Pa, Hs: Very high Pa indicates marked distrust and aloofness (combined with Hs it indicates sour hostility).
>
> ICL–(4) High 4th octant in Self, completely vacated in Ideal, connotes sharp conflict about her feelings of suspiciousness and inability to relate.
>
> DAP–"Piercing look" on DAP suggests distrust and pushing others away or destroying them.

She went with her husband for four years. When he did not get a divorce from his first wife, she triggered the issue by joining the WACS as a medical technician and leaving the country. Still loving her husband-to-be, she "got involved with a captain patient" of hers but left another country to escape this second involvement.

> MMPI–Pd: Her peak (and extremely high) Pd indicates her gross sense of resentment towards family (and, by extrapolation, society) and the impulse, therefore to defy or flee via action.

Returning home, she found her husband-to-be divorced. They had odd wedding plans. In their Nevada honeymoon he was accompanied by his two elder brothers and their wives. The wedding was sandwiched in between gambling. The sisters-in-law were jealous of the flowers the patient received. She said nothing but just sulked; she does not believe in expressing feelings. While they were still on their honeymoon, her husband wrote to his father; she added a greeting and he flew into a rage because she had butted in, but she just kept her feelings in. Although she rationally described her actions, her defiance and guilty tone accompanying this description were clarified for her.

ICL—(4) Does not express feelings because they are potentially too hostile, so sulks.

MMPI—Pa: Very high Pa indicates marked distrust and aloofness (combined with Hs it indicates sour hostility).

In discussing arrangements for appointments twice a week, she brought up the fact that her husband handled all the money and that she is helpless in this situation. It was indicated that her feelings about this might be discussed further, but at the same time it was suggested that she assume responsibility for the therapy bill.

MMPI—K: Low K demonstrates her claim to weakness.

MMPI—PdMf: Extremely high Pd and extremely low Mf point to her strident claims of helplessness and even marked masochism (Pd, resentment directed at self; Mf, weak and feminine).

Second Session (4/28): The patient phoned to cancel therapy completely. She wondered about the efficacy of it, the therapist's age, the expense, etc. I suggested that she come in and talk about it.

MMPI—Pa, Hs: Very high Pa indicates marked distrust and aloofness; combined with Hs, it indicates sour hostility.

ICL—(4) High 4th octant in Self, completely vacated in Ideal, connotes sharp conflict about her feelings of suspiciousness and inability to relate.

TAT—Gloomy theme of almost every story.

The patient did come in and we explored her feelings. Begrudgingly, she said that she had considerable emotional difficulty. She had a great deal of trouble talking with people but handled it by compulsively talking about many little things.

She would like to practice as a medical technician again because she likes to feel useful. At home, she feels depressed by her family and the demands placed upon her.

MMPI—D: High D indicates dysphoria, a sense of being buffeted by the demands of others, by one's environment, and by internal conflicts.

Near the end of the hour, she told of the following dream: "Very funny." Her husband's Cadillac was parked on an incline where she parks her car ("usually in everybody's way"). The car rolled free and into a lagoon, where a 16- or 17-year-old boy found it in a picket fence—just a "shiny shoe of a car" (toy size). She took it out and showed it to her husband.

Associations: She has wanted a new car for some time and has been dependent on her husband taking her places. I asked whether she was talking about a wish to have greater independence and to confront her husband with this. (Phallic significance was not touched upon).

> MMPI–Pd: Her resentment is expressed by indirect or passive hostility.
>
> DAP–Aggression: Powerful, threatening quality of drawings suggests both fear of aggression and her being the aggressor.
>
> Rorschach–Destructiveness: Destructive quality of most of her Rorschach responses.
>
> ICL–(3) Both quantity and quality of items chosen by her for 3rd octant describe her suppressed aggression.
>
> Rorschach and TAT–Frank confusion on these tests seem to be centered around her conflicts concerning autonomy.

She wanted to come once a week for awhile.

Third Session (5/5): The patient was fifteen minutes late. She wondered whether she and her husband shouldn't discuss a schedule and budgeting as other couples do. It seems that they cannot talk about any of these things; her husband does not want to, so she does not push it. He treats her like a child with respect to running the household and money matters. She is considering acquiring more independence by getting a job.

> DAP–Male more powerful, she more helpless and childish. (Thus, female is a high school girl and male 25 years old–but then she disparages and weakens his position.)
>
> TAT–(1) Theme of submissive child.
>
> MMPI–K: Low K demonstrates her claim to weakness.
>
> MMPI–PdMf: Extremely high Pd and extremely low Mf point to her strident claims of helplessness and even marked masochism (Pd, resentment directed at self; Mf, weak and feminine).

For years these situations have gone on. She rationalized the situation by suggesting that she follow the path of least resistance, avoiding fights. But she was able to see that while her husband believes that he wants her to be more independent, he needs her to be like a child. Similarly, although she believes that she bitterly resents the lattr, she apparently needs this too.

> MMPI–PdMf: Extremely high Pd and extremely low Mf point to her strident claims of helplessness and even marked

masochism (Pd, resentment directed at self; Mf, weak and feminine).

Having mulled this over, she began to speak of her increased chest pains, her lack of sleep and her poor appetite.

MMPI–Hs: Extremely high Hs indicates her enormous focus on somatic complaints (and means of avoiding commitment to interpersonal relationships).

ICL–(8) Very exaggerated and peak representation describes her claim to hypernormality, which frequently leaves only somatic arena for person to battle out his conflicts.

TAT–(10) Grave illness is what keeps couple clinging together.

Rorschach–Somatic, diseased responses.

The emotional patterns expressed during the session were summarized. Despite her difficulty in starting, she still was talking at the end of the hour and spoke of coming the following week.

Fourth Session (5/12): The patient was a half-hour late. Her car wouldn't start. She mentioned that she had hired another woman for the household. Other people in their home serve to inhibit her husband's temper. Moreover, he is appeased when the house is clean. The defensiveness and rebelliousness with which she said this was pointed out.

ICL–Sadomasochistic relationship: Contrast between her masochistic representation of her Self (stress on lower half) and sadism of husband (stress on upper half but especially his exploitiveness in octant 2).

She brought up the point that she is fearful in front of groups and has been since she was a child. Yet she always got A's in school. Now she has a problem because she is being pressured to be and wants herself to be president of the PTA.

Rorschach–Phobic features, gruesome fantasies, particularly on IX.

Fifth Session (5/23): Patient absent, no call.

Sixth Session (5/30): She phoned to cancel therapy a half-hour past appointment time.

MMPI–K, Pt: Low K, or sense of weakness, and high Pt, or anxiousness, combined indicate phobic orientation.

MMPI–Pa, Pd: Very high Pa indicates marked distrust and

aloofness; combined with Hs it indicates sour hostility. Her peak and extremely high Pd indicates her gross sense of resentment towards family (and, by extrapolation, society) and the impulse, therefore, to defy.

(7/1): The referring physician informed me that patient suddenly died, cause undetermined. This occurred a few days ago. He indicated the possibility, which could not be discounted, of toxic substance intake in a suicidal act.

MMPI—D, Pd, Ma, F: (see psychological report warning of serious break): Extremely high D describes marked depression; Pd morbid resentment; moderately high Ma indicates she is not immobilized and can and does act (but with insufficient energy to pursue her ambitions); and high F feeling different and rebellious. Add to this pattern PdMf, or directing of aggression against oneself, and her checking of item "At times I have strong urges to do something harmful or shocking," and a suicidal potential is portrayed.

Comments

The psychological evaluation presented the poor prognosis unfortunately proven in the outcome and it warned that the patient's defenses were so poorly integrated that she might well regress into serious psychopathology. The suicidal possibility was also suggested by the evaluation. From a more dynamic approach, the MMPI, ICL, and DAP considerably clarified her markedly distorted view of herself and others and the Rorschach and TAT indicated her morbid preoccupations and sense of rage and helplessness. When these attitudes were expressed in therapy, therefore, it was much more possible to understand them, although there was little success in dealing with them.

CHAPTER EIGHT

A CASE OF DENIAL: HYSTERICAL CHARACTER DISORDER WITH COMPULSIVE FEATURES

I

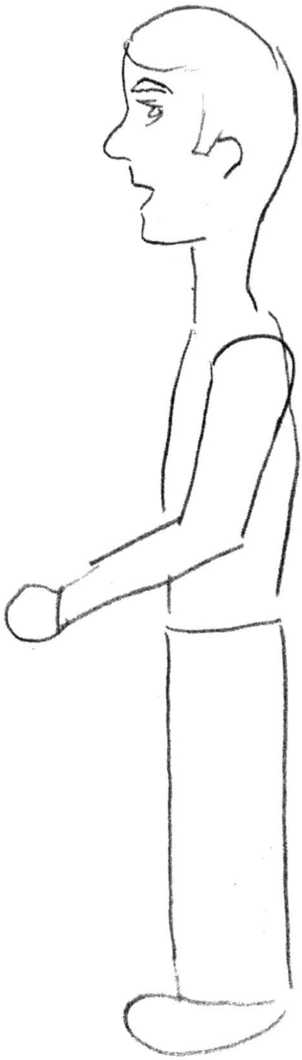

DIAGNOSTIC OVERVIEW:

Hysterical Character Disorder

with Marked Compulsive Features

The distinction between an hysterical neurosis and an hysterical character disorder is at best subtle, since each category merges into the other. Neurotic symptomatology, however, is relatively insulated from the character structure and generally serves specific functions that are not conscious (for example, a paralysis or convulsion that serves to avoid threatening emotional situations). Character disorders, on the other hand, are ingrained patterns of attitudes and behavior that often are part and parcel of the self-concept (*e.g.*, the world has given me a raw deal so I don't give a damn about anyone else—I can't help or really care about what I do, that's how I am).

This patient demonstrated hysterical features in that her emotional reactions were dramatic, and there was massive repression of experiences, marked naivete, childlike relatedness, and stereotypic attitudes. These characteristics were less symptomatic than characterological because they seemed ego syntonic and were of very long standing, rather than alien manifestations of, say, someone else's personality. Moreover, equally ingrained in her character structure were compulsive defenses. Under stress, when both hysterical and compulsive maneuvers failed, deep depression set in. One further note relevant to the characterological make-up of this patient: her emotional reactiveness was demonstrated primarily in interpersonal contexts rather than in response to generalized stimuli. (Thus, on the Rorschach color was not particularly responded to; and the Hy scale on the MMPI was not especially high.)

Hysterical components were suggested in the test material by attitudes that were overconventional and even stereotypic and dependent (representation of 7th octant in ICL; conforming themes on TAT, particularly story; low K on MMPI; and P's on Rorschach as well as childlike fixation on animal responses on latter); by repression of sexual, hostile, and other emotionally charged data (on WAIS discrepancy between verbal and performance IQ's in favor of the latter, with relative superiority on tasks emphasizing concentration and attention but relatively free of emotional material—Digit Span, Digit Symbol, and Object Assembly; avoidance of sexual or aggressive content on TAT cards 13MF and 18GF; and rejection of Card VI on the Rorschach); and by manifest anxiety, pointed to by D, Pt on the MMPI and representation on ICL octant 6.

Compulsive features were indicated by the peak Pt on MMPI and such items as fear and repulsion of dirt, fear of disease, inability to decide, compulsive habits, etc., and by anality on Rorschach such as squatting position on card III. The depression was notable on the D scale in the MMPI, and themes of sadness on the TAT. Judgment faltered when she revealed contaminated (fused concepts) thinking on Rorschach card II.

The psychological evaluation delineated the patient's ego resources that prognosticated her ability to withstand the pressures and stresses of uncovering therapy: the well conceived DAP drawings, MMPI and ICL profile, within reasonable non-pathological limits, striving response of climbing animals on the Rorschach, and TAT and Rorschach on the whole devoid of serious distortions. (Other resources such as a devoted husband, parents, friends, and healthy attractive children were propitious factors for her.) The test material indicated her yearning for, and reaching out to, people. Important clues were provided to assist her to understand her repressed hostilities and confused picture of herself. When these attitudes came up, frequent referral by the therapist to the test material clarified what was taking place. Most significantly, the evaluation underscored the necessity for the patient to avoid even the usual stresses of family life until her defenses were strengthened.

PSYCHOLOGICAL EVALUATION:

A Case of Denial

Patient, female, age 27, married, two children	Education: one-half year of junior college
	Occupation: housewife

Referred by: her psychotherapist, Dr. Blank, for personality evaluation, with special reference to "quality and quantity of pathology."

Tests Administered:

Minnesota Multiphasic Personality Inventory (MMPI) and Interpersonal Checklist (ICL) (administered and reported earlier), Rorschach, Draw-a-Person (DAP), Wechsler Adult Intelligence Scale (WAIS), Thematic Apperception Test (TAT).

Interview and Test Behavior:

The patient was friendly, although somewhat reserved and emotionally bland, except for occasional instances of animated speech. At a superficial level she was quite cooperative, but expressed bewilderment about why she was being tested and responded to the projective tests in a cautious, evasive fashion. She became quite upset during the verbal part of the WAIS, complaining that she doesn't read the news and had never liked school-like tasks, and also complaining of difficulty in concentrating on items requiring thinking. From time to time during the testing she responded to the examiner's further questioning of a response by a mildly haughty remark suggesting that her original response was perfectly adequate and needed no elaboration.

Evaluation:

The tests reveal an immature, hysterical character structure. The patient characteristically seeks to defend herself from anxiety by repressing sexual and aggressive feelings and by restricting her awareness greatly in such a way as to avoid contact with any thought content that might be related to these feelings. Her cautious, evasive responses to the projective tests reflect this pattern, as do her scores and responses on the WAIS. She obtained an over-all IQ score of 96, within the normal range of intelligence, but scored only 89 on the verbal scale, while scoring 105 on the performance scale. Such a discrepancy between verbal and performance IQ's is typical of hysterical patients, and in this patient is largely the result of an extensive restriction of interests in order to avoid possibly disturbing content. She is able to perform with considerably greater adequacy on more content-free activities, such as repeating digits.

The patient's hysterical defenses have not been successful, however, and she has been flooded with anxiety-laden repressed emotions and thoughts. She cannot tolerate this material and has resorted to more primitive obsessive-compulsive mechanisms to allay her anxieties. Thus, at present she wavers between hysterical mechanisms of avoidance and obsessive-compulsive mechanisms to deal with what she cannot avoid. Sexual material appears prominent in the material that has emerged, and she seems to deal with this by fragmenting her perceptions in a way that prevents constructive use of her thought processes, and that also could lead to confused thinking.

At a preconscious level, strong dependency needs play a major role in the patient's dynamics and in the internal pressures which weaken her defenses. Basically, she would like to be taken care of by a nurturant person, and she greatly resents having to assume adult responsibilities. Her dependency motivation also makes abandonment by those who can satisfy these needs a threatening prospect she is unable to cope with. She appears pessimistic about gaining dependency gratifications through relationships with other women, and hostility toward female figures is indicated. She seems to look to men to take care of her, rather than seeking more mature sexual relationships.

At a conscious level the patient is at least partially aware of her strong dependency and would like to be less so. She also finds unacceptable her feeling that she is treated unfairly by others, and the consequent suspiciousness and distrust she experiences. She would like to be a more responsible, assertive person, who can help and care for others.

At present, the patient seems to be in an extremely vulnerable condition. While she seems to be able to function reasonably well, although in a hysterical way, in the nurturant ward atmosphere, her usual repressive defenses are weak, and stress of the sort she would encounter upon resuming family responsibilities would be likely to increase her obsessive-compulsive mechanisms to a disabling degree and to subject her to intense anxiety. Prolonged psychotherapy in a life situation in which she is relatively free from pressures until she is better able to handle them is advisable.

Diagnostic Impression:

Anxiety and obsessive-compulsive reactions in a hysterical personality.

THERAPY NOTES

(Patient had been hospitalized for a week prior to this interview when she complained of disabling depression to her physician.)

First Session (10/9): The patient said she was anxious and depressed. She explained her cheerful appearance as a means of conveying to other people that she was all right. She said that it was hard for her to concentrate and that it felt like there was a fog between her and other people.

> MMPI—D, Pt: Extremely high, and peaks on D and Pt convey depression and anxiety.
>
> Rorschach—II Response includes feeling of tears. Also she dehumanizes her human response (like a fog between people).
>
> Rorschach—III Again dehumanizes.
>
> TAT—Themes: People alone, not really relating or, at best, arguing.
>
> DAP—Profile suggests avoidance of direct relationships.

Saying that she loved her children and husband, she was puzzled about her anger towards them. Exploring this anger brought tears to her eyes.

> ICL—(3) Third octant represented even higher for Ideal than Self, suggesting pressure to express aggression.

Second Session (10/10): The patient is preparing to leave the hospital. She is afraid of hurting her children or of suicide, although her only conscious feelings are of hopelessness.

> MMPI—Pa very low, D, Pt, Ma: Markedly low Pa is suspect and usually may be interpreted as if profile were turned upside down. Thus, very high Pa would suggest projection of her feelings and impulses onto others. High D, Pt to which can be added pessimism and sense of immobility expressed in low Ma. Last suggests weak activation of suicidal impulse.

She revealed that she "pulled" fainting spells in order to get her husband's attention and convince him how sick she was. Although eulogizing him, she indicated he expressed little feeling and was hard to get close to.

> TAT—Themes: People alone, not really relating or, at best, arguing.
>
> ICL—(4) Well represented 4th octant in Self pulled back in Ideal suggests conflict about relating to people.

Both the patient's parents have been institutionalized. They were good parents but never demonstrated affection.

> TAT—(7GF, 12F, 18GF) All three stories describe lack of affection between parent and child.

Third Session (10/18): The patient appeared well-dressed and poised. She said that she was somewhat nervous caring for her younger child. Her husband makes demands on her to be responsive. More generally, she strains to be sociable and would prefer to be her natural shy self.

MMPI–Pa: Markedly low Pa is suspect and usually may be interpreted as if profile were turned upside down. Thus, very high Pa would suggest projection of her feelings and impulses onto others.

ICL–(4) Well-represented 4th octant in Self pulled back in Ideal suggests conflict about relating to people.

The patient never had any responsibility until she was married. The birth of the second child caused tremendous strain. All her energies have been wrapped up in her oldest son, and she has little left for her husband and much less for the infant.

MMPI–K, Ma: Very low K connotes weakness psychologically, and markedly low Ma describes sense of physical debility.

With considerable difficulty, she reported her fear that her husband's affection would lead to lovemaking, of which she feels incapable. She is concerned that this may indicate loss of love on her part. Both were ignorant of sex before marriage—they never have had satisfactory sex relationships (6 years). Her husband is "too reserved" and always has a rapid climax, while she seldom ever reaches climax. She has resigned herself but has mixed feelings of disgust at her husband and guilt at her own inadequacy.

Rorschach–VI Rejects card that often presents sexual stimulus, suggesting sex avoidance.

TAT–(13MF) Avoids any reference to very possible sexual or hostile theme.

MMPI–K, Mf: Markedly low K and Mf suggests that her conception of sexual role is of weakness and literalness (stereotyped) but devoid of fuller meaning.

DAP–Hands near genitals: Sexual conflict suggested by position of hands.

Fourth Session (10/25): The patient had hints of desires to do and be things she finds unacceptable. This was summed up by her comment, "Why did I get into all of this" (last child, first child, responsibilities of marriage).

ICL–(9) Self vs. Ideal: Exaggeration and peak representation in 8th octant for Ideal as compared to lower representation in Self indicates her conflict about assuming responsibility as well as her strivings to be hyperresponsible.

She told of her approval of women who put family and housework before themselves; therefore she disapproves of herself. Her mother is of the former type.

ICL—(9) Ideal: Same.

Fifth Session (11/1): She is in a tremendous bind—she feels that her husband is not acting like a man—too passive. She has to be too aggressive and dominant. She would like to be treated more like a woman, having him take over. Even a beating would give her some satisfaction. Yet she appreciates that on the rare occurrences of usual sex roles (husband aggressive, she more passive) she feels frightened and disgusted.

ICL—Lower Hemispheres in Self and Ideal: Self stresses lower hemisphere while the converse is presented in the Ideal, demonstrating her conflict between presenting herself as weak but aspiring to dominant behavior.

MMPI—K, Mf, Ma: Very low K connotes weakness psychologically, and markedly low Ma describes sense of physical debility. Markedly low K and Mf suggests that her conception of sexual role is of weakness and literalness (stereotyped) but devoid of fuller meaning.

In general, she has demonstrated lessened inhibitions: hired a baby sitter to help care for the children, especially during therapy; spanked the children; and went out Saturday night with her husband, relaxing with a few drinks. However, she was uneasy about this change of behavior.

Sixth Session (11/13): The patient's husband phoned to report that his wife had tried to cut her wrist with a knife. Both came in. She complained about her husband's stopping her and insisted that she wanted to take her life—then he could remarry a fit wife and mother for the children. She persisted in this view so that we discussed the advisability of hospitalization. Although she did not want this, she did see it as the only alternative, even though it would prevent her from taking her life—the only thing she wanted. Something inside her made her want this. Hospitalization was decided on.

MMPI—D, Pt, Ma, K: Markedly low Pa is suspect and usually may be interpreted as if profile were turned upside down. Thus, very high Pa would suggest projection of her feelings and impulses onto others. High D, Pt to which can be added pessimism and sense of immobility expressed in low Ma.

TAT—(13MF) Wife and mother dies—husband will just have to go on.

The husband seen alone, was notably calm. He thought the situation was unfortunate but had seen depression coming on for a long time. He almost completely lacked insight and was defensive about himself. He reported that his wife did not sleep well last night and spoke about ending it all but he thought it was just a little worse than before. She called him from work and he came home and matter-of-factly made lunch for his son. She pulled a *butter knife* from her sweater and ran into the bathroom and hacked at her wrist (there was no observable scar). At first he said he got angry, but then he denied this and said he wanted to shock his wife so he yelled at her. When he saw it was a butter knife, he didn't believe she was serious. He had thought that the treatment was going along very well and that his wife had been very satisfied with it.

The patient seen after tubs was able to talk calmly and rationally but did make reference to her need to punish herself.

Seventh Session (11/13): (Same night) The patient was even more calm. She said she called her husband because she had been saying "no" to everything he asked, such as kissing and making love. That was terrible because she did not want him to think she did not love him, "My poor husband!" When he came home, she said that she could not take care of the children; he said that of course she could. Some time after this, she grabbed a knife and wished it were sharper.

> Rorschach—VI Rejects card that often presents sexual stimulus, suggesting sex avoidance.
>
> TAT—(13MF) Avoids any reference to very possible sexual or hostile theme. (4) Underlying hostility of wife toward husband.
>
> ICL—(3) Third octant increases in Ideal substantially suggesting aggressive urges.

A few nights before, she went dancing, which she loves above all else, but did not enjoy herself because of the people she was with—her husband, his brother and wife, and their friends. Her husband hardly dances at all, but she did enjoy dancing with the bandleader. She does not know if she loves her children but thinks so; she has considerably more doubt about loving her husband.

> Rorschach—II Response includes feeling of tears. Also she dehumanizes her human response (like a fog between people). (III) Again dehumanizes. (VI) Rejects card that often presents sexual stimulus, suggesting sex avoidance.

Eighth Session (11/14): The patient assumed a dutiful child's attitude toward the therapist about medication, eating, etc., although she still spoke of wanting to take her life. Once she showed a flash of anger, when she recounted that the nurses had told her that she had everything to live for but she could at least consider her husband and children. She had answered angrily that she had considered them only too much. She is not so dismayed (if at all) by the ward as might be imagined.

TAT—(7GF) Manner in Rorschach and TAT conforming yet passively resentful, childish attitude.

Ninth Session (11/15): The patient came to the hospital office. The point came out that she was tired of assuming responsibilities of living, particularly since she could not feel like an individual. She blurted out that she had had her period and was relieved because she feared pregnancy even though they had not had intercourse for four months. (However, during her first pregnancy, the doctor told her that she had been pregnant during her period.) The patient wondered whether she loved her husband. She could scream when he touches her yet he is "so good." She denied feeling any anger towards him and then told how he brought her the wrong clothes and shoes that hurt.

ICL—(3) Third octant increases in Ideal substantially suggesting aggressive urges.

TAT—(4) Underlying hostility of wife towards husband. (13MF) Avoids any reference to very possible sexual or hostile theme.

Tenth Session (11/16): The patient felt bad because instead of loving her children she felt like running away. She saw her own mother as completely selfless, subjugating her own interests, if any, to her family and particularly to her children. She remembered that as a child she turned to an older cousin for being tucked in, hair brushed, etc., because her mother was too impatient and nervous. She got some insight into her conflict between seeing her mother as all giving or giving too little of love. The latter aspect made her anxious, particularly in her re-enactment with her own children. She then told of how pigheaded, unreasonable, and parsimonious her father was. Realizing the anger with which she expressed this, she told of how charitable he could be, but then told of how frightened she grew when he yelled and called her stupid. She saw some transference of these feelings of helplessness and protestations of stupidity to the therapy situation.

TAT–(1, 7, 10, 12, 18) All themes describe lack of affection between mother and child and even suggest hostility.

Rorschach–III, VII On both cards inhibited interpersonally, she only produces responses additionally on card where easy to see people. Finally, does see human responses but bestializes.

Eleventh Session (11/17): The patient was very restless and agitated but could not say why. She does not want to see her husband or parents; when he did come last night, he chewed gum and stared into space. She wasn't angry about this, only sorry that she is hurting him (and, by implication, making him helpless). She became preoccupied with my office furnishings and with questions about me. This seemed to be related to the fact that she did not expect to see me on Saturday.

Twelfth Session (11/19): She still complained about not wanting to live, but indicated that she did not want to feel any other way—above all else she wanted to run away from her feelings.

ICL–(7) Her marked hysterical orientation (gross 7th and 8th octants and receded 4th octant in Ideal) points to her massive denial—in this context—of hostility.

Rorschach–Color cards: Overreactivity to color also stresses her hysterical orientation.

Thirteenth Session (11/20): The patient appeared to be, and said she was, considerably more relaxed. However, she reported that the only thing that she enjoyed was smoking—"puffing and inhaling."

Rorschach–VII Lamb's leg may suggest oral needs especially in "Mother" card context.

She expressed ambivalent feelings toward her husband but cried when we touched upon the idea that she could be angry or want to hurt her husband, because "he's so good." Yet she thought of her mother scolding her father when he feel asleep watching TV, and feared acting similarly towards her own husband.

ICL–(3) Self stresses lower hemisphere while the converse is presented in the Ideal, demonstrating her conflict between presenting herself as weak but aspiring to dominant behavior.

She considered the possibility that her husband, like her father, was inconsiderate, in his chewing and staring, and particularly in sex. She could hardly conceive of his having unsatisfactory sexual experiences, although he suffers from premature ejaculation "among other things." She begged off this topic because of a headache which she guessed was psychological.

> TAT—(13MF) Avoids any reference to very possible sexual or hostile theme.
>
> Rorschach—VI Rejects card that often presents sexual stimulus, suggesting sex avoidance.
>
> DAP—Hands: Sexual conflict suggested by position of hands.

Earlier in the week she dreamed that she and Mrs. C, another patient, were locked in an elevator. An attendant tries to get her to play cards and do things; this bothers her. She is not as sick as Mrs. C (who is the same age and very withdrawn). We discussed whether she felt that I bothered her, and she said that, on the contrary, I was the only person to whom she wished to speak.

Last night she dreamed she was driving a car and her son was looking out of the window. When she does drive with him, she prevents him from going near the window because she is afraid that he will get hurt. We discussed whether she felt that her being in the hospital might hurt her son.

Fourteenth Session (11/21): The patient looked quite relaxed and even smiled several times. She wondered what I had to discuss with her husband. (He came in earlier to talk a little about how things were going with them.) She told of playing solitaire, watching TV, and reading but always being obsessed with the idea of "wanting to end it all." When I told her that I would be away several days on a trip, she asked such questions as whether I was married, and at the end smilingly said, "Have a good trip."

> TAT—Themes of dependency cravings.

Fifteenth Session (11/26): (The patient was presented at ward rounds: consensus was a Character Disorder, Hysterical Acting Out. The recommendation was to encourage positive transference, even erotic manifestation, but at the same time to encourage expression of all feelings, including negative ones, to others.) The patient was quite relaxed and laughing. While trying to remember if she had been agitated before her hospitalization, she recalled that her husband kept watch on her in the car to prevent her jumping. (We related this to her last dream.) She never thought of jumping while the car was moving because she did not want pain and would only pick a painless way of suicide.

ICL–(7) Her marked hysterical orientation (gross 7th and 8th octants and receded 4th octant in Ideal) points to her massive denial–in this context–of hostility.

She turned the conversation to her sister-in-law's jealousy of her mother giving the patient more food, thus showing she loved her more. When a child she was more hopeless and needed more love; she got her mother to admit she loved the patient more than her older sister (who died).

Rorschach–VII Lamb's leg may suggest oral needs especially in "Mother" card context.

MMPI–K: Very low K connotes weakness psychologically, and markedly low Ma describes sense of physical debility.

TAT–(7) Behind screen of disgust, yearning for love from mother.

The patient planned the birth of both children; pregnancy and delivery were enjoyable and thrilling. After their births, particularly the second child, she no longer felt happy or that she had a purpose in life. With excitement and pleasure, she considered the importance and creativeness that were hers in bearing children.

Rorschach–II The depressive quality (tears) of the response.

Sixteenth Session (11/27): The patient revealed that she was uneasy only with the student nurses because she felt they were young, only girls–not too far removed from herself (given full battery by psychology intern yesterday). She was able to muster annoyance at them; these were people with whom she could be annoyed because she identified with them and disparaged herself in the same way.

ICL–(3) Undercurrents of TAT stories: Third octant increases in Ideal substantially suggesting aggressive urges.

When she was about 20, she worked with a female office manager. The patient felt she was taken advantage of and given all the dirty work because she was the "baby" of the office. Although angry and resentful, she would only sulk–then the manager would tell her how cute she was and how good her work was, making it even more difficult for her to express her feelings. She has remained friendly with this woman since. Recently, the latter offered her a part-time job, praising her work, but the patient felt she was considered a sucker who would do all the dirty work. She had similar experiences with her sister-in-law. Despite talking of helplessness, the patient laughed and expressed wry humor.

MMPI–Pa indicates feelings of being taken advantage of.

ICL (4) Well-represented 4th octant in Self pulled back in Ideal suggests conflict about relating to people.

Seventeenth Session (11/29): The patient revealed indirectly that it was important to her to feel that she did *not* care when her parents and husband did not visit her. From her continued protests to the contrary, it developed that she was furious with them and felt she was continually hurting them despite her opposite conscious hopes (e.g., by her hospitalization, by not being a good wife, mother, or child, not wanting to see them, love them, etc.) or a return of the repressed.

She told of how she quarrelled with her husband once and they called each other names. She had called him something "horrible" which infuriated him. Very reluctantly and then blurting it out despite herself, exclaiming, "You made me say it!" She revealed that the word was "cocksucker—something you never call a man." Only with considerable anger had she been able to release her latent hostility, hitting back at him in a way that would really get to him by accusing him of not being a man. With support, she worked through her anxiety about this and displaced her anger to the hospital situation.

ICL–(3) Third octant increases in Ideal substantially suggesting aggressive urges.

Rorschach–VI Rejects card that often presents sexual stimulus, suggesting sex avoidance.

MMPI–Mf Avoids any reference to very possible sexual or hostile theme.

Eighteenth Session (11/30): She dreamed that her brother's best friend got into an accident with his convertible. The victim changed into another fellow who was smashed into pieces. The patient kept wishing it was herself. Associations indicated that she felt to be vulgar or sexual is to be bad—for which you can be punished (smashed to pieces). Yesterday, she talked about being vulgar; she felt I made her be so and was therefore myself vulgar and bad, and she resented me. The final victim (who had my first name) was punished. All males are vulgar and dirty. When females are vulgar, they are like males; often males are not men. She needs her husband not to be a man yet part of her craves him to be manly.

MMPI–Mf: Markedly low K and Mf suggest that her conception of sexual role is of weakness and literalness (stereotyped) but devoid of fuller meaning.

Rorschach–VI Rejects card that often presents sexual stimulus, suggesting sex avoidance.

DAP–Both drawings: Sexual conflict suggested by position of hands.

Nineteen Session (12/2): There were many pauses and silences, with an evident attempt at suppression. Finally she revealed her concern that I and other people would misinterpret her relationship with a male patient five years younger than she, believing that she flirted with him. Actually, she encourages him to feel that life is not hopeless, although she is worried that her own pessimism and suicidal ideas might influence him negatively. She guessed she did flirt with him somewhat. She then admitted she had told a particularly obnoxious patient, who suggested this flirtation to her, to mind his business.

ICL–(2, 3) The greater representation of octants 2 and 3 for Ideal suggest her potentiality for being more assertive and even aggressive.

Twentieth Session (12/3): Last night she laughed heartily when an attendant laughed hard. This bothered her because it was inconsistent with the fact that she was a "depressed" patient.

She remembered her mother beating her with a broom during an argument about a doorstep flirtation with a married milkman when the patient was 17. Her parents were very strict and distrusted her in matters of sex, yet she learned that her mother had been pregnant (with brother) before her marriage. The patient had always considered all her family sexless until she learned that her brother had contracted a venereal disease. She was so shocked and shamed at these discoveries that she could hardly face them.

DAP–Execution and conception of drawings demonstrates an intactness of ego.

MMPI–Pa: The depressive quality (tears) of the response. Pa indicates feeling of being taken advantage of.

ICL–(4) Well-represented 4th octant in Self pulled back in Ideal suggests conflict about relating to people.

Rorschach–VI Avoids any reference to very possible sexual or hostile theme.

Twenty-first Session (12/4): The patient was concerned that psychological tests will show her as dumb. Because she felt dumb, she blocked in the tests and in school and would not cooperate even though this made her seem more stupid. She always felt her brother to be more intelligent; women, if they were feminine, were dumb and helpless. Both her father and her husband would call her stupid when they were angry. When threatened or anxious, she seemed to act dumb but otherwise was able to discuss things quite intelligently. Thus, in the area of sex, she expressed vast ignorance because it was so threatening—the less she learned about something like that, the less threat and anxiety there would be. Only her self-esteem was hurt by this.

> WAIS—Verbal and Performance pattern: The significantly higher Performance score suggests her intellectual potential. Her hysterical orientation blocks out information because some of that might be sexual and because to be "intelligent" is to be more adult (i.e., more of a woman).
>
> MMPI—K: Markedly low K and Mf suggests that her conception of sexual role is of weakness and literalness (stereotyped) but devoid of fuller meaning.

Last night, she heard some lullaby played on children's toys and got upset and cried. Yet she feels she hasn't changed. She wants to see her husband only to ask for clothes and money; she felt this was not right in light of her utter selfishness.

> TAT—(3GF) Longs to love and be loved. (9GF) Yet opposite side of coin, fleeing from relationships.

Twenty-second Session (12/6): The patient said that things were going fine, and a regular schedule of three times a week was arranged.

> DAP—Execution and conception of drawings demonstrates an intactness of ego.
>
> ICL—Self & Ideal: ICL's despite exaggerated aspects, are fairly well balanced demonstrating good degree of integration.

She cannot bear speaking to husband and especially being touched by him. She didn't think she loved him or would again. Exploration revealed that she had found sex with him boring and unsatisfactory at best, and thought it would always be so.

> MMPI—Mf: Markedly low K and Mf suggests that her conception of sexual role is of weakness and literalness (stereotyped) but devoid of fuller meaning.
>
> Rorschach—VI Avoids any reference to very possible sexual or hostile theme.

Although being treated like a child angered her, she gained some satisfaction from such childishness and a means of expressing such feelings as petulance, sulking, etc. Apparently, she learned to express anger by making others feel sorry. Just before the patient got ill, her mother would complain over the phone but without saying anything too much. The patient would angrily tell her mother she did nothing to help herself, but then would feel guilty. The patient's condition might be considered similar. She was disappointed and angry with people important to her and particularly with her husband; they would feel sorry and helpless because she was sick. This made her feel even guiltier and more hopeless since they were such well-meaning people, and so, a vicious cycle.

ICL (5) Scoring into second circle of octant 5 suggests fairly strong sense of guilt.

MMPI–Pt, Mf: High Pt, low Mf connotes pattern of anxiousness and guilt.

Twenty-third Session (12/9): She wondered how sick she was and what it consisted of, comparing herself to another very disturbed patient. She said that all she wanted from life was death, that she was confused as to what she was and what she expected from life. The hour was devoted to her discussing her confused identity.

DAP–Execution and conception of drawings demonstrates an intactness of ego.

Rorschach–II The depressive quality (tears) of the response.

ICL–Self and Ideal: Contrast between figurations of Ideal and Self indicate search for, and confusion about, identity.

Twenty-fourth Session (12/11): The patient revealed that she has been plagued with constipation since childhood (when anxious she reverts to diarrhea). Her mother was always concerned about this and plied her with cathartics and enemas (constipation worsened during pregnancies). Patient always has been anxious about bowel movements—she requires privacy, is tense even then, and must read a magazine. Her mother also suffers from constipation. The patient's condition becomes exacerbated when she is tense. She was surprised but readily got at the fact she was anxious about the entire anal area to the extent of considerable conflict with respect to toilet-training her own children. She worked with the idea that her inability to let go of her emotions and her bowel problems might be correlated.

Rorschach–II Anal aspect conveyed by squatting position and fingering rears of figures.

MMPI–Pt: High Pt connotes compulsivity which, dynamically, may include anal conflicts.

Twenty-fifth Session (12/13): The patient spent the previous day outside the hospital and enjoyed it. She discussed how she kept her feelings in. She did not want to keep talking about how hopeless and miserable she felt because this would push other people away; she was concerned I would feel that way.

> MMPI—D, Pt, Pa: Extremely high and peaks on D and Pt convey depression and anxiety. Markedly low Pa is suspect and usually may be interpreted as if profile were turned upside down. Thus, very high Pa would suggest projection of her feelings and impulses onto others.
>
> ICL—(4) Well-represented 4th octant in Self pulled back in Ideal suggests conflict about relating to people.

She thought that she did not love her husband because she never wanted to see him. This brought out the fact that she never expressed her feelings unless they were extreme, and then there were always counter feelings submerged. Thus, she was completely wrapped up in her first child (now she does not think of him). She was very concerned about his coming into contact with dirt or germs and took elaborate precautions. She is a zealot in her home about dirt and dust. Her parents, however, are slovenly.

> MMPI—Pt: High Pt connotes compulsivity which, dynamically, may include anal (orderliness, cleanliness) conflicts.
>
> Rorschach—III Anal aspect conveyed by squatting position and fingering rears of figures.

Review of Succeeding Psychotherapy

1/3: The patient came to and left the office from the ward by herself.

1/13: She went on pass with her husband and had a few beers.

2/17: The patient took an apartment one block from hospital. She is associating with a group of patients who have also located near hospital; she is on an outpatient basis.

2/26: Her husband brought the children to see her. She is on a once a week basis in therapy.

3/12: I note that I have been having feelings of irritation with the patient, expressed by impatient, if not scolding confrontation of her defenses (e.g., helplessness, resistiveness, denial, blocking, etc.).

4/9: The patient visited her children at home.

5/21: She spent the weekend at home and even slept in the

same bed with her husband. She revealed that just prior to hospitalization she had suffered a tonsillectomy, a bad fall during pregnancy, and a rash; also, both her parents had emotional breakdowns.

5/28: She had sex relations with her husband.

9/10: Although still uncertain of her feelings for her husband, she has positive feelings about life and has moved back into household.

12/3: Very frank Oedipal feelings manifested.

7/1: (Following year) Because of clinic move, patient made plans to see me privately once every other week. Now lying on couch.

10/7: The patient terminated with sense of confidence and ability to handle affairs. During the past few months, rather than working through her Oedipal conflicts and blurred identity, of which most of previous therapy consisted, she has consolidated her defenses, tested reality, and manifested considerable positive feelings toward husband, children, parents and friends.

Concluding Comments

Despite the depression, agitation, and withdrawal aspects presented by the psychological evaluation, there was also conveyed an ego intactness and defensive structure able to tolerate the pressures and probing of intensive psychotherapy (the "good" drawing, "reasonable" MMPI and ICL, and TAT and Rorschach devoid of serious distortions). She also indicated on these tests her yearning for, and reaching out to, people. Another important clue was the need to concentrate on her understanding and working with her tremendous hostile impulses and their relationship to her sexual identity. When this material came up in treatment, frequent referrals back to the test material helped clarify for the therapist what was going on

CHAPTER NINE

HYPOCHONDRIA: CHARACTER DISORDER WITH MARKED HYPOCHONDRIACAL FEATURES

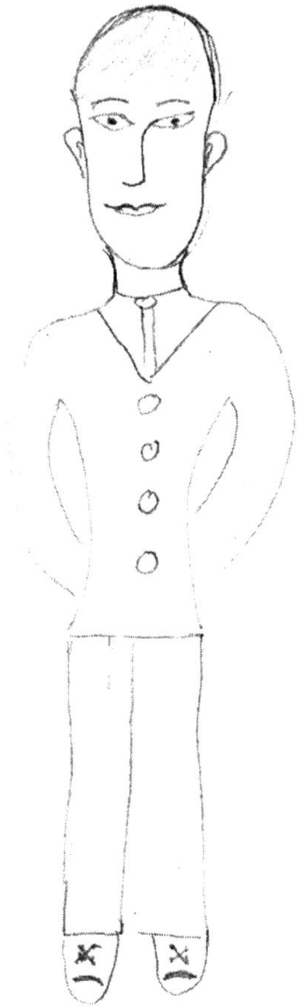

I

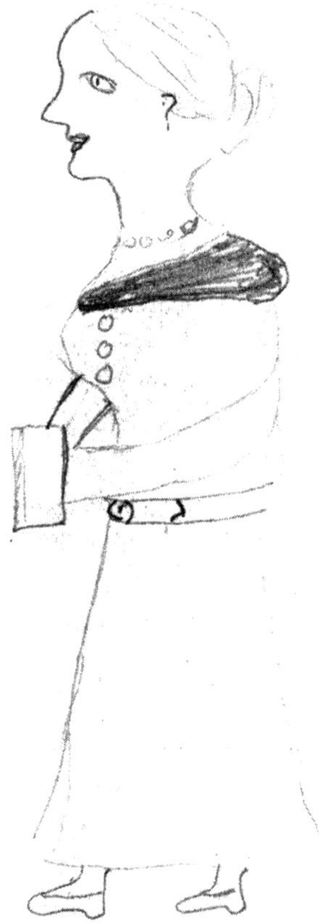

DIAGNOSTIC OVERVIEW:

A Character Disorder

with Marked Hypochondriacal Features

Hypochondriacal features may be present, in varying degrees, in any of the diagnostic categories. When they are so pronounced, however, as to be a person's most distinctive orientation to the world, then there is either a character disorder and/or a symptom-laden facade covering psychosis usually of a paranoid schizophrenic nature. (See Chapter 7, where a character disorder had sadomasochistic and hypochondriacal features quite similar to this patient and where the psychotic underlay was more evident.) This patient uses withdrawal into her soma as an escape from the anxiety-provoking outer world or her threatening inner drives. Her vitality and considerable resources enable her to act out the latter impulsively without pausing to consider their implication for her. This is typical character disorder behavior. But with increasing age and changing family circumstances, the acting out became less possible, and focus was more and more placed on somatization. When one cannot accept oneself in terms of conflicting psychological forces and in intimate relationship to others but rather as a complex of aches, pains, and diseases, then a warped self-concept is bound to develop, as it did with this patient.

She initiated and continued referring in her interview to a fantastically long and varied list of somatic complaints, illnesses, and surgical procedures. When she was not ill, her husband or other close family member was. Associated with this was Hs as one of the peaks on MMPI (ranking with D and quite higher than Pt suggesting only vague anxiety); and enormously exaggerated 8th octant on ICL (over-responsible, over-generous, or psychosomatic orientation); and TAT story (1BM) that was peculiarly circumstantial and related to surgery.

The "acting out" behavior was stressed by her account of carrying on two love affairs simultaneously, concurrent with her avowed love for her husband; TAT stories of rebellious and asocial themes; high F Sc on MMPI, and caustic interaction with the examiner (*e.g.*, only thinly veiled hostility expressed during beginning of Rorschach); and turning of Rorschach cards often preferring the upside down perspective. The corollary of this impulsive behavior (also suggested on the Rorschach by intense reaction to color, C, CF, and even failure on color cards) was the considerable degree of hostility percolating from the patient—which she denied at the same time. Thus, she disparaged all and sundry—including her family—in the interview; DAP I story was disparaging and supercilious towards males; Rorschach card II dealt with teeth (oral-sadistic) and destruction concepts such as on card V; and peaks of Hs Ma on the MMPI suggested open expression of hostility.

Her grossly distorted self-image was indicated by the very exaggerated representation in every octant of the ICL for both Self and Others Seeing Her; by her masculine identification (participation in masculine, contact sports; drawing of male first on DAP; and male dancer on Rorschach card X); and such concepts on the Rorschach as turtle under exposed shell (Card II) and withered, fallen leaf (Card IV). Most significant was her shallow relationships to others described in the interview, conveyed by high Pa on MMPI, by distantiation from others on TAT (*e.g.*, story 4); distrust suggested by large ears of male and question mark ears of female on DAP; and almost all human responses dehumanized "H" on Rorschach where her forced affect (color forced into inaccurate form contexts as on card X) was demonstrated.

The psychological evaluation, therefore, pinpointed the patient's poor ability to relate, her basic distrust, and her tendency to flee or to withdraw into her soma. Particularly the MMPI constellation of high F, Hs, Pa, Sc carried poor prognosis. Further, there were indications of questionable judgment (somewhat of a failure on emotionally stimulating Rorschach card V, circumstantial thinking in TAT story 8BM, and her confused love affairs). On the positive side, her imagination and intellectual capacity were clearly manifested in all test material by good conceptualization and inventiveness, her success in organizations and in colleges, and the ability to bounce back that she showed on card X of the Rorschach where she gave an excellently conceived human movement response and utilized color well in one response (evidence of mature and socialized thinking). Moreover, probably due to increased age and environmental factors, she was growing more depressed and vaguely uneasy (High D on MMPI, diffuse K on Rorschach card IV, and suicidal theme on TAT story 3). Here was more than enough forewarning, perhaps insufficiently heeded, that therapy had to proceed cautiously with her until she might be able to substitute other defenses while being propped up in the interim.

PSYCHOLOGICAL EVALUATION:

A Case of Hypochondria

Patient: female, age 53, married, two grown sons
Occupation: housewife, volunteer work
Education: high school graduate
Referred by: Dr. W for personality evaluation in light of fantastic history of physical illnesses and surgical procedures and of current psychological complaints.

Tests Administered:

Rorschach, Thematic Apperception Test (TAT), Minnesota Multiphasic Personality Inventory (MMPI), and Draw-A-Person (DAP).

Behavior:

Mrs. H, a woman looking younger than her age, was cooperative, friendly, and frank. Although evidently highly intelligent, she was self-depreciatory. In like vein, she illustrated her shyness with many examples of acute stage fright extending to any group situation where she was the center of attention. Yet she seems eminently successful in becoming a cynosure.

Apparently, the onset of both her physical and psychological symptoms began following the death of her fiance when she was 18. This occurred in a car accident in which she suffered an injured shoulder. Within recent weeks her complaints have become very aggravated: "As if I am not getting enough oxygen, lying on one side my shoulder hurts, on the other my heart palpitates, and there is an intense apprehension *as if I just missed being in an accident.*" (This, 35 years or so after the car crack-up.) In addition, she has been insomniac, unable to concentrate, her thoughts racing, with crying jags and acute depression with some suicidal content. "For so long have I felt confused and all let out as if a pin was stuck in me that maybe it is mental."

She described an extremely lonely childhood indicating strict, aloof, old-fashioned parents. Although not expressing her rage directly, she emphasized how spoiled and favored her brother was for his intelligence, while her father suggested that she also should have been a boy. Even now, she said, her brother is acting obnoxiously and is an SOB (stated almost without malice). Consequently, she has always let off steam in athletics and frankly masculine sports. On the rebound after the death of her fiance (of whom her parents disapproved), the patient married a man favored by her mother and father. For eight years, she and her husband cared for his mother, sacrificing their own social life. For an additional ten years she spent considerable time and travel caring for her own invalid mother. These periods coincided with a tremendous incidence of medical and psychological difficulties for her. Initially picturing her 60-year-old husband as letter-perfect, she then added that he could have spent more time with their children, had neglected her for long periods of time because of business, had never satisfied her sexually, and for the last two years has been impotent. He was, she thought, not very masculine and more mental whereas she was more physical. Consequently, she has been involved in enormously complicated and anxiety-provoking affairs. She stated her desire to be happy and worthwhile and to contribute—"Life has seemed pretty worthless."

Evaluation:

The patient appears to suffer from a severe character disorder. The features of her maladjustments are more pervasive, chronic, and characterologically defective than warranted by a neurosis. She has always felt keenly lonely and rejected and has responded to stress situations and crises in indirect, ineffective, and self-defeating ways. For example: she apparently never has recovered completely from whatever the death of her fiance meant to her; she has suffered silently, not even admitting to herself, the trials and tribulations of 18 years of caring for ill and demanding relatives—what she *did* manifest was an interminable list of somatic and psychological complaints; and rather than coping directly with her circumstances and airing her dissatisfaction with her marriage (with suggested submission to, but resentment of, her parents and husband), she has rebelliously and very guiltily become involved in extremely complicated affairs.

Mrs. H has never accepted herself as a female. Only by being a male or being like a male she has unconsciously fantasized, could she be truly loved and respected. This is what she believed her parents, and particularly her father, wanted. It almost seems as if she has tried to prove that she is a better man than her brother, husband, and in the final analysis, her father. And yet she seems to search constantly for the love and approval of the latter (*e.g.*, via athletic accomplishments, affairs with older men, etc.).

Environmental circumstances and age itself are limiting the acting out which has served as an escape valve for her confused identifications and repressed emotions. Currently, she feels more depressed and anxious than ever before. Her self-concept, blurred as it is, emerges as a picture of a withered, helpless, fallen person with self-destructive fantasies. Extremely impulsive, she has been forced in affect and stilted in relations to others—although she puts on a great act. She does have great resiliency and can be very successful at times, even demonstrating a good degree of social maturity. Mostly, however, she represses considerable potential for creative and social adjustment. Her tendencies for warmth and love are repressed except when accompanied by guilt and self-punishment. There are no gross distortions of judgment, other than those mentioned above, or any impairment of orientation. However, if she continues as she always has or if additional pressures arise, more serious psychological and/or physical illnesses (*e.g.*, involutional disorder) or self-destructive behavior may be expected. Long-term intensive psychotherapy is recommended.

THERAPY NOTES

First Session (5/17): Mrs. H, the patient, expressed all sorts of reservations about therapy. She has not been told anything new, or anything that she can't help herself, and it would be inconvenient as to time. Would I just tell her about outlets? We discussed the meaning of this and she was able to see the resistance aspects.

> DAP—Ears: Suspicion and distrust suggested by large ears of male and question-mark ears of female.
>
> MMPI—Hs, Pd: Extremely high and peak Hs, especially when associated with high Pa, indicates sour, even sullen, distrust. Unable to deal with people satisfactorily, she uses soma as a shield.

Dream: Three or four men were taking her sportscar but she had the key. One of the men had dark, greasy hands. Associations: She told of various things going wrong with her sportscar and of several men wanting to fix it. Her lover has been instrumental in getting her this car, which was easier to drive with her illness. (She, herself, saw the car as representing love. Different men were fighting over her and/or different doctors wanted to help but she held the key passively—and resistively.)

TAT—(2) People significant for her (mother and lover) fight over her while she, passively, but firmly, decides the issue.

In telling of her involvement with her lover, she presented herself as being drawn in helplessly although she admitted great interest. Her contributions (quite evident to me) were not accessible to her.

MMPI—K, Mf: Very low K indicates acute self-criticism, and very low Mf a sense of helplessness. In association, they paint a feeling (or overprotestation) of being overwhelmed by others and by her environment—the weak female.

Rorschach—II (2) Helpless and exposed beneath her hard shell.

TAT—(8BM) Unaware of contributions to situations, tending to project interpretations and motives in the most flimsy circumstances (*i.e.*, anxious about story so she interprets figure with "abnormal glandular").

She paid cash for the session and asked for a receipt because "I can't keep track of the hours."

MMPI—Pa: High Pa, which presents her basic mistrust, shown here by her request for receipt (in the very first hour).

Second Session (5/17): We discussed the matter of how she paid fees. Considerable anger was expressed indirectly and she pulled away from me sharply. She said she paid each hour because she felt that I did not trust her and wanted to be paid each time. Further discussion not possible since the conversation became sticky—she associated to prominent psychoanalysts whom she knew and who were "mixed-up," to doctors and dentists who had done her harm, and so on.

MMPI—Ma: Very high Ma suggests open hostility, especially when combined with high Hs and Pa.

Rorschach—I (2) An almost overagreeableness at first hints at possibly the converse. VI (1, 2) Destructive attitudes or fantasies (skeleton of bug, skin "laid open").

MMPI—Pa, Sc: Pa associated with fairly high Sc suggests a highly personalized, even illogical interpretation of her circumstances.

She described her husband as perfect, but on questioning got to his neglect and her loneliness. She then spoke of her loneliness as a child and of being treated harshly and unfairly, particularly by her mother who was always too socially active or ill "like me" (even had a number of operations) to have time for the patient. The patient seemed to require support.

> TAT—(2) Treated unfairly and criticized by mother.
> MMPI—K, Sc: Fairly high Sc connotes sense of differentness. In association with low K, convey feeling of loneliness.

Third Session (5/23): She was much more congenial. Twice, she said, she experienced palpitations and shortness of breath on planes. She associated this, in content if not with insight, to her husband's illness (embolism and possible cancer), to an aunt's possible heart condition, and her father's heart condition, of which he eventually died and in which illness she was very involved.

> MMPI—Hs: Very high and peak Hs describes enormous preoccupation with soma.
> TAT—(8BM) Handles anxiety with surgical solution and very loosely thinks of glandular disturbance.
> ICL—(8) Fantastic exaggeration (scored every item) of 8th octant in both Self and Ideal portrays her claim to be extremely responsible—even perfect—the psychosomatic orientation.

The patient went on to deny vigorously that all of her life has been a tribulation. Her "compensation" was her father who was a "rock" and who hunted and fished with her. Her mother was just fluttery and helpless. She indicated indirectly that she saw herself as a rock when everyone around her got ill.

> DAP—1 and 2: Euphemistic associations for both drawings.
> MMPI—Mf: Really confused identification. The "flitting," helpless mother is her own self-concept (low Mf) alternating with that of a rock (herself as a male).
> TAT—(6) Goes along with dominance of other. (12) Central figure passive and suggestible (asleep or hypnotized).

She talked a good deal about illnesses, and at the end of the hour mentioned her inability to sleep and to concentrate.

> MMPI—Ma: High Ma indicates irritability and restlessness.

Fourth Session (5/25): She feels much better. She told the referring physician that I "play her like a violin," which she laughingly admitted was a backhanded compliment.

She "physically loved" her first fiance, and 15 years later experienced that same feeling towards W (an older man with whom she has had an affair for 16 years). In opposition, she indicated that she and her husband were virgins when married (she was 24 and he 31). Indirectly, it came out that she has always felt that her husband was cold, aloof, and withdrawn. He is always correct in an intellectual and platonic sense. But he is fanatically devoted to business with little time for her and the children.

She was surprised to think now that her husband seems to have needed her and still does, rather than the opposite. Her lover provided warmth and understanding and physical contact.

> DAP–1: Despite some denial ("even younger" male about 10 years older and a teacher), the male looks childish and not described very warmly.
>
> TAT–(4, 7, 10, 13) In all themes, something always amiss in love situation–distance, separation, third party, amorality, etc.

Fifth Session (5/26): Always when she needed and wanted attention, her husband would compete for it more actively by acting very much like a child. She then retreated from this comment, pointing out how successful and efficient he has been in business.

> DAP–1: Despite some denial ("even younger" male about 10 years older and a teacher), the male looks childish and not described very warmly.

We focused on the great pains the patient took to paint herself as unintelligent, and how this seemed to be related to her feeling that men are smarter. Her father, brother, and husband are more intelligent–women, such as her mother and herself, are flighty. She said that she could not accept a compliment. When leaving she complimented me on a plant in the office.

> MMPI–K, Mf: Very low K indicates acute self-criticism, and very low Mf a sense of helplessness. In association, they paint a feeling (or overprotestation) of being overwhelmed by others and by her environment–the weak female.

Sixth Session (5/31): She wondered where this therapy was taking her, and whether the hours should follow more of a sequence, be more orderly, etc. I talked supportively about this and she responded.

> Rorschach–I (2) Her compulsive drive for order and systematization.

This equation emerged: She wants everyone to like or at least to approve of her, and she hopes to achieve this by keeping her feelings completely under control, no matter how provoked. But she can't always abide by this (*e.g.*, irritations on golf course, etc.). She expresses herself and then is bothered. She remembered that when she was a debutante, she was knock-kneed, and her mother, instead of being supportive, was critical. She has lacked confidence since then.

> ICL–Right hemisphere: Extremely exaggerated representation of right hemisphere portrays her craving to be approved.
>
> Rorschach–IX, X Diffuse handling of color indicates hysterical aspect of suggestibility and dependence on other's approval.
>
> TAT–(2) Treated unfairly and criticized by mother.

She has an early memory of being in a crib, rustling white starchy clothes. Her brother is in the room, she is lying on her left side. Her brother slapped her for doing something wrong–looking at and teasing her? There was a bathtub in the room. Associations: She had a nurse-governess. Once she had hives and plunged into a cold tub to get rid of it so as to get to school. She was caught by her nurse whom she begged not to tell. Her parents were prudish about sex, and she never even saw her mother undressed. She was curious about this and, with a cousin about her brother's age, she stood behind bushes to look at people undressed–but only discovered that they had hair.

> DAP–2: Both sexual and hostile feelings denied in female by her Victorian aura and association to female as "motherly."
>
> TAT–(13) Seemingly frank confrontation with sex but indicative of disturbed conceptualization (more precisely, feeling integration) in this area.

She has another memory of sitting in a cherry tree with Joo Joo candies, staring into a very blue sky and wondering about infinity. Association: Her grandfather dies and she was told that he had gone to heaven.

> MMPI–Sc: Deeply introverted, perhaps highly idiosyncratic thinking suggested by high Sc.

Seventh Session (6/1): The patient has a tremendous focus on physical ailments. She never felt so low physically: pressure and pain on chest and neck, palpitations, shortness of breath, etc. She smiled inappropriately while listing these complaints. We looked at her ability to weep after her considerable talk of the need to be stoical. She was apprehensive of cancer and discouraged by the lack of effects from treatment (physical) and wondered about capability of doctors.

> MMPI–Hs, Pa: Extremely high and peak Hs, especially when associated with high Pa, indicates sour, even sullen, distrust. Unable to deal with people satisfactorily, she uses soma as a shield. Very high and peak Hs describes enormous preoccupation with soma.
>
> ICL–(8) Fantastic exaggeration (scored every item) of 8th octant in both Self and Ideal pórtrays her claim to be extremely responsible—even perfect—the psychosomatic orientation.
>
> TAT–(8BM) Handles anxiety with surgical solution and very loosely thinks of glandular disturbance.
>
> Rorschach–VI Morbid, pathological fantasy.

I reinforced a comment of hers that referred to talking so much about physical symptoms, and suggested the possibility of diversionary motives. She froze and grew very hostile, but would not admit this, even to herself. However, with encouragement, she said, "You're talking through your hat!" Then more relaxed, and somewhat tearful, she told of her inability to sleep and asked what to do about these things. I was supportive.

> MMPI–Ma: Very high Ma suggests open hostility, especially when combined with high Hs and Pa.
>
> Rorschach–II (3) Stingray concept suggests aggression and use of white space, oppositional tendencies. VI Destructive attitudes or fantasies (skeleton of bug, skin "laid open").
>
> MMPI–D, Ma: High D indicates her depressive state. High Ma indicates irritability and restlessness.

Eighth Session (6/3): She asked about taping sessions. This seemed to reflect the issue of confidentiality and whether I was really interested in her and remembered what we talked about.

> MMPI–Pa: High Pa, which presents her basic mistrust, shown here by her request for receipt (in the very first hour).

Exploration revealed that the patient felt that I was a "cold fish" and looked on her only as a case chart. This was related to last hour when I was not sympathetic to her physical complaints. Moreover, I "pounded" away at her feeling of crying or depression (*i.e.*, was punitive and sadistic even if "for your own good"). She saw some of this but directed most of her venom at the referring physician; she felt he callously disregarded her allergies to medication—she has only gotten worse. Therefore, after submitting and being taken advantage of, she will now rebel (leave him).

> MMPI—F, Sc: High F conveys rebelliousness, Sc sense of differentness. Both in association suggest feelings of victimization.
>
> TAT—(2) People significant for her (mother and lover) fight over her while she, passively but firmly, decides the issue.

She was able to relate some of these feelings to her mother. She got at an equation that efficient women are also "cold fish" and not feminine, but she was confused at the mixture of these characteristics in her mother (and herself). She told of how slavishly she took care of her mother because of duty. It was pointed out how upset she grew when her mother's condition grew worse. Defiantly, she said that she never even visited her mother's grave but countered this with how obligated she felt to care for an aged couple who had cared for her mother. She tried to explain her guilt by the experience of others and then admitted it in herself. (She could not hold onto this insight.) At the very end she reported that she told her husband off for going to sleep so early because of what we talked about previously in therapy; she then felt sorry.

> DAP—2: Both sexual and hostile feelings denied in female by her Victorian aura and association to female as "motherly."
>
> MMPI—Mf: Really confused identification. The "flitting," helpless mother is her own self-concept (low Mf) alternating with that of a rock (herself as a male).
>
> TAT—(7GF) Conflict between duty and wish to hurt, between love and guilt.

Ninth Session (6/6): Again she began the hour with physical complaints and discouragements, and mentioned her decision to return to a physician who had helped her several times in the past.

Eventually, she worked around to psychological matters. Her husband really shares nothing with her as a wife. After dinner he falls asleep watching TV. He does this even when they have guests. But when he invites even a casual business acquaintance, he is a dynamo sparkling with interest. The lack of sharing extends even to financial matters, where things have been doled out to her, and she is not now a full partner. She showed flashes of disappointment and irritation about her husband "not being a man" sexually or in any other way, but she blamed herself for the marriage in the first place.

We worked on her contribution somewhat and her pessimism in changing the situation. Particularly, we focused on her resentment and grievances (*e.g.*, going to a boring cocktail party) when she might be able to suggest and bring about choices.

DAP–1: Despite some denial ("even younger" male about 10 years older and a teacher), the male looks childish and not described very warmly.

MMPI–Mf: Really confused identification. The "flitting," helpless mother is her own self-concept (low Mf) alternating with that of a rock (herself as a male).

TAT–4, 10, 11) In all themes, something always amiss in love situation—distance, separation, third party, amorality, etc.

Rorschach–III (1) She is just a puppet.

Tenth Session (6/8): The patient sailed into me. My office was a dark, stuffy dump and my smoking takes away what little air she has. Furthermore, therapy is not helping in the least, and she does not know if she needs it anyway. Perhaps another person, "say a more sympathetic woman psychologist, would be better." She had also gotten angry with her husband. He fell asleep and she told him she was fed up and wanted a two-fisted male, which he wasn't. He responded with a wounded look. I wondered whether she felt my remarks had anything to do with her exploding against her husband and she said yes. Why didn't I provide more tangible "guideposts"? She feels that she has made the most of her circumstances.

Rorschach–I (2), II (3), VI (1, 2), X (2): I (2) An almost overagreeableness at first hints at possibly the converse. VI (1, 2) Destructive attitudes or fantasies (skeleton of bug, skin "layed open"). II (3) Stingray concept suggests aggression and use of white space, oppositional tendencies. X (2) Phallic aggression (animals holding stick).

MMPI–Ma: Very high Ma suggests open hostility, especially when combined with high Hs and Pa.

She went on more calmly to tell of many circumstances in which she has been treated unfairly. (One would expect this patient to score very high on Pd in the MMPI. Perhaps her marked denial—MMPI Hy, ICL 8, Rorschach II (1a)—masks this tendency.) The paramount situation is that of her brother robbing her of her share of her mother's estate, and her helplessness in this. She is very bothered by this and said the estate represented not money but her share of things, and it would "build my ego." She was able to relate this to her getting her share of love from her mother, which her brother originally took from her. We talked of her expecting the wrong things from the right people and the right things from the wrong people.

> MMPI—F, Sc: High F conveys rebelliousness, Sc sense of differentness. Both in association suggest feelings of victimization.
> TAT—(2) People significant for her (mother and lover) fight over her while she, passively but firmly, decides the issue.

Eleventh Session (6/10): The patient was very congenial, working at therapy. She related her sense of inadequacy (stumbling over or forgetting words) to the harsh critical attitude of mother, who told her she literally and figuratively was tongue-tied.

> TAT—(2) People significant for her (mother and lover) fight over her while she, passively but firmly, decides the issue.

She revealed that her mother ill-prepared her for interpersonal relations. With insight (and apology for mother), she guessed that her mother was ill at ease in this area (*e.g.*, flutteriness). This led to the patient's incredible lack of preparation for sexual role and motherhood. She explained this by her parents' Victorian, old-fashioned attitudes reinforced by her strict secular schooling. She agreed she could either rebel or submit, and she chose the former. But we looked at indications of the latter as well—she is "reserved," "English," etc.

> MMPI—F, Sc, K: Fairly high Sc connotes sense of differentness. In association, convey feeling of loneliness. High F conveys rebelliousness, Sc sense of differentness. Both in association suggest feelings of victimization. Very low K indicates acute self-criticism and very low Mf a sense of helplessness. In association, they paint a feeling (or overprotestation) of being overwhelmed by others and by her environment—the weak female.

Positive transference was manifested during this hour by her hearty concurrence with my analogies and so on. This may have been expedited partially by my listening, to even encouraging, her usual introductory physical complaints, and by the possibility that she let off steam last hour (*i.e.*, she is still seeing the referring physician).

Twelfth Session (6/13): Theme: her tremendous drive to compete and be on top and to be approved of, versus her sense of being attacked and despised in that position. Associations led to the extreme critical attitudes of her parents. Father instilled drive in her, a sense of being hated by brother and parents (probably mostly mother). These feelings are now symbolized in her need to share in the estate.

> ICL—Upper half: Exaggerated upper hemisphere. Tremendous drive to dominate and compete.
> Rorschach—I (all), II (3), VII, X (2): Aggressive and striving quality in all these responses.
> TAT—(7GF) Conflict between duty and wish to hurt, between love and guilt.

Thirteenth Session (6/15): She began with an angry criticism of her gardener, accompanied by guilt. Then she blocked. This was followed by memories of her brother not being all bad and, indeed, of his coming to her defense on occasion. As a matter of fact, they each resented the other's spouse, demonstrating concern for each other. This led to her marked ambivalent feelings for her family and especially her mother. She said that she could see both love and hate for her mother but evidenced little emotional insight into the conflict and guilt involved. We talked about how guilty she felt when she criticized her husband, his wounded look. Unwittingly, in this context she laughingly told of her contempt for her dog who was very dumb but her guilt for feeling this way. The sequence was pointed out and she added that her son made her feel guilty, too, with his doleful look. I suggested that this was a powerful weapon in her family.

> ICL—(5) Exaggerated 5th octant indicates sense of guilt.
> Rorschach—VI (1, 2) Destructive attitudes or fantasies (skeleton of bug, skin "laid open").
> TAT—(3) Sense of either self-destructiveness and/or sadism.

Fourteenth Session (6/17): The patient protested that she could not breathe in my smoke-filled office. She was finished with therapy —it did not help her. Her problems were primarily biological. She has the strength to handle her emotions. And so went the hour.

> TAT—(8BM) Treated unfairly and criticized by her mother.
> MMPI—F, Hs, Pa, Sc: This pattern especially as exaggerated in this profile, because of the rebellion, distrust, and acute alienation from others, prognosticates very poorly.
> ICL—(8) Fantastic exaggeration (scored every item) of 8th octant in both Self and Ideal portrays her claim to be extremely responsible—even perfect—the psychosomatic orientation.

She insisted that I had set a "two-month period of intensive treatment and a three-week trial period"!!! Nothing I could say would convince her otherwise. She only got into therapy to get the other doctors out of her hair.

> Rorschach–V and color cards: Fails on card that presents most difficult emotional stimulation as well as diffuse reaction to other emotional (color) situations.

(6/20): Mrs. H phoned to terminate treatment. She said she had a question about her confidence in me and perhaps in anyone else (although she did take the names of several people I recommended). She alluded to some "unhappy" remark that I had made last hour and complained that I did not give her an "aptitude appraisal." She seemed angry that I would not ship the protocols of her tests in addition to a report to anyone that she might designate.

> Rorschach–III (1), VII (1, 2) and color cards: Orality in the responses suggest a craving, even devouringness, which was not satisfied at all in therapy.

Concluding Comments

The psychologicals were accurate in pinpointing the difficulties in the patient's ability to relate, basic distrust, and tendency to flee or withdraw into her soma. Particularly the MMPI profile, F, Hs, Pa, Sc suggested an extremely poor prognostication. However, they also presented fair warning, perhaps insufficiently heeded, to the therapist to proceed very cautiously until the patient could substitute for her defenses and first get as much support as possible from treatment.

CHAPTER TEN

MISS FANTASY: EMOTIONALLY UNSTABLE PERSONALITY WITH PSYCHOTIC POTENTIAL

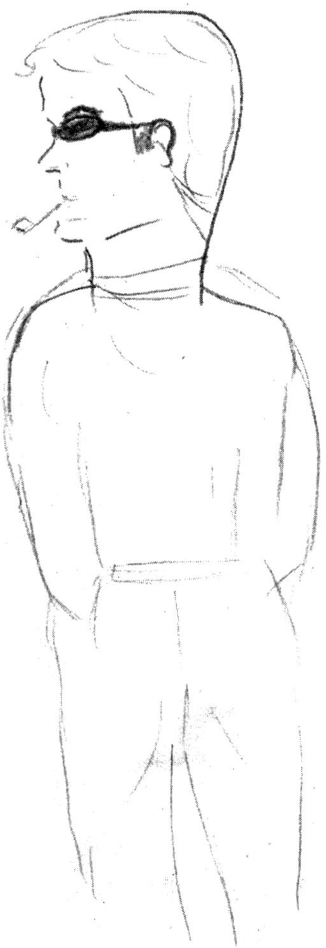

I

DIAGNOSTIC OVERVIEW:

An Emotionally Unstable Personality with Psychotic Potential

The differentiation of psychosis from character disorder is often a tenuous one, particularly when there is stress. The differentiation in the case of an Emotionally Unstable Personality is even more blurred. The classification is applied to individuals who react with excitability and ineffectiveness when confronted by minor stress. Judgment under stress may be distorted, and relationships to other people are continuously fraught with fluctuating emotional attitudes, because of strong and poorly controlled hostility, guilt, and anxiety.

With this patient, a case could be made for a diagnosis of psychotic reaction. She dwelled in a world of fantasy, was more preoccupied with symbols and magical considerations than with practical reality, and was tempestuously emotional almost all of the time. The fact remained, however, that she appeared at all times to be capable of discriminating between reality and her fantasy even if she was loath to do so. This feature had its corollary in test material in "content distortion." That is, the content of Rorschach, TAT, and other test responses was wild and loose, but the formal aspects of the test situations were not abused—emotions were rampant, fantasy unfettered, and imagination ran wild, but her thought processes seemed always to pull in the reins when it was required.

The instability of this patient but, more precisely, her figuratively screaming, "See how terribly sick and helpless I am" was connoted by her exaggerated "floating" MMPI profile (the many scales well above 70) and by marked stress on the lower hemisphere of the ICL. On the Rorschach, this was presented by her proneness to symbolize and by self reference, as well as by extreme reaction to color with many C's and CF's. She unleashed a veritable flood of fantasy in her TAT stories, Rorschach content (and a great number of M's), in the interview, and during psychotherapy. Other severe pathological elements were her bitter distrust, tantamount to a paranoid degree (extreme representation in 4th octant of Self and Other ICL; Pa above 90 in MMPI; and figures in DAP with dark glasses—virtually, fear of direct confrontation of others); her preoccupation with sadistic and masochistic ideas (many TAT stories; almost all of associations to Rorschach responses; and comments in the interview); and her impulsive and rebellious acting out (the many acting out and rebellious TAT themes, including prostitution and her homosexual stories on 6BM, 9GF, and 12BG, and incidents described in the interview.)

It would be easy to dwell on the pathology of this patient since it was exuded in huge blobs like octopus ink, probably serving much the same function. Her positive features, on the other hand, in view of her extremity of thinking and behavior, were even more interesting and revealing insofar as the utility of the psychological evaluation for psychotherapy. Thus, despite the histrionic fantasy and bizarreness in her tests, productions were always rich and well detailed: no F minus on the Rorschach; no violation of reality consideration on the TAT; and good conceptualization on the TAT. On the WAIS, her highest score, at the Superior Adult level, was on Similarities, a task of abstract reasoning. On the MMPI, her general lack of defensiveness (very low K) and her high FSc (differentness) score were mitigated by the safety valve of awareness and anxiety (very high Pt) and HsHyMa within the normal bounds of 50-70. (This MMPI pattern suggest the possibility that these very tendencies —somatization and hostility—might have been trouble spots and necessarily defended against.) She indicated a yearning and reaching out for other people to depend on (Upper and right hemisphere of ICL—Way-I-See-Clinic ICL; story of strong prizefighter on TAT 3BM; Rorschach card VI; Rorschach and TAT content of lovers depending on each other, even if hostile, and story of little child hurt by, but still needing and apologizing for, parent).

The psychological evaluation stressed her rich imaginative ability and capacity to grasp and uncover complex motivation. The evaluation prognosticated her forming a dependent, relatively stable relationship in therapy. The patient was unhappy, wanted to change, and was hungry for sympathy and understanding. The evaluation was most valuable in stressing the need to focus on reality and capitalize on the transference relationship—emphasis which appeared to pay off in psychotherapy.

PSYCHOLOGICAL EVALUATION:

A Case of Fantasy

Patient: female, age 18, unmarried

Interviewed by: intern psychologist, Outpatient department

Occupation: dance student

Referred by: Dr. S—"There is question about the psychotic potential of this patient and about her diagnosis more generally."

Tests Administered:

Wechsler Adult Intelligence Scale (WAIS), Rorschach, Thematic Apperception Test (TAT), Minnesota Multiphasic Personality Inventory (MMPI), Draw-A-Person (DAP), Interpersonal Checklist (ICL).

Interview Behavior:

Miss F, a young girl of frail and wan appearance, came to the clinic three times for psychological testing. During this time there was little communication except for the tests, to which she responded very fully. If the examiner had not occasionally drawn her into conversation, there would have been none. She seemed willing to talk when this was asked of her but was unable to initiate even the smallest interpersonal contact. If someone asked her to enter a relationship she might pour herself into it, but without a direct bid she would remain aloof.

She talked of being terribly confused and of not knowing what to believe. Everyone tells her something different and she believes each one at the time. At her school everybody believes in something (Yoga, Zen, God) and each convinces her until she talks to the next forceful person.

The third day she came in looking quite agitated and spoke of being involved in a divorce suit because she had been dating a married man. Her account of what was happening and of how she might be implicated was very confused, but she seemed to be both distressed and elated over being involved in this. Her speaking of dating this man does not square with her account of being friendless, nor does the above account of being told what to believe by everyone at the school. It sounded rather as if everyone was trying to direct her and give her advice, taking her under their wings. This would agree with the impression this examiner obtained of a lost little girl who subtly pulls for and probably gets a lot of advice from others.

Personality Evaluation:

Miss F's performance during the psychological examination could be characterized as a veritable flood of fantasy—fantasy that was extremely rich, sensitive and well detailed. She is a person who is aware of and takes into account the world of objective reality only for purposes of building onto it a tremendous superstructure of fantasy. The objective world provides her with very little in comparison with her dreams, and it is through her dreams and fantasies that she relates to people.

An overall intelligence quotient indicates that she is functioning at an average level, but this is highly misleading. On some subtests her performance was at the level of the Superior Adult; this is perhaps closer to her capacities as judged by projective techniques. Her score on the intelligence test was lower for a number of reasons, but one reaction was particularly interesting: she responded in a very emotional, personalized manner, as if she knew the conventional response but simply didn't bother with it. For instance, when asked what she would do if she saw a fire while sitting in a theater, she replied that she wouldn't tell anybody; she might leave herself but she wouldn't say anything because she might be wrong—there might not be a fire. Similarly, she said that if she were lost in a forest she'd just stay there, and if no one came that would be all right because she would like being there alone. Such responses are characteristic of her, and she is surprisingly ignorant in many areas because she disregards conventional reality unless it is presented to her in such a way that she must deal with it.

In her beautifully elaborated fantasies she tells of many conflicts; first of all, the conflict between conformity and unconventionality. This seems to involve her rebellion against her mother, a flight into the Bohemian life to punish a mother who always rejected her—or so she perceives it. Then there is the conflict about what it means to be a woman; men are much sought after because they can help a woman become a woman, but these men are, after all, fairly weak and must be helped and supported by women all the way lest they fall apart. She sees female sexuality as a hostile weapon; women are hard provocateurs who use men for their own purposes. About this she is fairly glib, but she is completely unable to deal with the positive aspects of sex without either intellectualizing or else becoming extremely romantic and almost telling a fairy tale. Even more fundamental than the problem of what it means to be a woman is the problem of just who she is. This is a girl without any sense of identity, lost between her hostile attitudes toward everyone she knows and her sentimental dreams of what relationships should be. She knows neither what she is now (in any concrete way) nor what she would like to be or can be.

It is difficult to answer the question of possible underlying psychosis, largely because virtually nothing is known about the realities of her situation. A period spent with her in taking a careful, developmental history would probably shed more light on this than anything else. Her reaction to psychological tests suggests that, although her problems are very serious, she is not now psychotic and would not too easily become so. This is based on her ability to take reality into account without distortion even though it means little to her and she goes on to build a web of fantasy around it. She is capable of seeing things as they are when necessary; furthermore she is well-organized. At all times she is in control; her emotional reactions are always within well-defined limits and never leave her disorganized. It should be reiterated, though, that her problems are serious and that a schizophrenic break is within the realm of possibility.

She is in need of therapy as soon as possble. Because of the very dependent relationship she will probably form, a therapeutic relationship that would be stable over a period of time seems necessary. She will probably relate in therapy by outpouring of fantasy material; this is her major avenue for relating to people and, in fact, her main defense. Focusing on reality instead would probably be of great help to her—too much indulgence in fantasy would not only strengthen the defense but might dangerously blur distinctions between real and not real. She appears to be repressing the positive experiences in her life—the times when people cared for her, the times she felt worthwhile. A major therapeutic task will be uncovering these. This is an extremely creative and sensitive person with rich potentialities; she will understand the task of therapy comparatively easily and should profit from it. While she feels helpless and threatened, she demonstrates ability to deal with emotional material and still maintain control.

Diagnostic Impression:

(1) Emotionally unstable personality manifested by fantasy and acting out behavior; and (2) psychotic potential.

THERAPY NOTES

First Session (3/12): Miss F, the patient, was a mousy, scared, intense 19-year-old, with black hair and extremely white skin. She squinted and bowed her head forward when I spoke. When she spoke, she was voluble and rapid, and stammered.

> MMPI–K, Pt: Extremely low K (self-criticism and screaming "I'm sick") and her high Pt (manifest anxiety) describe her acute anxiety reaction.

She revealed that she is an extremely miserable and lonely girl who wants to come out of her shell and is paying a terrible price in the attempt—an attempt via interpretive dancing in the theatre.

> MMPI–Pa, Pd, Sc: Marked peaks on all three scales, Pa (inability to relate), Pd (alienation from family and others), and Sc (different and isolated from others) in a pattern that describes her loneliness and misery.
>
> ICL–(4) Grossly exaggerated and peak 4th octant convey her inability to relate warmly to others and even paranoid tendencies.

Her parents were separated when she was born. An alcoholic father fled at the responsibility of a child. The mother resented the daughter yet had wanted the baby to save the marriage. She has been sadistic toward the patient although the latter conceded that as a child she was extremely dependent on her mother. (The mother apparently is extremely neurotic if not psychotic; e.g., disheveled appearance, cluttered house, blurts everything out, etc.)

> MMPI–Pd: Extremely high Pd indicates marked sense of alienation from family (and society).

The mother and daughter have not spoken to each other since the patient was 12 years old—they keep food on separate sides of refrigerator, and the patient reports "stealing" food from her mother.

> DAP–Orality conflicts suggested by male smoking and stressed lips of female.
>
> Rorschach–IX Hollow inside and consuming like a fire testifies to her fantastic and pathological oral drives.

The patient attends dance school, and describes the director (a woman) in the same terms as her mother. She directs the patient's life and exposes her before everybody. Nevertheless, the patient completely depends on her for job placement.

Miss F gave the impression of being a very anxious young woman but one able to relate and to be aware of reality even though she reported things such as her troubles largely being caused by being "born under a bad star." She was tremendously masochistic without realizing the extreme dependent and hostile implications of this.

> ICL–(5) Gross representation of 5th octant describes masochistic and guilty feelings.
>
> MMPI–Pd, Mf: Tremendous discrepancy between high Pd (resentment) and low Mf (feminineness and weakness) sends this message, "See how weak, helpless and feminine I am–and it's your fault."

Second Session (3/19): The patient told of several relationships with men of two types: (1) married men whom she chased or "crawled" after; (2) unmarried men who chased her and in whom she found defects that repelled her. In any event, she craves some relationships, even a girl friend. The last two weeks she has had no friends at all. She still worships Jimmy the fighter and wants to maintain this on a level of idolatry. She spoke fluently and animatedly for most of the hour, revealing flashes of superiority over, and disdain toward, men; these were attitudes that she really did not appreciate in herself. Near the end of the hour, she talked academically about homosexuality and beatniks. She wondered whether I would continue to see her and apologized for talking so much.

> TAT–Stories demonstrate some themes of unconventionality in all, but especially sexual, areas.

Third Session (3/26): She told with pleasure how she enjoys hurting people. However, she also told with considerable feeling how such people as her teacher, the teacher's husband and her own mother relish hurting and ridiculing her.

> Rorschach–III, IV Both responses describe delight in hurting and in victimization (sadomasochism).
>
> TAT–(6BM) Everybody involved is hurt, crushed, shocked, etc. (12MF) Father sadistic to son.

Since she was 13 years old, she has had to clutch a chain and an empty paste bottle while reading, listening to radio, or similar activities. She cannot go to sleep without them. Originally, she used the paste bottle when pasting pictures of a movie couple in an album; the chain represented their being bound together in marriage. She worshipped this couple and lived their lives, sexually and otherwise, including their fighting. At times, she wished they would take her to live with them but, of course, she was "not young enough." So she wished she could be their bird.

> Rorschach—V Enormous craving to belong to and be loved by parents attenuates her judgment to highly tenuous degree.

Before she was 13, she had been tremendously attached to her mother and was constantly in panic that something would happen to her. Her mother just laughed. At the end of the hour, the patient wondered whether she could do something about people laughing at her.

> Rorschach—I, III, IX: All three responses convey her preoccupation with significant figures (usually mother) laughing at or hurting her.

Fourth Session (4/2): She wanted to kill either her teacher or herself. She decided on the latter. All week she was ridiculed by this teacher, other teachers, and her classmates. She would not kill her teacher because she would get caught and she would not quit school because that would hurt her uncle. She did not kill herself because she thought she should talk it over with me first.

> MMPI—Pa: Extremely high Pa indicates projection of feelings and motives and definite paranoid tendencies.
>
> ICL—(4) Grossly exaggerated and peak 4th octant convey her inability to relate warmly to others and even paranoid tendencies.

The patient feels that everybody hates her, that she is cold, ugly, mean, a "slut," and so on. This is what she thinks of herself. Her mother was always ugly and ridiculed (because mother shaved her head). After a while, the patient was able to see positive things about herself.

> MMPI—F, K, Pd, Sc: Marked peaks on all three scales, Pa (inability to relate), Pd (alienation from family and others), and Sc (different and isolated from others) in a pattern that describes her loneliness and misery. Entire MMPI configuration of "floating profile" (terrifically high scores).
>
> ICL—Lower half: Exaggerated lower half carried over to Ideal present her claim to helplessness and "sickness."

She agreed to talk over with me any urgent need to act; she also expressed her positive feelings towards her therapist.

> TAT—Men always "so good"—positive feelings towards men transferred to therapist.

Fifth Session (4/9): The patient was very disturbed and agitated. She felt like killing her mother (not her teacher this time). She described the crazy and dirty behavior of her mother and then her own eccentric behavior which she rationalized in this way: she examined her food for fifteen minutes to determine that there was no dirt, ate on the floor because it was cleaner there, and set fires in the sink to experience some danger and excitement which she can't get otherwise.

> Rorschach—VIII, X: Dirt and vermin association on these responses suggest her self-concept (and conceptualization of mother).
>
> DAP—Orality conflicts suggested by male smoking and stressed lips of female.
>
> MMPI—F, K, Pd, Sc: Marked peaks on all three scales, Pa (inability to relate), Pd (alienation from family and others), and Sc (different and isolated from others) in a pattern that describes her loneliness and misery. Entire MMPI configuration of "floating profile" (terrifically high scores).

Although she feels terribly deprived and would like a cleaner home, cars, men, food, etc., she must continue in school and thus is unable to work or to leave home until June. Then, with fame and money, perhaps she can buy some respect from people—they still won't like her but she cannot settle for mediocrity. She sees nothing likeable about herself.

> MMPI—K: Extremely low K (self-criticality and screaming "I'm sick") describe her acute anxiety reaction.
>
> ICL—Lower half: Exaggerated lower half carried over to Ideal present her claim to helplessness and "sickness."

With effort she reported that, although she has gone with many men (even undressed before them), she is still a virgin. She laughed at her "cleverness," but felt this proved her hatefulness. At end of hour, she asked if I was mad at her.

> DAP—2: Saucy even whorish quality of drawing—exhibitionistic sexuality.
>
> TAT—(13MF) Flaunting of sexual behavior ridden through with guilt, punitive actions, and expiation.

Sixth Session (4/15): Miss F discussed her need to make a clean geographical break from her family, the school, and her general surroundings. So in August, she will go to New York and lose herself in the big city. We worked on the implication of this "big jump." Despite her judgment, she felt I was just like her teacher. (She held her hand before her face most of the hour.)

> TAT—(2) With characteristic projection she at first sees people "running away from themselves" but then central figure flees from her home and bounds of reality. The big jump to New York may connote something of the same.

She wondered about the reason for the moving of the clinic and the termination of treatment. (She had been informed initially that the clinic was to move at the end of June.) Contrary to her judgment, she felt rejected by me. She actually thought that I might be her woman teacher—that is why she held her hands before her eyes. Yet she also expressed a very positive feeling.

> MMPI—Pa, Sc: Very high Pa and Sc, especially in combination, indicate poor judgment and loose hold on reality.
>
> Rorschach—Rorschach content approaches bizarreness and distortion of reality concepts.
>
> DAP—Front view: Male figure looking away and with blinders on. Female poses front view but has dark glasses and only behind brittle facade of a tart.

She was told that an additional hour per week was available. (This possibility had been considered at the beginning of therapy.) Although she had a problem of timing with school, she appeared overcome with gratitude.

Seventh Session (4/23): Miss F was very upset because her cat was taken away by the SPCA and destroyed. Her mother told her that it was because the cat had a stomach tumor, but she felt mother did it because she hated the patient (despite her mother's caring for the cat all these years). She then expressed hate at her mother and everyone else. She even vented her rage at the teacher's dog, and pushed a lady in a bus because lady had pushed her, creating a scene. However, she would not cry because that is too weak.

> MMPI—K, F, Pa: Combination of low K (weak ego), high F (opposition to environment), and high Pa (distrust and projection) presents a configuration of distorted thinking and loose hold of reality.

At this point, she said that she knew by "rays," "voices," "sensing," etc., that I hated her—she seemingly wanted to be convinced otherwise but at the same time resisted this. She then told with chagrin of everybody laughing at her because they hated her. However, she indicated that she contributed to this by blurting out sexual ideas and, at the same time, being quite inhibited in expressing sex in any of her dramatic roles. She fled from looking at her own contributions in these matters.

> MMPI—K, F, Pa: Combination of low K (weak ego), high F (opposition to environment), and high Pa (distrust and projection) presents a configuration of distorted thinking and loose hold of reality.
>
> Rorschach—I, III: Weird notions and symbolic flavoring, even in context of human responses, portray her wildly imaginative, even paranoid thinking.

Eighth Session (4/27): She told of how lonely and frightened she was in dealing with her environment. She attempted to ascribe this to: (1) how miserable people are; and (2) how miserable she is, for she was born that way, etc. Very supportingly, I tried to get her to look at life more realistically and at both the historical and current reasons for this situation (including some specific talk on how she might make friends). She became angry and, feeling that I was angry with her, resorted to fantasy and spoke of suicide.

> MMPI—K, Sc, Pd, Mf: Pattern in association describes fright, loneliness, and isolation.
>
> TAT—(3BM) Despair and self-destructive theme.

Ninth Session (4/30): Last night she awoke late and felt that someone was in her room. She went into hysterics. Although gleeful at frightening mother and neighborhood, she was fearful at her lack of control. There was some talk of good and bad spirits which, with exploration, she changed into some sort of ESP phenomenon.

> MMPI—Sc: Her peak Sc (up in the 100's) demonstrates such acute sensitivity that she loses her hold on reality.
>
> Rorschach—Rorschach content so exaggerated and loose in logic, suggesting her near panic state.

Most of the hour was spent in having her look at reality without (hopefully) overly challenging her. For example, she hoped that her mother, her teacher, and everybody else she cannot get along with would die. Rather than hoping for such unlikely occurrences and devoting her energy to such unrealistic fantasies, I wondered how she could focus on what she could do to make the most of her situation. We talked a little about her need to feel clever or at least not completely powerless, which resulted in her playing "mean" tricks or making wishes.

> MMPI–K, F: Combination of low K (weak ego), high F (opposition to environment), and high Pa (distrust and projection) presents a configuration of distorted thinking and loose hold of reality.
>
> ICL–Lower half: Exaggerated lower half carried over to Ideal presents her claim to helplessness and "sickness."

Tenth Session (5/4): She described her increasing anxiety and fear of the world and her own reactions and of losing her mind. Considerable support was given, and her positive features and accomplishments, despite the extreme deprivation of her environment, were stressed.

> MMPI–F, K, Pd, Sc: Marked peaks on all three scales, Pa (inability to relate), Pd (alienation from family and others), and Sc (different and isolated from others) in a pattern that describes her loneliness and misery. Entire MMPI configuration of "floating profile" (terrifically high scores).
>
> MMPI–Sc: Her peak Sc (up in the 100's) demonstrates such acute sensitivity that she loses her hold on reality.
>
> MMPI–K, F: Combination of low K (weak ego), high F (opposition to environment), and high Pa (distrust and projection) presents a configuration of distorted thinking and loose hold of reality.
>
> Rorschach–Rorschach content so exaggerated and loose in logic, suggesting her near panic state.

She went on to describe her need for love and the desperate bids she makes for it. From this, she went on to talk of Jimmy the fighter in a daydream fashion (suggesting that this "romance" may be largely, if not almost entirely, fabricated from her fantasy). Indirectly, she also presented her own identifications with this glamorous version of the tough, fighter-poet (*e.g.*, Odets' "Golden Boy") who has received many beatings–like herself.

> TAT–(6BM, 9GF) Both stories depict cravings for love and desperate but inefficient bids for it.
>
> DAP–Draws male first (tough looking), suggesting a male identification.

Eleventh Session (5/7): The patient was in a considerable bind about (1) concentrating on a dance program which means so much to her; and (2) getting involved with another student, Ted, which would distract him from the dance. If he encouraged her, she would get involved but, if he was indifferent, it would be worse. After telling how lonely she was and how she needed love, she went on to describe the fantastic involvement she might have with Ted. He has a very jealous wife and needs to be mothered by an older woman; he does not like the patient; he has homosexual tendencies; his friend, F, who is a homosexual, voyeuristic, and so on, would also be involved.

MMPI—Entire MMPI configuration of "floating profile" (terrifically high scores).

Rorschach and TAT—Rorschach content so exaggerated and loose in logic, suggesting her near panic state.

Since she seemed to be floating along on fantasies as well as capable of acting out, I suggested the following: This three-ring circus did not appear calculated to secure her the love and attention she wanted, but instead only headaches. To say the least, it would also confuse the issues; since she did want to succeed in the dance, why not concentrate on that? She seemed enormously relieved and ready to follow any structure. I thought that perhaps the dance was making her anxious because it meant so much to her; but this was understandable. However, displacing this anxiety to these other situations would not appear to solve anything for her.

ICL—Therapist: Sees therapist (or clinic) as providing warmth and guidance (stress on right hemisphere, particularly octants 7 and 8) strength conveyed by stress in 1st and 8th octants.

TAT—and Rorschach—Quality of creativeness and ego strength.

Twelfth Session (5/11): The patient's theme of the hour was that daydreaming was her only real source of gratification. We looked at how this had come to be in light of her having no father and an extremely disturbed mother. However, she was able to see that her daydreaming was a very inefficient way to gain gratification, at times, and that when in direct conflict with reality, could invoke great confusion. In this vein, we looked at some of the possible intentions behind her planned move to New York: the idea of "being born again" and everything being rosy was clouded by its daydream aspects; she would still be the same person whose techniques of getting love and approval must be improved.

> ICL—Lower half: Exaggerated lower half carried over to ideal present her claim to helplessness and "sickness."

Thirteenth Session (5/14): She feels that the world, rather than herself, is bad because she is always disappointed and things turn out poorly for her. We tried to focus on her passive expectations (including those of inevitable disappointment).

> TAT—(2) With characteristic projection she at first sees people "running away from themselves" but then central figure flees from her home and bounds of reality. The big jump to New York may connote something of the same.

I had the hunch that she felt I was scolding her and accusing her of being stupid because of clarifications of her distortions. She inquired why I did not call her by her first name. We explored this somewhat.

> MMPI—K, Sc: Low K, feelings of being criticized, and high Sc, hypersensitivity, in combination presents sense of vulnerability to, and constant interpretation of, being criticized.

Fourteenth Session (5/18): A large part of the hour was devoted to her god-like adulation of Jimmy and her intense need to cling to this dream. She told of being extremely happy because she found out where he will fight next and will send him a telegram. (Her laughter and mannerisms connoted anxiety despite her avowed joy). She revealed that her kidneys bothered her, which happens when she is upset. She is fighting with her mother, who upsets her by insults and by cutting off her (the mother's) hair. We considered what might be going on in her mother. The patient assumed that everything would change when she leaves. We hoped for some amelioration in this respect but considered internal problems as well.

> Rorschach—VII Sharp conflicts between strivings for love and conventionality and fleeing, fighting, or bohemianism. The response on this card suggests possible relation of conflict especially to her mother.

Fifteenth Session (5/21): The patient was in a positive state of mind because her hero won his fight and because she met a fellow at school who likes her and with whom she can flirt. However, her side hurts her intensely again. On 2/12, she had severe pain and came to the medical school. Kidney pathology was diagnosed but only pills were prescribed. She had created a scene because of the pain; subsequently, her own physician ruled out kidney disease.) She did not want to do anything about it because nobody else believed that there was anything wrong. She was not sure herself, but the pain was real enough.

> MMPI—Low Hs: Relatively very low Hs belies patient's stress on somatic complaints. May speculate that when her Pa tendencies are submerged because circumstances are going well, she reverts to somewhat less primitive somatic defenses. Often when probings are premature with Hs patients, they become Pa-ish (see cases of Miss Hypochondria and Miss Pollyanna).

She felt like two persons in conflict (two parts of herself)—the reasonable one and the wild, imaginative, impulsive one who distorts things and is ultrasensitive. The latter usually reigns, but both want to go to New York. A friend of hers is there; this friend whom she met at school, had problems and everyone teased her about her affairs. The patient empathized with and helped her.

> Rorschach—VII Gross ambivalence expressed in this response in right and left symbols, parts of a person.

She then told of her aversion to close contact with people in buses, particularly heavier older women.

> ICL—(4) Grossly exaggerated and peak 4th octant convey her inability to relate warmly to others and even paranoid tendencies.
>
> MMPI—Pa: Extremely high Pa indicates projection of feelings and motives and definite paranoid tendencies.

Sixteenth Session (5/25): The patient was very upset about a doctor's appointment this afternoon: (1) If he finds nothing, he'll laugh at her and think her a liar; or (2) if he does find something, she would be terribly afraid of the hospital—the pain, other women seeing her, nurses touching her, etc. She is aghast at the possibility of a scar. She was very agitated and indicated very low tolerance for pain or even for thinking about it.

> TAT—(6BM, 12M): (6BM) Everybody involved is hurt, crushed, shocked, etc. (12M) Father sadistic to son.
>
> MMPI—Entire MMPI configuration of "floating profile" (terrifically high scores).

She went on to describe her apprehensions about other women looking at her clothes, people staring at her when she eats, and so on. We considered the feelings of stupidness and messiness which were engendered by her mother and generalized by the patient to other situations. We worked hard on her focusing on positive features in herself.

> MMPI–K, Pt: Rorschach–VIII, X: Dirt and vermin association on these responses suggest her self-concept (and conceptualization of mother).

Seventeenth Session (5/28): She had a fight with her mother and with a girl who called her neurotic and evil-minded (because she criticized a famous actor, for flaunting his homosexuality). She also lost a sales slip, and broke an ashtray; these were all parlayed by her into catastrophes. She spoke about no one liking her and her wanting to kill everyone. By exploration, gentle teasing, and exaggeration (burlesque), she was able to look at herself and see her own contributions more reasonably. However, the theme of homosexuality became more prominent and phobic.

> MMPI–Entire MMPI configuration of "floating profile" (terrifically high scores).
>
> Rorschach–Color, content exaggerated: Rorschach content so exaggerated and loose in logic, suggesting her near panic state. Over-reactivity to color indicating her overreaching (hysterical) to emotional situations.
>
> ICL–(4) Grossly exaggerated and peak 4th octant convey her inability to relate warmly to others and even paranoid tendencies.

At the end of the hour, she again questioned whether I liked her, though she said she knew I wasn't mad but perhaps was disturbed with her. The answer was left up to her.

> TAT–(12M) Theme indicates her ambivalence about trusting her father versus fearing sadistic (or at least rejecting) behavior from him. Apparently transferred to therapist and other "authority" figures.
>
> ICL–(4) Grossly exaggerated and peak 4th octant convey her inability to relate warmly to others and even paranoid tendencies.
>
> MMPI–Sc: Her peak Sc (up in the 100's) demonstrates such acute sensitivity that she loses her hold on reality.

Miss F's dancing teacher called before the hour began to see what she could do to help. She felt guilty about "kidding" the patient, but wanted to have her come out of her shell more and correct her inadequate interpersonal relations. However, she said that Miss F was a marvelous dancer. I tactfully obtained her agreement that she would concentrate on the patient's dancing ability, while I worked with the emotional factors.

TAT and Rorschach—Creativity

Eighteenth Session (6/1): The patient told about nearly having intercourse with a boyfriend. She said only "nature" prevented completion of the act. She was very happy about this affair and intended to pursue it further. Rapturously, she expressed her need to be desired psychologically and physically, not to mention the pleasure involved. However, she revealed no knowledge and care about contraceptives; exploration of this subject brought out tremendous dismay that such behavior could result in pregnancy. I carefully went over this with her.

TAT—(2, 3BM, 12) All three stories deal with sexual themes of a rebellious nature.

She revealed further a more or less unconscious need to shock her mother and teacher (and me), evidenced at least in her fantasy. The patient wants her children to know that she had sexual needs and acted emotionally in this area, since her mother never achieved this communication with her. Further clarification demonstrated her intense need to be liked and accepted by teacher in and beyond her dancing—although she fights frenetically to deny this.

MMPI—F, Pd, Ma: High F connotes oppositional tendencies, Pd morbid resentment; in combination they suggest acting out against the environment.

Nineteenth Session (6/4): Again she nearly had an affair, and again "only my period prevented completion." She indicated that she wanted me to say yes or no to this behavior of hers, but that in any event she would go ahead with it. In light of all her confusion and anxiety, I suggested that she wait and first try to understand what her feelings were. She described her immediate need for warmth, affection, etc. However, near the end of the hour she confided that she had cried on the above occasions.

ICL–(7) Confusion and naivete about sex is characteristic of hysterical reactions.

DAP–2: Sexual exhibitionism, desperate attempt to relate.

I again reiterated my suggestion that she proceed slowly and cautiously, but assured her that in any event I would still be here to talk with her.

Twentieth Session (6/8): She was very anxious about an abortive attempt at intercourse with her boyfriend. At a crucial point, she "stopped" and yelled at him to stop beating her although he had been quite gentle. When we tried to examine her feelings, she became quite upset and felt that I was laughing at her.

MMPI–Pd, Mf: Tremendous discrepancy between high Pd (resentment) and low Mf (feminineness and weakness) send this message, "See how weak, helpless and feminine I am—and it's your fault."

ICL–(5) Gross representation of 5th octant describes masochistic and guilty feelings.

Rorschach–II, III, IV: These responses all tell of victimization.

She was determined to prove again that she was not a "failure" and that she could love and make a male happy. Otherwise she would always be alone and in despair. We worked the entire hour on getting her to see what the urgency was about and what had to be "proved" right now (we also considered this in relation to the approaching termination of therapy).

TAT–(13MF)–Only way to win male is to give self sexually.

ICL–(4) Grossly exaggerated and peak 4th octant convey her inability to relate warmly to others and even paranoid tendencies.

MMPI–Sc: Her peak Sc (up to the 100's) demonstrates such acute sensitivity that she loses her hold on reality.

Twenty-first Session (6/11): Rather defiantly, the patient insisted that she was going to go ahead with her affair and tell her uncle that she was leaving for New York. She manifested considerable ego strength despite the rebellious aspects. While I pointed out the rebellion, I gave much support to her self-expression—and she blossomed under it. She emphatically made the point that she wanted to try proving several things for herself: (1) being a woman sexually, and (2) getting a job and dance experience away from home.

TAT–(2) With characteristic projection she at first sees people "running away from themselves" but then central figure flees from her home and bounds of reality—the big jump to New York may connote something of the same.

It may be very important for her to be given her freedom, but there is the danger of how she will respond to the bumpy road.

Twenty-second Session (6/11): She appeared to be in an even better psychological state—assertive and relating more directly and warmly. She described sexual experience with her boyfriend, and said that the act of going through with it has made her feel that she has proved herself. She does not have to get involved again or even dwell on "dirty jokes." (This is all despite very awkward proceedings in the act, wherein her boyfriend ultimately "landed in the wrong place.")

Contrary to her expressed good feelings, she also was very anxious and experienced somatic difficulty (kidneys, headaches, etc.). With absolutely no realistic foundation, she was apprehensive of being pregnant. She also felt very guilty; we explored her sense of guilt and dirtiness about sex (at least on an unconscious basis—for example, she slipped with "odor" for "order," "in-stink" for "instinct," etc.) Her mother had always told her that sex was sordid and dirty. The patient said she could not bear to have others touch her.

TAT–(13MF) Theme indicates that although she might experiment and defy with sex, she suffers severe guilt and self-punitive reactions.

Rorschach–X Morbid preoccupation with dirt (e.g., here vermin). Her blurred sexual discriminations thereby have been "contaminated." (Probably, she is very influenced by primitive sexual interpretations and fantasies of a cloacal nature; namely, that genital and anal apertures are one and the same.)

Twenty-third Session (6/18): The patient has met with her uncle, who first attempted to persuade her to remain in the city for a year before making such a big leap. However, she convinced him of her sincerity and planning. He arranged for her to move to a guest house for the next few days until she goes to New York. She felt very guilty about taking advantage of her uncle, particularly since she was so bad (especially with respect to sex) despite his desire and ability to help her. For the first time, she expressed positive feelings about her mother. She dreaded being cruel to her—i.e., leaving her residence (and the patient was truly ecstatic about living in her own quarters, eating with other people normally, and so on) and going to New York. "After all, I have lived with her for 19 years!"

> TAT—(12M) Theme of story portrays her ambivalence of craving love, wanting to adulate parents, but having experienced and always anticipating brutal rejection. Nevertheless, in this therapy hour, because of mollified anxiety, the positive feelings re-emerge.

Twenty-fourth Session (6/22): She has moved into a new apartment and is feeling good about things. She expressed the conviction that she feels much better than when she began treatment, and I said I thought so too. However, interspersed within this positive material was a leit-motif of hatred for her teacher. I pointed this out, and she agreed that this was "a big black mark" that prevented her from being happy. When she flowed from her teacher to her mother, I pointed out the link and possible displacement. Since the mother has been so nice, and the patient for the first time had expressed positive feelings towards her, perhaps this explains the need for her teacher as a target.

> TAT and Rorschach—Projective quality

Twenty-fifth Session, Termination (6/25): Her pregnancy fears began to reappear three days ago as "punishment for being bad" (sexual incident). Otherwise, she is getting along very well. I gave support to her accounts of eating and watching TV with other people. She asked for and was given referral sources in New York.

> MMPI—Positive features: Hs, Hy and Ma within normal limits. Pt not too discrepant with Sc. Hs, Hy, and Ma within normal limits suggest that she can maintain control, resiliency, and mobilize sufficient energy and optimism (Ma) to cope with her environment. Although she has extremely high Sc, her very high Pt serves as an escape valve—that is, she is aware of and anxious about her emotional difficulties.

She expressed positive feelings about treatment and me and said that she no longer feels that I want to get rid of her. However, she did say that she would have a hard time trusting another person.

> TAT—No F or formal distortion on TAT despite wild hysteria on both tests. Despite "content distortion"—that is, wildly imaginative, bizarre, and histrionic associations, she never seriously distorts formal aspects—that is, she always uses form correctly on the Rorschach (no F minus) and does not misperceive people

and objects on the TAT. Consequently, we would expect a wildly imaginative person but one who has contact with reality. This latter presents a working base for therapy.

Concluding Remarks

In this instance, the psychological evaluation was invaluable, particularly in light of the short period of time in which treatment could be conducted. The recommendation to focus on reality with the patient and to capitalize on the transference relationship seemed to have paid rich therapeutic dividends. As an illustration of the value of the test clues, refer to the last two items in the therapy explanatory comments.

CHAPTER ELEVEN

CONCLUSION

At this point the contributions made by the psychological evaluations may be considered. However, for this consideration to be meaningful, allowance must be made for such nebulous factors as these: differential diagnosis, personality strengths and weaknesses, interests, talents, hobbies, tolerances, interaction with the particular therapist; and the fortuitous circumstances with which the patient may be involved before, during, and after the course of treatment. Let us consider several of these factors with respect to the case histories that have been presented.

One fact must be underscored—eight of the ten patients did not seek psychotherapeutic treatment but were "convinced" by their referring physicians to try therapy when they complained of physical distress. The other two initially sought psychological treatment—and these two were among the successful cases.

FAILURES

Diagnosis

Three cases were considered therapeutic failures—Pollyanna (chapter 3), Sadomasochism (chapter 7), and Hypochondria (chapter 9). Each had a diagnosis of character disorder, a lifelong pattern of maladjustment characterized by lack of closeness in interpersonal relationships. All had exaggerated hypochondriacal features. They all had myriad somatic complaints from which they either were unable or not inclined to disentangle themselves. This feature was most marked in their notably high Hs scores on the MMPI. This commonality appeared to be associated with the exaggerated eighth octant (Psychosomatic classification) on the ICL. Two of the three also had peaks on Pd and Pa in the MMPI. (The configuration HsPdPa has been interpreted as a sour, gloomy, alienated, suspicious person and the bane of medical practitioners). (7)

All three produced Rorschach protocols in which human responses were dehumanized (that is, "M" and "H"). The protocols were characterized by morbidity, again related especially to the interpersonal sphere.

Most important of all, each of these patients was strenuously propelled into treatment by his physician.

It may be speculated that these three patients utilized such a primary first-line defense projected by their soma that they were, in a sense, fanatically resistive to psychotherapeutic treatment. They wanted to relieve their physical symptomatology, to be sure, but not at the expense of relinquishing their defense against the more painful anxiety of facing their internal conflicts. Suspicious in their relationships to begin with, they practically had to be coerced by the referring agent into attempting with a therapist a most intense relationship based on trust. They may well have sensed that, if their defensive armour were pierced, they might be overwhelmed by the emotional turbulence which would flow out. One fact became prominent—a result pointed to by the psychological evaluations before the course of treatment—this therapist had little success with the patients presenting this syndrome unless they became extremely motivated (*e.g.*, symptoms posed a threat to life or treasured interpersonal relationships). There may be an implication that other therapists can prognosticate in similar fashion from test data as to those patients with whom they can be more or less successful.

Fortuitous Circumstances

An external factor in the case of Hypochondria was the patient's unlimited funds which she could (and did) apply to travel and even for surgery in order to flee introspection. That she had high social standing and realized positions of responsibility paled in significance in light of her constant flight. Her self-concept was of a "rock" resistant to change. In the case of Pollyanna, the patient fortuitously had the solicitous (guilt-laden) attention from her mother and the economic wherewithal to garner the secondary gain of staying away from work because of illness. Her self-concept was very narcissistically tinged and the danger of risking anything but a looking-glass reflection was too great for her. The patient in the case of sadomasochism had an extremely trying and malignant environment. If her untimely and sudden death (of possible suicidal nature) had not taken place, it seemed that something would have to give (if that, indeed, wasn't what happened)—either her emotional balance or her resistance to treatment. Her self-concept was so extremely morbid that she could not tolerate self-investigation.

PARTIALLY SUCCESSFUL

Diagnosis

This group consisted of the cases of Amorality (Chapter 1), Orality (Chapter 2), Shakes (Chapter 4), and Dysphoria (Chapter 5). They presented a mixed diagnostic picture: Masochistic character with hysterical features, character disorder with hysterical features, anxiety reaction, and hysterical personality, but all had hysterical features, as did the more successful cases. Hysterical might be defined operationally as Hy peak on the MMPI, stress on the 7th octant on the ICL, well-conceived but exhibitionistic DAP, overreaction (or shock) to color on the Rorschach, and overly dramatic, naive, or superconventional content in interview, TAT, and Rorschach.

More dynamically, hysteria, as it is interpreted here, is fluidity of affect, running hot or cold (but usually hot) emotionally, a veneer of warmth of relatedness sometimes quite thick in depth but always masking hostility; and, most pervasive, a childlike quality revealed especially in attempts to seduce (charm, flattery, exhibitionism, etc.) or extort (play one person against another, become piteous, tantrum behavior, etc.). Related to this description was the marked immaturity demonstrated by all of these patients with hysterical features. They had childish fears, phobias, expectations, and primitive moral strictures (which they managed to circumvent in a most innocent fashion). Their combined self-concept seemed to be of a childish but omnipotent person who had received love but who still felt he needed and in fact demanded, much more.

Fortuitous Circumstances

Both character disorders characteristically acted out, primarily sexually. In the case of Miss Amorality, the patient garnered considerable secondary gain not only from such action but from her physical attractiveness, family background, success in her vocation, and her superior and creative intelligence. It might be stated, rather vaguely, that her personality resources demonstrated a degree of resiliency and strength that was commensurate with her test protocols. The patient in the case of Dysphoria, on the other hand, presented a much more sterile personality and intellect, only marginal success vocationally, and a rather perverse satisfaction at frustrating her mother and sister by using therapy as an excuse to attack them; she attempted to frustrate the therapist also by "not getting with it." (This hostility was pronounced in all of her test protocols.) But she did seem to get an ego boost from treatment.

The other two cases, both very dependent people, could not stand up to their family members who became threatened by the personality changes beginning to be effected by treatment. The patient in the Case of Orality seemed to be far more desirous of clinging to his mother than ridding himself of anxiety attacks. Although he was very apsychologically minded and very weak in resources, he had begun to display some initiative. The patient in the Case of Shakes, on the other hand, had far more personality resources and life experience at her disposal, and had worked out somewhat successful (if neurotic) ways of displaying her individuality (hostility). She was able to take a longer look at herself and made deliberate changes in the way she related to people close to her. She is specified as only partially successful because she terminated before it could be determined whether her "insights" would be translated into behavioral changes.

SUCCESSFUL

Diagnosis

Each one of these cases—Rebellion (chapter 6), Denial (chapter 8), and Fantasy (chapter 10)—had pronounced hysterical features. Each one also tended to establish an intense relationship with the therapist. They did at least as much "acting in" therapy as they did outside of treatment. (The term here signifies more emoting rather than Zelig's (25) concept of posturing.) Each was consciously very unhappy with his picture of himself (on the MMPI, D and D, Pt–Pd not an isolated peak) and wanted to understand and change this picture.

Interestingly enough, two of these cases (Denial and Fantasy) were among the most seriously disturbed insofar as nosology was concerned; the patient in the Case of Denial was the only one to be hospitalized. Therefore, it was easier to detect more dramatic changes and to experience less hesitancy in pronouncing success. Moreover, these were the only two patients who initially asked for psychological treatment. The patient in the case of Rebellion was an hysteric with acting out tendencies and epileptic symptoms.

Fortuitous Circumstances

The patient in the case of Rebellion had high intelligence and, even more important, a sense of humor—he could laugh at himself. What seemed to keep him in therapy, however, was his parents' guilt (they were reinforced in this by the family physician's confronting them with the emotional implications of their son's behavior) and peer rejection resulting from his physical symptoms and school failure. Moreover, he yearned for the setting of limits, even the little provided by therapy.

The patient in the case of Denial had very nearly hit bottom. If she had any intention of changing her situation, she had to take a look within herself. Her lifelong characteristic had been a prodigious effort to get people to like her. She attempted the same with her therapist, and then had to repay his interest and approval by "getting better." A solicitous husband willing to put up with almost anything, two attractive children, family, and many friends were other available resources.

The patient in the case of Fantasy was impoverished and highly unstable. But she hungered for understanding and a sympathetic relationship. She also was able to utilize a superior intelligence and tremendous creative ability in exploring herself. Fortunately, she had one (and really only one) area of success outside the therapy situation: she had dancing talent and was gaining some recognition for this. The author's hunch is that this success and these abilities were indispensable for her to tolerate and benefit from outpatient treatment.

SUMMARY

In summary, on a diagnostic basis, the least successful cases appeared to involve hypochondriacal and/or distrustful attitudes which were reflected in the test results. Somewhat more success was experienced with patients who, although they had chronic character disorders and tended to act out, had hysterical features and related to people (and especially to the therapist). The most successful cases had pronounced hysterical features but related warmly and intensely to people—particularly to the therapist. In half these cases, the patients had initially sought psychological treatment.

What have been called fortuitous circumstances may be indicated by the psychological evaluation and in particular by the interview, TAT themes, and Rorschach content. The reader may judge for himself from the data how much this is the case and to what extent they were alluded to in the reports.

Post hoc analysis, rather than prognosis, proved to be rewarding. The author found that in reviewing his treatment notes, the psychological evaluation often provided a condensed and revealing summary of what had transpired. That is, apparently confusing and disjointed therapy data were lent meaning and consistency by referral to the test material. The reader may judge from the material presented to what extent the information provided in the psychological evaluation, and referred to from time to time during the course of treatment, can be very meaningful and permit a more purposeful career of therapeutic intervention.

APPENDIXES

APPENDIX 1

MISS AMORALITY
CHAPTER ONE

TEST DATA
AND INTERVIEW

Diagnostic Interview

The patient, a 30-year-old divorcee and mother of two, was referred by a psychologist and an obstetrician for personality evaluation to determine the advisability of a therapeutic abortion.

She began by reporting that she was four to five weeks pregnant and that she had made a great mistake in becoming involved with her lover. He earns, she said, too little to support her, and besides she would lose out on her property settlement trust fund. She said she lived with an unhappy marriage for eight years, having married her husband only for his money; she got divorced a year ago. Now she felt she had a great opportunity to support herself and further her career—a baby would destroy this.

> Immediately she presents rather inappropriate affect, sense of values, and relatedness to significant other people. She shows no conflict or defensiveness, suggesting a disordered personality feature that will not be very amenable to threapeutic intervention.*

The lover is a Catholic but is in favor of an abortion. He is a homosexual (which she discovered after the affair began) and might not be able to adjust satisfactorily to marriage. He is compassionate, shares her artistic interests, loves children, and is very sensitive. But

* Interpretive comments by the interviewer are set apart from the text of the interview and the test data in this manner.

he is irresponsible—at the age of 31, after seven years on the job, he has not advanced at all. She chose him because he was available. She loves him but then she loved her husband in the same way, as one loves one's sister or brother. However, she also is sexually attracted to him. The stronger of the two, she "feeds" him.

> She disparages her lover but indicates a need for a sensitive, feminine or childlike mate, suggesting her confused sexual identity. She continues to present callous, amoral orientation.

She was born in a large midwestern city in the early 1930's. Her father a mathematician, was from a very prominent family. This was his second marriage; he had three children from the prior one. Before, during, and after his marriage to the patient's mother, he philandered and finally left home when the patient was a year old. The patient met him only once, when she was ten. Her mother is in the performing arts and served in responsible political positions. Her mother loved the father so much that she never remarried and resented children. She is a tremendous source of energy, very aggressive, and far more interested in making a life for herself than for her children. The mother made the patient feel she loved her only for her accomplishments rather than for herself although, because of her artistic talents, the mother favored her over her sisters. The mother has spent her life pursuing men and, when they wanted her, she did not want them and thus punished them. At the age of 17, the patient felt "squeezed out" of home when her mother was too busy.

> Strong ambivalent feelings toward mother. No solid relationships even in family. Men to be feared and hated.

The patient has two sisters: A, 35, and D, 34. She loved the latter "madly," and still does, but A, the oldest, was like a mother towards them and was resented by her sisters.

> A sense of alienation from everyone but sister. Although latter may serve as a mirror image and thus reflect strong narcissism, here is evidence of ability to love.

Her childhood was happy but her adolescence was dreadful. She never felt that she belonged, and her grades suffered because of her inner turmoil. Rebelliously, she went with unpopular fellows or just with girls. This made her feel even more out of the in-group. When she broke her neck in the gymnasium, she had no social conflicts and got straight A's (as if to suggest physical problem relieved her interpersonal anxieties). In her junior year, she suffered a "breakdown" which consisted of her crying uncontrollably for no reason. Finally, she collapsed on a basketball court and could not breathe. She convalesced in Florida for a month.

> Defenses have collapsed in past when she felt left out and when she had to contend with adolescence crisis and school pressures.

At 17, she won a scholarship to a first-rate girl's college. She was lonely there, and left when her counselor fell in love with her, although this is what she had planned. She left because she did not feel this school would equip her for a job.

> Suggests how she handles an authority figure and possibly the therapist.

So she enlisted in an art institute where she remained for four years (four weeks short of the full time). Both she and her husband "rebelled in Bohemian fashion" against getting degrees—it did not mean too much vocationally.

> Can be very practical and amazingly impractical, almost simultaneously.

The patient met her future husband as a fellow student at the institute. She was rooming with his fiancee, whom he did not love but on whom he was dependent. This man then became a "puppy dog" for the patient; once she even hit him and accused him of being weak. When he said he did not want her, she wanted him. The money from her father's trust had been running out, and this man was potentially wealthy, tremendously intelligent, and of the same background and religion as she was. Prior to this she had loved all sorts of unavailable men, such as older and married men.

> Family triangle theme where male is inaccessible or if he is accessible, he is disparaged and despised.

They were married when she was 21. He remained up all night (and still does) drinking with their landlord. They went to the movies three times in one night, just did anything. (She conceded that "anything" was often drinking.) They both still managed to get to eight o'clock classes until they left the institute when she was 23. (Then her husband constantly sat in front of TV reading the Wall Street Journal.) During the last year at the institute she was very lonely and fell in love with a "very sensitive" student. He was a mutual friend of theirs, a homosexual, who had come to live with them. He was put in the living room but they kept a bedroom for their dog. The man became a companion for her. The student represented everything her husband was not: warm, loving, and friendly—he reminded her of her present lover. After several months, the roomer left, although she was still in love with him. The affair was continuing; at the same time, her husband was jealous of her friends and even the dog. They had lots of childish fights. When they left the institute, they bought a home in the suburbs and were happy for a while. Her husband just puttered around the house for two years. Both were extremely happy, and her husband went to work for a business his mother bought for him. However, he soon began running around with older and wilder men. He bought a yacht and engaged in a social flurry. They both moved in different sets and the rift widened.

> Her first significant relationship after her family—marriage—was a miserable failure. Her husband was totally inadequate, offering her a rationalization to seek out yet other inadequate males.

When she was three months pregnant, she fell in love with a "married Catholic doctor who had his own family." Her husband would not touch her while she was pregnant and instead went around with other women. She was very depressed for three months after the birth of the baby. He gave her no money to secure help for the very large house. Although extremely irresponsible with money, he allowed nothing for the household. The baby boy was four months old when she became pregnant with her daughter. *"I was vulnerable to contraceptives, I mean to conception."* Her husband was drunk at the time. He did not want the daughter at first. Patient made nothing of this because she was used to his philandering. (Relevant to the slip, she related this obscurely to the possibility that she wanted to break her neck in the gym—apparently she felt that she had made a slip here which I may have missed. Thus, she seemed to be saying both behaviors were self-destructive.) But she was happy being pregnant and thought that she could make her husband happy and more home-loving. She looked to her doctor lover and his "wonderful homelife" and aspired to the same for herself.

> Paints vivid picture of how she is helpless before events—a leaf in the wind. She suggests her self-destructiveness in every

way including slips. Again she indicates she must master a "father figure" and may try to do so with her therapist.

Things kept up the same way. In the sixth year of marriage, her husband beat her up because she paid the grocery bills. They slept in separate rooms; and then she left him and stayed with her mother and children in very small quarters. She left the children with her mother, who hired a nurse while the patient traveled to get over her depression and exhaustion. By this time, her husband was a confirmed drunk and philanderer. She even contracted "crabs and a venereal disease" from him. The doctor's wife began to suspect, so she pulled away from the doctor and her whole crowd and felt terribly lonely. Her husband then wanted to reconcile. She went to a psychiatrist for three months to understand her "messed up life." It didn't help at all because too many things were going on. Her husband began beating her again. So he went into treatment for about four months. A psychiatrist told the patient that the husband's therapist was interested in him but that he had "no will power." The husband did give up a mistress. They spent two happy weeks in the following summer. Then he stayed away from home and she fell in love with a man (in the same occupation as her mother) who encouraged her to file suit for divorce.

Enters treatment but "pot boiling" prevents insight, a warning for future treatment.

That year, she discovered that she was pregnant again. She thought that it was a result of the two happy weeks that she spent with her husband. She could not tell him about it because of the divorce, so she had an abortion. She could not explain how and why she became pregnant. Throughout this year, during her separation, she was carrying on an intense affair with the artist and paying no attention to her children, for whom she had hired a girl. The divorce was effected 8 years after their marriage. She stopped loving the artist who had a family of his own; both were glad to give up the affair.

The pattern of her pregnancies suggests that they represent a means for her to act out extremely strong unconscious conflicts. They seem to represent in part attempts to punish herself, significant others, and to prove she is a woman.

For a year following her marriage, she was employed in her field. Offered a job personally by the owner of a large concern, she accepted and moved West. The owner has more than a platonic interest in her but she does not want to hurt her lover who also works there. Both would lose their jobs if the owner knew about them. She works five hours a day and has a woman take care of the children and the apartment. She loves her job and the possibility of a career.

> Positive features and ego strengths in making such a move, finding work satisfaction, and caring for her children.

MEDICAL HISTORY

No serious illnesses. She did have pneumonia when she was 14 and was hospitalized for a month. She had a spastic stomach before marriage and during schooling; her husband actually had ulcers. She has sleeping problems—on sleeping pills, tranquilizers, and dexadrine; she takes Equanil (a tranquilizer) three times a day. She doesn't drink much and smokes "less than two packs a day." She has headaches once in a while.

> Use of drugs commensurate with diagnosis of character disorder and suggests this is what she uses to hold herself together.

IDIOSYNCRASIES

The patient doesn't care what anyone thinks with respect to right or wrong because she feels so wrong herself. She is very amenable to advice and suggestion. Everybody gives her advice but she does what she wants. She is bothered by heights, because she feels she would fall off. However, she used to be a high diver. She has never had a satisfactory relationship because she was never able to give herself because of her fear of being hurt and left. "Probably because father left." She enjoys sex but never experiences an orgasm during intercourse.

> Seeming insight about not being able to give may have been gleaned from sister who has been in treatment. Or worse, it may be integrated into her character structure and self-image. Same refers to her frank discussion of sex so early and admission of her inability to relate in any meaningful way.

DREAMS

Repetitive nightmare: She pushed A (her oldest sister) off a cliff. During her marriage she had many nightmares from which she awoke screaming.

She also dreamed of a man dressed up like a woman and wearing lipstick coming after her. There was a student who attended the institute with her who was a "paranoid in treatment with the VA." (Considerably elaborate and confused detail followed.)

Before her marriage she dreamed about horses. The other day, she dreamed about a parrot with a very large beak who became very excited by her, ruffled its feathers and sat on her shoulder. She was given a horse when she was nine and she gave it away. She always dreamed of a black stallion who loved her but might hurt her and she always felt this way about horses, she had the same feeling for the parrot with the large beak. She added that her lover "preens" himself. She had him sign a note that he would discontinue any homosexual activities but she is pessimistic about this. Questioned about the incidence of such men in her life, she said, "Possibly I'm afraid of manly men, of the dominance and submission. I would have to perform and therefore lose my identity and security. Obviously, I am afraid to have a mature man because I do not know how to hold him." (This was said very glibly, and she conceded that she had gleaned most of these ideas from sister who had been in treatment.)

First dream may describe her ambivalence towards mother represented by sister who acted as mother.

Second dream continues her theme of confused sexual identity.

Third dream is very aptly, if glibly, interpreted by patient herself.

Psychological Tests

DAP

She worked long and hard on the figures. She questioned whether she should draw clothed or undraped figures and then proceeded to do latter.

Drawing I

Rather Greek or Roman type female figure and face structure. Voluptuous, sensuous, serious. Although she looks rather heavy, the position suggests she is rather graceful. Mature, reserved—not very outgoing, but kind. Rather moody. Generally a rather wise, reserved woman devoted to some cause or other; rather aloof, self-confident, and quite at peace with herself. Late 30's.

DRAWING II.

A man. Rather powerful, many of the same attributes that the woman has. Profound, thoughtful, seems to know what he wants and able to go after it. Neither is gregarious; they would rather live their lives apart from people, although they have interest in mankind and man's welfare. Most significant thing about them is their rather quiet, unassuming, somber way. Intelligent and kind, compassionate although not overly friendly; engaged in activities that benefit not only themselves but mankind. Early 40's. (You lumped man and woman together, are they related?) Could be man or wife or sister and brother. (Which?) Man and wife. Don't consider them very beautiful . . . quite out of proportion.

General Comments

The nude figures, in that they display the body openly, suggest exhibitionism. The patient also indicates her flaunting of sexual conventions by her emphasis on sexual detail. Defiance is suggested by the aforementioned features as well as by the thrust forward of the bodies (literally bulling herself into interpersonal situations) and the front view (looking-you-straight-in-the-eye orientation). She seems to overreach into her environment (very long arms) in a desperate attempt to make contact. Yet she *pushes* away (turned-away position of hands) and is aloof from people; she mixes superficially and is depressed (feelings expressed in her associations to the figures). Her conceptual ability is excellent (demonstrated in fine execution and over-all conceptualization of the drawings).

RORSCHACH

CARD I

1. Immediately asked if she could turn card (6″) Couple of figures twirling.

Inquiry: 2 spinning figures, capes flying and hoods. (What else?) Looks like they're defecating. They are men. Wings rather than capes. (Action?) Looks like Goya etchings—expression of biological urges.(?) Habits, rather.

Comment: Immediately aggressive but still conforming to authority, moderately rebellious. Turning card suggests manipulating environment but asks permission. Initially perceptive of people with considerable tension. Content distortion; i.e., form or reality adhered to but interpretation or quality of content of logic is strained. Seemingly oriented to environment, but her thinking is extremely pathological with respect to people. Must "express biological urges," in this case anal. Thinking somewhat contaminated i.e., men with wings suggests disturbed logic.

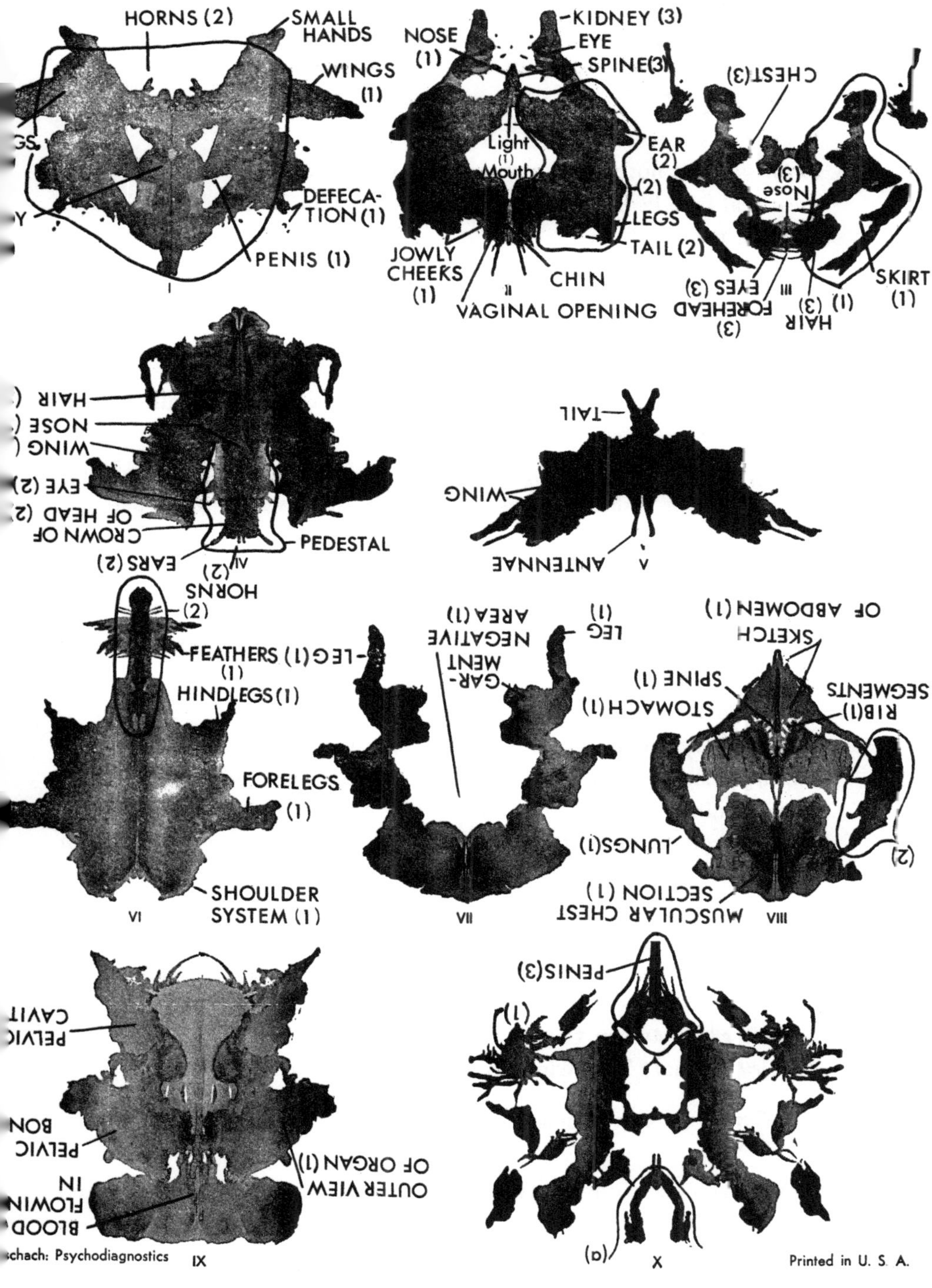
HORNS (2)
SMALL HANDS
WINGS (1)
DEFECATION (1)
PENIS (1)
I
NOSE (1)
KIDNEY (3)
EYE
SPINE(3)
Light (1) Mouth
EAR (2)
(2)
LEGS
TAIL (2)
JOWLY CHEEKS (1)
CHIN
II
VAGINAL OPENING
CHEST(3)
Nose (3)
EYES (3)
FOREHEAD (3)
HAIR (3) (1)
SKIRT (1)
III
HAIR
NOSE
WING
EYE (2)
CROWN OF HEAD (2
EARS (2)
HORNS (2)
IV
PEDESTAL
TAIL
WING
ANTENNAE
V
(2)
FEATHERS (1)
(1)
HINDLEGS (1)
FORELEGS (1)
SHOULDER SYSTEM (1)
VI
LEG (1)
GAR-MENT
NEGATIVE AREA (1)
LEG (1)
VII
SKETCH OF ABDOMEN (1)
SPINE (1)
STOMACH (1)
SEGMENTS
RIB(1)
LUNGS(1)
(2)
MUSCULAR CHEST SECTION (1)
VIII
PELVIC CAVIT
PELVIC BON
BLOOD FLOWIN IN
OUTER VIEW OF ORGAN (1)
IX
PENIS(3)
(1)
(a)
X
schach: Psychodiagnostics
Printed in U. S. A.

2. ∨ ∧ Also a beetle. Anything else? (Whatever you see.)

Comment: After initial impulsivity can be more cautions, i.e., little speculation and meager use of form and content.

CARD II

1. (4″) It's a face.

Inquiry: Eyes, nose, open mouth, jowly cheeks, and chin. (?) Macabre, theatrical face lit from below (M or F?) female; (age?) oldish; (lit?) light on nose section.

Comment: Unusual, almost bizarre interpersonal concept. Macabre effect, old female, eerie, disparaging, oral (oral because of open mouth).

2. And a pelvis bone, x-ray.

Inquiry: Vaginal opening, kidney, spine. (Color?) Yes, all colored ones where saw anatomy.

Comment: Morbid response—emotions carry her away, break somewhat with reality content-wise. Preoccupation with vagina, pelvis, and other anatomy.

3. < Couple of rabbits ∧ ∨ < ∨

Inquiry: Dark area (usual)

Comment: Again recovery with near-conventional and soft, child-like response.

CARD III

1. (5″) Very much two ladies facing one another.

Inquiry: Ladies with bosoms and high heels. Look windswept therefore spinning, holding purses. Look like blown from behind. (Why?) Direction of ink, smooth outer line and flowing inner line, skirt blown forward.

Comment: Excellently conceived women indicating creativity and sociability, but again with much tension (leaf in the winds); woman nurturant or wish to be (nurturant because of emphasis on bosoms).

2. Butterfly between them (held at arm's length.)

Inquiry: (usual) Two wings and body, except upside down.

Comment: Conventional but not completely conforming (upside down).

3. ∨ Sort of a monster with his arms over his head and kinda red bow on his chest (sigh!).

Inquiry: Two black eyes, enormous chest, bowtie on white vest. (Red bowtie?) Just a bowtie. (Rest of head?) Gray fuzzing hair around ears, forehead, no mouth or chin.

> *Comment*: Weird response suggesting strained logic (bow on monster's chest.) Phobic re: people (monster). Again related to old people (gray hair).

CARD IV

1. (17″) Also sort of a monster with great big feet sitting on a pedestal with rather small arms.
Inquiry: Soles of feet exposed, sort of turned up, beak-like nose and ears coming out. Obviously sitting on something, feet off ground, looks bottom-heavy. (Monster?) Arm-wing or whatever.

> *Comment*: Again a monster, phallic-like beak (suggesting aggression and aggressive sexuality), monster put on pedestal (anal, because of seated position).

2. ∨ (4″) Bony animal with a rather goaty type head.
Inquiry: A flying, goat-like figure, hair (much detail).

> *Comment*: Again contaminated thinking (flying goat—strained logic).

CARD V

1. (4″) ∨ This is a butterfly. That's all I see. ∧
Inquiry: ∨ Wings, antennae, tail.

> *Comment*: Conventional.

CARD VI

1. (6″) This is the skin of an animal like a cowhide and mounted like an Indian might with painted feathers on top.
Inquiry: [much detail] feathers. (Why?) color or shading. Looks like tips of feathers painted as if in colors, would be in many colors, about six feathers.

> *Comment*: Conventional with added artistry, perhaps hostile twist (Indian suggests aggressive figure). Can be tactful and seek affection in a controlled way (good use of shading).

2. ∨ ∧ And a kinda Indian weapon or symbol or wand or what-have-you, handing down from top.

> *Comment*: Phallic (long object hanging down) and hostile concept (weapon).

CARD VII

1. (35″) V Λ < V This is hard. Only thing I can think of is this creature I used to dream about as a child. Exploded horizontally standing up on tip toes. Only a dream moved in constant kind of vibrating way.
Inquiry: (Explosion?) Negative area between two blots (White Space). Horizontally shaped with no face.

> *Comment*: Chimera from childhood. Absolutely phobic and terror-stricken.

2. Λ Also two busts of ladies with great hairdos staring at one another.
Inquiry: (Staring?) Chins jutting out, obviously not smiling, eye to eye. (Unfriendly?) Passive not necessarily unfriendly, although don't look terribly kind. Additional response (a) Also looks like caricature of donkeys with one hoof (same as VII, 2).

> *Comment*: Women disparage, are passively hostile and unkind. Additionally on "Mother" card woman is disparaged "caricature of a donkey" (mother's politics).

CARD VIII

1. (3″) (arm's distance) Looks like an anatomy drawing, nerve, blood vessels and spinal diagram. V Also heart and lungs, stomach, abdomen, and muscular system on chest.
Inquiry: (Lungs?) Because that's where it is. (Color?) Wouldn't look like lungs if gray or blue.

> *Comment*: Practically overwhelmed by emotional stimuli and resorts to second-line anatomical defense (only projection, delusion, and hallucination more primitive defenses).

2. < Also couple of mountain lions or wolves or bear.

> *Comment*: Recovery to conventional (if aggressive) predatory animals.

CARD IX

1. (14″) V All of colored ones remind me of innards and sort of pelvic region.

2. Λ This one looks like an enlargement of portion of other in anatomical way, bare structure, possibly lungs, portion of spinal column and blood flows through.
Inquiry: Both responses vague and much emphasis on blood flowing and anatomy.

Comment: Even poorer with pelvic emphasis and extremely vague. Stress flowing of blood (implication of fluid emotionality and, in this context, diffuseness of sexual concept)—sexual context.

CARD X

1. (2″) Crabs—four in fact.

2. Kinda sketchy outline of chest, neck, and shoulders (muscle and bone detail.)

3. A penis and a pelvic section. < V (a) Seahorses. (b) Where ribs meet.

Comment (1,2,a,b): Start somewhat conventional but regresses back into anatomy; (3) ends up preoccupied with sex.

General Comments

Although the patient is generally well-oriented to her environment, her thinking, particularly with reference to people, is markedly distorted. Her judgment becomes extremely impaired under emotional stimulation, dissolving into impulsivity, first-line anatomical defenses, and surrender to immediate gratification—usually biological urges. She is extremely phobic about, even terrified by, relations with people, particularly authority figures. She attempts to deal with this, unsuccessfully, by disparagement, acting out, and assumed sophistication. Another cover is aggression, even rebellion, appearing to cope with situations while concealing her temerity. She is potentially creative but her superior intellect is blurred by her defensive preoccupation with sexuality.

TAT

CARD 1.

This child is blind, unhappy, and moody. Very gifted child, prodigy but does not relate to world around him and is very much alone. Seems that his violin will be his only source of joy in life and his music.

Comment: Blind, unhappy, moody prodigy. Instrument only source of joy.

CARD 2.

Rather peaceful scene of good hard-working people who have somehow managed to make the earth yield to them. Mother figure leaning on tree looks pregnant and divinely happy. They apparently have been able to provide for young girl to study and it really looks like it is a cooperative venture. Man too young-looking to be a father, yet working in the field with others, and this is the life he is leading or has chosen. (Not father.) Might be brother. (Is there a father?) Yes, somewhere. (?) (laughs) Might be in background.

> *Comment*: Mother pregnant and divinely happy. Father not in picture—somewhere in background.

CARD 3.

This woman has just shot the one person in the world she loves most—a man—and she is completely despondent about it. (Why shoot?) Because he hurt her in some way. (How?) Disappointed her, might possibly have fallen in love with another woman. (Outcome?) She does not recover, goes through life in sort of daze but goes on.

> *Comment*: Woman shot one person she loves in world, converts this to man. Is it really mother? Completely despondent and goes through life in a daze. Hurt by one she loves.

CARD 4.

This woman is trying to restrain this man from doing something very evil and yet she does not. He looks the more intense and compassionate of the two. She looks very much as if she is very calculating and I'm not too sure as if he would be making a mistake—she does not look like she would be worth it. (What is he contemplating?) In a sense she does not look like she is related to him. He looks like he is going to murder some other man for horning in on his girl. But she does not look like the girl but rather friend who is trying to dissuade him (What happened?) He . . . wrenches free and slugs the guy and walks out.

> *Comment*: Woman calculating, man weaker and impulsive. Woman not worth the attention. Ends in violence.

CARD 6.

Well, this is a man and wife having a discussion. He looks very kindly and intelligent as if he cares very much for her. She looks very skeptical about what he has to say. Might be some question about the children. He seems to be wiser than she, and he is helping her make a decision about them. (What?) Whether or not to let John go on to study in some expensive school. (What do they do?) He tells her that it would be best to leave John there; he seems to be gaining more than she realizes from the fine schooling. She probably feels that they cannot afford to waste money this way, and he thinks it is probably worth it.

Comment: Man wiser than wife about children. Mother doesn't want to waste money on *son* applying himself; father thinks it's worth it.

CARD 8.

Story of a young boy who dreams some day of becoming a great surgeon and probably will.

Comment: Can be conventional, but with effort and by restraining self.

CARD 10.

This is a scene of a very tender moment between two people. Man and Wife I would say. Love and compassion and understanding for one another and peace and harmony.

Comment: Same as 8. Also, can express tenderness.

CARD 12.

This is a portrayal of a hypnotist and a patient. Patient looks a little as if suffering and hypnotist is . . . although hypnotist looks rather evil, he is making an effort to relieve him. (Suffering how?) Pain, physical pain. (If hypnotist is evil why is he helping?) He is experimenting because technique is relatively new.

Comment: Hypnotist (doctor, therapist) evil looking. Helping suffering patient only because of experiment. She had reported that her physician was interested in her sex life with a homosexual because of experimental interests.

CARD 13.

(Longest pause) This boy has just strangled a woman because he hates women and, although he regrets the act, he would probably do it again and he probably made her want him and did not seduce her. Instead he strangled her. (Why this particular woman?) Could be any woman and attracted to him. (Was she a casual contact?) Yes. (Outcome?) Sort of Raskolnikov episode. Probably the woman is no good and he probably feels he brings a form of justice to society. Probably will suffer some sort of guilt for act and yet not ever be truly sorry.

Comment: Man seduces woman not for sex, but only to strangle her because women are no good and he is an agent of justice.

CARD 18.

(Long pause) This woman has probably just pushed this man down the stairs and is lifting him up to see if he is still alive. Man figure looks rather womanish and she has spite and revenge on her face (Why?) That he does not give her the kind of love and compassion she needed. He might've been a professor and his work has been his life, or he might've been a homosexual.

> *Comment*: Woman attempts to kill feminine male because he is wrapped up in his work and because he is a homosexual. Relevant to current relation with lover and her last remarks in interview.

General Comments

She can be conventional only by restraining herself with considerable effort. Otherwise, she has tremendous feelings of bitterness, depression, and violence. Women are calculating, revengeful creatures seeking to destroy or emasculate males because they are so wrapped up in themselves. Males, and herself, also wish to destroy women who are all no good. Mother divinely happy to be pregnant—no father. Doctors only wish to experiment with their patients.

Starke R. Hathaway and J. Charnley McKinley

Name______________ Age______ Sex______ Date Tested______________

Address______________ Occupation______________

Education______________ Marital Status______________ Referred by______________

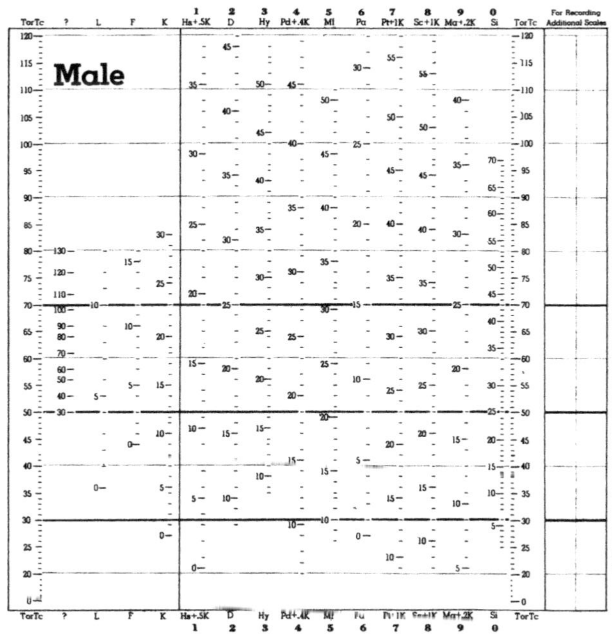

Fractions of K

K	.5	.4	.2
30	15	12	6
29	15	12	6
28	14	11	6
27	14	11	5
26	13	10	5
25	13	10	5
24	12	10	5
23	12	9	5
22	11	9	4
21	11	8	4
20	10	8	4
19	10	8	4
18	9	7	4
17	9	7	3
16	8	6	3
15	8	6	3
14	7	6	3
13	7	5	3
12	6	5	2
11	6	4	2
10	5	4	2
9	5	4	2
8	4	3	2
7	4	3	1
6	3	2	1
5	3	2	1
4	2	2	1
3	2	2	1
2	1	1	0
1	1	1	0
0	0	0	0

Raw Score ___ K to be added ___ Raw Score with K ___

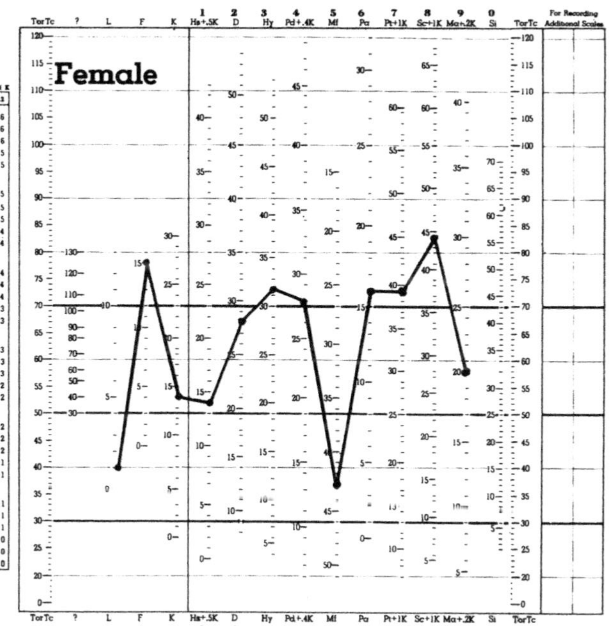

	?	L	F	K	Hs+.5K 1	D 2	Hy 3	Pd+.4K 4	Mf 5	Pa 6	Pt+1K 7	Sc+1K 8	Ma+.2K 9	Si 0
Raw Score		1	15	14	7	28	32	22	43	16	25	30	17	
K to be added					7			6			14	14	3	
Raw Score with K					14			28			39	44	20	

Signature______________ Scorer's Initials______________ Date______________

THE PSYCHOLOGICAL CORPORATION
304 East 45th Street, New York 17, New York

Printed in U.S.A.

60-141S

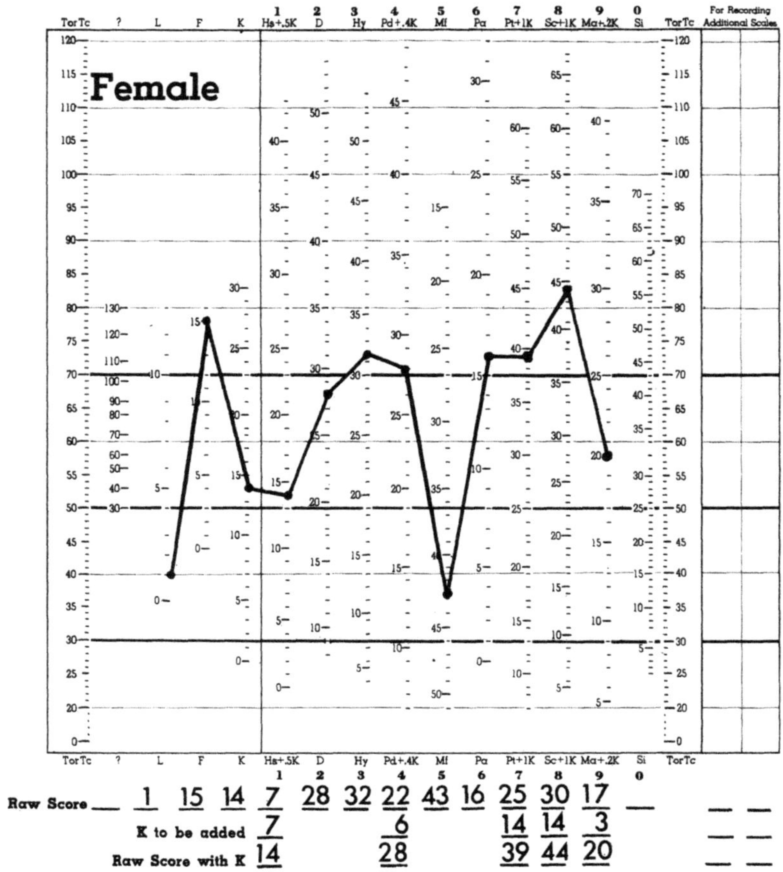

MMPI

A serious personality disturbance that approaches psychotic proportions. More precisely, her extreme oppositional tendencies (F) and hypersensitivity (F,Sc in combination) distantiate her from her environment. She feels so different and alienated from others (Pd,Sc) that she is unable to trust or comprehend the motives of other people (Pa). She tends to act out and be carried along by her impulses (Pd,Hy). Her femininity or sexuality is only a means of relating—and more probably like a weapon than effective communication (F,Pd,Mf—rebelliousness, impulsive rashness, and weak and feminine pleas, in that order).

APPENDIX 2

A CASE OF ORALITY
CHAPTER TWO
TEST DATA AND INTERVIEW

Diagnostic Interview

The patient, an only child, was born in a large Western city in the early 1940's. His father was a longshoreman who moved to a large farm with his mother and grandmother when the patient was a little child. The father, the patient said, is a nice guy and thoughtful but easily led and "too good." He does not show love or feelings. His mother, he added, is the best woman in the world but she "gets nervous and hollers a lot," particularly when he does not do well in school. He did fine in grammar school until the eighth grade, when he stopped studying because he felt tired and didn't care. Now he is a high school junior and has been left back both in parochial and high school. He said that about two or three years ago (actually five), his father decided he liked farm life, his mother city life, so they got divorced.

> Confused and contradictory feelings about parents. Considerable indications of his pain and anxiety related to his broken home.

When he was six, he was very heavy but it did not bother him. At about ten or eleven, he was teased and grew self-conscious; he became ashamed to go swimming. He was doing well in school then. He said that he is still self-conscious, but has a lot of close friends, dances well, and has a couple of good girl friends. He commented that he does feel nervous and gets rashes on his hands. He told of feeling tense at times, with his muscles jumping (e.g., in his legs), but that he sleeps like a rock for about eight hours. He manifested a noticeable head tic (observed as shaking his head as if he were saying no, which became more exaggerated when his attention was called to it). He said his father was nervous also and then complained of a nervous cough. Sex, he said was not a problem, only his weight, which kept him from "fitting in." (The patient could not add anything to his medical history—the referring physician reported that he suffers from gout and weighs 335 pounds, reducing only 5 pounds in the past seven months.)

> His great weight, sexual problems, and anxiety seem somehow related, but covered by massive denial.

He admitted that his mother was overprotective. She did not let him go on trips. He saw her point because he was her only child and only responsibility. So he does what she wants. When he was a child, people used to say to his mother, "Where is your shadow?" referring to him. When he was 13 or 14, he put on a burst of weight and had to give up baseball. This was about the time things were brewing between his parents. His mother remarried about seven months ago, and he has gotten along great with his stepfather.

> His weight problem, and his mother and the satisfactions and resentments in their relationship all seem intermingled.

The patient said he did not dream much. He has dreamed that he used to live in his father's farming town. Sometimes he has dreamed that he has been caught in an old building by himself; he also dreamed that he fell off a truck.

He listed his interests as both popular and classical music, passing his time by playing pool or pinball machines, and collecting shotguns and rifles. He said that he was a good shot, but that he needed money for duck hunting and the upkeep of his car. On weekends he has gone to his father's ranch and hunted; he loves the outdoors.

> Slightly implied confused self-image, conflict between masculine and feminine identifications, and between passivity and aggression.

The mother phoned to ask how her son should answer the MMPI. She reported that when he was two he was bitten by a dog. He first manifested a weight problem at six—even then there was a strain between her and her husband (she married her third cousin when she was 18). Her husband's mother was mean to her, and he was illegitimate (sic). Her husband's side was not interested in the boy; the marriage was unhappy from the start—her mother-in-law was mean and a matriarch. She had a difficult pregnancy with the patient, 2½ days of labor and a Caesarean delivery, while her husband remained on the farm. They had been married 14 years when they were divorced when the patient was 13. The patient saw his father living with another woman right after the divorce; this disturbed him very much. A year ago he asked his mother about masturbation; she told him not to—he would get ill. (She seemed morbidly interested in her son's sex life.)

The mother's dominant and neurotic relationship with son is evident.

Psychological Tests

DAP

Drawing IV

Looks like one of those guys they hang up if they do not like—a fizzy. (Effigy?) Yeah, effigy of a gangster! (How about a real person?) Looks like a boxer or wrassler. Looks like a rough character—not mean. Big head, all broken nose, mouth all cockeyed. Looks like a stupe.

Drawing V

Mona Lisa. Reminds me of a hermit girl all out of shape. Stupid girl lives in the hills. Does not know anything. Awkward looking girl. Built like a man almost.

General Comments

Considerable disruption of judgment (sketching, poor space orientation). Tendency to be expansive or inhibited (first very large drawing with minimal detail and which he rejected). Grossly immature (very childlike, simple detail). Male pathetic, dependent, and inhibited with arms rigid to side. Self-image ugly, misshapen. Considerable destructive hostility directed at males and self (stories). Female very masculine, fearful, and depreciated (drawing and association to it).

WAIS

Subtests	*Scaled Scores*
Information	10
Comprehension	13
Similarities	10
Vocabulary	9
Verbal	42 Pro-rated 63 Verbal *106*

General Comments:

High average verbal intelligence with probability of even higher performance functioning in light of his hysterical features and understressing of speech. *Relatively* superior common sense (comprehension score).

RORSCHACH

CARD I

1. (3″) Looks like some kind of butterfly.
2. Some kind of big bug.

Comments (1,2): Conventional, poor (vague), critical cut off parts of blot, inhibited (not very productive).

CARD II

Is this right up? ∨ What the hell! Don't know what this could be.

(120″) Don't remind me of anything.

Inquiry: Still rejects.

Comment: Cannot handle first "easy" emotional (color) stimulus. Rejects.

CARD III

1. (16″) Reminds me of a skeleton-like mask.

Inquiry: ∨ Skeleton, blood on side, two eyes, frame of head, brain, blood on sides. Skeleton head mask you wear on Halloween.

Comment: Hysterical (reaction to color and blood response), judgment fails, impulsive (response not defined by form). Morbidly pathologically.

CARD IV

1. ∧ ∨ ∧ ∨ (65″) Carpets like bear, skins lying on floor.

Inquiry: (What about skin?) It's flat and head cut in or shot.

> (a) Looks like frog on its two hind feet.

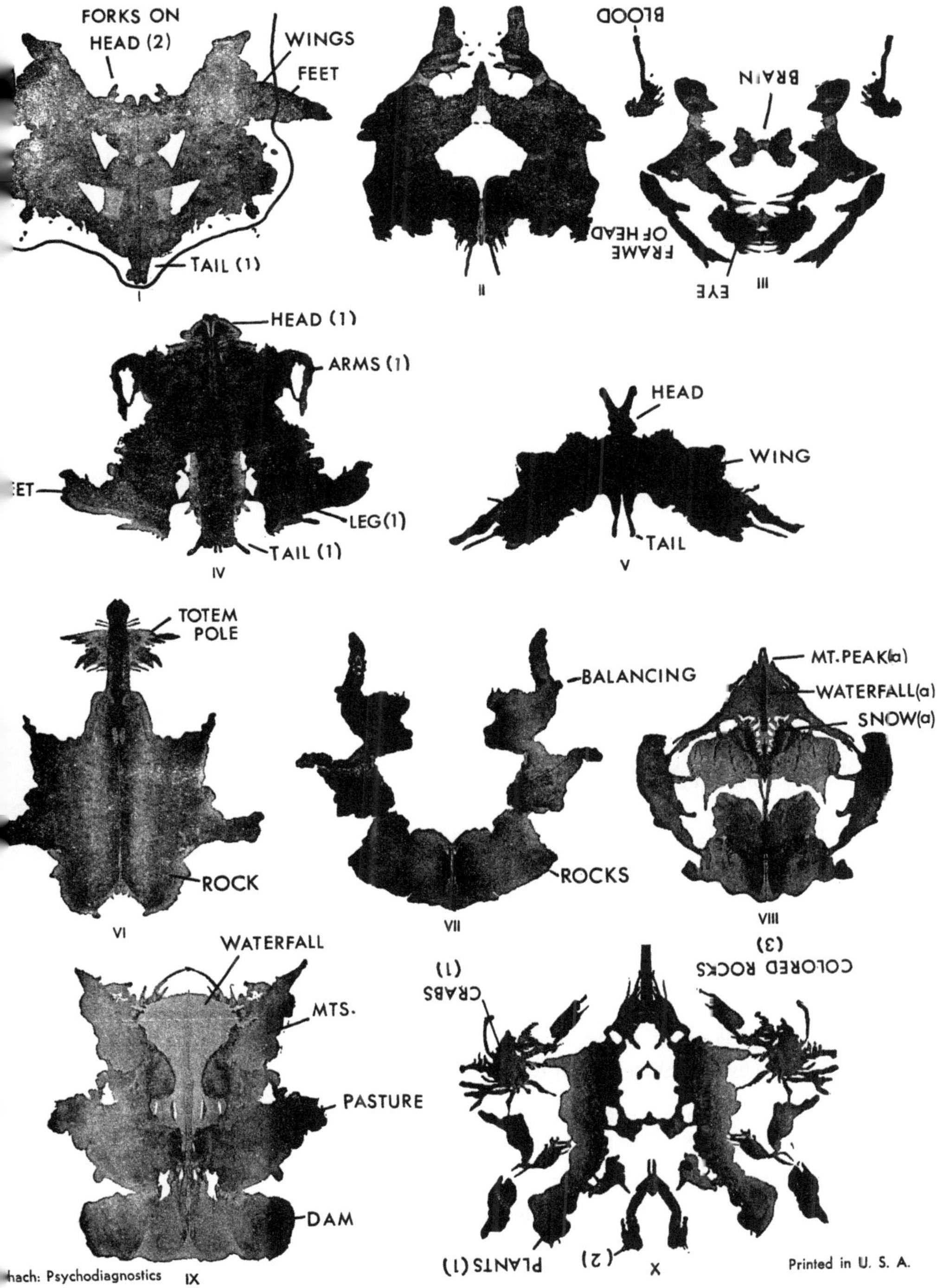
FORKS ON HEAD (2)
WINGS
FEET
TAIL (1)
I
II
BLOOD
BRAIN
FRAME OF HEAD
EYE
III
HEAD (1)
ARMS (1)
ET
LEG(1)
TAIL (1)
IV
HEAD
WING
TAIL
V
TOTEM POLE
ROCK
VI
BALANCING
ROCKS
VII
MT. PEAK(a)
WATERFALL(a)
SNOW(a)
VIII
COLORED ROCKS (3)
WATERFALL
MTS.
PASTURE
DAM
IX
CRABS (1)
PLANTS (1)
(2)
X
hach: Psychodiagnostics
Printed in U. S. A.

Comment: (1): Handles situations impulsively if not rebelliously (manipulation of card). Very inhibited (little elaboration), destructive but in conventional bounds. (a) Inhibited anal tone (squatting position.)

CARD V

1. ∨ (40″) (Turned to back of card and back) Looks like a bat.

Comment: Conventional, inhibited.

CARD VI

1. ∧ ∨ (40″) Looks like a big rock, a goofy bird on end of it, like a totem pole.

Inquiry: Rock, Looks like a bug, tarantula with totem pole on end of it—sounds stupid. (Totem?) The way it's shaped, colors in there.

Comment: Possible sexual stimulus (sex response frequently given to this area of card) becomes phobic (tarantula-mother, goofy-self?) phallus depreciated, judgement confused but mitigated by awareness.

CARD VII

1. ∨ ∧ (20″) Looks like odd shaped rock with empty space in middle. Like an arc.

Inquiry: Looks like rocks balancing on other rocks.

Comment: tension, conflict (Mother-rock?) Card often elicits responses associated to mother and childhood—does he see mother strong as a rock?

CARD VIII

1. > (13″) Looks like an ice cream cone. Rainbow colors.

Inquiry: Ice cream. Color of it, whole thing.

Comment: Impulsive (diffuse use of color), oral.

2. These look like two bears.

Comment: Even mundane fantasies inhibited.

3. Big flower, snow mountain peak, waterfall. (Snow?) White. (Flower?) Colors and formation.

Comment: Pushing inhibition aside, impulsive but creative fantasy life. (Enuretic, because of falling water?)

CARD IX

1. ∧ ∨ (6″) This looks like big mountains, waterfall coming through middle.

Inquiry: Spilling into dam or green pasture (mountains orange, dam pink)

Comment: Very impulsive but imaginative. Possibility of enuresis and/or nocturnal emission and concern thereof (second successive response of waterfall and spilling).

CARD X

1. ∨ ∧ (12″) Looks like underwater aquarium plants.

Inquiry: Because of colors.

2. ∨ Seahorses.
3. ∨ Fishes.

Comment (2,3): Less inhibited, recovery from emotional shock (using colors effectively).

General Comments

The patient finds it difficult to relate meaningfully with people. His judgment at times fails but recovers in the long run. Very impulsive, sexual difficulties. Inhibited but has creative and increased intellectual potential.

TAT

CARD 1

Looks like a young kid who'd like to go out and play. Mother makes him play, or father. Looks disgusted—like me. Does not want to play but parents forcing. Rather go out and play. Mad they're forcing him, not going to play for meanness. Ends up in future years playing the violin.

Comment: Disgusted and angry over conformancy to parental demands. Rebellion ends in conformancy.

CARD 2

That's supposed to be a girl? Yeah. Looks like she has no parents. Left alone and does not know what to do. Has no one to get advice from, becomes a tramp on the streets. Ends up a prostitute, don't care anymore, a big pig. Knows doing wrong but goes on doing it.

Comment: Identifies with girl, no parents to give advice, ends up bad and big pig.

CARD 4

This here looks like a girlfriend and a boyfriend. Probably got in an argument. She loves him, and yet he likes someone else and, she's trying to hold him. He probably lets go the girl he's thinking of (background?) and falls in love with this one. Lives happily ever after.

Comment: Girl settles on second choice. Mother and him?

CARD 6BM

Well, this guy looks like he got in fight with mother. Maid looking at mother. He probably did something to mother—she's standing in front of maid. He has head down in shame and mother does not want to talk to him. (What did he do?) Probably went with a gang of guys and left home. Ten years later came back and mother don't want to see him. (What will happen?) Mother don't want to see him anymore. (Woman in picture is maid, mother not in picture.)

Comment: Mother rejects him if he "does something to her". Mother just a maid.

CARD 7

Father and son having a talk. Father wants son to do something wrong. Son mad, does not want to do it but his father (sic). Father wants him to kill mother and get in fight with father. (Why does father want this?) Probably looks like they're separated and wants son all to self.

Comment: Almost verbatim, almost self-referrent.

CARD 7BM

Son has a gun—planning to kill father. Thinks if he kills father he can see (sic, think?). Two guys taking bullet out of him and pain father in. Can see two guys cutting father's side and getting bullet out and father in great pain. Probably ends up he does not kill father even though gun there and tempting him. (Why kill?) Looks like father has been mean to him—probably has no mother. Ends up father really likes son after all, in fact sends son to school.

Comment: Treated mean by father, sadistic revenge by son. Other component of wish for father-son love wins.

CARD 10

Here it looks like man and wife. Making love to each other but husband really does not like wife. He married wife for money and then goes to other girl he really likes.

Comment: His interpretation of parents' split. Does not see affection even where strongly indicated.

Card 12M

Father and son, son sleeping. He's planning to kill him, and chokes him. Probably jealous of son. Probably ends up kills son to get revenge on. Probably does not like father. (Jealous?) Son does not like, he likes mother and never looks at him. Mother probably mistreated father, and to get revenge on her, he kills son.

Comment: Continues interpretation of parents' split. Preference for mother, father's revenge, patient as a pawn between both.

Card 13MF

Girl laying in bed, guy probably raped her and left her after raped her probably killed her. He does not know what to do. Probably ends up gets caught, executed or something.

Comment: Sex and violence—guilt and punishment.

General Comment

Preoccupied with relationship to mother and rage and yearning for father. Rebellion and conformancy are combined with guilt and sexual confusion themes.

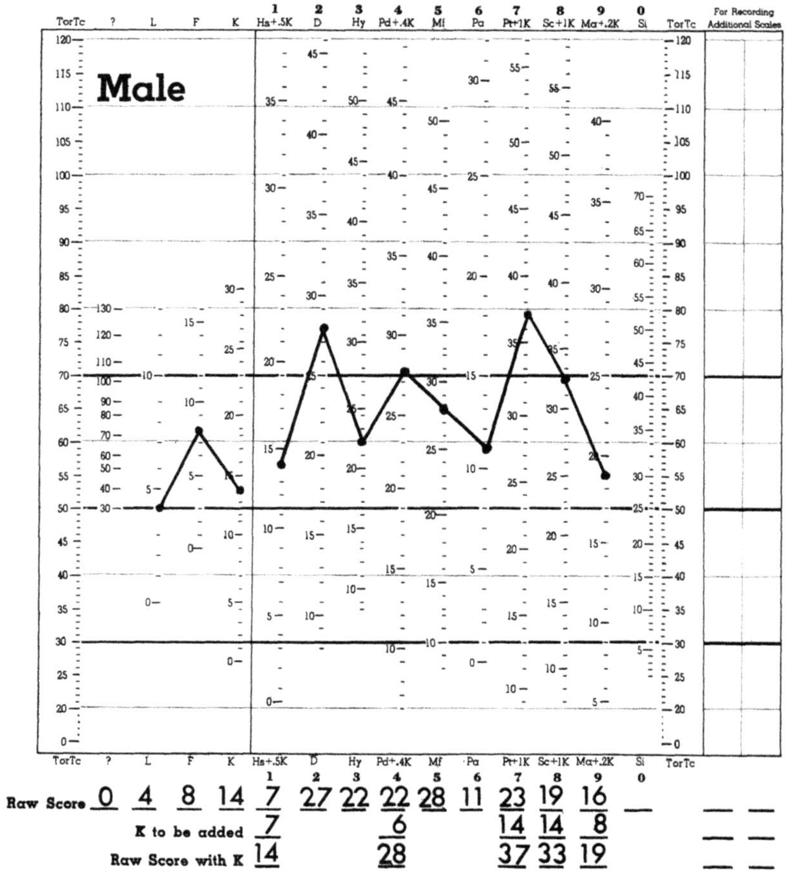

MMPI

Significant Sc Items: Sex life unsatisfactory, no one understands me, not as happy as others

Depressed and anxious, neurotic profile (D,Pt)

Feels different, very sensitive, inadequate (Sc, K)

Compulsive (item: even steps over cracks) (Pt)

Impulsive and brooding but turned inward (Pd,Ma,D,Pt)

(Inward and brooding because of the high D and Pt)

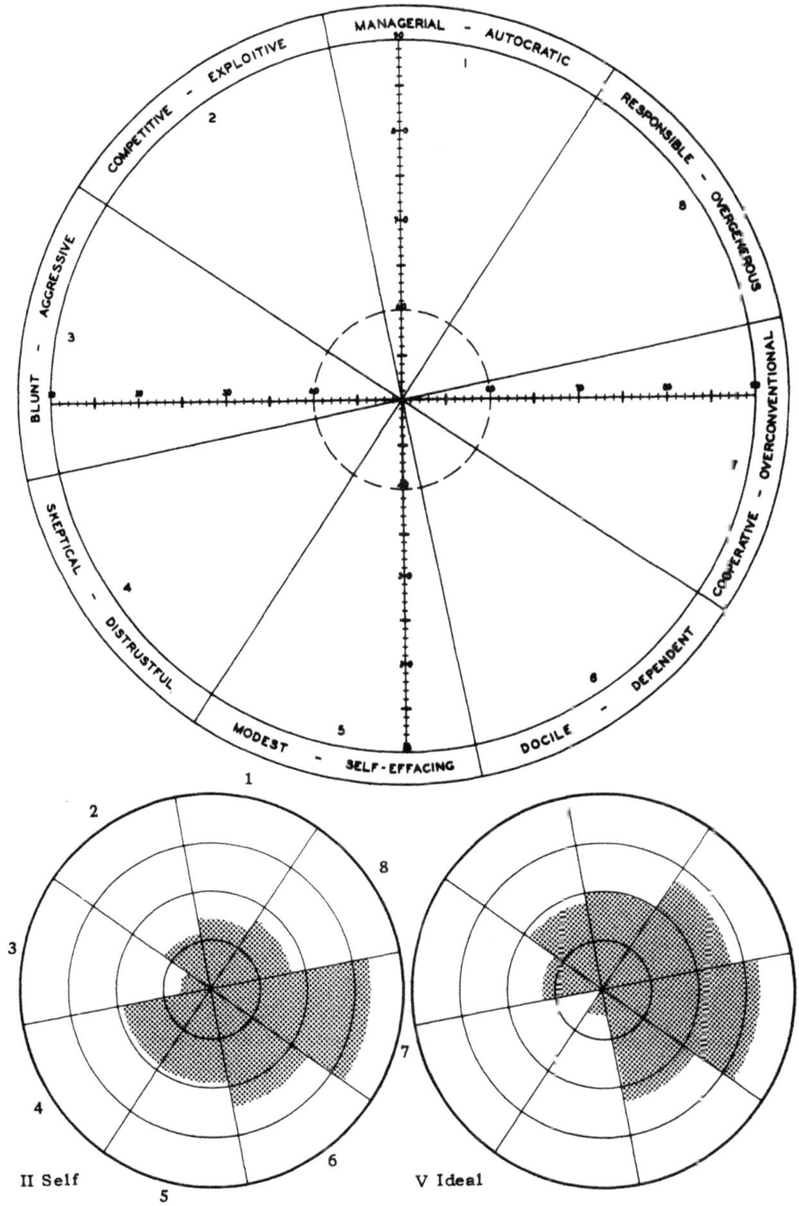

ICL

Presents self as conventional (7) and stereotypic—Hysterical (7) with considerable phobic and dependent features (6) conflict about bitterness, uneasiness with others. Complete absence of octant 4 in Ideal as compared to self suggest the conflict and self effacing tendencies (4 and 5) and discrepancy with Ideal.

APPENDIX 3

POLLYANNA
CHAPTER THREE

TEST DATA
AND INTERVIEW

Diagnostic Interview

The patient immediately initiated the interview by reporting that she has been under the care of Dr. R for low grade rheumatic fever: muscle pain, swelling, weakness, highest fever 102 (mostly in the daytime), upper back pain, headaches top of the head, etc. (Syndrome very suggestive of mononucleosis.) Primarily, she said she takes penicillin and aspirin. Last June she was put on cortisone and bedded for five weeks because of a "heart murmur." She wanted to work. In December, the patient and her sister had flu. She was getting sicker, so she was taken off cortisone and referred to several doctors at a medical school. Dr. R had called her employers and given them the impression that she was a worrier, so they switched her to another branch. They thought she was calm but suggested that she recuperate for a few weeks since she had lost weight. She is 5′ 5″ and her normal weight was 133 but now she weighs 107. Dr. R could not decide between rheumatic fever or emotional disorder but Dr. E felt that it was organic. At this point, she mentioned that she felt unwell before menstruating; she presented a long list of physicians and considerable knowledge of all sorts of illnesses.

> Immediate and long list of somatic complaints, doctoring, and medical knowledge suggests hypochondriacal orientation.

Three weeks ago she checked into another medical school for

diagnostic procedures and was taken off medication. She lost weight rapidly, was nauseated and had a bad cold. She was there seven days, checked out on her own, and was disappointed that Dr. R did not phone her there.

Implication that she may flee treatment.

Nobody, not even her parents, has "hurt or interfered" as much as Dr. R, even though he preached that she could be independent and happy. Actually, "he babied me more than anoyone else." (Her tone and wording took on a vindictive quality.) She became disillusioned with him. "I'm afraid I'm getting a doctor's complex." Dr. R said she should clear up the psychological factors. She used to be energetic before she was sick but now she is always tired.

Forms intense relationships but underscored with deep distrust; again, problem for therapy relationship.

The patient was born in New York in the early 1930's. She lived there for a year with her mother. Her father, stealing from his business, got into trouble with the law; he was a philanderer as well. Her mother got divorced when the patient was about a year old; she had no memories of her father. When she was six, her mother sent the patient to her grandmother in Germany because the patient was unhappy with her nursery (the mother was working). Her sister, a year and a half younger, was not sent because she was too afraid of leaving her mother. Patient remained with her grandmother for 2½ years and forgot her English. When the grandmother died, she stayed with her aunt in Germany. Mother had told her she would be going along with her on the boat and then sneaked off.

Early broken home and absence of father figure.

She had a happy, loving time in Germany and gained a lot of weight.

Frequent stress on orality or its derivatives.

At the age of eight, she was sent home because of the political disturbances. Her mother had remarried but had tuberculosis and was short of money, so she had not sent for her sooner. (The patient had always expected her mother to bring her back). The patient said she was and still is close to her mother. Her mother showed affection although her stepfather showed less. She gets along well with her sister. Both live at home. Patient considered her childhood was happy and that she is cheerful and not overly sensitive.

Actually rejected by both parents.

She liked high school, did well there, and even "bossed" her sister. Her mother was very generous and encouraged her to study piano. The patient took care of the housework while her sister lay around (their mother was still working). Although this took considerable time, she still wanted to do it. She associated exclusively with her sister, because other girls did not like the things that she likes. She attended socials but had little time for boys, although she dated occasionally. After graduation, she worked as a bank bookkeeper and then as a teller. Her last job, which she held for two years, until around Christmas, was a bookkeeper-teller. She would like to return to this job or to another bank. Her social life was more active when she was younger. After working her first six months, she developed symptoms of fatigue and fever, and her arm hurt. She has no friends now, though she did go steady once and would like to get married. She feels insecure about holding her job but she wants to work and study the piano. For recreation, she reads, watches TV, goes to the movies, and takes care of her birds. She likes to dance but then she gets sick.

Paucity of relationships.

IDIOSYNCRASIES

There followed an enormous amount of somatic complaints or at least sensations. At times she feels as if she is falling and avoids high places; she can't do anything in moderation (e.g., eating and playing piano); she is fearful of the dark and of being alone.

Phobic

She sleeps a great deal when she is listless; she sees herself as a dancer or pianist; and she gets depressed when doctors or nurses make remarks about her being shy and not going out with boys. Sometimes she is afraid of losing her mind. She has always had faith she would find the right doctor. At times, she feels like a burden to her family and would "like to have a new body." She became more inactive when she was about fifteen, when her periods began. They used to be very irregular.

Keen sense of alienation almost somatic delusion. Symptoms began with very late menarche.

DREAM

She had a mask over her face and was not getting enough air.

EXAMINER'S IMPRESSION

The patient gave the impression of being shy, introverted, and evasive about details and her interaction with others. She stuck to concrete situations or symptoms. Speaking low, she demonstrated a German accent and so was difficult to understand at times. She was dressed in a fairly tight sweater and skirt. Seemingly unaware of her seductive gestures, she rubbed her arms, chest, etc. Very restless, she wriggled in her chair, ate Sen-Sen, and frequently played with her hair.

REFERRAL INFORMATION

The patient was born here and taken back to farm in Germany. The father died or disappeared. Her mother tried to give her away, then took her back; the mother has profound guilt feelings with respect to the patient and had invalided her, but she may have a mild rheumatoid arthritic condition, "probably a schizoid personality." Her mother made her give up piano and clerical job.

Psychological Tests

DAP

She took an extremely long time and was compulsive on drawings, making many false starts. She even counted on fingers. After a long time, she was encouraged to discontinue, but I almost had to pull drawings away (similar to response on Card X on Rorschach).

Drawing I

Young girl about 18. Happy girl, couldn't make her smile. Healthy girl, friendly, enjoys being alive. Sees life on the bright side. Wanted to draw her nice looking but she came out not bad. Average intelligence. Girl that likes to sing.

DRAWING II

Wanted him to be athletic type, loves sports, smart, school age, knows what he wants in life. Big career ahead of him. Very active.

General Comments

Pollyanna on surface (as in Rorschach). Counterreactive, "smiling on the outside, crying on the inside."

Deals with people openly (front view, friendly expression). Tackles environment (hands reaching out), but with assistance of extremely compulsive defenses (taking a long time, emphasis on detail).

Same with respect to identification. Facade of great femininity but reaction against masculine strivings (male just does not look athletic and appears childlike, if not effeminate).

Very anxious but able to channelize and show little external psychopathology. (Extreme length of drawing time, enormous preoccupation with last little line and leaving strokes but final product very well conceived.)

RORSCHACH

CARD I

1. (12″) God! At first glance these look like two Santa Clauses.

Inquiry: Fat Santa Clauses, dancing around.

Comment: Immediately, powerful magical being from childhood. Active fantasy (active movement).

2. Looks like two hands holding something or trying to pull something apart.

Inquiry: Hands, mittens, either dancing around or pulling something like in a game. (Tug O' War?) Yes. (Dancing or pulling?) Pulling.

Comment: Pronounced internal conflict (tug o' war).

3. Couldn't be real person, this has no head.

Inquiry: Like seamstress' dress, not human being.

Comment: Again dehumanizes (seamstress' dummy).

CARD II

1. (8″) Looks like they're having a dance. First thought it was bears. Hand holding something together. Not a hat.

Inquiry: Clapping hands, party hats.

Comment: Again not quite human. Very active fantasy life. Frequent dancing response suggests reaction against depressive mood.

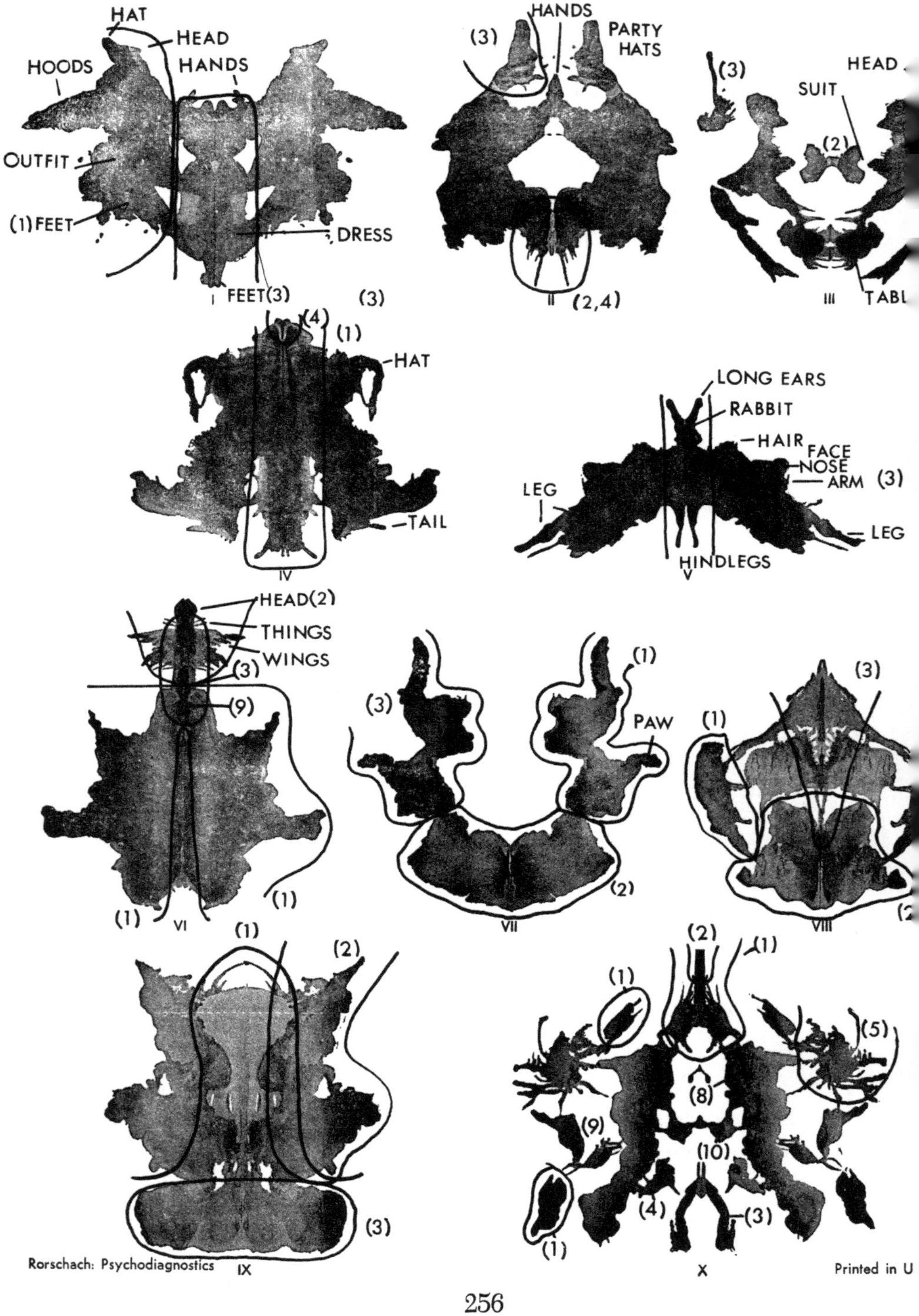
HAT
HEAD
HOODS
HANDS
OUTFIT
(1) FEET
DRESS
FEET(3)
(3)
I
HANDS
PARTY HATS
(3)
II
(2,4)
(3)
HEAD
SUIT
(2)
III
TABL
(4)
(1)
HAT
TAIL
IV
LONG EARS
RABBIT
HAIR
FACE
NOSE
ARM
(3)
LEG
LEG
HINDLEGS
V
HEAD(2)
THINGS
WINGS
(3)
(9)
(1)
(1)
VI
(1)
(3)
PAW
(2)
VII
(3)
(1)
VIII
(1)
(2)
(3)
IX
(2)
(1)
(1)
(5)
(8)
(9)
(10)
(4)
(3)
(1)
X
Rorschach: Psychodiagnostics
Printed in U

2. Could be fire. They have no heads, do they?
Inquiry: The color and the way it comes out. Has some form.

> *Comment*: Impulsively emotional (diffuse handling of color), somewhat controlled.

3. They could be little dogs. Looks like they're having a good time.
Inquiry: With fur and legs.

> *Comment*: Able to channelize need for affection (tactual fur), provided object is little.

(a) Could be firecrackers you throw on floor. Not kind that would burn house down.

> *Comment*: Inhibited aggressivity, firecrackers-sparkler.

CARD III

1. (2″) Looks like they're enjoying themselves, good time dancing around table.
Inquiry: Gentlemen dancing. (Men?) Suits, collars are white.

> *Comment*: Well-seen people, able to relate and identify (with male?). Dancing again.

2. Bow or ribbon
Inquiry: Fancy ribbon, fancy knot, some men make bows. Might be girl's bow.

> *Comment*: Sex conflict. After seeing men sees male tie but can be feminine.

3. Two men
Inquiry: Things hanging down (Why?) Shape.

> *Comment*: Back to men, helpless, hanging down (men impotent).

CARD IV

1. (26″) First reminds me of a rocket, shoot off and explode. Not like it because clouds higher up.

> *Comment*: Explosive expression of feelings and tensions.

2. This thing looks like dogs with ears leaning against whatever that is. Straw hats, tail in back.
Inquiry: Hats dwarfs wear. Dogs with quite a bit of fur standing on hind legs with hats on. (Hats?) Crazy (laughs), but do not look like men; they have tails.

Comment: Dogs seen in human fashion. Laughs at her contaminated thinking (human-like activity). Thus can accept and be creative about neurotic impulse. Sensitive and sensual (good use of Fc, fur).

3. Flower on top.

Comment: Explosion converted into passive flower—aggression becomes passivity.

CARD V

1. (1″) My god! In middle looks like rabbit ears and feet. Holding two things.
2. Looks like fox.
3. Could be like a man, an Eskimo, just lying there. Little bit shaped like human. Could be two hunters trying to catch rabbit and fell asleep; and he's right there and they do not know it.

Inquiry (1,2,3): In between two figures, hunters lying asleep, arms crossed, hair, face, nose, eyes. Rabbit holding them up, maybe just standing between.

Comment: Confused thinking, rabbit fools hunters, actually holding them up. (Nice example of "masochistic attack." "Victim" really attacks or controls persecutor.)

CARD VI

1. (8″) Looks like a rug you see in some home. Bearskin rug.

Inquiry: Looks like hair sticking out, feet sticking out.

Comment: Reveals sensitivity (good handling of Fc, hair).

2. Two little things (whiskers) Have two eyes, wings, snake.
3. Vase, but the rest do not look like flowers. First thought of butterfly but did not have faces like that. Two heads sticking out of vase with wings. Guess snakes don't have wings, must be butterflies, moth.

Comment 1,2,3: Phallic (elongated objects in usual sexual context) preoccupation associated with suspiciousness. Result: confused thinking, phobic, hysterical (snakes sticking out of vases). Again corrects such thinking. Recovery strength.

CARD VII

1. > (30″) Looks like two lions on two hind feet like in circus doing tricks.

Inquiry: Two lions dancing on hind feet.

Comment: Card involving responses to Mother gives lions rather than usual lambs, performing.

2. Butterfly

Comment: Conventional

3. Could be two dogs with long ears with little paws looking at each other. Dogs show entertaining. Can I turn it around? > V
Inquiry: Graceful with paws.

Comment: Graceful and entertaining for others.

CARD VIII

1. (7″) Omigosh! Pretty colors. These two look like some kind of animals, very pretty.
2. Beautiful stones, colored.
Inquiry: Nice shape and pink ones and orange ones.
3. Or very fancy decoration.
Inquiry: Fancy vase. Something in it that spreads out.
4. Certain lamps, hanging.
5. Butterfly
Inquiry: Shape

Comment, all: Hit by affect (color) and never does completely recover, but after giving poor and rather hysterical responses (passive sort) can be fairly creative (vase).

CARD IX

1. (26″) Reminds me of a candle or light.
Inquiry: Candle supported by base.

Comment: Handles card initially well, phallic detail (elongated object).

2. Looks like a face, not like clown's, but like you go to a masked ball. Have funny nose on and pointed hats, maybe firecrackers, just dancing around.
Inquiry: Woman in a masquerade and man. Woman has hair all up like older woman and dress. He has overcoat (confused masking sexual differences). Throw firecrackers, shooting out (holding sparklers).

Comment: Sees derogated people, ingeniously handles a sexual confusion, explosive emotionality, channelized (firecrackers to sparklers).

3. Stone holding candle.

Comment: Part of comment for 1.

CARD X

1. (10″) Beetles, nice-looking ones walking on their legs (made finger motion).
2. Vase. Looks like have fun down here.
3. See in garden green things. (What?) Pretty, not really grasshoppers because no legs. (Tomato worms?) Something in that line.

Inquiry: Don't know what putting face against.

4. These two little yellow look like French poodles.

Inquiry: Hair and thin legs.

5. Insects
6. Green leaf.
7. Leaves turned yellow in fall, brown leaves.
8. Beautiful rock stone where dance around.
9. Two little plants or animals (What?) Animals holding something in air, balancing selves.
10. Fancy bulb.

Comment: Counterphobic (beetles are nice, cute). Persevering with vases. Dancing and fun suggest contrary feeling. Good handling of affect, ability to be sociable. Compulsive (had to be asked to discontinue).

General Comments

Good recovery and some creativity. Hysterical and counterphobic features. Masculine striving and identification. Can relate well and deal with affect (sociability) but inhibited in these aspects. Considerably tense and emotional, but denies and converts into opposites. Many strengths, but loose and very idiosyncratic thinking.

TAT

CARD 1

Boy looks at his violin. His father bought it for him for his birthday; he'd always wanted to play. Dreams of becoming a great musician. Most likely gets early start and becomes professional violinist. Even if it could not turn out that way, would still be very happy because get so much fun out of it. Makes life so much richer.

Comment: Father assists son in getting success and richness from life.

CARD 2

Very young girl, probably still going to school. Lady leaning against tree could be her mother, meditating. Looks like farm country. That young man on horse could be her brother, also could be young man interested in girl. She likes him too. Looks like she's thinking about her future, day when she gets older and will get married and he will be able to take over land.

Comment: Conventional story of love and marriage.

CARD 4

Looks to me like two people in love with each other. She's trying to make him see something her way. (Problem?) Maybe their careers so different best to forget each other. (What?) She could be movie star and he working man but very nice and she loves him. Most likely come out good for both of them—because she really loves him, tells him doesn't matter about careers.

Comment: Woman a star, but willing to sacrifice career for man.

CARD 6GF

Looks like young lady. This man looks older, could be father, very good friend, or doctor giving advice. Must be suggesting something to her. (What?) Could be she's married and she shouldn't break up with husband (Why?) After people married so many years. Might be husband travels and his beautiful secretary, harmless flirtation. He advising that it's foolish to make move she would regret, could be doctor explaining to her husband only human.

Comment: Again woman understanding of man, listens to doctor's advice that husband only human (adulterous).

CARD 7

Very young girl holding doll in hands. Wonder how it would be like taking care of baby. Thus her mother . . . or . . . yes, her mother reading to girl and girl sees herself in story in future.

Comment: Girl tries to identify with mother and become a mother.

CARD 9GF

Two young girls out on ocean beach. One has magazine and towel. Other one running, looks like she's mad; this one watching her. Kinda look alike. Could be sisters. Maybe had an argument before scene, other wants to make peace. (Argument?) Maybe young one—the mad one—very much in love with boy. This one told her this boy insecure, playboy. In end, glad that friend meant well and gave good advice.

Comment: Again male insecure and unfaithful.

CARD 13MF

Very young girl, man. Must be feeling very bad, covering face. Must have loved her a lot. Either she's sleeping or he found her dead when he came home. Don't know what to do. (What happened?) Doesn't look like from illness, could be somebody broke in house, no clothes on, maybe attacked her. (Relationship?) Hard to say, wasn't her fault—nice girl, was going to get married. He discovered this scene.

Comment: Woman attacked sexually, and killed.

CARD 10

Looks like older couple. Could be husband and wife. Looks like he's comforting her. Could be she had son and he had to go to war and she feels bad and he's trying to let her see other side, wonderful things doing for country and know he will come back. Boy returns home again.

Comment: Conventional happy ending.

CARD 18GF

Looks a lot like middle age. Grieving, could be a man she's holding. Looks almost like she lost someone dear to her. That could be her mother. Don't know if person died suddenly, standing in nightgown.

Comment: Mother grieving over sudden death of daughter, sexual confusion.

General Comment

Conventional, trite fantasy life that is also colorless, cold and empty. Men are unreliable and women are victims. Only hope is tie with mother.

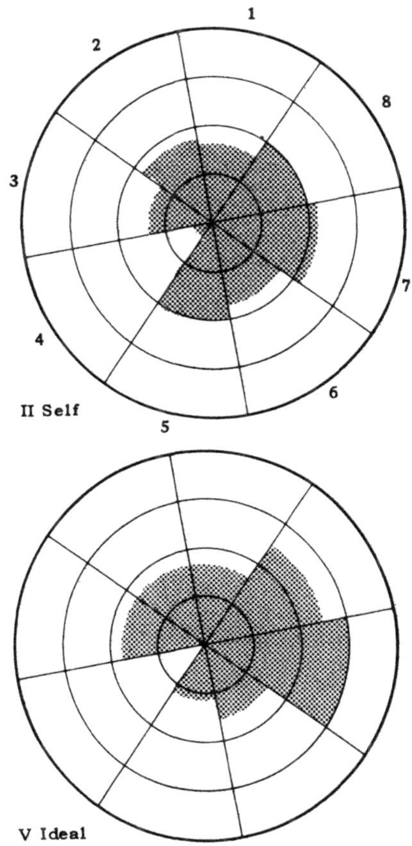

ICL

Presents self as responsible, self-sustaining person (8,7) who is overly anxious to please others (7,8,6) and is self-effacing and ingratiating in the process (5,6). She has little insight into the exaggerated and symptomatic aspects of this orientation because Ideal ICL even more exaggerated. Particularly her distrust of other people which she cannot admit even to her (4) self. Consequently, she is eager to please people even more than she thinks she does now.

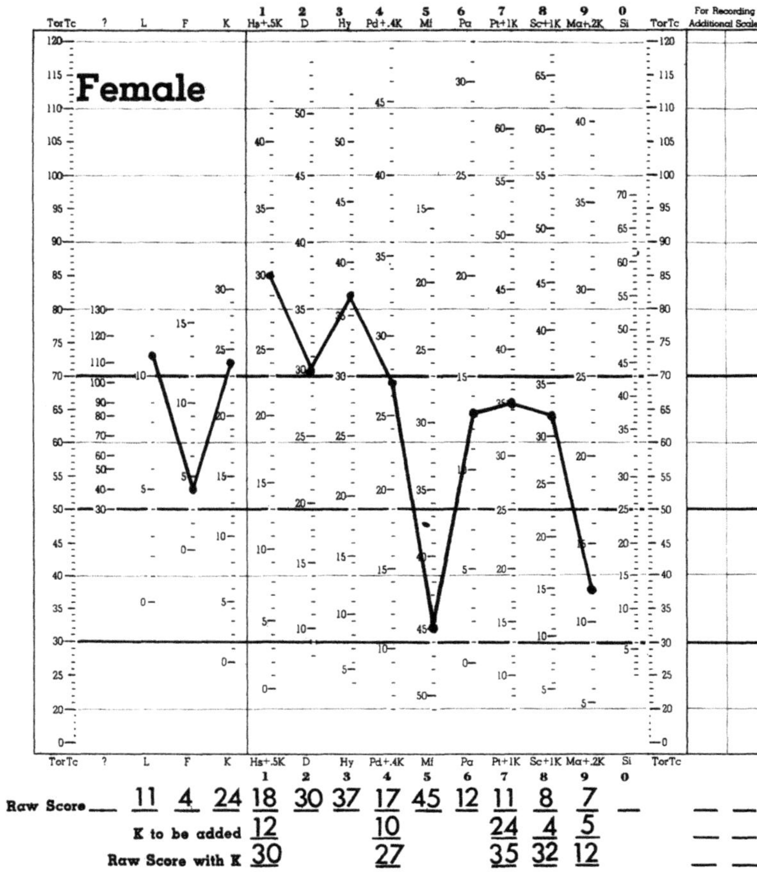

MMPI

Rigidly trying to appear in a good light (K,L) (L items: Always tell the truth, likes everyone she knows, never procrastinates, etc.)

Defensive, denying (Hs complaining, D not anxious, Hy denial). Very neurotic, definite psychosomatic (pronounced inverted V–Hs, D,Hy.) Dysphoric but not manifestly anxious (relatively lower D and yet lower Pt).

Superfeminine—possible unconscious masculine strivings (extremely low Mf, High K).

Stubborn, pessimistic (Hs, Pa)

Sense of immobility (Ma)

Impulsive, acting out (Pd)

APPENDIX 4

A CASE OF SHAKES
CHAPTER FOUR

TEST DATA
AND INTERVIEW

Diagnostic Interview

The patient began by reporting that she suffered bursitis in her right shoulder in March. It progressively worsened, making her more nervous. In the month before, she had developed pain in the small of her back "that physically handicapped me." She could not lift her baby or stand up. Seven years ago, she also had back trouble for three or four days; she had the same difficulty for several days before her marriage.

Enters new situation by listing somatic complaints possibly to convert her anxiety.

She then went on to say that she becomes very tense and shaky in certain situations, such as buying tickets. This occurred frequently, and she offered physiological causes for the shakiness, since candy alleviated it but chocolate did not. She was still waiting for a diagnosis from Dr. N.

Manages to get to psychological factors but retreats with denial.

The patient was born in a small Western mining town in the early 1920's and moved to a large western city when she was 12. Her father, "is a wonderful man and closer to me than my mother." She could always speak to him. He was very "undemonstrative," but her mother was just the opposite, nervous and upset by the least little thing. Her father was very strict, but her mother would reprimand her without reason. The patient would cry bitterly as a child when her parents went on trips; at those times, she would run away from people. She remembered that when she was seven, her brother was born, and she had to get rid of her dog because he jumped on and licked the baby. She didn't get along with her brother until he married at 26 or 28. She presumed that she was jealous of him. Her mother has always favored her brother while her father, she added, was impartial.

Jealousy of brother.

She remembered having many friends as a child, but actually her first twelve years were pretty much a blank. According to her mother, she used to fall asleep in kindergarten. Her parents were angry at her poor marks and she did not want to bring her report cards home. Her grades were poor because of a lack of interest.

First 12 years amnesic.

Her social life was terrible in high school, where she was a wallflower. She never brought home a girlfriend of whom her mother approved. She wasn't allowed to go out with boys—her first date was at graduation at 17. Mother never told patient "a blessed thing" and she resented this. Thus, when she menstruated at 14, she was completely surprised. Her periods were regular but were accompanied by cramps until after the birth of her first child.

Hostility towards mother and sexual anxieties.

She went to a Catholic college for women and intensely disliked it. She quit for a year and worked as a salesgirl and fashion model—she could not wait to get back to school. The patient then attended a Catholic college in the midwest, to be away from home and pick out her own friends. She graduated at age 23, majoring in psychology. She loved it there and became "independent despite the strictness of the sisters." There was little social life but she did begin to date. After graduation, she obtained a clerical job with a bank for several months. The patient came down with rheumatic fever one half year later, and was hospitalized for three weeks and in bed for six months. She got up gradually and has had no physical restrictions since. However, her physician told her not to return to work, which involved pressure. Consequently, for six months she attended graduate school in philosophical studies. She then worked for her father as a secretary, which she loved, until she married in 1948.

Gets sick soon after she begins working.

At 26, she met her husband on a blind date. She could not stand him at first but went out with him again on the suggestion of a mutual girlfriend. They knew each other for a year before they married. She claimed that she has a very happy marriage. Her husband, a vice president of a large company, has a very demanding job and is very conscientious. He is away from home a great deal because of long hours and occasional travel. She was petrified when she met his boss. She has fights and arguments with husband. The marital (sexual) relations are poor and that bothers *him*. She felt that she is too tired because of all the housework. This was not the case before they had children. Her husband had a heart attack nine years ago and was hospitalized for eight weeks. He had been in the navy. He had to give up sex for several months, and was retired from the service. He is 41 now. At the same time he suffered the attack, she discovered that she was pregnant. He must keep away from excessive physical strain but has no other restrictions. (Patient's sequence of events.)

Displaces sexual difficulties onto husband.

Both she and her husband were happy about the pregnancy. The daughter was born eight years ago and the second girl four years ago. They are not planning to have any more children. The first child is quite intelligent and quite a problem—the patient can't handle her or reason with her because she out reasons everybody and is "too smart for her own good." She still has "accidents" (bowel movements), and had one in school last month when the patient was in the hospital having her teeth removed. The patient was upset about this. Her husband and she agreed on the procedure of raising their children. The younger child so far so good but she tends to have a temper.

Can't handle children.

The patient's mother lives five minutes away. (When questioned if this was a coincidence, she immediately answered no.) The patient wishes she lived further away—she sees her mother once a week but talks to her on the phone all the time. Her mother gets her mad, the patient resents her mother never babysitting, but still spoiling the older child. The patient can't win out over mother.

Since the patient frequently thrust her left ear forward, she was questioned as to whether she had a hearing difficulty. She answered that she has been conscious of this but so far no organic problem has been found.

Mother's influence reigns on.

Psychological Tests

DAP

Drawing I

Happy person. Happy normal person about 17 or 18. Average intelligence. Average looks but attractive.

Drawing II

Age about 20. Intelligent, happy, normal, nice looking. Goes to school. Very nice guy.

General Comments

Very childlike, immature drawings (lack of detail, general impression). Superficially outgoing and frank in dealing with people (front view). However, basically suspicious (large ears), with repressed hostility (teeth, spread fingers). Tendency for exhibitionism (no clothes). Poor sexual differentiation (only gross distinction is hair on female, both figures have broad shoulders and flare hips).

RORSCHACH

Card I

1. (3″) A bat (turned card over). (Else?)
Inquiry: (Whole with detail)

Comment: Conventional first approach to situations.

2. Just a big blob. Looks like a woman, a witch.
Inquiry: Woman with hands up above head, buckle at waist. (Old?) Her figure, beady eyes and pointed nose.

Comment: Well-seen human. Immediately alert to witches, fearful of women.

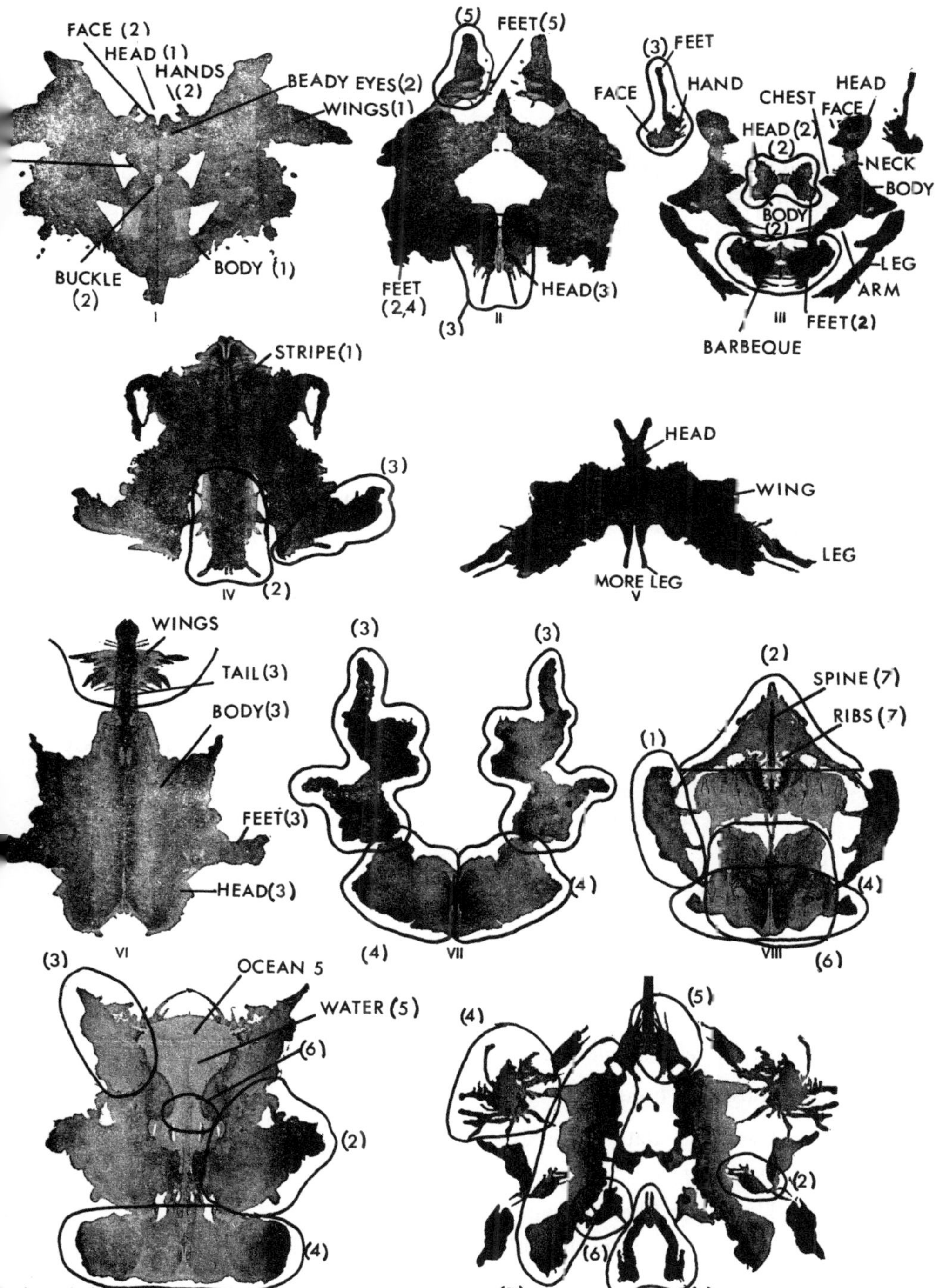

ach: Psychodiagnostics

Printed in U. S. A.

Card II

1. (4″) Well, Blood.
Inquiry: All red.
2. Dogs
Inquiry: (all black) Head, feet, tails.
3. Spider.
Inquiry: Think of tarantula, great big thing.
4. Also couple of elephants
Inquiry: With trunks. Baby elephants. (Why?) Little.
5. Caterpillars. May I turn this anyway I want? > ∨ That's all.

Comment (1-5): Hysterical (blood, color), phobic, smothering mother (tarantula), immature child-like fantasies. Phallic preoccupation in an emotional context (elongated caterpillars).

Card III

1. (2″) Two people leaning over a barbecue. Reminds me of places, outdoors.
Inquiry: Reminds me of ourselves in these places. (Who?) Me and husband, just guessed, could be either.

Comment: Able to relate well to people but exceedingly egocentric—no sexual differentiation.

2. Dog
Inquiry: French poodle (Why?) Looks like all hair shaved off body, rest of it fuzzy.

Comment: Sensitive, masochistic, strips potency away.

3. Angels
Inquiry: Head, body, arms, feet.

Comment: Childlike, magical fantasy.

4. > Beach at (an island). See the driftwood.

Comment: Self-referent need-press finally results in poor judgment. Has to refer to self even if inappropriate—probably does so socially.

5. Bones, dog bones

Comment: Rather morbid.

Card IV

1. (3″) Looks like bearskin rug.
Inquiry: Head standing out. Fur on either side of spine. (Why?) Looks soft.

Comment: Sensitive, able to control needs for affection (good use of Fc).

2. A cow

Inquiry: Just head, eyes, horns.

Comment: Rather than the frequent aggressive response here, hers is phlegmatic.

3. > Lambs

Inquiry: Fleecy fur (excellently seen).

4. Part of it looks like bearskin, part like tiger-skin throw rug.

Inquiry: Because of stripes going this way (horizontal stripes at top).

Comment (3 and 4): Sensitive, even sensual, but displays tact and some aggression (good use of Fc, very tactual, bear aggressive animal).

CARD V

1. (5″) Looks like bat again. Looks like one I saw before. Just looks like bat.

Comment: Conventional

CARD VI

1. (7″) What are those big bugs that fly over swimming pools?

Comment: phobic in possible sex context (i.e., responses often given to this card). Self-referent.

2. Remind me of swimming pool

Inquiry: Don't see swimming pool, just associating to bug.

Comment: Again self-referent, resulting in loose judgment (very poor judgment).

3. ∨ Dogs >

Comment: Same as for 2. Preoccupation with dogs. Very poor (form not sharply defined).

CARD VII

1. (½″) Clouds.

Inquiry: Whole seems fleecy white

Comment: Bids fairly strongly for affection (tactual quality very strong).

2. Sky

Inquiry: All around it. (White Space)

Comment: Diffuse and poor.

3. Seem to have dogs on the brain.
4. Scotties.

Comment (3,4): Again dogs in possible maternal context (childhood and "mother" responses often given to this card).

CARD VIII

(5″) Color!

1. (12″) Mountain Lion.

Inquiry: Climbing up

Comment: Impulsive (color exclamation) and aggressive (lion and climbing).

2. Mountains
3. Water

Inquiry: Color, shape, and ripples.

Comment 2,3: Handles fairly well with some tension (inanimate motion).

4. Sun

Inquiry: The color, orange.

Comment: Rather overwhelmed by emotional stimulation (form almost inundated by color affect).

5. Trees
6. Lava

Inquiry: Along with red (patient made reference to her island home).

Comment: Lava may connote anal concern–semiliquid expulsion.

7. Spine

Inquiry: Lines down center, ribs going off.

Comment 6,7: After much impulsivity and self-reference, last ditch resort to anatomy (again anal implication because back anatomy).

CARD IX

1. (6″) Rainbow color.

Inquiry: Colors remind me of rainbow because could almost be an arc.

Comment: Passive response to emotional stimulation.

2. Ocean.

Inquiry: The color.

Comment: Poorly controlled impulsivity, but characteristically passive.

3. Portugese man o' war.
Inquiry: Shape, looks like little jelly things.

Comment: Self-concept?

4. Coral.
Inquiry: Color and shape

Comment: Better handling somewhat, can be sociable (more mature emotionally). (Affect-color defined by form-reality considerations.)

5. > Swimming.
Inquiry: Because see ocean and water.

Comment: Impulsive (lack of form and planning) but handles.

6. > Fish
Inquiry: (Very good inner area).

Comment: Recovers with well-seen concept.

CARD X

1. (7″) Can't think of correct word but in museum you see butterflies in box—all kinds.
Inquiry: Patterns and colors.
2. Caterpillars.
3. Deer.
4. Crab.
5. Lobster.
6. Shell.
7. Coral reef.

Comment for all: Impulsive but reasonably well-handled. Good use of affect and productive with emotional stimulation (utilization of color).

Association to dogs: Used to have dogs but couldn't bring home. They had a boxer for 4½ years before baby was born. When the child was going on three, they gave the dog away because it was jealous of baby.

Association to pool: Once I imagined I saw the skeleton of a fish in my swimming pool, got scared. Also I'm self-conscious of my figure in a bathing suit. Now I swim in my husband's boss' pool.

Association to island: In the Carribean for three years—too long, no enough to do. Do not care for armed service people. Pretty boring, got homesick.

General Comments

Hysterical, very impulsive and phobic. Resorts to anatomy when denial fails—this often results in poor judgment. Denies aggression and handles emotions phlegmatically. She is self-referent and egocentric, but has ability to relate and to be sociable. Very sensitive and striving for affection, at times successfully. Masochistic, childish, with magical notions.

TAT

CARD 1

Little boy is taking violin lessons and is very unhappy at idea, does not want to. Has to practice and is sitting with idea in mind—"Do I have to practice?" I can remember mother telling me her father made her stand in corner and practice despite tears running down from her eyes. I think the child is going to practice to please *her* parents but not because he wants to. I don't think he gives a damn whether he becomes a violinist or not. Looks like someone of years ago that would probably be 60 or so now.

Comment: Self-referent. Child must conform to parents even if miserable. Her mother was forced to do so by patient's grandfather.

CARD 2

This is a farm and a young girl is about to go off to school. Her mother is standing by the tree by herself. Daughter looks like a little bit worried and would like to talk to her. Mother looks completely selfish, interested in her own problems, period! Man represents hard work. Believe daughter appreciates it—don't think mother does. Father doing it for farm. (Outcome?) Cause see myself here and I know what girl would like—stand on own two feet and make her own decisions rather than be criticized and doubts put into her. Mother represents my mother, father my father who works hard for all of us. Don't know outcome.

Comment: Self-referent. Mother completely selfish. Only daughter appreciates hard-working father. Daughter yearns for independence, ability to stand on own two feet.

CARD 7GF

Well, this looks like a mother trying . . . don't think child particularly cares about dolls, mother trying to make child like dolls: see how cute they are, how she loved them, and how she should love them. Girl turning away wishing she could do what she wants to do. I think this is the only way mother thinks she can be closer to child temporarily. Also mother got book in her hands so after she interests child in dolls, she can go back to her book. Child looks lonely like she does not have playmates, very sad. Incidentally, this woman looks very much like my mother used to look. Little girl dressed well.

Comment: Self-referent. Mother attempts to make daughter assume her wish fulfillment as a way of getting closer, but also wants to get back to own interests. Daughter very lonely.

Card 4

This looks like Ava Gardner and Clark Gable. Reminds me of movies that I have seen. Very dramatic, very emotional. Maybe people of not highest morals because of calendar tacked on wall back of man. (What is going on?) This man is about to give in in disgust because he has heard something from his wife. I said disgust, I meant hurt. Woman looks like begging to be forgiven. (What has he heard?) That she was engaged once before and should have married man she was engaged to before she met him. Here I go dragging family in. She looks like she is trying to get him to stay for her good, trying to make amends and I don't think she has hurt just him. (Family?) My mother had been engaged before she met my father and one night she got mad at father and started making remarks at dinner table—said in front of children. Hurt me for her to say that after so many years of marriage. Found out one of mother's diamond rings is one this fellow gave her. *She* never did any begging or pleading. Think she should have. She has wrong values in life.

Comment: Self-referent. Her mother throws up to her children that she does not love their father but someone else. She hurt father before children but didn't beg forgiveness.

Card 6GF

This is definitely my mother and father at home. My mother wants something, to keep up with Mrs. Jones. Father trying to tell her there is something like money. She's a person who just won't face realities of situation. I think man getting absolutely no place with her. She's just a selfish person.

Comment: Self-referent. Mother does not face realities of life. Father cannot get any place with her selfish, childish views.

CARD 7

All of them seem mother and daughter to me. Have you done this purposely? (Laughs) Think daughter trying to escape mother's clutches and influence on her. I'm telling you about (her own first name). Seems mother trying to interfere with her all of the time and make her feel guilty. (The patient told her mother about MMPI, and she said, "I hope you answer it intelligently.") Mother never told people I had teeth pulled, all except lower six. I have told everybody. When my parents found out I was pregnant, mother gave impression something wrong about sex, and daughter had nothing to do with it and same with her son. Wish I could tell her to go jump in the lake.

Comment: Self-referent. Her mother is constantly critical and makes her feel guilty. Her mother even thought her pregnancy was wrong.

CARD 10

Mother and father. Shows great love for one another. Way I would like to see my mother and father. Woman looks like extra thoughtful and would do anything for husband, for whole family. Would be mostly willing to sacrifice things without making big show of fact.

Comment: Self-referent. Wish for affection between parents and mother to be more meaningfully maternal. Herself too?

CARD 13MF

Leaves me kind of cold. Like a woman sound asleep in bed. Man comes home tired and he's gonna go to bed.

Comment: Denial of sex or aggression, not explicitly but implicitly.

CARD 18GF

If this is supposed to be another woman or a man or child . . . I'll imagine it's a child and mother leaning over listening to her daughter. Reminds me of myself in place of mother. I'm so worried that I'll turn out having so little understanding like my mother with me. So conscious of it, that I try so hard; it gets the better of me, I have screaming meemies and yell at my child. Should be closeness between mother and daughter.

Comment: Self-referent. She is afraid of duplicating mother's lack of understanding and aggression towards daughter, and is leaning over backwards to avoid ending up the same.

General Comments

Extremely self-referent. Mother selfish, controlling, childish, and unreasonable. The patient would like to declare her independence of her mother but can't. Father just a poor victim. The patient indicated that, in this interraction with her mother, there is a very gratifying, if neurotic, relationship. Conscious of imitating her mother but completely unconscious of her identification with her father. Denial of overt sex and aggression other than in verbal expression.

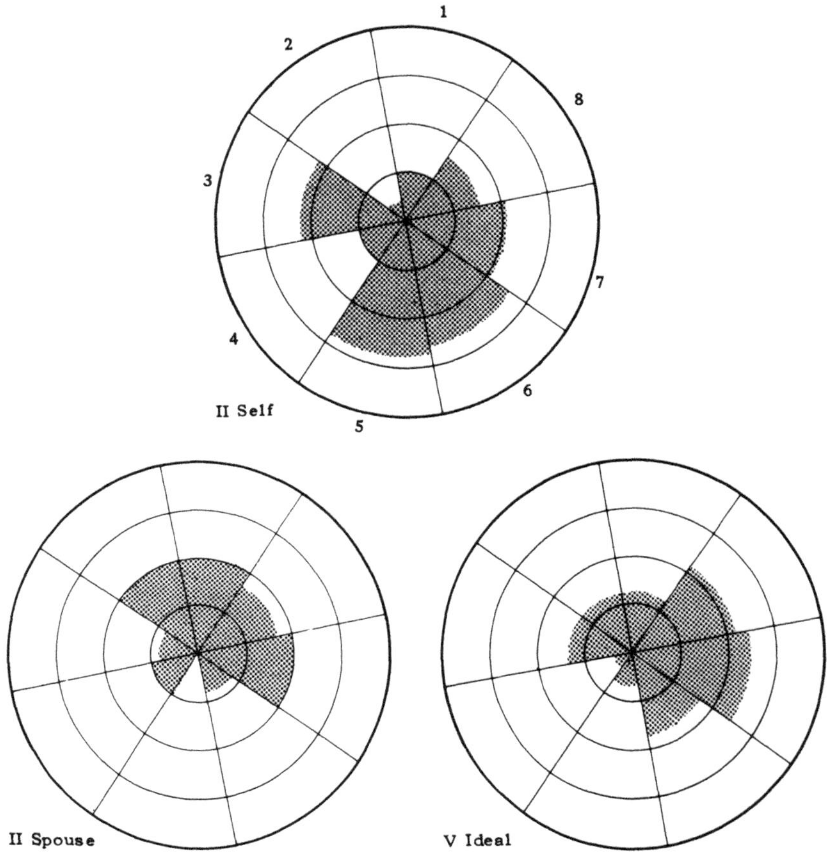

ICL

Presents self as extremely masochistic, self-punishing, doormat, spineless and passive (5). This makes her feel helpless anxious, phobic and indecisive (6). But she also tends to be sarcastic and impatient with others (3). She would like to be more forceful, dominant (Ideal, 1,2,8), assertive rather than hostile and would hope to accomplish this by being so cooperative, friendly and colorless that everybody will love her and vice-versa. (7, Ideal)

Husband seen as dominant, forceful (1,2) and, with reservation, aggressive (Items in 3). A competitor pushing his own interests but friendly notwithstanding (7). She sees her husband much as *she* would like to be, except she would rather be less aggressive and selfish (more "feminine").

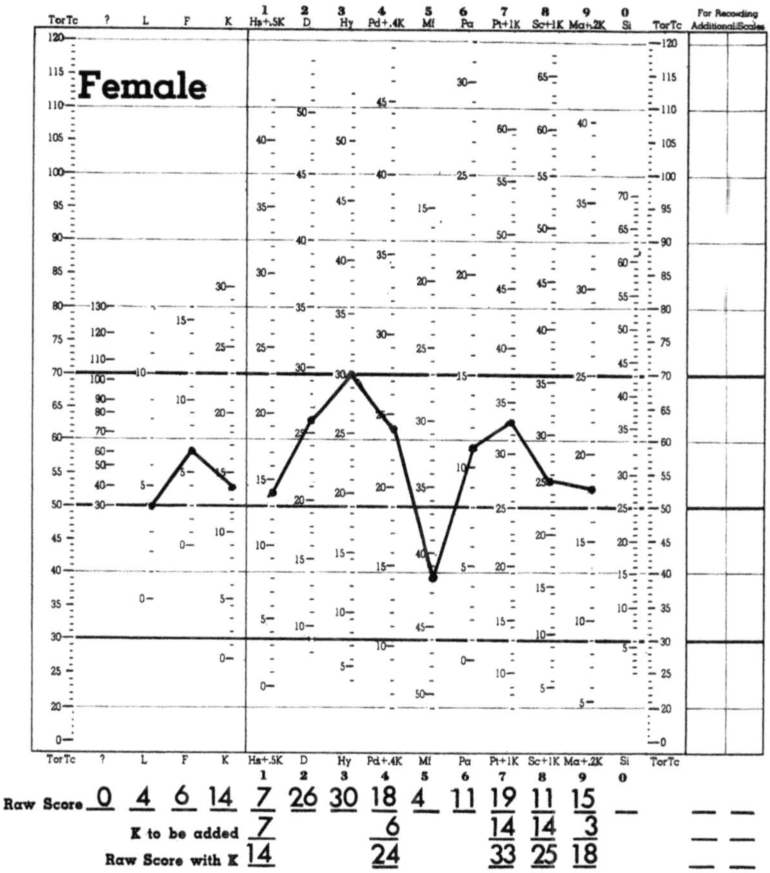

MMPI

Pathology not severe (profile within normal limits.)

Hysterical pronounced (peak—Hy at 70)

Anxious and tense (D,Hy,Hs,Pt) (All above 60)

Impulsive (Pd at 63)

Helpless and ultra feminine (Low K, Low Mf)

Masochistic orientation (Pd,Mf,K)

(Mf—"see how feminine," K—"see how helpless," and Pd—"I'm rather alone and alienated from family.")

APPENDIX 5

DYSPHORIA
CHAPTER FIVE

TEST DATA
AND INTERVIEW

Diagnostic Interview

The patient, a 20-year-old clerk, initiated the interview by rambling from talk of her overweight, depression, and somatic symptoms to various memories and complaints about her family. Currently, she said she is 5′ 7″ and weighs 188, and would like to weigh about 140. She has had a weight problem since she was 13. Three months ago she had an ulcer and put on 18 pounds because of the starchy foods given to her. Three months ago, she noted black and bloody stools and was hospitalized for 15 days. There was no further bleeding and not enough pain to disturb her. However, she stayed home for nine weeks until it cleared up. She did not know location or nature of ulcer. She was a little worried, but not much, and took it in stride—and had a good rest from work.

Somatic stress. Ulcer with indifference.

She was born in New York in the late 1930's. Her parents were divorced when she was nine because her father was an alcoholic (although this was hidden from the children). The patient was hurt and surprised when she learned of this, although she guessed she had some idea of his drinking. Her father who was a truck driver, was not home much, but when he was she would sit on his lap. "Funny how I cling to memories of him while I never saw much of him." She could express love to her father, but not to her mother and sister.

She said her mother was a very remarkable woman, very proper and straitlaced but in some ways lenient. She could never talk to her as her sister could, their mother favored the sister, and so on. However, in retrospect she could appreciate little gestures of affection from mother and knew her mother loved her. But as a child, when her mother would hug and kiss her, the patient would push her away and realize this hurt her mother.

> Identified more with father. Sense of alienation from family. Ambivalent attitude toward mother.

Her sister, who is three years older and more serious (the patient said), studies and does not date often. The patient said she, herself, took things more lightly. Her sister was not broadminded and ranted and raved when the patient came home late from dates. They never got along well, always fought, and still do. Although she disliked this sister immensely, the patient would do things for her because they were sisters.

> Intense rivalry with sister.

Her sister, a divorcee with two children, is at home and not working. The patient contributes about $40 a month and shares a room with her sister's 13-month-old son.

When the patient's parents were divorced, her mother sent the daughters to school while she worked at night, and the children saw little of her. The patient would start off well in school and then "louse" it up. When younger, she stuttered in class; the other children laughed, so she was frightened of speaking in class. She became more and more reserved and let people consider her stupid; she stopped trying.

> It pays to clam up and be dumb.

She was a grade behind while her sister skipped. She was not popular with both boys or girls, but she has dated frequently since she was 14. She barely made it in high school, finding it difficult to study both there and in parochial school. She graduated from school at 18.

> Not very popular but dates frequently.

After graduation, she worked as a clerk for an insurance company. She did not like this work and has not been successful, getting transferred from one position to another. She explained that her failure was due to her nervousness, transposing numbers, and inability to spell. However, she has been with the company three years and has been at the same job for 1½ years although her salary is still minimal.

Vocational adjustment, like her social, is marginal although she has been stable on job.

The patient dates a great deal. About a year ago she was engaged for six months to a serviceman she met at the U.S.O. He had to go to sea several times during the courtship, and two months ago he asked for his ring back because he wanted to go to college. She was hurt so she decided to have a ball, not caring about anything. She went steady with another fellow. One night after drinking, they drove to a remote area and spread a blanket on the ground. She passed out and woke the next morning. She saw him put her pants in his glove compartment, and the back of her dress was all covered with blood. Her sister questioned her about this but she remembered nothing but screaming and passing out. Before this, she used to be a "proud virgin," but then her morals changed and she became more intimate with "fellers"—she thought she could keep them this way.

Rationalizes her free expression of impulses by her sense of victimization. Frank and rapid reporting of sexual experiences suggest her rebellious orientation.

She never believed that other men loved her so she chased them away. She said that she went for the above man because he "took something from me that no other man has taken." She does not love or know what it is to love because her parents never showed any love to her.

Sense of alienation and defiance mixed.

Her sister thinks that she is wild and has a chip on her shoulder. Her mother doesn't know, because it would hurt her; the patient respects and has deep feelings for her mother even if she doesn't love her.

Again ambivalence towards mother.

MEDICAL HISTORY

The patient has had no serious illnesses, but has had many accidents. A truck ran over her foot once, and she has sprained her back and ankle on separate occasions which prevented her from going to graduation and senior prom respectively. (Questioned about possible connection, she laughed.) She said she suffered from constipation and used to have cramps when she first menstruated. She is still irregular, she said, but has no pains. When she said she wore glasses only for close reading, the ptosis of her left eyelid was pointed out but she had never noticed it. When upset, she reported she has an urge for sweets and goes "haywire."

Suggested somatic expression of psychological needs. Craving for sweets a craving for love?

DREAM

She dreamed of her girlfriends doing "crazy" things.

IDIOSYNCRACIES

She said she hated stuffy rooms, confining crowds, and small rooms. She reported she alternated between sloppiness and compulsive neatness, but she did like things to be in their place. She said that when not eating, she smoked a pack of cigarettes a day and also drinks. After evening adult education (typing) classes twice a week, she has been accustomed to three or four drinks, and on week-ends enough to get tight—between five and ten drinks.

Orality expressed in drinking as well as eating (also expresses defiance).

On her second visit, the patient complained of grinding her teeth at night. She said she did not have a "split personality" but felt two different ways: (1) happy and good looking, or (2) mean and moody. She said she was fighting over which one would come out. Therefore, she said, she daydreams a great deal of doing well.

Although only figuratively "split," her alienation, orality, marginal adjustment, and daydreaming suggest schizoid features.

Psychological Tests

DAP

She balked at first, then began to sketch, but got discouraged. Began a sketch of a stick figure but again got discouraged. Needed much encouragement. After two starts on male figure, drew female head, scratched out. Was concerned that examiner would keep drawings. Manifested considerable hostility at promptings.

Drawing IV

(Female) Looks like silly picture. (Why?) Girl in olden days, wear those hoop skirts. If person who drew was a good artist, might make her pretty good figure, very popular person, Age 22-23, average IQ. She has her moods. Sometimes can be nice, sometimes mean. Takes things lightly.

Drawing VIII

(Male) If artist good one—looks like funny man. Lot of jokes, lot of fun. Not good looking but nice. Average IQ, average looks. just average fellow.

General Comments

She is extremely anxious, evasive and resistive, but finally manages to conform. Figures are well conceived (no bizarreness). Childish and dependent (general impression, pockets, buttons). After initial resistiveness and evasion, she will deal openly but remain suspicious (test behavior, stick figures [rebellious], front view [open approach], large ears [suspicious]). Marked sense of inability in coping with environment or standing on own two feet (no hands, no feet). Superficially good discrimination between sexes, but female is seen as more powerful (associations to girl as good figure, popular, pretty—ideal?). Shift from friendly to mean, old-fashioned. The male is nice but funny. Hysterical flavor (female larger, childlike, Victorian, narcissistic).

RORSCHACH

Card I

1. (35″) Could be a butterfly or bat. Supposed to see more than one? That's all.

Inquiry: Little eyes, little feelers, wings, tail, body.

Comment: Cautious, conventional, counterphobic (minimizes size of bat concept).

Card II

1. Hm! (33″) Looks like inside of somebody. Like they have some kind of disease.

Inquiry: Red through here could be disease. Intestines of some sort. (Disease?) Maybe, looks like some kind of cancer, like eaten away (red blotches).

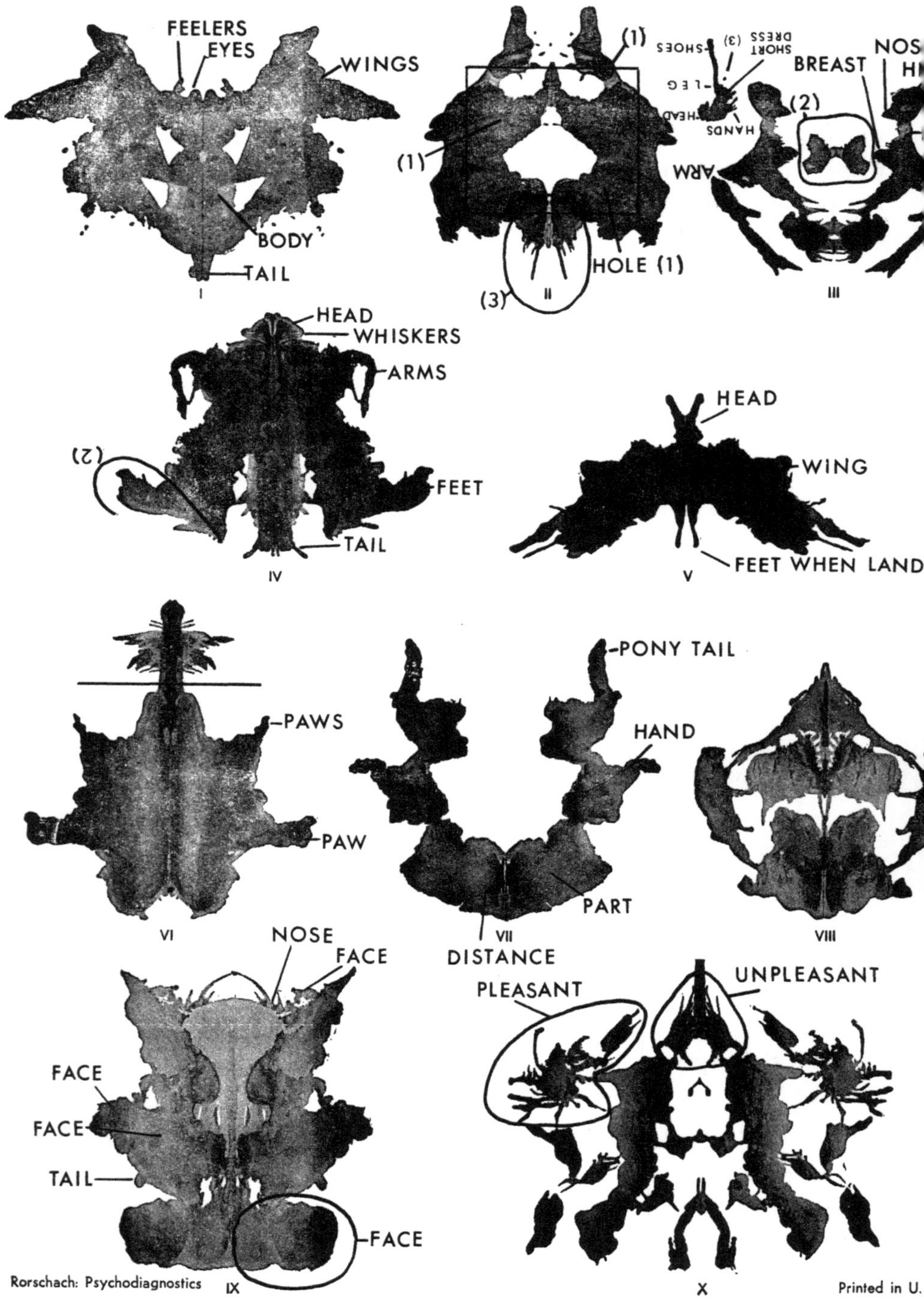
FEELERS
EYES
WINGS
BODY
TAIL
I
(1)
(1)
HOLE (1)
(3)
II
SHOES
SHORT DRESS (3)
LEG
HEAD
HANDS
ARM
BREAST
(2)
III
HEAD
WHISKERS
ARMS
(2)
FEET
TAIL
IV
HEAD
WING
FEET WHEN LAND
V
PAWS
PAW
VI
PONY TAIL
HAND
PART
VII
DISTANCE
VIII
NOSE
FACE
FACE
FACE
TAIL
FACE
IX
PLEASANT
UNPLEASANT
X
Rorschach: Psychodiagnostics
Printed in U.

Comment: Very responsive to emotional (color) stimulus, uncontrolled, symbolic of death.

2. Then on sides looks like maybe mad kind of painting, showing of death.
Inquiry: < (Cut off sides of black areas) Looks like painter trying to suggest death. (Why?) Grayish and shades look gloomy.

Comment: Looks at situations unusually (rare area) and morbidly.

3. There's my butterfly again.
Inquiry: Wings, little body. (Why?) How wings come down and color of it.

Comment: Recovers and handles emotion well and conventionally but counterphobic (again makes little).

CARD III

1. (5″) Looks like two women. That sounds funny if I say that. (Why?) Looks like going to play game like Ouija or tell fortune. Then looks like two people arguing.
Inquiry: (Ouija?) Table, sitting, like stern hands on table. (Stern?) Faces—like no expression, like mad, no feeling.

Comment: Well-conceived interpersonal (IP) relations, but tremendous projection (strong feelings with little explanation) and sensitivity, arguing, sternness, magic.

2. There's my butterfly again. They (people) both look mad.

Comment: Recovers conventionally.

3. May I turn it around? ∨ Two Ballet dancers.
Inquiry: Head, middle of step, hand behind legs, short dress, ballet shoe on toes.

Comment: Highly creative, oppositional (upside down concept), IP, woman.

4. ∨ Then looks like two women are mad, not talking to each other, turned their backs.
Inquiry: (Rare) Arm up, look mad. Impression of modern painting and interpretation so not all parts of body.

Comment: Tremendous need pressure turns her to another concept of women, mad, backs to each other (mother and her, sister and mother?).

CARD IV

1. This looks gruesome! (30″) Looks like a big monster going to come after you and get you.
Inquiry: (Why?) Head, whiskers, big body, arms, big old legs, big feet, and tail.

Comment: Phobic, fear big bad monsters.

2. ∨ First impression I get when turned it around is a mountain. Very unusual shaped mountain like those that hang from cave.

Comment: Runs to nature but phallic emphasis (elongated and hanging).

CARD V

1. (2″) This is my bird, something flying away again.

Comment: Conventional

CARD VI

1. ∨ (25″) Looks like a bear rug. < >
Inquiry: Skin 'em, paws, see no head on 'em. (Why?) How it skins jagged.

Comment: Conventional but castrating (skins, takes head off and in a frequently seen sexual area).

CARD VII

1. (5″) Those two women again. They keep popping up. Look like friendly now but still that distance, somethng between them. Either one can't get close. ∨ >
Inquiry: Pony tail, bangs, little pug nose, mouth, little hands. (Friendly?) Their features do not look so stern. (Distance?) This is here (bottom), part in there. Something between *us*, between them.

Comment: "Those two women popping up again." Excellent concept, extremely sensitive to woman. Friendly but distant—"between us, I mean them."

CARD VIII

1. Instead of two people, I see two people after each other, like trying to trap each other on a hunt. ∨ Either way I look at it, looks like still there and something dreadful is going to happen. They were once friendly though, pleasant.
Inquiry: Like trying to hunt each other going around mountain, on

top of mountain. (What?) Could be panthers or little mice. (Which?) One looks like mouse, one looks like panther. (Why dreadful?) Coloring strikes me that way (Why?) Gray not pleasant. (Once friendly?) Color back here (orange), going away from that.

> *Comment*: Aggressive, hunter and hunted. Phobic "dreadful" context, responding to emotion once friendly, now hostile.

CARD IX

1. Hm! ∨ ∧ (75″) Now looks like < two animals or individuals but more than one this time. Could be on friendly terms but could change. About four of them. (Turns card completely around). Looks like they're playing together! Yeah! ◎ Really having a good time. Having great happiness.

Inquiry: Animal or individual. Modern painting so can't distinguish. Looks like face of lion, then big and fat and tail. Very mean faces on these. This face (pink). Oh, looks like two little children. (Friendly?) Color of it.

> *Comment*: Responsive again to emotions (color). Sensitivity to people. Tries to make pleasant but cannot get away from "meanness." Highly autistic, rationalized.

CARD X

1. ∨ (25″) This looks like, won't say a big mess, I won't say that, but looks like a lot of people all doing something, all going someplace, real busy. Some are angry, fighting. Some are working together. (Turns card completely around)

Inquiry: (Mess?) All different colors together, doing something, running into each other. Don't really describe, looks like world a big mess, everybody doing something, or wish they could and can't, and everybody getting into way. Friendly people and unpleasant. All types of persons like two individuals everybody keeps from, like boss like there always is, but people around don't care because realize have to be someone over you, laws, and so forth. (Boss?) pink, vague (unpleasant?) Top. (Pleasant?) (Usual crab and grasshopper) Help each other.

> *Comment*: Again very emotional response, "big mess," tension. People running into each other, some helping, all resigned to "bosses," world a big mess, everybody doing something or wish they could and can't.

General Comments

Considerable creative imagination and active fantasy life. But also very autistic, extremely ruled by emotions and acutely sensitive to women. People argue, fight, compete, and run into each other. Morbid preoccupation with disease, death, and frightening concepts (big bad monsters.) Very pathological, but has ability to see world and people well, can be conventional when she wants to be.

TAT

CARD 1

Looks like little boy who wants to play violin, he's deciding. One day he's going to be a great musician. Going to have a lot of difficulties, maybe won't recognize his music right away but he'll make it. May write music. Right now looks sad. Doctor! I'm not in a good mood to tell stories about boys. Sometimes I can let my imagination run away. Maybe just finished a lesson, pouting about it, wants to play and has to study violin.

Comment: Ambitious despite difficulties. Mood sad. Patient became resistive. Pouting although conforming.

CARD 2

On a farm, girl's not very happy. Mother is very stern. There's a man in field who's working. Maybe girl and man are lovers. She's going to school or coming home. She's a very pretty girl, quiet, very intelligent. Man is goodlooking, big, tall. Could be very great love story. (Mother stern?) She's watching over her little girl.

Comment: Again heroine not happy. Mother is stern and watching over little girl. Desire to be pretty and intelligent.

CARD 3BM

A woman's crying. She's been hurt very deeply. Nobody around because that's how she wants it. (Hurt?) Troubles, something didn't go right or love affair wasn't good to her, maybe broke off with boyfriend. (Outcome?) She'll remember this day but live with it, keep on living. It clears up and she'll have more hurt.

Comment: Woman crying and hurt deeply by man in love affair. Gets over it but will be hurt again.

CARD 4

Like man and woman quarreling. They're lovers, could be big situation. Woman trying to explain to him how it is and how it could be, but he does not understand. But they will make up. (Quarrel?) Maybe she wants to get married and he does not. Maybe they had an affair and he's telling her it's over. Or maybe he could be one of those men who's here today and then gone, a traveling man, salesman. But he loves her. She'll never forget him.

> *Comment*: Again lovers quarreling. Man does not want to get married, he's leaving her after affair. One of those men here today and gone tomorrow but she loves him, and he her.

Card 6GF

Looks like story of a woman's home, doing something. Husband comes home and scares her, "Well, hi!" Like average home, happy. Not lovers, married, they have one child. Expression on her face startled, like he said, "Boo!"

> *Comment*: Distance from feelings, relative to people (possible father-daughter card). Husband, not lover, who just playfully startles wife. Have one child.

Card 8BM

This could be a plot of a good story. Boy has bad father and father has run away from law. Has a bullet in him, trying to get it out. Same old thing, maybe wife ran out on him, or he on her, or maybe she died. But he thinks a lot of father and will stick with him, good boy. (How shot?) Maybe running away, law shot him. (Outcome?) Father later realizes best for boy to go in good home and cops caught him. Everything turns out all right.

> *Comment*: Again distance. Father is lawbreaker; wife runs out on him or dies. Child still thinks a lot of father and will stick by him. Son put in good home by father who gets caught.

Card 10

Could be two people who just met and dancing, and he whispers sweet nothings into her ear. There again another love story. But he does not stick with her very long. Just passing fancy.

> *Comment*: Love story, but again man does not stick with her long. "Just passing fancy" for him.

Card 12

Well, she could be sleeping, she could be dead. Looks like he's going to call her or maybe wake her from sleep. Can't say much. (What else?) Maybe he's just waking her up, her father, could be his little girl, waking her up for dinner. (Relationship?) Oh, just fine.

Comment: Girl dead, changed to father waking up little girl for dinner.

CARD 13MF

What would happen if I could not think of a story. (Why?) Like now (Try!) Could be two, married couple. He wants to make love to her, and she refuses. Or be lovers just met. *He got it from her,* found out real nice girl, and now he's ashamed. (Outcome?) (long pause) Does not turn out very good. They weren't meant to be.

Comment: In sex-aggressive situation becomes facetiously resistive. Married couple—she refuses lovemaking. Or lovers just met—"he got it from her" that is, intercourse. Found out she's a nice girl. He's ashamed but it was not meant to be for them.

CARD 18GF

Mother and son and he's trying to explain boy something. Like he's trying to do something wrong, and he won't listen. Still goes out and does what he wants, but realizes at end she's right. Had to do it, find out for self. (What?) Could've gone out with wrong kind of girl, or business deal, like buying factory. If he weighed it, would not make mistake but has to go ahead. (Confused story and pronouns are verbatim.)

Comment: Mother and son—instead of two women. Son wants to do something wrong and won't listen, too stubborn; goes with wrong kind of girl, or business deal. But he has to go ahead and find out for self.

General Comments

The patient's mood was sad, with a sense of being taken advantage of, rejected, and deserted. Woman (child or lover) just passing fancy of men who love and leave her while she pines for them. Mother always stern or scolding, Father no good but child sticks by him (confusion among lovers, husbands, and fathers). Child wrong, stubborn, and must do things for self to find out. Few, if any, loving or meaningful relationships.

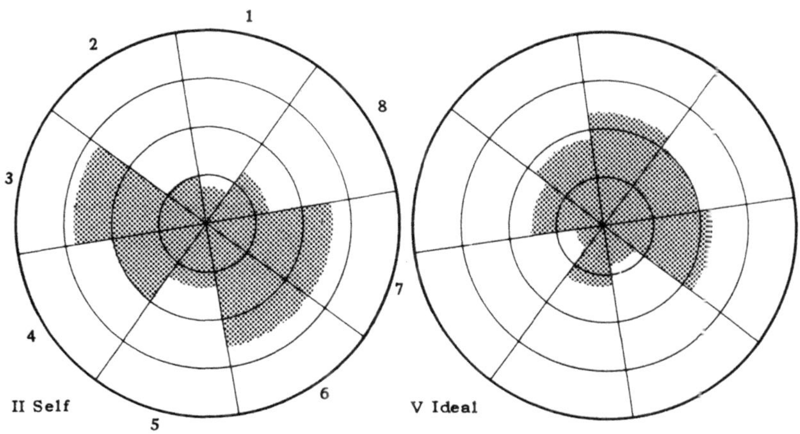

ICL

She presents a confused picture of herself (bow type profile). While she sees herself as very aggressive and selfish she also feels weak, obedient, easily influenced, wanting everyone's love, and too willing to give to others (self 6,7)

Ideal. She wants (1,8) to be much stronger to the point of managing others but *not* aggressively so (3). At the same time she does not wish to be excessively influenced, dependent on opinion of others (low 6).

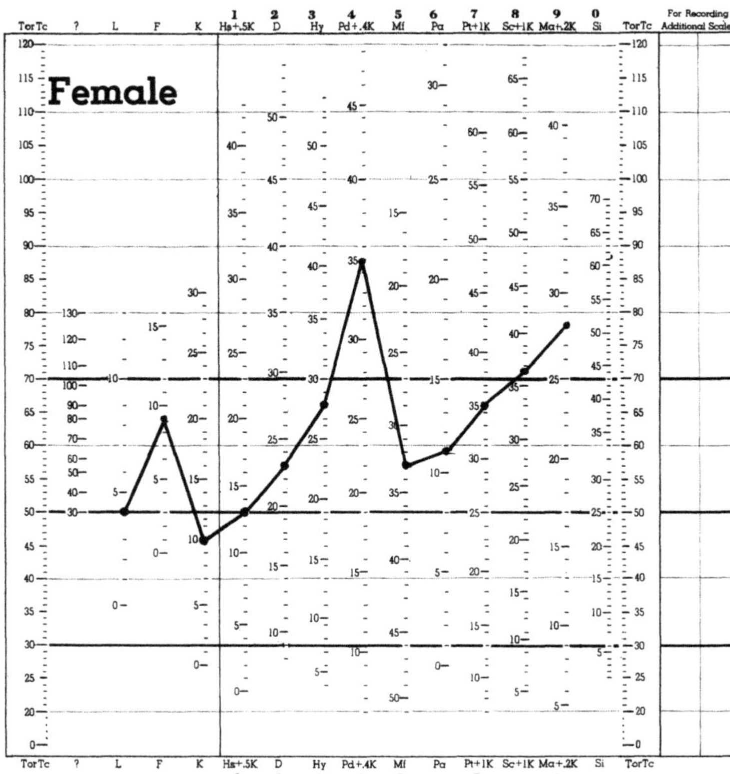

	?	L	F	K	Hs+.5K 1	D 2	Hy 3	Pd+.4K 4	Mf 5	Pa 6	Pt+1K 7	Sc+1K 8	Ma+.2K 9	Si 0		
Raw Score	—	4	9	10	8	23	28	31	33	11	25	26	26	—	—	—
K to be added					5			4			10	10	2		—	—
Raw Score with K					13			35			35	36	28		—	—

MMPI

Poor prognosis (Pd,Ma,Sc with D and Pt so relatively low) (Former demonstrates poorly internalized modes of handling frustration and aggression while latter indicates low anxiety or internal conflicts.)

Very alienated, immature, impulsive, adolescent, acting out (Pd), restless, mood shifts, aggressive and irritable (Ma)

Hypersensitive (F,Sc,Pd)

Low sense of worth (K) but sees self as feminine (Mf) if rather victimized (Pd Mf)

APPENDIX 6

THE RENEGADE—A CASE OF REBELLION
CHAPTER SIX

TEST DATA
AND INTERVIEW

Diagnostic Interview

REFERRAL INFORMATION

Vital statistics from referring physician: The patient, a 19-year male, is an only child whose mother is a nice person but hysterical; she picks on him all the time. A neurological consulation suggests idiopathic epilepsy wih a history of earlier fainting—he is on dilantin.

From vocational counselor: The patient scored in the lowest quartile in computational, verbal, and total performance on college achievement tests. The counselor felt that he consciously was giving false or inadequate answers in smart-aleck fashion. The patient admitted that he did this because if his parents knew he was smart, they and the school authorities would push him. He was told in grammar school that he had an IQ of 150. As the interviews progressed, he grew flippant and eventually told of fearing his father; he still was anxious when considering his problems. His mother complained that he had no friends except a group of pranksters and that, despite his large size, he was afraid of other youths.

Counselor saw him as smart-alecky, fearful, and then more trusting.

The patient began by telling of quitting school because of poor grades. He said he had "troubles and something I can't get rid of the rest of my life" (meaning epileptic attacks). However, he said he didn't worry about anything and had only had two attacks recently. On those occasions, he was not taking his pills and was staying out late with friends. In the first situation, he experienced a peculiar head-achy sensation at lunch and remembered dropping a bottle and coming-to a split second later. His friend was mad because he had to clean up the messed-up lunch (the same lunch which the patient had complained about before fainting). He went back to his room and tried to force himself to study for a math test. That was 11:45 A.M. and the next thing he knew it was 4:45 P.M. (He laughed enjoyably during this entire account). That was three months ago. Then, on the first day of school he was arguing with his mother about where his clothes were. He started banging drawers, then fell on the floor kicking his desk. A physician was called who thought he had hepatitis. He had a neurological work-up in a hospital and was put on dilantin by Dr. O. "Imagine! My parents almost collapsed, I don't know what's wrong with me." (He laughed heartily at this.) The only reason he was taking pills was because Dr. O would report him to the Motor Vehicle Bureau since three seizures legally define epilepsy.

At least secondary gain suggested by seizures, amusement rather than anxiety.

He was born in a large California city in the early 1940's. He has lived in the same house all of his life. His father, a big, massive man was just like a god to him. The father owns a very large ranch and has been away from home a good deal; his mother has hardly been home either.

Felt rejected by his parents.

His colored maid has been closer to him than his mother (laughed as he said this). His father was very nice to him when he was small but very strict. Although, he never took much personal interest in his son, he bought him everything. "And am I spoiled—an only child!" But he never had a chance to play with his dad so he had to look for friends. He has never been able to talk with his father—the latter becomes mad so easily. So the patient keeps things from him, and now his father, he said, is even more on edge. His mother was worried that he would not make this appointment and his father yelled at him to get here. He believed that his father wants to help him to be the best, but doesn't know how to talk to him. During the day, he said, his father is quiet, but he builds up his anger all day and then he takes it out on the patient—nagging, flying off the handle, criticizing him, and bringing up everything from the past. Therefore, he said, he stays away from his father, who, however, can be affectionate and calls the patient Shorty. "I have a lot to do with it, I'm no angel." (All of this flowed out compulsively.)

Keen ambivalence toward father. Pleasure at being spoiled child.

His mother, the patient said, was much better to him and able to handle him when he was a child. "I always was a terror in the neighborhood. You name it, I did it." (He laughed pleasurably at this point.) When he was eight years old, he threw a cherry bomb in some kid's fish bowl and blew it up (said with tremendous pleasure). His mother used to beat him with a brush and then a belt (still said with pleasure), and then could not handle him. At this point, and still with pleasure, he told of beatings by father and of how even now he was frightened of his wild-eyed looks.

Sadomasochistic pleasure.

The other night he shoved his father back viciously for the first time, and his father then looked very funny. Last week his father put it to him either school or a job. He threatened to take away his son's car (the latter owns a third of the car). This time, instead of hanging his head and making his father feel guilty, he spoke back to him. His father swung at him but he pushed him away, and his father was flabbergasted. Now the patient said he felt sick about it.

Open rebellion towards father.

He always found school easy but went through with C's and didn't work until he was a junior in high school. He got good grades in high school although he was still loafing (tone expressed self-contempt). *"I'm just not mature enough for college."* He added that he wanted very much to change. When he was little he had friends, but then he told of sadistic tricks he played on them. He said he had one pal now and several girl friends; he dates frequently, likes to neck, and gives girls "a line." He grew evasive when the conversation veered towards the sexual area, stating vaguely that his parents might find out.

Self-awareness colored by low sense of worth.

He has worked for an uncle who owns a chemical company, and liked it enough to want this as an occupation. However, he felt he would fail the required chemistry and thus "maybe unconsciously avoid college." His father has indicated he would like him to work for him, but patient cannot stand the business.

> Can evaluate his circumstances realistically if not with full insight.

He graduated from high school a year ago and has had only a few odd jobs such as taxiing planes around and washing them. He has thought of getting a job but is undecided about attending a junior college in his own city (a less rigorous school).

> Fails in academic and/or vocational adjustment

MEDICAL HISTORY

The patient has had no serious illnesses but did have tonsils and adenoids out when 6 and has had stitches over his eye. Six years ago, he had a serious case of "athlete's foot" and had literally to crawl about. (Here he presented a detailed and enthusiastic description replete with the "gory details" of cleaning scabs and pus, showing keen and informed interest in the pharmaceutical treatment.)

> Is somatically preoccupied. Anal sadistic orientation.

He presented a good many other somatic complaints, finally mentioning that he never had "attacks" before but had passed out from drinking (although he couldn't remember when he last drank). When he had the last attack three months ago, he had been drinking the night before and thinks he hit his head while drunk. Neither parent, he said, drinks.

> Acting out here expressed in drinking and possibly related to his "seizures."

IDIOSYNCRASIES

He bites his nails all the way down, chews on cut-off nails like chewing gum. He loves high places and has no phobias. He has crazy thoughts in order to go to sleep: reels off United States presidents and the dates; makes himself dream—e.g., his bed is built on a boat with levers and he shoots submarines via the levers—doing this since he was five. His room is terribly dirty and sloppy—he is not comfortable unless everything is a mess.

> Compulsive infantile fantasies of omnipotence and anal destructiveness.

DREAMS

Never forgot one dream years ago in grammar school. Dreamed he was superman.

> Omnipotence.

BEHAVIOR

He was very friendly. At times, he was facetious but then would say, "No . . . ," implying that he was withdrawing such hostility. He is definitely of superior intelligence, but he played this down and expressed contempt for himself, particularly about his goofing-off. Very intense, he laughed inappropriately and evidenced sadistic and masochistic pleasure on such occasions. During his second visit he was very much on edge; he handled this with compulsive facetiousness and inappropriate, uproarious laughter. Despite himself, words would break through that he would regret, so that although he always wanted to take back hostile, disparaging thoughts, he still kept on expressing them. He dealt with Rorschach, TAT, and DAP in a very obsessed manner. In conversation, he got mired down in circumstantial material, but spoke with desperate enthusiasm. He brought back the MMPI just barely started; he disappeared from the room where he had been working and shoved the test under the office door an hour later.

Psychological Tests

DAP

As in all other tests, the patient paid very compulsive attention to detail, with obsessive doubts and rationalizations that nevertheless indicated impulsivity pushing out. Could not let go of drawing, particularly nose, finally settled on "Schnoz Durante—young because of hair," which made him smile.

DRAWING I

It's me. If he looks like Schnoz Durante, has pretty good sense of humor. Anywhere from 17 to 20. Crummy looking, anybody playing has no intelligence—I played for two years and that's why I wear glasses—got hit with baseball bat too. He's a rat no good, a bum, illiterate, lazy. (Describing self?) That's what everybody tells me, I guess they're right.

DRAWING II

Started to look like boy and still does, crummy looking. No intelligence, would not date a girl like that, too flat. School girl, about 13. Good personality.

General Comments

Very anxious and obsessive. Aggressive but need for protection (helmet-shell on Rorschach). Disparages males and self, particularly regarding illiteracy and laziness. Female shows impaired judgment; he makes a harridan of her, cold and rejecting (flat-chested).

WECHSLER-BELLEVUE (administered 10/56)

Verbal	*Scale*	*Performance*	*Scale*
Information	14	Picture Arrangement	9
Comprehension	12	Picture Completion	13
Digit Span	7	Block Design	7
Arithmetic	10	Object Assembly	10
Similarities	12	Digit Symbol	8
Vocabulary	10		

Verbal IQ 125   Performance IQ 95   Full Scale IQ 112

General Comments

He shows superior verbal intelligence (IQ 125), but significantly poorer performance ability (IQ 95). Depressed general intellectual functioning but still Bright Normal (IQ 112). Anxiety seemed very depressing factor as well; his lowest scores were on tests of concentration and attention span, Digit Span, Block Design, and Digit Symbol. Academic skills are far below average (retarded achievement scores mentioned by counselor).

RORSCHACH

CARD I

1. (6″) Looks like a Cadillac emblem on a car (laugh).
Inquiry: Line down here (drew emblem, very vague).

Comment: Initially autistic, poor form, grandiose (Cadillac).

2. Looks like something dissected in biology, anyway looks like something I may have dissected—frog—so many pieces (laugh, suggesting he did poor job).
Inquiry: Just said that to be smart, stupid. Can remember one time in class really messed up a frog. (What?) Just as a feeling to it, looks like I want to puncture it and formaldehyde squirts out.

Comment: Destructive response (miserable form). Admits he made destructive mess. Extremely anal sadistic (mess, formaldehyde squirting out).

CARD II

1. (20″) Looks like a couple of people with their hands together. Hope I'm giving sane remarks. Looking at each other. Don't know what red splotch doing down here—unless feet, no, unless tail. (laugh) I'm crazy!
Inquiry: Flat head sticking tongues out at each other. Looks like someone threw ink or blood on them. Real morbid. (People?) Don't know. (Sex?) Could be either, woman because small hands. (Blood?) Red, don't have to be blood, red paint.
(a) Could be a couple of Martians, blasting with ray guns—no, having sort of a duel, standing on one leg, one amputated.

Comment: People (women) disparaged, seen in both oral (tongues sticking out) and anal (threw ink and blasting) sadistic manner. Very hysterical (blood), some insight into autism of response. Reinforces rage and sadism with another response of similar nature.

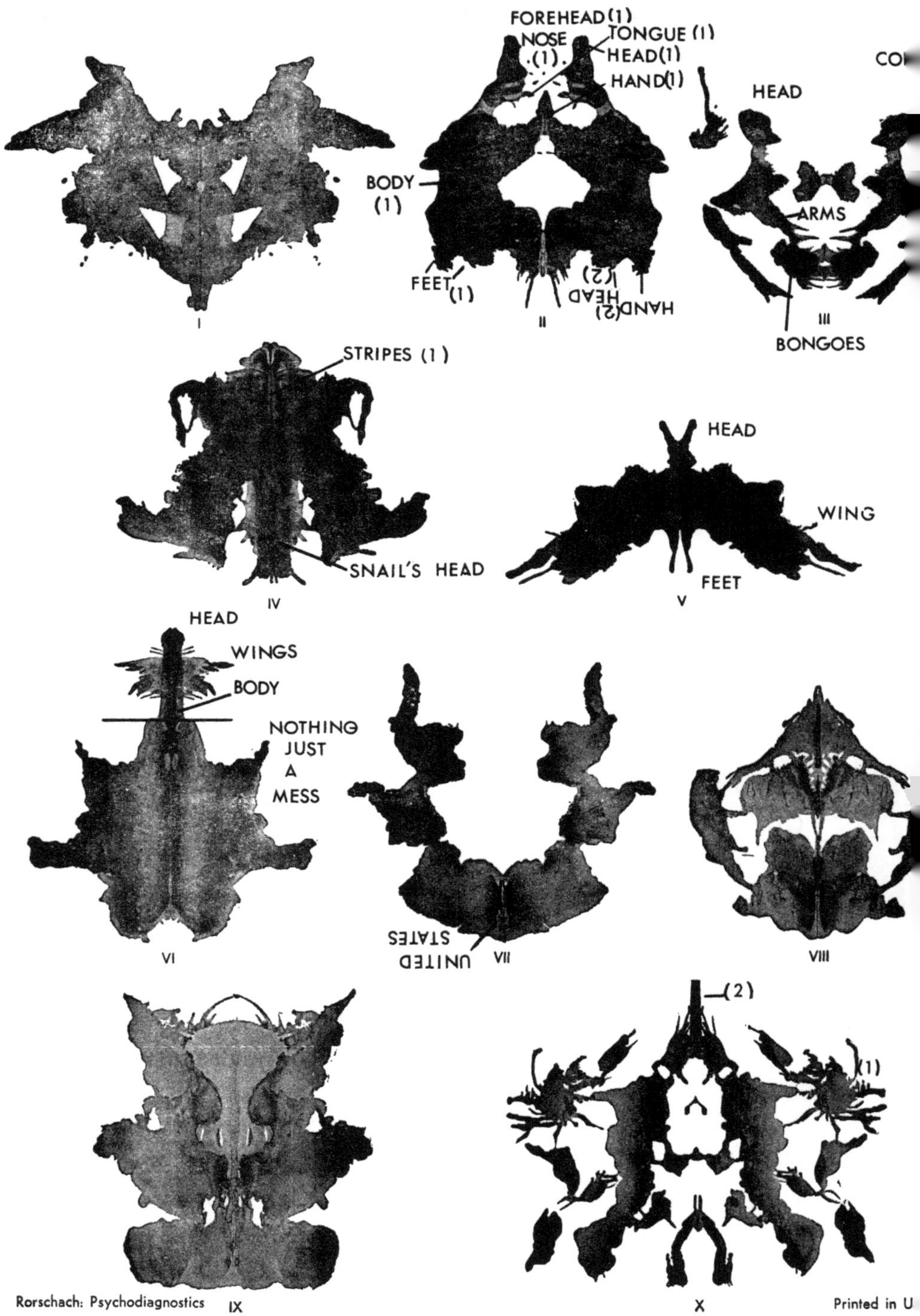
FOREHEAD (1)
NOSE (1)
TONGUE (1)
HEAD (1)
HAND (1)
BODY (1)
FEET (1)
HEAD (2)
HAND (2)
CO
HEAD
ARMS
BONGOES
I
II
III
STRIPES (1)
SNAIL'S HEAD
IV
HEAD
WING
FEET
V
HEAD
WINGS
BODY
NOTHING JUST A MESS
VI
UNITED STATES
VII
VIII
(2)
(1)
Rorschach: Psychodiagnostics
IX
X
Printed in U

CARD III

1. (3″) Couple niggers beating the bongo. With a couple of red lights on each side, no, not lights. I should have said Negroes, hope you didn't put down niggers.
Inquiry: (Negroes?) Because black, cause could be shadows on them. (Man or woman?) Women, smaller, smaller bodies, could be men—no hair. Could be fire down here. (Obsessively back and forth re sexes.) Could be warming hands over fire.
2. Gives impression of cord with light. (What?) Does not look like it, but it could be baby just born, umbilical cord, cause I'm probably crazy. (Light on it?) Does not look like light.

Comment (1): Again people (now minority Negro rather than woman) severely disparaged. Obsessive bind whether male or female. Aggressive action.

Comment (2): (Longing) just born with umbilical cord.

CARD IV

1. (6″) Top is nothing. Underneath is a shell and beneath that a snail or slug.
Inquiry: Snail in crushed shell, someone stepped on it—just imaginary shell—just mess on top of it.

Comment: Self-concept of snail stepped on—a mess.

CARD V

1. (1″) A bat, a bat with beat-up wings (laughs). (Concerned that the writing down of his verbatim responses would show him up as an "illiterate.")
Inquiry: Might be a bat hanging from a tree. That's impossible, bats don't sleep that way. Beat-up wings, not in good shape. (Told of keeping dried up bats in room to scare girls.) Looks like bat been dead a long time.

Comment: Conventional response not so conventional, beatup, dead; told of keeping dead bat to scare girls.

CARD VI

1. (30″) Can't see anything. (45″) Except maybe a couple of feathers, turkey feathers.
Inquiry: Now see second time, poor creature looks like dragonfly.

Comment: Somewhat blocked on sexual card but recovers somewhat.

CARD VII

1. (10″) What it looks like to me, I suppose I'm crazy, looks like bunch of isles to me. V This one looks like United States.
Inquiry: (itemized the states in U.S., naming all of them.) Don't know why U.S.—bunch of isles—could be Mexico down here, Alaska up here (Where is water?) Blank part the water.

Comment: Handles poorly, again concerned about emotional soundness.

CARD VIII

1. That's pretty! (3″) Modern art!
Inquiry: Modern art—nothing. (Colors?) No, except blend well.

Comment: Passive impulsivity.

2. Looks like skeleton of something with a tail bone.
Inquiry: Skeleton of a small animal, insect.
(a) Dragonfly but too crazy.

Comment: Morbid in emotional (color) situation.

CARD IX

A blob—don't write. Does not look like anything. (35″) Can't [Hold card a while]. Pretty! (Named colors.) Turns card completely around.) (2′5″) Can't see anything.
Inquiry: (Still rejects)

Comment: Can't handle emotional situation, responds vaguely to emotions.

CARD X

1. (2″) Couple of crabs.
2. Couple of crabs fighting for a stick.

Comment: First conventional, then in context of fighting.

General Comments

Extremely poorly handled for his intelligence. Extremely impulsive and even hysterical—unable to handle emotions—falls into autisms and grandiosity. Actually has self-concept of messed-up, stepped-on, insignificant creature. Raging and preoccupied with sadistic fantasies, severely disparages people, sexually confused, longing for early infancy, concerned about his emotional soundness. Poor form level and color naming suggests possibility of cerebral pathology.

TAT

Card 1

Once upon a story about a little boy. Mother wanted him to play the violin but he does not want to play it. (Very anxious and facetious, so he threw story out.) Title, "Very confused kid"—like me. Tommie came from a well-bred family, parents were intelligent, well-meaning people. Tommie's father was a concert violinist and he wanted his son to follow in his footsteps but Tommie was an illiterate bum. No, he had other ideas about his life, wanted to be a fireman, no, doctor. During early life, while in grammar school, Tommie acquired complex from parents, got idea parents wanted him to do things he wasn't capable of, made him take violin lessons. Tommie, now at age of 12, had been studying violin for past three years, and Tom has been growing disgusted. (Had to assist him out of his paralyzing obsessiveness, not being able to decide which story pattern to pursue.) Might really be story of self. This torture which has been upon him has driven him to intense hatred of parents which if not stopped soon will result in Tommie's . . . . in Tommie committing suicide. Real mixed up kid. (Outcome?) One day, Tom hated violin teacher, arguing with teacher, walked up behind him and broke violin over his head. Teacher in hospital with brain concussion and parents, I mean teacher's parents sued for $100,000 breaking Tom's father's bankbook and reputation. Whole family ended up on Skid Row.

Comment: Very anxious and facetious, cannot help but feel that he was getting involved but had to keep on. Admitted he was "confused kid" and "illiterate bum." Feels that parents want him to be other than what he wants for himself, so he rebels. (Parents expect him to be "more capable" than he really is.) Got bogged down in paralyzing obsessiveness. "Intense hatred of parents" because tortured by their dominance of him. Threatened rage converted into suicide (morbid). Instead bashes teacher over head (Acting on impulse equivalent to Pd on MMPI). Father ruined and whole family on Skid Row.

Card 2

Mary was a good girl, but she was treated mean by her parents. Mary had a fond desire to go to school but her parents were against it. She had been going to school for past five years. She wanted to finish high school but parents wanted her to work on ranch. Finally Mary's mother made ultimatum: she either stayed home and worked or went to school. So Mary went to school and lived with friend—never saw her parents. Ten years later saw parents at funeral—they died of Vino intoxication.

Comment: Again mean treatment of child by parents (morbid), exploitation as above. Again hate—she leaves parents, sees them years later at their funeral.

CARD 4

Jack was a hardworking man. He had been working in electronics plant for last ten years, ever since army discharge. Hadn't had checkup in long time. Got physical in plant, thought just routine. Doctor told him news, had cancer and was dying—let's say *brain tumor*. When Jack found out, walked for hours in dark misty streets of old New York. Thought of suicide but decided better things to do. Wife wondered what's wrong (gave heavy dramatic dialogue), he told wife. He kept on working for six months—then died.

Comment: Preoccupation with physical defect, brain tumor. Again suicidal thoughts. Again morbid.

CARD 6

Nick Nichols. No, Al was born in New York slums during early 1900s. Went to school for only few short years. Parents very poor and he had to go to work. He wasn't satisfied and organized a gang around 1910—numbers game, gambling, etc. Became very powerful and wealthy man. Hadn't been home for long time. Went to rooming house and asked landlady for Mrs. Capone. He was Al Capone. Mother told him to get out, no good rat. He came back and mother reported to police. Finally got sent up for tax evasion and mother died of heart attack while in prison. When he got out, built big monument for mother. Proves even when bad, still got a little good in them.

Comment: Mother feels son no good. Ambitious to be powerful but unscrupulous. Mother turns him in to police. Nevertheless built monument to mother who dies. "Proves little bit of good in bad." (Pd.)

CARD 7

Johnny and his gang had held up a drugstore. He and two other buddies leaving when police shot and killed two buddies. Druggist died of gunshot wound. Johnny up for murder. Lawyer leaning forward asking if he pleads guilty or not.

Comment: Pd (holdup), hopeless, convicted for murder.

CARD 8BM

(laugh) This picture just down my line. Johnny and brother Tommy grew up in slums of New York, Chicago to be different. Johnny very wild child, liked excitement and bright lights. Tommy liked law and order. While Johnny quit school, went out with gang and terrorized countryside, Tommy went through college and became policeman. (Very nervous laughter) Years passed and Johnny and gang still public enemies. On a warm sultry day on July 21, 1932, four men walked into First National Bank on Fourth Street in Chicago, Illinois. Ten minutes later shot rang out, four men emerged from bank (describes alarm in detail). Tommy and men came and blasted at them (Stopped after elaborate detail.) Tom followed one man to deserted shack. He's captured, take off shirt to torture him. Johnny walks in and kills friends between brother. Proves brother always faithful to each other.

Comment: Conflict between Id and Superego (throughout TAT). Despite this struggle and violence, family faithful to each other. (Suggested less detail, balked at avoiding obsessiveness but succeeded.)

CARD 10

Joe head of a syndicate. Lived for many years and made thousands of dollars, very strong-willed man. Does not confide in anyone but self. Met this girl he fell in love with. She found out he was head of syndicates and begged him to give it up. To amazement of comrades, he gave up and confessed to police, sent up for three years. Then he and wife had a grocery store and happy life.

Comment: Throughout extremely obsessive attention to detail. Pd, powerful crook. Only influence a girl who persuades him to lead useful even if mundane life.

CARD 12M

Young Frank's parents killed in plane crash. Parents worth quite a bit of money, all willed to him. Year later became legal guardian of elderly uncle. Uncle's plan to assassinate him and to acquire all this money, planning death for long time. Decided best way suffocate. One night when Frank asleep, uncle just about to lean over and smother *grandson* when had heart attack and died. Pretty morbid stories I'm giving.

Comment: Again parents killed. Old uncle plans to assassinate him, suffocate grandson (slip) but dies instead.

CARD 13MF

Don't know why holding hand over face unless she's dead (uproarious laughter). George very mean to his wife. They lived fairly well, had fairly good income. But George differs from other husbands, treated wife without mercy. No-good bum—no! Went on for years and she was becoming more disturbed mentally by his treatment. He complained about breakfast and slapped her. That night when he came home, found wife in bedroom lying in bed. She was cold and swallowed whole bottle of sleeping pills and his mind snapped. His mind snapped and he grabbed .32 and shot self.

Comment: Husband mean to wife, "without mercy," wife commits suicide, husband's mind snapped and shot self (even specifies gun).

General Comments

He was extremely obsessive about self and performance, paying sticky attention to detail. Uproarious and inappropriate laughter. Very morbid themes—hate and death wishes towards parents (because they exploit him, particularly father, and expect more than he can do), often turned against self in suicidal thoughts, or ineffectually coped with by obsessiveness and facetiousness as well as somatic preoccupation—such as brain tumor (cf. grand mal). But tremendous conflict between love and hate, moral and amoral impulses. Rage and rebellion seemed temporarily to have upper hand with some suggestion that right influence (girl) might switch his orientation. Self-concept that of an "illiterate bum."

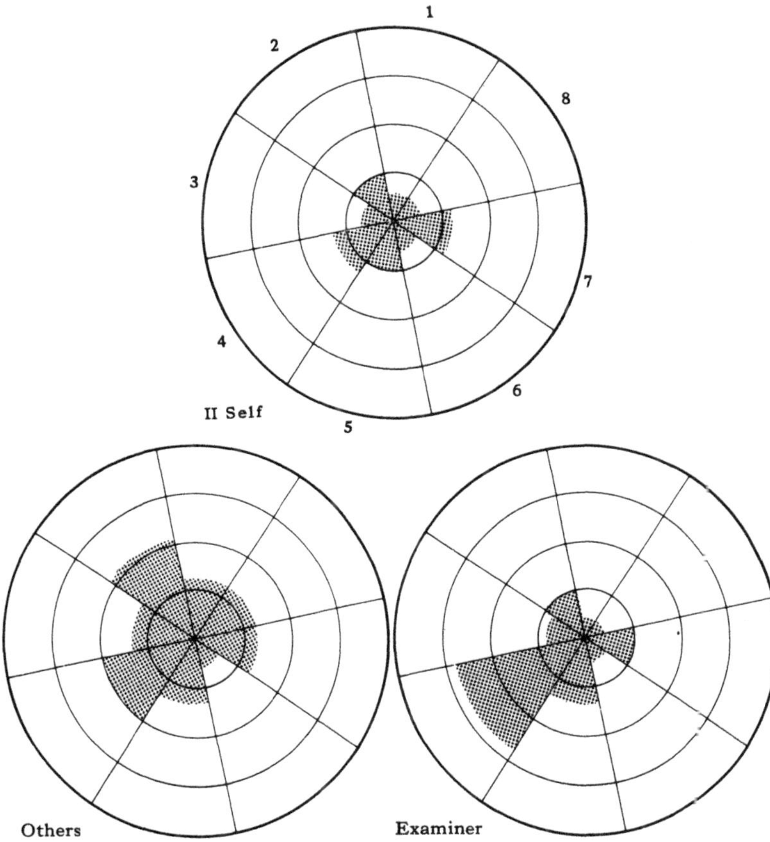

ICL

Presents self as an essentially integrated individual (mostly in inner circle) although he concedes he is cold and selfish and often unfriendly (items 3 and 4, self). He believes that others see him as a very brash, boastful, angry, bitter rebel (4). The examiner agreed with last impression but the rebelliousness and resentment (4) was seen in exaggerated proportion whereas his relatedness to others and self-confidence were not strongly represented (1).

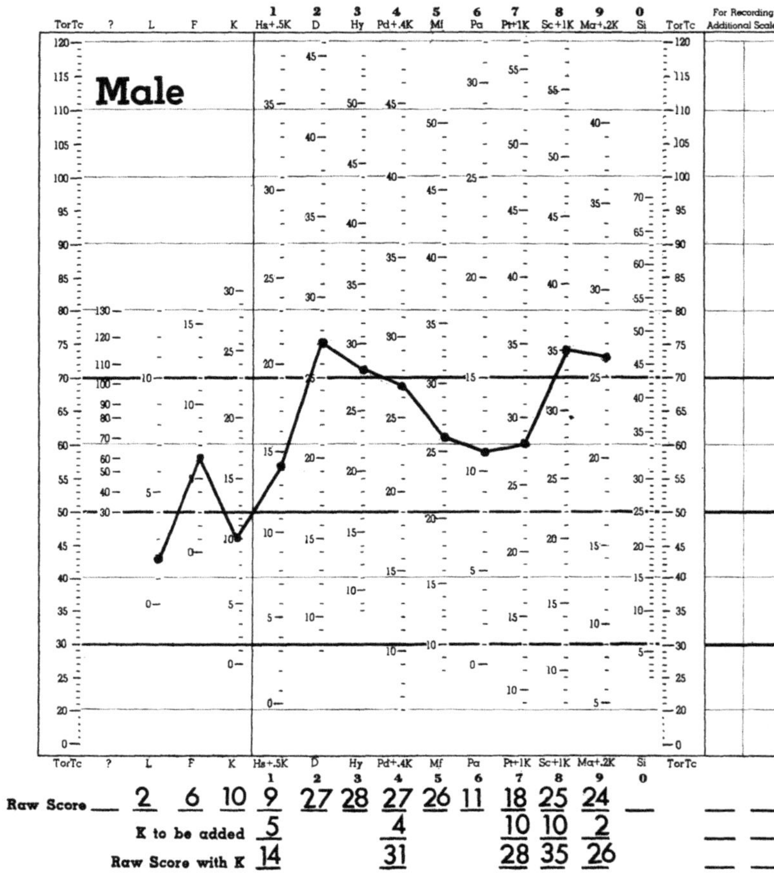

MMPI

Anxious and insecure (D, Pt)

Hypersensitive and sense of alienation to marked degree (Pd, Sc)

Very impulsive, even hysterical (Pd, Hy)

Acting out in rages or temper tantrums (Hy, Pd, Ma)

Suicidal or at least self destructive tendencies (D depressive, Pd impulsive and acting out, Sc thinks and acts differently, Ma hostility and rage)

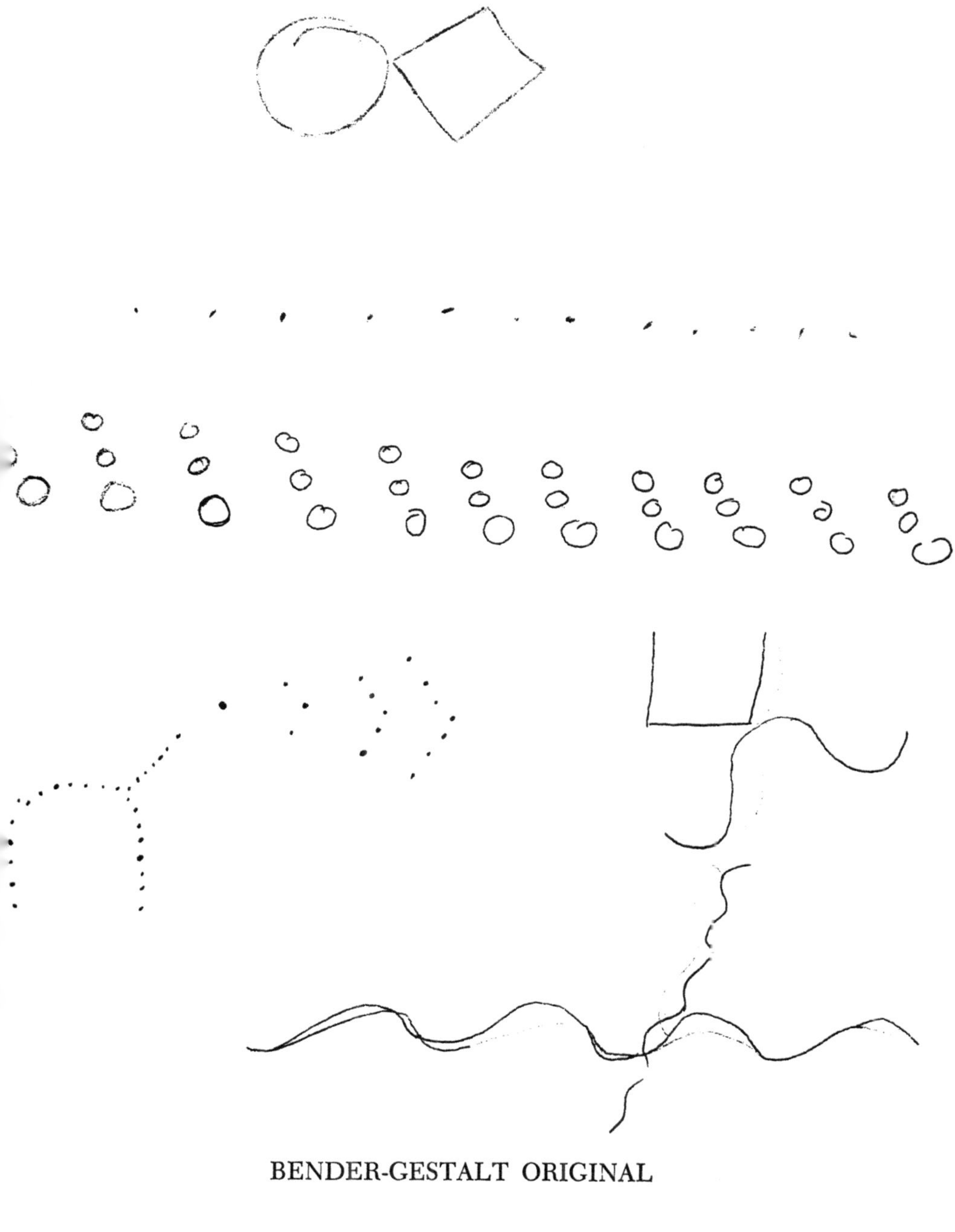

BENDER-GESTALT ORIGINAL

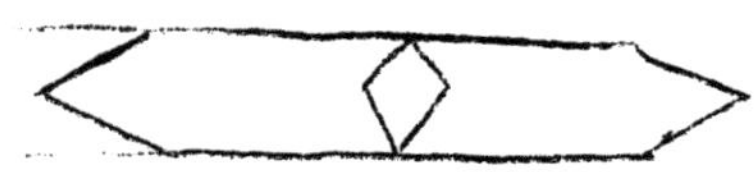

BENDER-GESTALT ORIGINAL, Continued

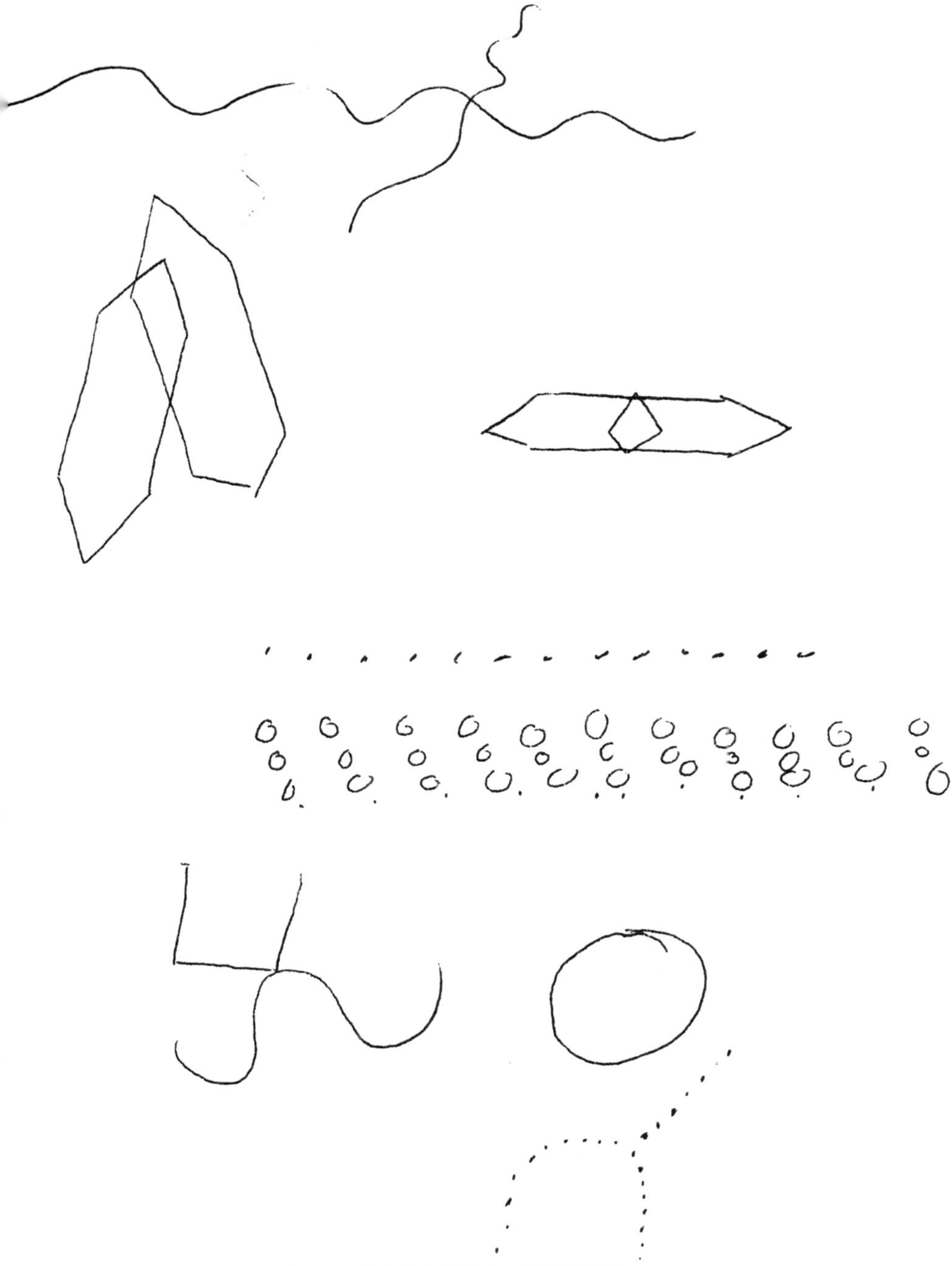

BENDER-GESTALT RECALL

APPENDIX 7

MISS
SADOMASOCHISM
CHAPTER SEVEN

TEST DATA
AND INTERVIEW

Diagnostic Interview

BACKGROUND

From referring physician: Thirty-six-year-old woman who has had myxedemia and is on thyroid. She drinks some. Recently, she came home intoxicated, had a big fight with her husband, and threatened divorce. She suffers from pain in her upper abdomen and has a demonstrable duodenal ulcer. Her mother died when patient was a child; someone in the family was a prostitute. The patient studied to be a medical technician. *At one time, she tried suicide by taking medicine, possibly barbiturates.* Husband is 48 years old and is retired, possibly as a result of selling his business for a great gain. He suffers from gout, recurrent uretitis, and spindolitis. He is president of a large sporting society and has very important, successful friends who are also heavy drinkers. His wife made him give up his friends. This is his second marriage; he has a teenage son by his first marriage and four children by his present wife. He is slow-moving and plodding; he gives his wife about $25 a month to get along.

From patient herself, seen in hospital: she told of her husband having to care for the children because of her hospitalization. Smilingly, she added that, "It will do him good and he will learn how hard it is." She has been talking back to him for a year now. She painted a picture of being practically a slave in the household. Her 7½-year-old daughter had polio at 2½ and is still taking physiotherapy.

Hostile secondary gain of illness.

One year ago, the patient experienced pain on her right side and around the back which lasted for two days and ached for a while thereafter. She had been hunting with her husband, when her dogs pulled her into a ravine and she was hurt below her chest. She has lost eight pounds so that now, she said, she weighs 92. She added that she has a hematoma on the spine. She felt fair until a month ago when she experienced tenderness of the abdomen. A week ago, she had a spasm in her throat and felt sore in the abdomen for an hour. She was hospitalized because her marriage was breaking up, she was in pain, and was just worn out. Physician just put down peptic ulcer to get her in but she had them! She could see the relationship of her ulcer to her marriage.

Varied and vague, somatic complaints.

They were married 9 years ago. She worked for her husband and dated him for several years. She was very much in love when she married. She reported that her husband is jealous and never allows her much money for her needs; he holds money over her head; she never knows his income; he is suspicious of her handling his money and never lets her know anything about these matters; they fight over money; her husband is very domineering. Their children, she said, are a girl 7½, a boy 6½, a boy 5, and a little girl 2½. Her husband's 18-year-old son by his first marriage lives with his mother and stepfather, but visits frequently. At this point, she added rather ashamedly that her husband has slapped her around for looking at other men.

Sadomasochistic relationship to husband.

When they moved into their new home two years ago (last week was the anniversary of this move), things got worse. She has been taking thyroid for eleven years because she was very tired and thin. When pregnant with the last child, she gained only four pounds. Moving into the new home with the infant, she felt normal. Then her husband began yelling and insulting her and she left for five days. He has painful arthritis. He retired two years ago at the age of 49 because he was not getting a sufficient return for his investment. Now, she said, he just hunts or sits around and reads, and the children fight or are irritable because of the parents. She has been screaming at them too, losing her patience. She has threatened divorce to calm things down. Her husband, she added, is a very harsh disciplinarian. They haven't gone out socially for seven months, and she has mostly her own friends.

> Sadomasochistic relationship to husband.

The patient was born in a rural California city. She did not remember much of her childhood. Her father's business building burned down when she was a child. Her mother died when she was ten. She had two younger sisters, a younger brother, and an older brother. Her mother hemorrhaged after childbirth. The children were taken away from the father and given to a social agency.

> Very pathogenic early history.

Her father was always good to her and backed mother up. He took the children to picnics and saw them once a month. He died eighteen years ago of *cancer of the stomach.* The patient did well in school, going through high school in three years with A's and B's. She worked after school hours and also played on the field hockey team. Her last foster mother got her a scholarship as a medical technician. She loved being a medical technician and worked at it until nine years ago when she got married. Before this she had dated and was even engaged but broke it off when she met her husband.

> Male identification (especially since she has father's symptoms).

Psychological Tests

DAP

Drawing I

Looks like a high school girl, a student. An OK personality. Hair is a bit stringy, fair-looking. Normal intelligence. Active, sports and things.

Drawing II

He's a hopeless case, it's my drawing. Average, normal man. Seems happy enough. He looks older, 25 or so. Fair-looking, intelligence may be just a little below normal. The eyes I drew on the poor soul!

General Comments

Drawings are powerful and threatening (large size and intent stares).
Female powerful figure (large size, broad shoulders).
Female awkward in coping with environment, turns efforts back into self (position of arms and hands.)
Female indicates patient's sexual conflict (hand in proximity to genital area).
Female indicates her impaired judgment, perhaps primarily in relation to sexual matters (same hand in transparency through skirt).
Female narcissistic (ornaments and a "high school girl"). Male extremely threatening (piercing eyes and tense posture of arms), combined with depreciation and immaturity "He's a hopeless case," "poor soul," intelligence below normal).

RORSCHACH

CARD I

1. (2″) Looks like a bat. (Else?) No.
Inquiry: Tip of wings where they hang on (saw tail on bottom originally but withdrew this location).

Comment: Potentially can see things the way others do, but gives own twist. Needs something to hang on with.

CARD II

1. ∨ Can you turn it around? (3″) Looks like a hermit crab this way, don't see crabs unless come up on beam.
Inquiry: (Whole) antennae, head, claws, tail. Claws clamp down.

Comment: Deals actively with, even manipulates environment (manipulation of card). Again concerned with clamping down (hanging on).

CARD III

1. (3″) That looks like two people (laughs). Actually looks like two South Africans over their pots.
Inquiry: South Africans because of lips. Feet look odd to be barefooted. In spite of fact it looks like female, thought of male right away. Protrusion of bust, could be animals on side of body. Males because of shape of body and thin hips. Women don't take part in boiling.

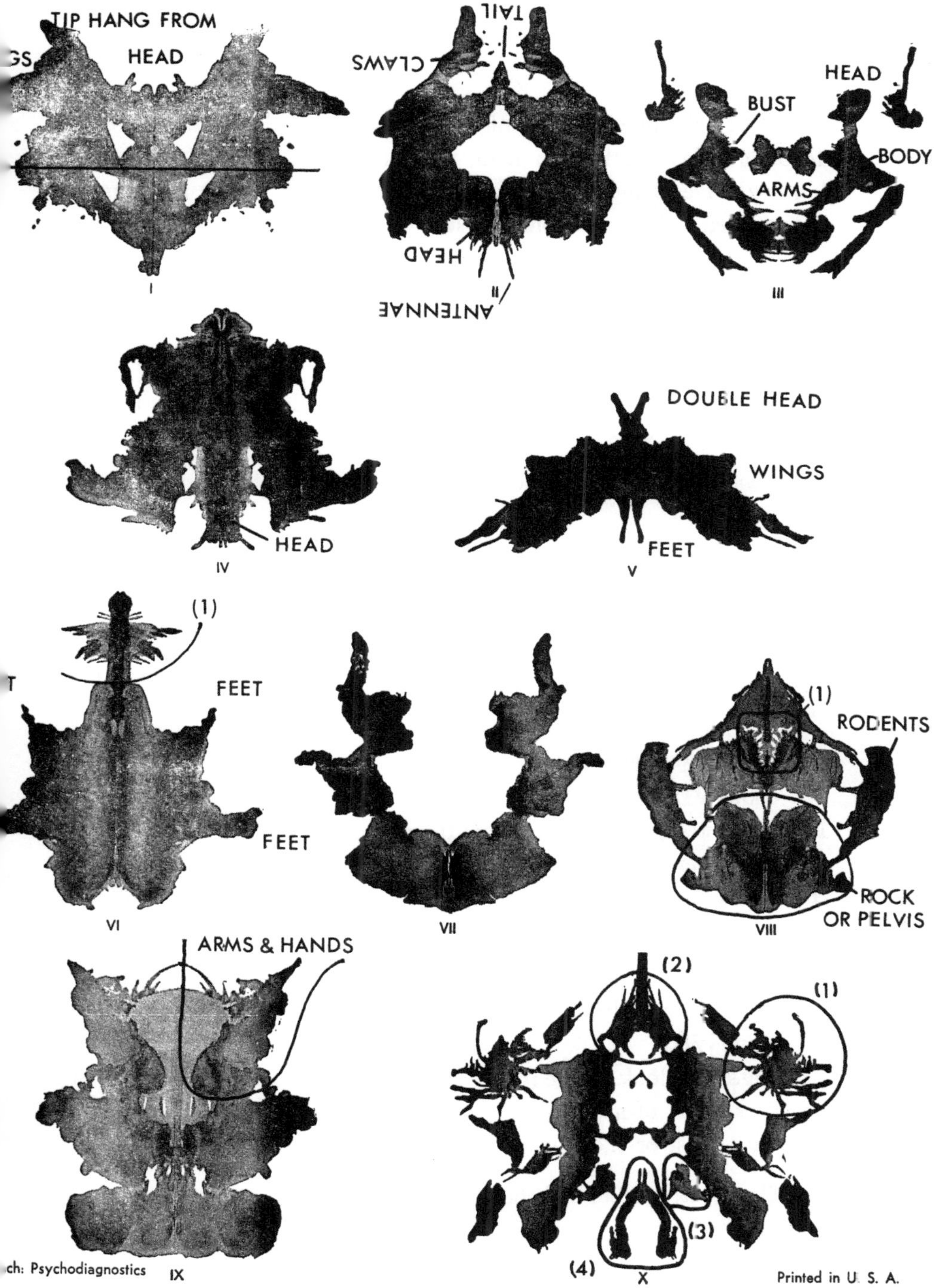
TIP HANG FROM
GS
HEAD
I
TAIL
CLAWS
HEAD
ANTENNAE
II
HEAD
BUST
BODY
ARMS
III
HEAD
IV
DOUBLE HEAD
WINGS
FEET
V
(1)
FEET
FEET
VI
VII
(1)
RODENTS
ROCK
OR PELVIS
VIII
ARMS & HANDS
ch: Psychodiagnostics
IX
(2)
(1)
(3)
(4)
X
Printed in U. S. A.

Comment: Sexual confusion but women must keep their place (if reversed).

CARD IV

1. (2″) Looks like skeleton of something. Reminds me of something dead, half-dead rotting in field, vultures eating them.
Inquiry: (Dead and rotting?) Difference of color. Looks like some of it has been eaten and some of it hasn't (spine, head).

Comment: Morbid, sense of rotting decay. Extremely pathological affectional craving (stress on texture).

CARD V

1. (1″) That looks like a bat too.
Inquiry: Double head does not look like a bat, do have many types of bat.

Comment: Again conventional but with idiosyncratic twist.

CARD VI

1. (24″) Top part resembles a worm.

Comment: Phallic

2. Bottom part resembles a bear rug without a head.
Inquiry: Looks like rug because all spread out with feet where they are.

Comment: Conventional.

CARD VII

1. Does not suggest much of anything except . . . (15″) Coral, have you ever seen coral?
Inquiry: Looks like coral growing. (Coral?) Coral grows in different shapes, pretty and frothy looking. (How?) Lacy, wavy, or delicate.

Comment: Strong affectional (texture) strivings not too well handled. (Getting hostile—"have you ever seen coral?")

CARD VIII

1. Longer you look, worse it gets. (10″) Center, it looks like a ferocious beast, skeleton of a cow.
Inquiry: Beast or skeleton staring out.

Comment: Morbid, sadistic, destructive (self?).

2. Rodents or weasels standing on pelvis.
Inquiry: Rock or pelvis. (Why?) General shape divided in two.

Comment: Contaminated, distorted thinking (incongruous concepts—weasels on pelvis), sexual.

CARD IX

1. Oh dear! Does not suggest much of anything. (25″) Top two figures, two Halloween witches.

Inquiry: (Halloween?) Suggestion of arms and hands, how gruesome drawing around Halloween time, hat. (End of inquiry asked about color. She said she thought of it.)

Comment: Fearful, gruesome fantasy.

CARD X

1. (2″) Hermit crabs again.
2. Top looks like crawfish.
3. Birds, yellow things. We must have too much crabs on our beach.

Inquiry: Shapes, bill, rounded head. (Color?) Yellow with orange spots on.

4. Green below looks like horsefish. (Seahorses?) Yes.

Inquiry: Long curled body. Pretty pictures!

Comment: Uses affect well, can be sociable (color defined by form).

General Comments

Although can deal with people and situations, extremely morbid emotional life. Sense of just hanging on and rotting. Thinking distorted (especially in the affectionate and sexual areas) with destructive or self-destructive fantasies.

TAT

CARD 1

Looks like a little boy coming home from school. Mother told him he has to practice the violin. He is in room looking at, does not want to practice. He wants to go out and play baseball with the other boys. He wasn't one to practice the violin. His parents wanted him to; they forced lessons on him, But he ends up by practicing anyhow (sigh!) and going out to play. Does not seem too unhappy.

Comment: Submission

CARD 2

She looks like a girl that has been terribly sad or in trouble of some kind. Probably just left her boyfriend, split up, and really still loves him. Very heartbroken over it. Time heals all wounds. (Breakup?) If she had been one to break up, she wouldn't feel like that. Probably he has found another girl he thinks he likes better. She'll go on working and find someone else. Looks like a fairly strong girl.

Comment: Couple breaks up, woman tossed aside but she struggles on.

CARD 4

Looks like having argument over something. Maybe wife trying to get husband to cooperate and he's disagreeing completely, not listening to her. Must be something fairly important from the look in his eyes. (Something?) Probably something that she wants, maybe a new dress, hat or TV. She's sort of coaxing him along. Will probably get it.

Comment: Marital discord, woman successfully coaxes husband.

CARD 5

Mother coming to answer the doorbell. She has a slight frown on her face. An older mother. Probably expects someone she wouldn't be too friendly with or not ready for, house very neat. Does not look too anxious to answer door. Probably be all right when she meets the person. Probably forgets her problems and excuses "my dirty house" like most women do.

Comment: "Please excuse my dirty house." All women feel this way.

CARD 6

Suggestion not married couple. Older, I mean, 30-35 year old couple seeing each other, talking over something seriously. Very close to each other, have grave problem to talk over. Both strained. (Why?) Maybe their marital problems. Maybe she is divorced and has children or maybe he has. Probably very intimate but must solve problem first. They look sensible and probably work it out.

Comment: Not really married. Children the complicating problem. Work out sensibly.

CARD 10

Older couple. Probably married 40 or 50 years, maybe facing a very grave illness of either one. Very devoted. Holding onto one another praying. Probably will accept God's will as to what will come out.

Comment: Grave illness keeps couple holding onto one another.

CARD 13

Suggests a soldier, head looks like a helmet. Probably killed this girl. Probably he was getting too amorous and ashamed of what he's done in his or her room, not a house. The fact that he is ashamed means that he will go to the police and tell them what he has done. (Why kill?) Getting too amorous, she resisted, and he killed without realizing.

Comment: Sex leads to aggression leads to sadism of male.

CARD 18GF

Man coming home late. Must be a little smaller than his wife. He came home late and intoxicated. She, fairly robust, has him pinned down by her. She is tired of waiting night after night and so she shakes him. Lot of unhappiness in her face. Probably will keep on taking it from him, same life. She looks like she is right in a rut.

Comment: Again sexual confusion (does not see usual two women). Man makes woman unhappy (drinking). She is the stronger and can "pin him down" physically. She stays in the same rut, taking it from him.

CARD 7GF

Mother and little girl, probably fondled and held too close. Little girls that age don't hold that way to Italian dolls. She probably wants to run out and play. Overdressed and coddled. Doubt she'll ever be able to get away from her mother and associate with other children. Probably have to make a quick break.

Comment: Overloved by mother, never can break tie (longing fantasy?)

CARD 12MF

Gee! More stage, not real life. Not quite real—acting out from a story. Dressed in costumes to portray certain people. Boy looks awfully feminine, don't see people dressed in long hair like that unless an artist of some kind, suggests femininity to me (two women actually.)

Comment: Sexual confusion—feminine boy.

CARD 9GF

Two sisters go out to meet some boyfriend and he is not leveling with them. One sister heard other sister and is hiding in woods.

Younger sister scampering out to meet boy. Older sister does not want to be seen and probably deception of some kind. Probably have to work it out. Gives up boyfriend completely—he's no good.

Comment: Competition with younger females (children) for man (husband or father).

General Comments

All relationships are fraught with hostility or are sticky rather than warm. Marriage is viewed as a sadomasochistic affair—only illness can hold people together.

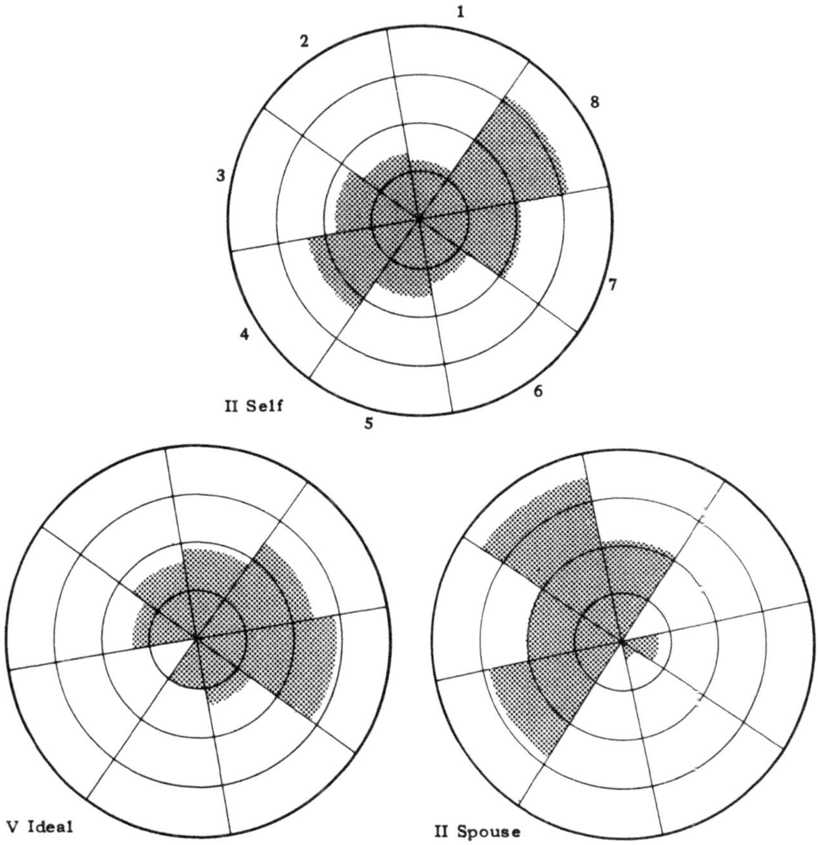

ICL

Presents herself as extremely responsible and generous person (8) who is quite cooperative and conventional, compulsively so (7) (in other terms she has psychosomatic orientation and is hysterical). However, she is suspicious of others (4) and often quite aggressive (3).

Ideal. She would like to shed even a trace of distrust (4) (real conflict here) and assume an exaggerated conventional milk and honey attitude toward people (7) (hysterical-compulsive orientation).

Implications for transference. She sees husband as a ruthlessly exploitive person (2) who does not trust others (4) and whose sole dealings with them is to manage (1) or manipulate them (2). She sees him as a narcissistic (2) and even sadistic personality (3).

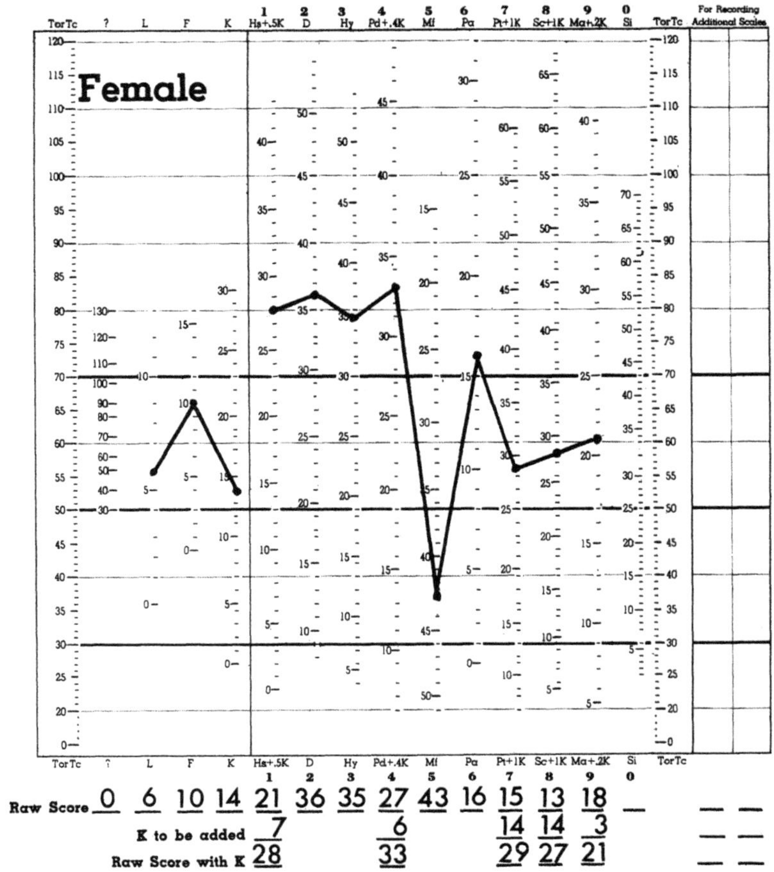

MMPI

Very serious character disorder profile—extreme stress on left side but peak Pd and Pa as well.

Hysterical—Character Disorder, Acts out and/or somaticizes (Hs and Hy as high as D, relatively lower Pt indicates depressive features but little manifest anxiety)

Particularly emphasizes how feminine she is (Mf) and how weak and ill treated (Low K, Mf, Pd)

Quite distrustful of others, making for sour outlook and cynical idea of being used and pushed around (Pa). *Acts on this distrust by fleeing or pushing away from others (Pd Pa)*

*Significant items (at times—have a strong urge to do something harmful or shocking; my memory is not all right)

*Pd Items (I get a raw deal from life; no one understands me; I have been in trouble because of sex behavior)

APPENDIX 8

A CASE OF DENIAL
CHAPTER EIGHT

TEST DATA
AND INTERVIEW

Psychological Tests*

RORSCHACH

CARD I

I mean it doesn't remind me of anything. Just put it down? (Anything?)

1. (30″) Butterfly, but I had to look at it carefully first.

Inquiry: The whole picture. The body here and . . . (points to wings). (Looks like?) I just feel like the whole picture, nothing else that's what I think it looks like.

CARD II

1. (21″) The head, this part up here reminds me of two roosters. And two bodies.

Inquiry: Rooster head. (Why?) With the crow—what is that deal? [comb] And the bill, with its mouth open. [Comb] Exaggerated a bit however. And the eyes, light marks. And the body with hands together. (Rooster?) No, did I say that? A human's body. (Separate?) Yes, rooster's head on a human body, with their hands together and

* This patient originally was administered the MMPI and the ICL by the author and subsequently seen in treatment by him. After therapy was initiated, he referred her for full psychological evaluation to a psychologist under his supervision. Hence associations to the Rorschach, DAP and TAT are not reported, nor are there interview notes, but reference to the projectives is made in conjunction with the therapy notes.

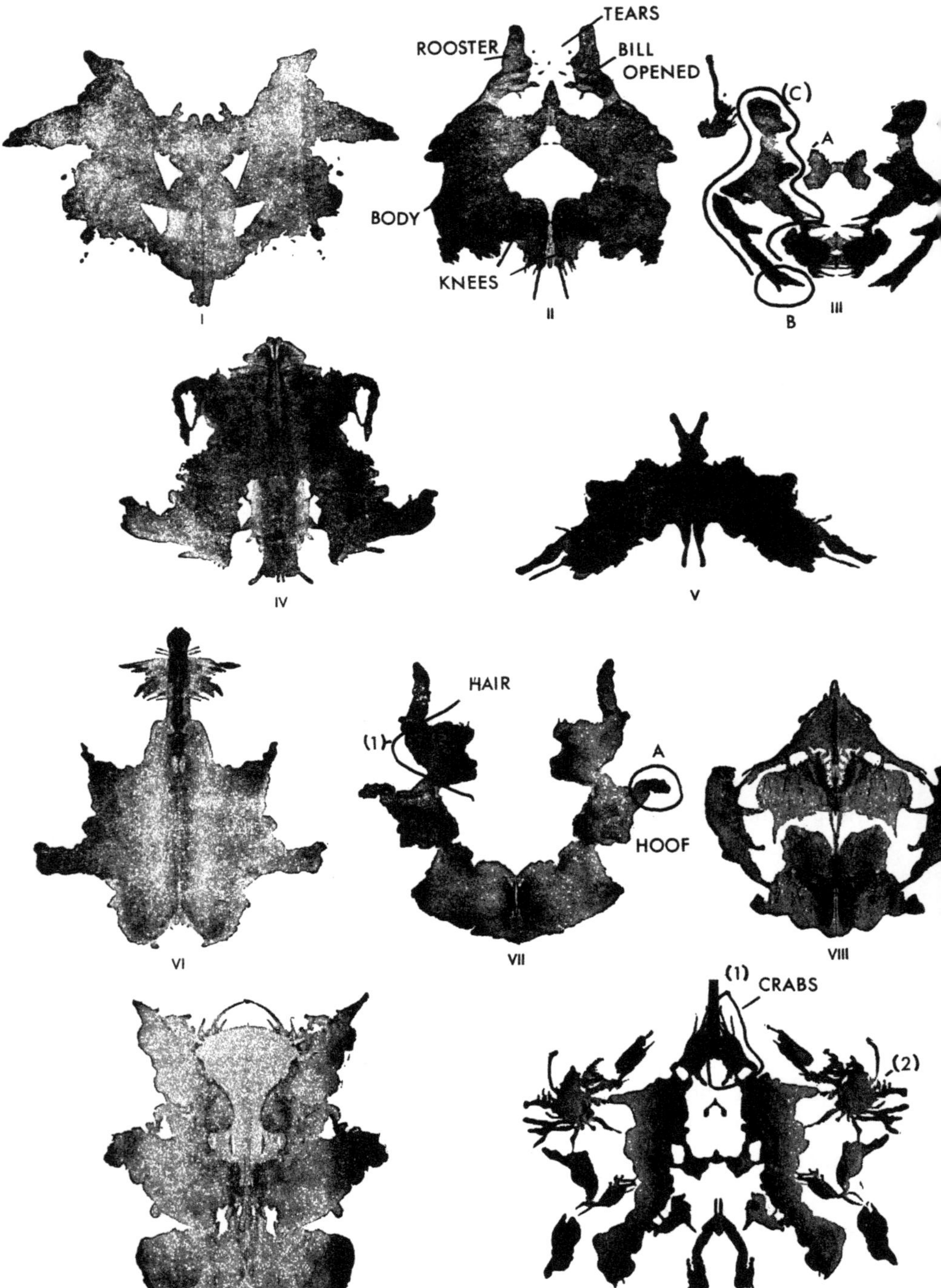

Rorschach: Psychodiagnostics Printed in U.

their knees together. And they're sitting. (How?) Whole picture. I notice other thing now. Little spots up there remind me of tears. (Why?) I don't know. (Something to do with rest?) Yeah, uh huh.

CARD III

I don't know (25″). I can't make anything of that (41″).

Inquiry: I don't know, that doesn't, I can't visualize anything there (perplexed), except this bow as I look at it.

(a) As a ribbon tied.

(b) Now that I'm studying it more I think of this as horses' hooves. (Why?) I'm not saying they look exactly like 'em. I'm just saying similarity. (Ribbon?) It's a ribbon that's tied, or bow tie.

(c) Now I look at the rest of it. I wouldn't know what kind of a head that was. I can take it for a head. (Anything about it?) Neck, a woman's bust line going down, the arms, Sort of in a squatting position (fingers around rear end). (A person?) Practically. But I don't know about head. The big nose . . . Makes me think of a chicken in a way.

CARD IV

1. (17″) Well, this part here reminds me of two feet!

Inquiry: I don't think I made that one out. (Two feet?) Feet and part of a leg up to here, I guess. (What else?) Well, I shouldn't . . . I said feet, didn't I? I should say shoes (Why?) They remind me of shoes, looking at them.

CARD V

1. (8″) That reminds me of a butterfly.

Inquiry: Head, with the two deals that come out. I don't know what they call them, the wings. That's all. (What else?) I see it as a butterfly, not as a perfect butterfly (indignant sound).

CARD VI

Doesn't remind me of anything (18″) [Generally patient should be encouraged to hold card for a minimum of 60″ and even more if possible: L.B.]

Inquiry: This one's blank to me (shakes head). I don't get . . . I don't see anything in this one . . . No.

CARD VII

1. (12″) Two heads.

Inquiry: Hair, outline of face. (Sort of heads?) Well, I never thought

. . . A woman's head . . . Well, now this part here . . . I'm studying it, it would remind me of a lamb's leg. But this doesn't (left) so I'm not going by it. Small hoof. I guess they call 'em hooves. (Why?) That's just the way it looks.

Card VIII

1. (5″) Well, this part here reminds me of two bears, two bears climbing.
Inquiry: Reminds me of a bear, the whole part here, climbing. That's all. (Where?) This part here reminds me of the head and its four legs.

Card IX

Doesn't remind me of anything (17″)
Inquiry: No, that doesn't remind me of anything. I can't think of anything.

Card X

1. (12″) Well, this part here reminds me of two crabs.
Inquiry: Whole thing, the crab legs going out. (How?) Crawling, yeah.
2. Feeling I got when I first saw the two blue ones was spiders. That's it there (signifying finished looking at cards).
Inquiry: Somehow they remind me of spiders. But just a similarity of a spider.

TAT

Card 1

Never told stories. A little boy sitting there, wishing he could be outdoors playing with his playmates, instead of having to practice on his violin. (Led up to this?) The way the little boy's sitting there looking at the violin, he has sort of that sad. (What happened before?) His mother made him practice, or take his violin lessons, when he wanted to go out and play. (Outcome?) He will probably end up playing the violin.

Card 3GF

This sort of reminds me of a woman, crying, maybe because her loved one walked out on her. She's left there all alone. (Outcome?) I don't know what *will* happen (smile), but she could've been real happy at one time, but I don't know what will happen after this.

Card 4

(Sigh!) . . . Husband and wife had an argument. The wife is trying to apologize to him, and right at the moment he's not in the mood to accept the apology. That's it. (What will happen?) They probably will make up. (Argument about?) Should I make something up? Well, I'll just say over that picture on the wall. (How?) The husband is attracted to the picture and he wants to keep it up, and the wife wanted to remove it.

Card 6GF

A married couple. And the husband is telling something to the wife, and she's listening to him. That's all I get out of that. (Telling what?) I don't know, want me to make something up? He's asking her to go out to dinner with him. (End?) Probably have a nice evening out.

Card 7GF

Little girl and her mother. The mother wants to read a story to the little girl but the little girl doesn't particularly want to hear the story. She'd much rather play with her doll. By the look on her face she most likely will end up playing with the doll. (Why?) She has that disgusted look where she doesn't want to be read to. (What led up to this?) I think I said, where the mother wanted to read the story. (Anything else?) No.

Card 8GF

This is a married woman who'd once been . . . no, not who'd once been married, who'd had children and all have left home And she's thinking of the days when they were little and is rather lonely. (What will happen?) Well, she'll stop being lonely and she'll go on with her life.

Card 9GF

Well, the woman had been sitting on the beach, and she wanted to be alone. Along came another woman, which annoyed the one, being as she wanted to be alone. So she got a little angry and left.

Card 10

. . . Well, it's time to go to bed, and the son is kissing his mother good night. Did you want me to make more? (Smile) I don't know what else to say. It's kind of hard to concentrate. My mind keeps wandering off, as I try to look at this and try to think of something. (We can go on . . .) Well, it's time to go to bed, that's all.

CARD 12MF

(Yawn) . . . Two women, one rather young and one quite old are listening to a conversation . . . period! (What are they listening to?) Well, someone is telling a rather funny story. The younger woman doesn't seem to be enjoying it too much, but the older woman is getting a little laugh out of it.

CARD 13MF

Are there many more? Well, this has been . . . a very happy home at one time, but the wife got very ill and suddenly one night she passed away . . . Trying to think, I don't know what else to . . . (Thoughts or feelings?) Do I have to talk about this one? (Why not?) 'Cause I don't have any feelings, really. Well, it seems to me the husband is grieving right there. (What will happen?) Well, the husband will just have to go on and learn to be happy. That is, if he can be.

CARD 18GF

Well, let's see (sigh). See, I find it so hard to concentrate, my mind just wanders off. I'll start something, I'll say that . . . the woman was going down her apartment stairway, she fell down the stairs. Neighbor in the next apartment heard her tumbling down and rushed down to see her. She picked her up in her arms to see if she was still breathing. She was. She still rushed to the telephone and called an ambulance. That's all. (What will happen?) They take her to the hospital. (How happened to fall?) She tripped.

WAIS

Verbal	*Scale*	*Performance*	*Scale*
Information	9	Digit Symbol	12
Comprehension	7	Picture Completion	10
Arithmetic	7	Block Design	10
Similarities	9	Picture Arrangement	9
Digit Span	12	Object Assembly	12
Vocabulary	6		

Verbal IQ 89 Performance IQ 105 Full Scale IQ 96

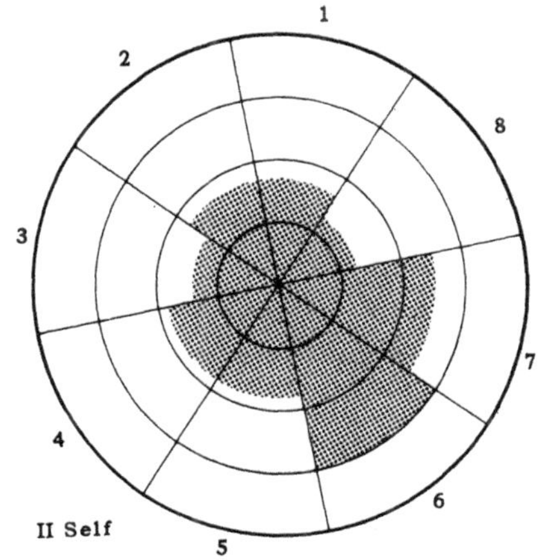

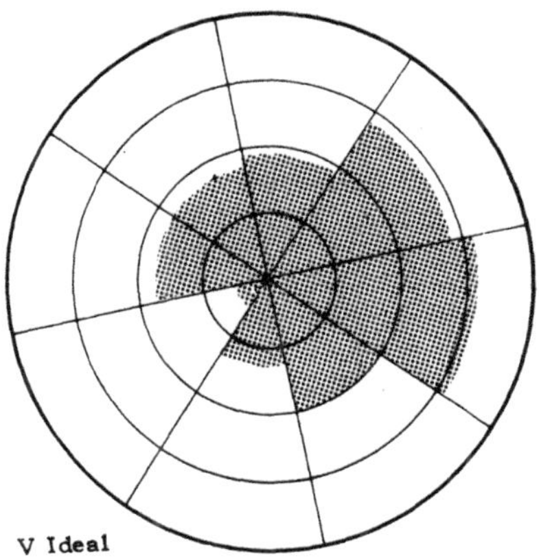

ICL

Anxious and submissive orientation (6) (anxious and phobic) with good deal of overconventional features (6) (hysterical).

Ideal. Wants to be (and, probably when well, functions at) hypernormal, responsible, psychosomatic level (8) and even *more* hysterical over-conventionality (7). She admits to but is highly conflicted over (discrepancy between self and ideal) distrustful, suspicious motivations (4). She would like to deny all of this.

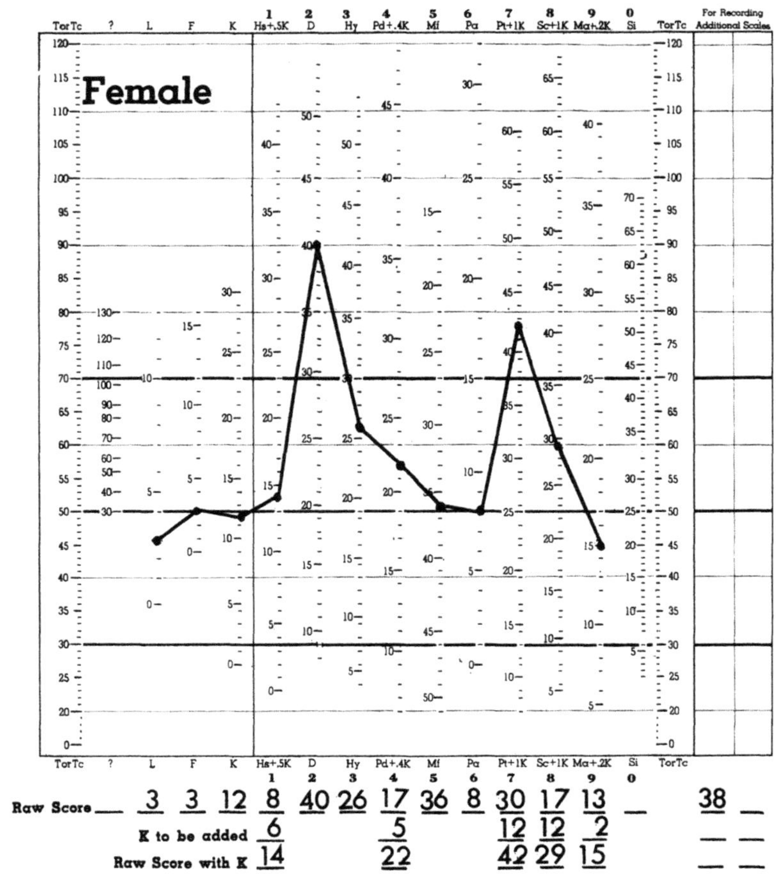

MMPI

(Low K) Overconventional, even stereotypic; (Low K,Mf) Weak, helpless, *superfeminine;* (D,Pt) Depressed, anxious, pessimistic, (Ma) Complaining, listless, at times almost immobilized.

(Very Low Pa is suspect) Denial of suspicion and distrust of other as well as any tendency to be overly aggressive or obnoxious. Very low score suggesting unconscious tendency to be all of this.

Compulsive Items (High Pt) (Fear and revulsion of dirt, fear of catching disease, compulsive habits, inability to decide, taking too much work on).

APPENDIX 9

HYPOCHONDRIA
CHAPTER NINE

TEST DATA
AND INTERVIEW

APPENDIX 9

Diagnostic Interview

The patient was seen in the hospital. She told of feeling nervous and apprehensive just before she went to Hawaii. She was unable to concentrate although able to complete things. She felt all in and tired even though she was an athlete. She suffered from intestinal stress during her menopause (had hysterectomy six years ago). She has been allergic to pollens, grasses, etc., with headaches, not sneezing. She was all right if she remained in her room.

> All in, nervous, apprehensive, allergies, gastrointestinal problems (O.K. if in room).

Her husband had been quite ill. She hasn't been able to do ordinary things, including her golfing and gardening. She is suspected of having hyperthyroidism and diabetes and is on a strict diet. In February, a tumor on her hip was removed and Dr. W suggested she vacation at their summer residence from beginning of March through last week. Her husband joined her two weeks later, suffering from a case of shingles. Her husband has had many serious illnesses recently. Consequently, during this vacation she had to cook and clean rather than relax. She swam every day to gain strength but her shoulder hurt so she had to cut down somewhat.

Either she or husband sick.

She felt increasingly worse, as if she were not getting enough oxygen. Most of the time she felt as if she had *just missed having an accident,* a tense feeling. She was tired but could not sleep or read; things kept pouring through her mind. She got very depressed. Previously, the depression came in cycles; this time she did not pull out of it, could not cope with things, and had desperate feelings (a forced laugh accompanied these descriptions). She was taking medication to reduce her goiter.

Felt as if just missed accident (Cf. symptoms and fiance's accident), worst depression.

Two nights ago, she was crying, gnashing her teeth, and even felt like suicide, "only of course I wouldn't." She knew of no reason for all of this, just felt like a watch all wound up. Dr. W thought it best to hospitalize her for tests and a rest. She feels a little better now but all let out as if a pin had been stuck in her. She is so confused she wonders if it is mental.

Agitated suicidal mood.

The patient was born in a large California city 53 years ago. Her parents were a very "intimate couple." Her father was English and her mother "Scotch-Southern." She has a brother 7 years older; her mother died a year ago. Her brother dislikes the patient intensely, does not even want to see her to divide their inheritance. She used to love him, but maybe he was jealous of her because he was quite spoiled. He was a "brain", she was a "dumb bunny." He had special tutors and was favored by their mother. Their father was quiet but disposed to the patient, saying that she should have been a boy instead of a girl. Sometimes the patient would be annoyed by her mother's favoritism to her brother and would let off steam athletically by swimming. Her father, a lawyer, owned a company and made many friends. He was the strong one in the family, and all his brothers and sisters depended on him. Her mother was a "Southern Belle" type and knew nothing of business. The patient's father showed affection in his way, and sometimes took her and another girl swimming. She did not have too many friends because she had a governess. Her father was very busy and very close to mother so the family as a whole did very few things together. Her mother was affectionate, but the patient was unable to talk to either parent about personal matters. They were so old-fashioned, stressing the credo "children should be seen and not heard."

> Brother and sister rivalry. Brother mother's favorite, she father's, who treated her like boy, and she was a tomboy.

When the patient was a child, she complained to her grandmother about having no friends; she even climbed over the fence and played with the newsboys. Then she exploded by squashing a banana in her book, "Reading Without Tears." The next day they placed her in a private girls' school. She loved it, had lots of friends, could integrate with the group, and felt normal. She was not a "brain wave" because she was more interested in playing games, and just about passed. She was in that school until she was 14 or 15, when she entered a girls' school to finish high school. They really piled on the work, but she found out that she was not so dumb as she thought and did very well (said in a self-depreciatory way). She loved athletics and had to get good grades to play on teams—baseball, swimming, hockey, diving, etc. She graduated at 18 and meanwhile had started recording work in a hospital, as a part-time volunteer.

> Rebels

During this time, she had gotten engaged. Then her fiance was killed; they were all in a car and she was thrown out with only cuts and bruises. She had told her fiance that night that she would not see him for six months while she went to Europe following her debut because her family disapproved of their engagement. He became angry and sat in the back, while she was in front (otherwise she would have been killed, too). She felt pretty bad and from that time on had colitis for years. For a while she "felt a hundred years old" and lost interest in things, and it was difficult for her to snap out of it. However, she was still active in charities, ran horse shows, and participated in various volunteer work.

> The accident and onset of symptoms.

A year later, she became engaged to her husband, whom she had known before her fiance. They were engaged six months because he did not have enough money. Her family wanted her to marry him all along. Laughingly, she indicated that her rebellion and resentment kept her from appreciating her husband in the first place.

Husband on rebound and bows to family.

They were married thirty one years ago and the Depression began soon afterwards. They took an apartment in the city. He was starting a business and it was a real struggle; they lived quietly. They wanted children but did not seem to have any. His father died so they went to live with his mother in a nearby city. The patient accepted this, liking his mother and passively going along with what she felt was the right thing. They stayed there five years and couldn't see many people. On questioning only, did she realize that she chafed a bit in these circumstances.

Unaware of resentment of in-law.

Twenty-seven years ago they had a boy and three years later another boy. The second birth was difficult. She developed carbuncles and did not feel well for some time. Then she had two operations for appendicitis and hernia and was not able to walk well. She felt sick, suffered colitis: abdominal pains, mucous discharge but no blood, and diarrhea. She also had several allergies (as did her mother).

Long term colitis after second birth.

They continued to live quietly, staying with her mother-in-law for eight years when they got their own house. She was still not feeling well (she presented a tremendously long symptomatic history replete with diagnostic terms). About two years later, she had vaginal surgery and one ovary removed. She began to feel better and not so dragged out, but had family cares. About six years later, she began to feel ill again and had a hysterectomy because of a tumor; she also had foot problems. However, she played tennis a lot and won a championship (notably, she played down this accomplishment). But she did have to cut down on her very active civic participation. She felt exhausted and could hardly drag herself around, even when they traveled in Europe.

Eighteen years of living with invalids.

Ten years ago her mother became an invalid, so that the patient, in addition to supervising the care of her own home, had commuted 40 miles twice a week, and whenever else called upon, for *ten years.* This was "kind of" depressing, especially since her brother complained about money being spent for trivia, even though it was his mother's money. On questioning, she admitted anger though she did not reveal it. Her brother would not cooperate; for 10 years he has refused to probate their father's will. She called him an SOB but excused his being born that way. Her brother and his wife are alcoholics and have no children; she pities them. She also felt sorry for herself with no way out and nothing to show for all of this. Her sons are both professional men.

Her husband, the middle one of three brothers who are all outstanding, has done a terrific job running his company. He is, she said, a remarkable man with great understanding and intelligence. She didn't think he had a single fault, but wished he did because she had so many. She did regret that he spent so little time with their children. It has been a very good marriage with no problems.

Builds perfect picture of husband, admits his neglect.

(Here she hesitated relevant to the question of confidentiality.) She has loved another man for 15 years—no one, including her husband, has known about this, and no one would ever think this of her. Most of her friends have been men. These extramarital sexual relations have ended recently because her lover, who is 15 years older than she is, suffered a stroke and heart attack a year ago. She's been pretty upset about this. She did not know how it began, since she still loved her husband, but she was left alone and felt neglected because her husband was away frequently on business trips. It was an unresolvable situation—her lover was married too, with a wife much older than himself. Thus both had mates who were dependent on them. This situation had very insidiously sapped her strength and made her anxious. She would never do it again. Maybe her husband did know but he never said anything. She was more sexually interested than her husband, and he was never able to provide as much as she needed or was interested in. He is not too masculine—he is more mental and she more physical. She never saw a boy alone until she was 17.

Affair with older man. Loves husband too.

Two years ago she began another affair, with a friend of the family she had known for thirty years. She is trying to break this up but hasn't succeeded yet. Her lover was sick when this affair originated. *She had her hands full with these three men,* but thought that everything would work itself out. Her husband, now in his sixties (though he looks younger), had a prostrate operation a year ago and has been impotent for two years.

Two affairs concurrently. Husband never satisfied her.

IDIOSYNCRACIES

She likes to be left alone to pull herself together. She doesn't like to work in her house but loves the outdoors. She used to love to read but now can't concentrate on it or retain anything. She likes philosophy, and nature, and is very observant (*"I take in about everything"*); she likes to be with people but is not able to make good relations with them. She gets angry but then feels guilty—expresses her anger verbally or with tears.

DREAM

When she was a child she had a recurrent nightmare of a big man or ogre; she would run to her mother. Her last dream, which she can barely capture, was about a feeling of falling and crawling up from a pit.

ASPIRATION

She wants to be happy and worthwhile, to contribute. So far, life has seemed pretty worthless. She remembered a piano recital as a little girl when she was very frightened and shy. She outgrew this, but when 15 she was playing a piano and could not play a chord or even read the music. She lost confidence thereafter and was not able to participate in any dramatic production. Similarly, she had been vice president on many boards, but would get out of or resign from the presidencies. She cannot even read a treasurer's report because her voice dries up. She took a nurse's aid course and had to answer questions in public; she got through this but was scared silly.

Much self-accusation and embarrassment.

Psychological Tests

DAP

Drawing I

Looks kinda smug. Rather neat, precise, around 30 or 40 or even younger. Not too intelligent. Yet looks kinda keen, seems to be correct, straight-forward. Seems to be looking at you. Just an average kind of person (Occupation?) Could be a teacher.

Drawing II

Looks like a happy woman, simple, motherly—but take that back, isn't. Could be pretty. Around 30-35, old-fashioned 'though, way dress is—doesn't have any style. Think she could be pleasant, easy to talk to. Think she looks intelligent.

General Comments

Conceptual judgment quite good. Male identification (male drawn first), yet hostility toward males and sense of superiority (in story for I). Woman old-fashioned (Victorian), motherly, with no style. Both sexual and hostile feelings denied in marked fashion (attire, hands behind back). Dependency needs are prominent (buttons, buckle, purse), as well as suspicion or distrust (indicated by large ears of male, question-mark ears of female).

RORSCHACH

Card I

1. (2″) Looks like a fox face.
Inquiry: Looks a little cross-eyed. Just ears and eyes.

Comment: Foxy and self-depreciatory (cross-eyed).

2. Could be a butterfly. Should I turn it over? (Why?) Could see lot more things. (What?) Guess that's all. That's a pretty one.
Inquiry: Antennae, markings on wings.

Comment: Almost hostilely agreeable. Compulsive ("Could see a lot more").

Card II

1. ∨ ∧ One way or turn upside down? (32″) Butterfly on bottom.
Inquiry: Two wings, shape of Monarch butterfly but not colored, never saw that color.

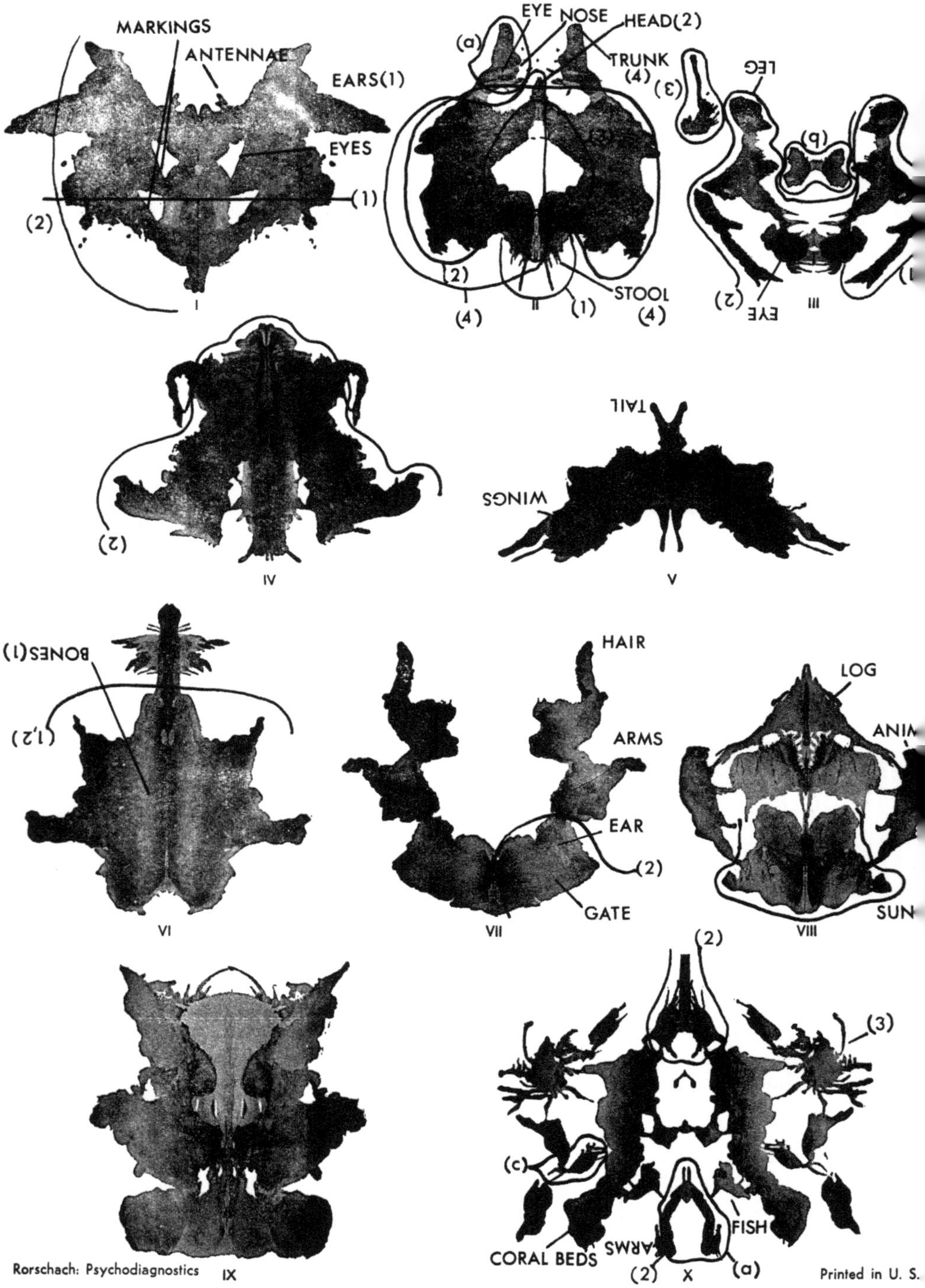
MARKINGS
ANTENNAE
EARS(1)
EYES
(1)
(2)
I
EYE
NOSE
HEAD(2)
(a)
TRUNK
(4)
(3)
(2)
(4)
II
(1)
STOOL
(4)
LEG
(b)
(3)
(2)
EYE
III
(2)
IV
TAIL
WINGS
V
BONES(1)
(1,2)
VI
HAIR
ARMS
EAR
(2)
GATE
VII
LOG
SUN
VIII
Rorschach: Psychodiagnostics
IX
(2)
(3)
(c)
FISH
CORAL BEDS
ARMS
(2)
X
(a)
Printed in U. S.

Comment: Very emotional (reaction to color), even as denies in conventional context.

2. Or a turtle, can't figure out red things.
Inquiry: (all black) snout, small head, flippers on side. Upside down, way natives turned them, somewhat farfetched.

Comment: Different, helpless as exposed beneath shell.

3. Looks like stingray in there or manta ray.
Inquiry: (White space) pointed tail (through red) but they're dark, this is white.

Comment: Aggressive in phallic sense (elongated concept), oppositional (manipulation of card and use of white space).

4. Couple of elephants, dancing. Feel so ridiculous.
Inquiry: Trunks, ears, standing on little bench, one leg on stool.

Comment: Can be creative (and at same time depressed—empirically, dancing seems to represent fight against depression) but feels ridiculous.

(a) Up in here could be two faces, eye, ear, nose, mouth, like partial teeth.

Comment (a): Emotions related to her "partial mask." Hostile (oral, teeth).

CARD III

1. (9″) Looks like two puppets holding a pot.
Inquiry: Two puppets holding a bowl. (Puppets?) Angle which suspended (What?) Dressed-up monkeys, small ones 'cause legs rather long. Monkeys don't have . . . like vest on breast area. Actually fishtails base of leg.

Comment: People are puppets or monkeys even in nourishing context (or especially so here).

2. ∨ This way looks like a beetle. That's it!

Comment: Helpless again. See things differently, a bit peculiar, not morbid.

(a) These could be little dancers, sea horses.
(b) Could be butterfly but never see that color. ∨

Comment (a, b): More productive when recovers somewhat, although not completely, from emotional stimuli.

CARD IV

Oh, I don't know (murmured).
1. (28″) Mountain or some clouds.

Comment: Diffuse, vague anxiety.

2. Fir leaves or leaf that's dropped to ground or fallen.
Inquiry: Curled-up leaf, withered and dropped off.

Comment: Sense of being withered or fallen.

CARD V

1. (1″) Looks like butterfly or moth. All seem to be pretty much same shape with variations.
Inquiry: Wings and tail. Really this way. ∧

Comment: Conventional

CARD VI

Suppose to notice minute details?
1. ∨ (35″) Looks like skeleton of some bug.
2. ∨ An animal skin on floor.
Inquiry: Laid open, leg pieces of skin when tanned. It could be a deerskin except for tail.

Comment (1): Rather morbid, pathological fantasies.

Comment (2): Even her well-controlled bid for affection (Fc) is in morbid (destructive) context.

CARD VII

1. (8″) Looks like topiary where they clip hedges into two women with Bobby tails up in air. Cute, good description!
Inquiry: Topiary, English. Two women's faces facing each other with hair blown up, arms held back. Say on either side of gate.

Comment: Again dehumanized but in very creative manner.

2. < Looks like dog there, on both sides, two dogs nibbling on some biscuits. Cute!
Inquiry: > Eye, ear flipped up. [Nicely detailed]

Comment: Only perfect animal, permitted to nibble on food.

CARD VIII

1. < (8″) Looks like some kind of animal climbing over rocks with lake beneath. Climbing one rock to another. Say, reflection. Good workmanship on that!

Inquiry: Must be sunset. (Why?) Because color of red, reflection, water. [All center color.] Coming to drink I imagine. Evening they usually do. Possibly a log. Supposed to be a Herald . . . someone's coat of arms. [Reaction to color.]

> *Comments*: Very impulsive but deals fairly well with emotions. Striving, ambitious (climbing) and even gets somewhat grandiose (coat of arms).

CARD IX

Colors just look pleasing!

1. < (42″) Just looks like reflection of water. Feel reflects one to another. Can't make out exact figures. Cloud effects. Can't see particular animals. Must be something but don't see it. [Held more than two minutes.] Feel I'm coming up with such dumb answers.

Inquiry: Just another reflection. (Why?) Water in one area and reflection of clouds. Although clouds not that color. Colors are pleasing. Must be able to see something out of this. Can't!

> *Comment*: Emotions (color) too much for her. More or less fails.

CARD X

1. (23″) Almost looks like tide pool with different color coral in it.

Inquiry: [Whole] As if looked into clear water and see things, almost fantasy.

> *Comment*: Some recovery but still very impulsive.

2. Looks like peculiar animals holding up a stick.

> *Comment*: Phallic aggression comes to fore.

3. Blue lobsters or crabs with green claws.

Inquiry: Crabs are blue but see shapes with green claws.

> *Comment*: Force affect but some insight (color forced into inaccurate form context).

4. Fish

Inquiry: Yellow fish, coral beds with water coming through.

> *Comment*: Recovers to demonstrate social maturity and tact (good use of color).

(a) Green worms. Couple of eyes and horns. (What?) A little rabbit (laughs).

(b) This way could be man doing a dance with pieces of chiffon, silk—pure silk—light that would float, man's arms over head.
(c) Could be deer leaping from here to here.

Comment (a, b, c): Highly original, different way of looking at concept, and breaks through with good interpersonal if *male* identifications (repressed, comes through only additionally).

General Comments

Relates to people in inhibited, stilted fashion. Her affect is forced but she has some awareness of this. Although at times she tends to be vigorously aggressive, and can be foxy and hostile in her very agreeableness, she feels withered, helpless, and a fallen woman. Very impulsive, she generally does not handle her emotions well although she demonstrates her resiliency in her ability to snap back and even be productive and socially mature. A chronically anxious and depressed person with self-destructive fantasies, she still has potentially superior, creative, and even interpersonal skills which she suppresses unless she can feel more acceptably "masculine."

TAT

CARD 2

Looks like a farm, they're sowing the fields. This girl probably a school girl going off to . . . Oh, you want it dramatic (spontaneous). This is the mother, this man young . . . Imagine young couple in love with each other. Mother here obviously pregnant and the man looks rather young and muscular. Think love between the two but mother does not approve of because girl wishes more education and he tilling fields. Girl her daughter, possibly, say she does not approve of daughter marrying this man. Probably she will marry him, looks calm, poised, and knows what she wants. Looks like land good farm, lead good life, looks like good soil, plenty of acreage. Girl looks pretty sensitive for farm girl with her hands.

Comment: Sensitive girl but self-willed and rebellious towards mother who disapproves of her marriage. Optimistic outcome.

CARD 3

Looks like woman very dejected. Looks like some pistol or something. Maybe trying to shoot herself and wasn't able to do it. She collapsed, did not kill herself but did not know where to go. Looks like woman but man's hand. Great dejection, almost looks like in institution. (Dejected?) Wouldn't know. (Why?) Looks like had utter, complete exhaustion—too many things. (What?) Looks like hadn't much pleasure in life, worked hard, rough simple clothes. Does not see much future. Probably ultimately make up mind what to do—won't kill self. Does not really solve it.

Comment: Suicidal theme. Sex confusion. Dejection to the point of mental illness. Not much pleasure from life. No suicide but does not know what to do.

CARD 4

Not very good stories. (What?) Looks like scene in movie—actor and actress. She would probably like him to do something but he probably has goals, at least in movie that he has things to do. She does not disagree and she understands but there is more or less of a parting, but don't think permanent. Send some place special if job to do but he'll return. Just talking it over. Love and understanding between them.

Comment: Separation, love and understanding, but all distanciated by movie.

CARD 6

Two people. He in love with her, probably told her, except he wouldn't have pipe in his mouth. She rather surprised, has known him for some time. Agreement but surprise. Rather masculine type, good looking. Or possibly could be asking what he could do for her, bending over couch. (Mutual agreement?) Yes, but she surprised. Great interest on his part.

Comment: Older man, friend, not husband (father?), loves her. She surprised but goes along with it.

CARD 8BM

Looks like operating on someone. Must be during underground. Looks like gun down here. Underground movement. Can't figure this (figure in foreground). Must be thieves or someone shot in burglary and they're removing bullet, and this other man looking on to see that they're not interrupted. Cannot tell what outcome—they're digging in abdomen but think he survives. (Technical explanation by her demonstrating why it is not a serious wound.) Such an odd face. (Why?) Don't like face, like someone with abnormal glandular, out of proportion.

Comment: Wrongdoing leads to abdominal surgery leads to OK outcome but feeling of being wrong glandularly. Serious projection thinking.

CARD 7GF

One woman seems to be hiding behind a tree watching another woman meet somebody. Tide coming in and she does not have time. Rushing to spot to meet. Other woman has been waiting (explained by book, etc.). Woman running, not happy about it. (Why?) Strain and suspicion. Could be this woman in love with whoever other woman's gonna meet. This other woman not eager (Why?) Because might know this other woman's wife (sic). Probably wrong relationship and she knows it. Does not want to make other woman unhappy, might be friends and know each other, woman there. (Outcome?) All right. Wife sees other woman is gonna terminate it.

Comment: One woman stealing husband of a friend—anxiety, strain for both. Guilt, does not want to hurt, and terminates affair.

CARD 10

Looks like two people in love, embracing. Seem to be mutually satisfied and relaxed. Woman very dependent on man. Can't see man's mouth or her mouth. Could be close friends, or lovers relaxed in each other's presence, and congenial, no strain, and everything all right.

Comment: Love, mutual satisfaction, relaxation—not married.

CARD 12

Looks like man lying down not sleeping, resting. His father gonna brush a lock of hair from his forehead, does not want him to know it, just responsive gentleness. Young man relaxed and tired. Maybe just want to touch him, been away for some time. (What else?) Or could be someone hypnotized. No, other.

Comment: Father responsive, loving, and gentle. Son relaxed and tired, away for long time.

CARD 13MF

He does not look very happy. Guess things did not turn out way he thought they would. Say some marital relationship and man not up to it, upset him. She certainly looks voluptuous enough (said with pleasure). (Outcome?) He is disappointed, possibly. Can't see whether he's young or old. Say would be someone want to have sex relationships if not able to function well sexually. So this particular result disastrous—would say it did not work out well.

Comment: First time a marital situation—does not work out well. Man impotent. Pessimistic.

General Comments

Very depressed record. Sensitive person with feelings of love and warmth but unable to express except in situations incurring guilt and self-punishing features. Very Oedipal, complicated by identification or unconscious fantasy to be son because that is more acceptable way of being loved by father.

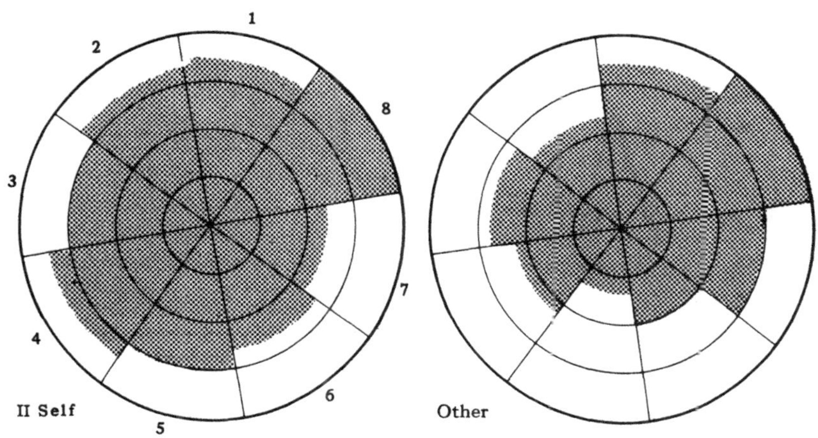

ICL

Gross distortion of self and way other people see her (tremendously exaggerated octants.) Does not know what to make of herself and only slightly more able to present better picture of what others think of her (others). Essentionally superresponsible person (8) who is conflicted between need for attention and dominance (upper half) and being liked (right Hemisphere).

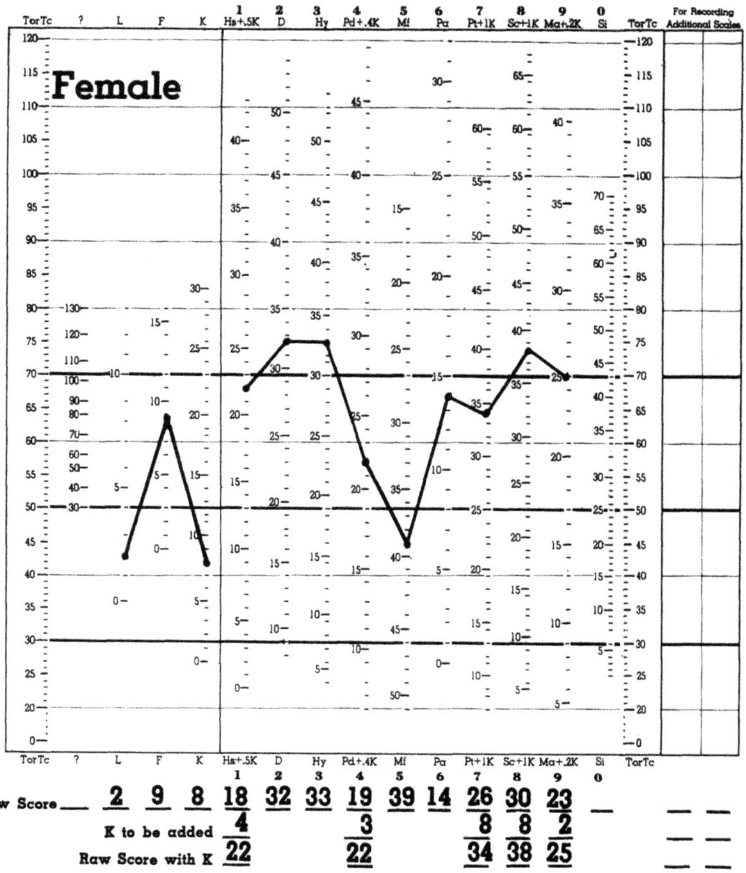

MMPI

Marked components of hysteria and depression (D,Hy). Hypersensitive person feeling very different (F,Sc) and helpless (K,Mf). Masculine protest extreme (Mf).

Question of severe character disorder rather than neurotic diagnosis (because bimodal profile and relatively low Pt and high Pa). (Sourness Hs, Rebellion F,Sc and open hostility Hs, Ma).

APPENDIX 10

MISS FANTASY
CHAPTER TEN

TEST DATA
AND INTERVIEW

Psychological Tests*

RORSCHACH

CARD I

1. (15″) Remind me of a person who has hold over me. Person who says they like me but they hate me. They almost kind of laugh at you, have control of you in every corner of your being.
Inquiry: Whole face in here, she has "ram-ish look," eyes, nose, mouth with sneer, horns out here, little feelers that come out. It's definitely her, horns and feelers dominate her. (Woman?) Nothing in blot, I've just seen more women like that. (Explained responses, asked about bat.) No bat, just ugly monster with face here (same response). (Anything else?) No, I can see their face.

CARD II

1. (20″) It's two broken hearts of two people. They're very unhappy, completely shattered. On top are two whole hearts of people that shattered them. Their whole life will be empty now. They tried to

* Since the bulk of the test battery was administered by a psychologist under the supervision of the writer, the interview notes and association to the tests other than MMPI, and ICL are not available. However, the interview is largely incorporated in the psychology report in the section "Behavior, Interview." References to the author's interpretations of the other test material are made in the therapy notes.

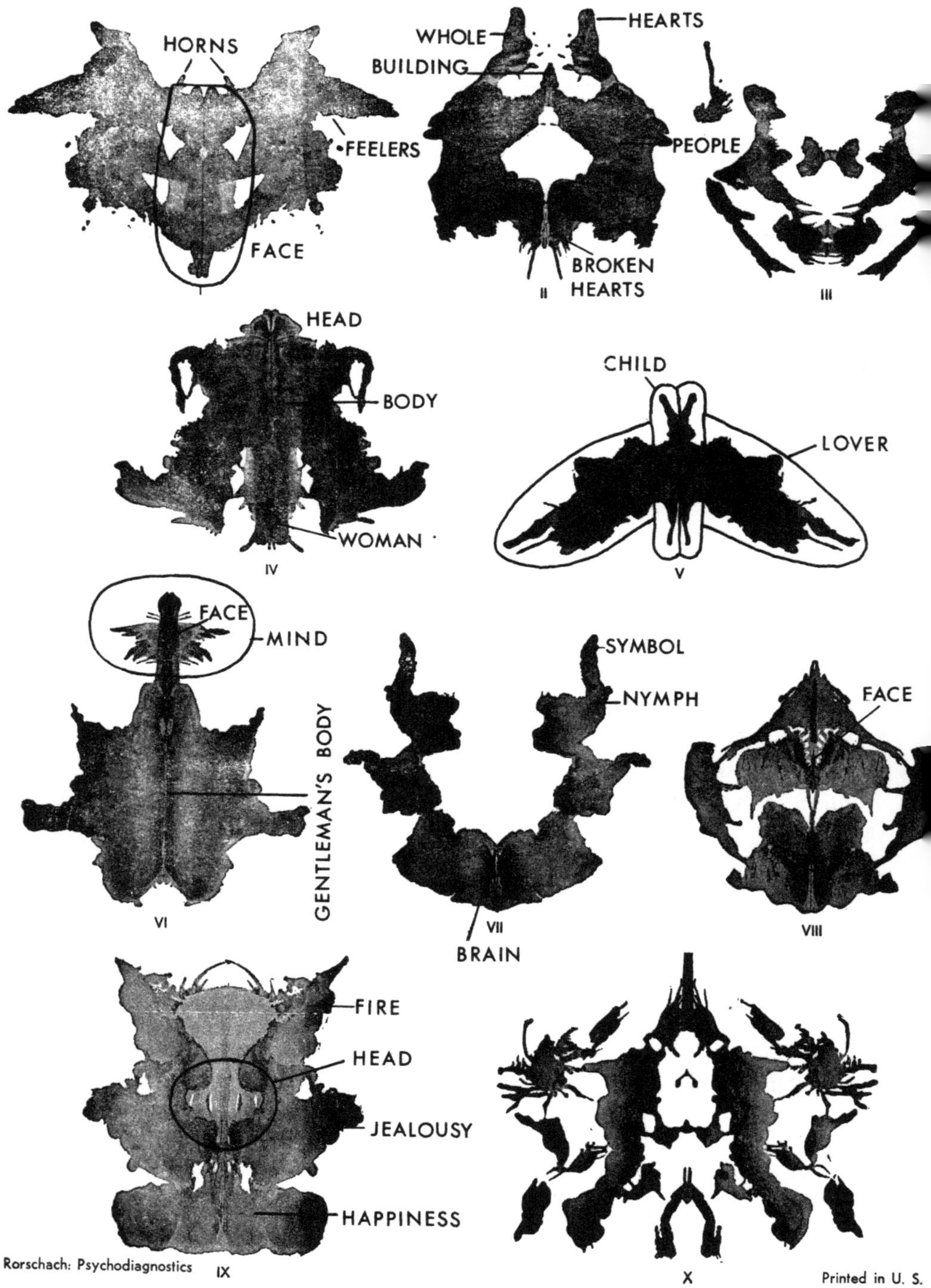
HORNS
FEELERS
FACE
WHOLE
HEARTS
BUILDING
PEOPLE
BROKEN HEARTS
II
III
HEAD
BODY
WOMAN
IV
CHILD
LOVER
V
FACE
MIND
GENTLEMAN'S BODY
VI
SYMBOL
NYMPH
BRAIN
VII
FACE
VIII
FIRE
HEAD
JEALOUSY
HAPPINESS
Rorschach: Psychodiagnostics
IX
X
Printed in U. S.

stay together but they couldn't, people who shattered them were too powerful, from every side. They almost had perfect union till those people came along. It was really going good.
Inquiry: Broken hearts down here at bottom. It's heart shaped and broken down center, and these two are people trying to build something up here, and this is empty void in center. Other two were broken, see blood all spilled over them. (Showed black representation.) Yes, it looks as much like it, can see everything in it.

CARD III

1. (2″) Those are two people who delight in hurting other people. Telling each other how many people they hurt today, how many lies. They keep trophy, pieces of broken hearts. Bragging about when can do more, one has power, other has charm. They even hang pieces of broken heart up on wall. And they have sacks to carry them in.
Inquiry: (Sex?) Each one is both man and woman. (How?) Have woman's breast and man's sexual organ. Woman's face and man's hair. Long neck and muscled arms. Can't see these are shattered hearts because they have lost form. These are sacks for weapons, weapons are power, charm, beauty. They have determined look, do what they want without thinking of anyone else, no softness or roundness about it.

CARD IV

1. (5″) That's man and he's ashamed because he can't solve his mind. Hurts people without meaning to because needs something for his ego. Sort of Jekyll and Hyde, has to show part of self not usually there to get people to see him. Needs this person to help him be man but will hurt them if he does. So wants to stay in airplane or somewhere far away where he'll never have to see anybody again.
Inquiry: Has man's build with unfolding arms, boyish-type crewcut, makes big impression, big stance. This is thing he's impressing, she isn't much, she's under him. Needs her under there so he can stand up like that and be masterful, not powerful enough to do it by himself. (What?) That's one of his women without power, he knows they're below him. (Looks like woman?) Well, small and slim, could have woman's apparel on, unassuming next to him.

CARD V

1. (5″) This is two lovers who can never be together because of children of one of them. Whenever they're together images of children

come to their mind. They come to certain point and children are there, which is silly, but it happens to them. They can't have anyone else but they can't have each other either.
Inquiry: Those two are lovers who can't join because children are between. They're crosswise, when children grow, they'll grow this way (up and down) so they'll never get together. (Lovers?) Outline of two heads, body, legs, reclining, can see they want and need each other.

CARD VI

1. (10″) This is fighter who was born with very powerful body, very gentle, sensitive man and good looks. Doesn't want to fight but body compels him to, and loves applause. Would like to be artist, loves nature, poetry, acting, but being sensitive is ruled by manager who won't let him out. But won't be great fighter because of mind, won't be challenged to do well, and will fight small fights until he ends up as waiter. Could be great artist if used will power to forget body.
Inquiry: This is big, powerful body. As it goes up it gets thinner, here is artistic mind and unassuming gentle face. Gentleness runs all way down but is outnumbered here by body which compels him to fate.

CARD VII

1. (8″) I think that's my mind, or a mind, seems to be right or wrong part of you. Right is good part to go and work in office, live normal non-Bohemian life. Other side doesn't allow sensation or really living emotion, be governed by society stereotypes, constant fight between symbols, like prizefight between two, only no intermission because person has to live 24 hours.
Inquiry: This down here suggests brain or all things in mind. This is good and bad, pointing in opposite way, up here are symbols they wear, like society and convention. More they fight, weaker mind down here gets, wearing down. Like two consciences. (People?) Like little nymphs in mind.

CARD VIII

1. (5″) That seems to be sample of happiness that's all rosy but doesn't last long. Happiness you dreamed of turn out miserable. Like some god says, "Here, this is what happiness tastes like." You get taste and then gray comes down. Surprising how fast the pink happiness can turn to gray.
Inquiry: Pink is happiness but only sample, because you can see it

leaves so quickly to go up and join grays and dull blues. Just taste of clean parts before they join all that's dirty. (Objects, people, animals?) Face in here sucking pink out and filling it with dirt. That is monster of some people you meet in life. Happiness even climbs out by itself, so it wasn't happiness after all.

CARD IX

1. (10″) This is woman who is very jealous, so very jealous it burns her like fire, ever-consuming everything else about her. When she's burned it out, she'll have to go out and look for some pink place, sample of happiness, and turn it into green and gray of anxiety, fear, and emotion. She'll have to do this all her life because she's hollow like a zombie, consumed by flame of jealousy.
Inquiry: Woman in middle, nose, hollow eyes, green-tinged head. When breathes, breathes out green jealousy that turns to fire, and here is little bit of happiness. She's contaminating. Just see her head.

CARD X

1. (8″) This is the building of a person and all the little vermin of people who had to put hand into building him. This person was nothing so even people who were very little came to put in their dominating, envy, evil, and other bad things. But with all this still not complete, could be two heads, one of insanity, one of conventional living. When head is put on little vermin will dance because of their contribution. (Choose head?) They'll try one head, put it on and beat at it, if it falls off, they'll choose other one. If it stays that means it can weather things.
Inquiry: Person just this little bit in background, gray and shadowy. All these are vermin, some that crush, some pull both ways. Here are things that look just alike—and they are alike, conformity and insanity.

TAT

CARD 1

He wants to be violinist. This a Stravinsky violin or something. He stole it and had taken it to his clubhouse but now he's afraid to play it and afraid of what will happen. But when he looks at it, forgets all that because it's so beautiful. (What kind of boy?) Mixed-up, wants to be violinist but doesn't want to be sissy. Lets hair grow too long, gets messy, and can rough it up with boys. Keep yearning to be violinist and himself. (How stole?) On display in museum, didn't plan it ahead, just saw it and had to take it. (What happens?) He'll break it, if he can't have it no one else will either. It'll make him go down in history for having broken so famous a violin, he'll do it out in the woods. (History?) Well, within himself. Everyone else will think vandals did it but he'll know why . . . He loves it, unobtainable but so close.

Card 3BM

Oh! (sighs) yes. She's had this boy friend and he was getting divorce from wife, annulled. She loved him now more than anything, never thought she could love until she met him, so she did everything for him, even cut her hair. He was a fighter, hadn't fought for a while, she went to see him and he won. This was bad because then wife would want him back. Saw him backstage and he was nice to her. But next day in paper said he had gone back East to rejoin wife, so now all is lost, she is just back where she started. Lying there wondering, her hand says, "What's the use?" She had very bad life, for once there was a chance. (What will happen now?) Maybe become prostitute. She's thought of suicide but hasn't courage to take the final step. (Why?) Prostitute is old way to get back at world without being physically lonely. Probably be good one too, maybe call girl. And that way she can send money to him without his knowing, to the gym.

Card 2

Oh. This is a girl who is very undecided. She's in school studying for career but doesn't want to work as everybody's telling her. They all say, "Work, work, don't marry." She sees through everyone around her who is working so hard and running away from themselves. She has very odd mother in background; whenever she thinks of stopping work, the image of her mother comes in, doesn't want to be like mother. But she wants to love, so when she works, she is unhappy. So she leaves it and she doesn't know what to do, through with working and with home, takes everything, sells some things for money, leaves family just when they need her most, when mother is most odd. Nice to leave people kinda gasping when they need you, makes you free, like coming up out of quicksand. Don't think she becomes prostitute, maybe goes to Europe, to Riviera, becomes great lady of evening, earns enough in six months to take off other six to quieter countries where maybe looks for husband. Doesn't lose capacity to love this way.

CARD 4

Hmm. This is a man who is very undecided. He's a very good man and because he's good, he seems to get in more difficulties than anyone else. He's married, this is his wife. She's very mean, married him because he has name in his profession. They have little boy. He wants to leave, has left twice before, but comes back because boy needs father and all that. Wants to leave again, she's just said something crushing that deflated his ego. But she only needs to say kind things to build him up again, he's like child in need of praise and feeling of worth. But she doesn't care a bit, she even has romances on side. (Why?) I just don't like her, she just doesn't care. Terrible to see someone so good being hurt like he is. (Outcome?) Maybe when he's older, he'll become more mature and think that staying and quarreling is worse for boy than divorce. I hope so. If she treated him like this for so long and he didn't mature, might turn to alcohol or narcotics for support. That would be terrible because he's so good.

CARD 6BM

Oh, I think this man wants to marry this woman's daughter and she's a little off. Has great hate and fear against all men because her marriage was so bad. Afraid he'll be woman chaser or drinker, and her daughter will be as bad off as she. But man doesn't see this at all, he's a little off because so religious, doesn't even like lipstick or anything, very rigid, goes through religious routines everyday. He's shocked, first crushed, self-esteem lowered because thinks he's so good. When walks down street thinks he's example of what good man should be. And mother is just crushed that daughter should want to marry after all things she taught her—so they're both practically hypnotized with shock now. (What happens?) Believe mother will go completely off and have to go into a home. Marriage won't take place because daughter will have to see him as he is in spite of his disturbingly good looks. She'll go away to another city. He meets homosexual and becomes homosexual but religion becomes more extreme and ridiculous. Homosexuality on high artistic level, woman didn't understand, but God granted him another man who did.

CARD 9GF

Oh. Girl in tree, she has Lesbian tendencies but doesn't practice them because feels she is very ugly, on inside not outside, would repel anybody she likes and so stays alone. Goes out on beach to be alone and see lovers playing. Doesn't notice man but woman is everything she wanted to be, good-looking, good figure, sparkles, and she wonders if she would have relationship with this woman if some of this would rub off. Doesn't want to do this but doesn't want to be alone either. Girl symbolizes youth and beauty but woman is angry because she doesn't seem to be fully aware of it and appreciate it, when she has never known such a moment. Thinks joys of life always given to ignorant who can't see it, annoys her that for this girl is only one moment of many. If it were she, she'd go home and write plenty about it. (Contact?) No, she goes home, never have strength to approach anyone. If approached first she might.

Card 12M

This is this boy's father. Father has always been good to him, too good, so good he had to be bad. Father didn't live with him, parents divorced, brought him everything, presents, everything but understanding. Boy very afraid of father, held up to him like a god, if he were to do something bad, father won't come anymore. Boy has had sadistic dreams father comes and attacks him or does something obscene sexually to him. Like fool he tells mother, and she says if he thinks this way father will leave him. One night father comes, he and mother have few drinks and talk of this, decide to play practical joke. Father creeps up to sleeping boy, touches him, leaning over with lecherous grin, mother in corner looking eerie. Boy wakes up, screams and cries, and runs out of house. Wakes up in police station, they think he is drunk. Mother comes down and still with sadistic gleam in her eyes says he's had a few drinks. So boy puzzled, doesn't know what happened, goes back to live with mother under same conditions as before. (Why?) They were a little high and like to tease boy—he's adolescent, neither man or boy, and they're both unstable. Both weak, father not sure of self, neither too intelligent, bored with their lives, meant it as practical joke, didn't mean to hurt him.

Card 12BG

This about girl who's never done much in her life and boy has started to be interested in her. Boy wanted to take her for ride in boat, she'd never been in one before. For first time, could truly say, "I am happy." But was very frightened because when you say this great unhappiness not very far away. Went home, he phoned every night, then one night said he'd gotten tired of her. This wasn't fair, to sample happiness and not be able to keep it. She wasn't lady, lacked sophistication and polish. They had much in common, shared much with each other, so she thought he might wait for her to catch up but he didn't. It was just a glance of happiness (?) She wasn't sure of herself, was higher person than those she grew up with, but not as high as those she wanted to associate with, so she almost had to stay alone. (What now?) Have to keep on living until another glimpse that will make life harder again. Could be suicide, but now just drifting. Resents ladies now.

CARD 13MF

This is a man who's just been unfaithful to wife for first time, with virgin who didn't care, wanted to lose virginity. She built him up, made him feel good—he taught her things about wines, read her palm, other things, just had fun. Now this guilt about wife, it's on paper that they're married, thinks that he should go back to wife, knows she's right for him but it can't be. So he'll go into next room and cut self to death with razor, but first will probably kill her because knows it more painful for her to lose him than to die in sleep. So he'll kill her, sit there and hold her hand as he's dying. But first he'll burn the Bible. (Wife?) She's no good, doesn't care, not enlightened, he brings money home, she has no concept of love and what marriage could be. Has gotten frowzy and slovenly, but he thinks because she's his wife he's chained to her for life.

WAIS

Raw Score	Scaled Score
Information 19	12
Comprehension 20	12
Similarities 20	13
Digit Symbol 54	10
Picture Completion 11	8
Block Design 28	9

Verbal PR IQ 114 Performance PR IQ 93 Full PR IQ 105

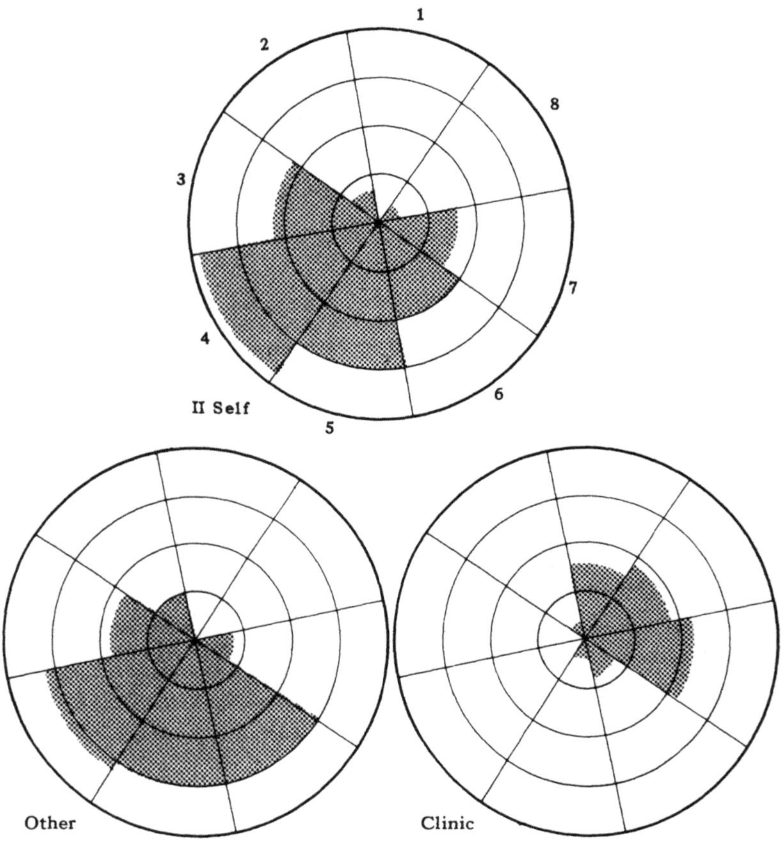

ICL

Exaggerated sense of weakness and helplessness (stress on lower half). Suspicion and distrust of others to paranoid extent (4 in *both* Self and Other). Masochism (5). Wants sympathetic, strong other person to relate to (Clinic right and upper hemisphere respectively).

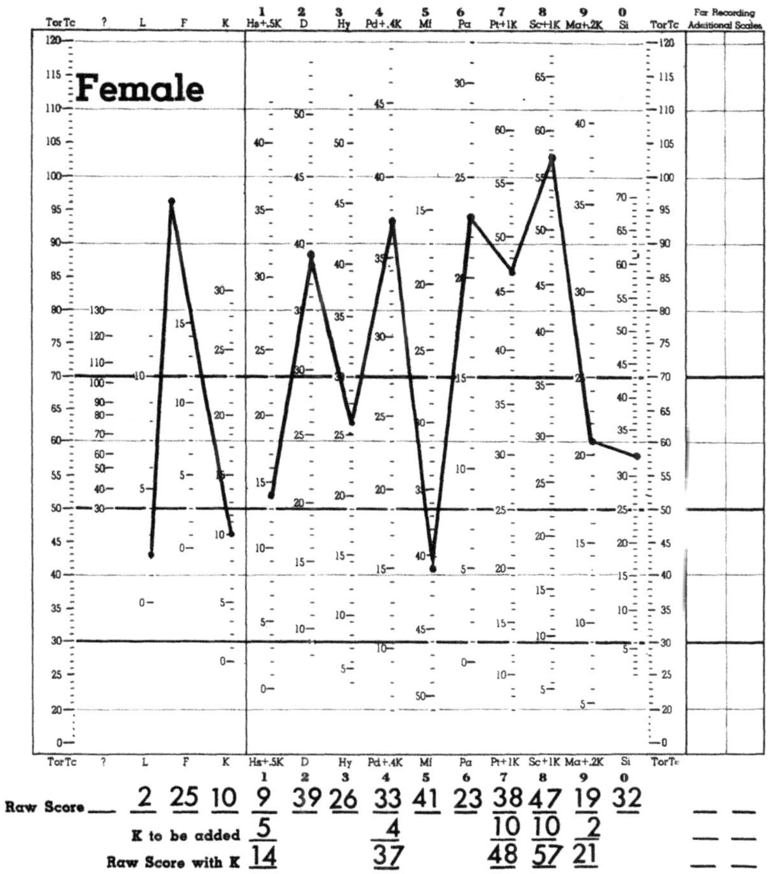

MMPI

See how terribly sick and helpless I am (entire, extremely exaggerated "floating" profile) (Pd,Mf).

Psychotic features not gross, or they are well contained. (Hs, Hy, and Ma within normal bounds, 50-70. It may be conjectured that these very tendencies must be defended against and are really the trouble spots.)

BIBLIOGRAPHY

1. Abt, L. E. and Bellak, L. *Projective Psychology,* New York: Alfred Knopf Co., 1952.

2. Anderson, H. and Anderson, G. *An Introduction to Projective Techniques.* New York: Prentice Hall, 1951.

3. Armstrong, R. and Harrick, P. "Sexual Identification and the First Figure Drawn," *J. Consult. Psychol.* (1961) *25,* 51-59.

4 Blank, Leonard. "Suggestions for Research with Projective Techniques," *J. Proj. Tech.* (1958) *22,* 263-264.

5. Blank, Leonard. "The Intellectual Functioning of Delinquents" *J. Soc. Psychol.* (1958) *47,* 9-14.

6. Dahlstrom, W. G. and Welsh, G. S. *An-MMPI Handbook.* Minneapolis: University of Minnesota Press, 1960.

7. Harris, R. E. & Lingoes, J. "Subscales for the MMPI: An Aid to Profile Interpretation." (Unpub. Manuscript) Langley Porter Clinic, San Francisco, 1955.

8. Hammer, Emmanuel. *The Clinical Application of Projective Drawings.* Springfield: Chas. Thomas Co., 1958.

9. Hathaway, S. & McKinley, J. *Minnesota Multiphasic Personality Inventory: Manual* (rev. ed.). New York: Psychological Corporation, 1951.

10. Healy, W. & Bronner, A. *The Structure and Meaning of Psychoanalysis.* New York: Alfred Knopf, 1930.

11. Holtzman, W. *Inkblot Perception and Personality.* Austin: University of Texas Press, 1961.

12. Klopfer, Bruno, et al. *Developments in the Rorschach Technique.* New York: World Book Co., 1954. Vols. 1 and 2.

13. Knight, Robert (ed.). *Psychoanalysis, Psychiatry and Psychology.* New York: International University Press, 1954. Vol. 1.

14. Laforge, Rolfe & Suczek, R. "The Interpersonal Dimensions of Personality 3: An interpersonal checklist," *J. Pers.* (1955) *24,* 94-112.

15. Leary, Timothy. *Interpersonal Diagnosis of Personality.* New York: Ronald Press, 1956.

16. Machover, Karen. *Personality Projection in the Drawing of the Human Figure.* Springfield: Chas. Thomas, 1949.

17. Piotrowski, Z. A. *Perceptanalysis.* New York: The Macmillan Co., 1957.

18. Rapaport, David. *Diagnostic Psychological Testing*. Chicago: The Yearbook Publishers, 1945. Vols. 1 and 2.

19. Rapaport, David. "The Theoretical Implications of Diagnostic Testing," in Knight, *Op. cit.*, 173-195.

20. Rapaport, David. "Projective Techniques and the Theory of Testing," in Knight, *Op. cit.*, 196-203.

21. Shafer, Roy. "Psychological Tests in Clinical Research," in Knight, *Op. cit.*, 204-212.

22. Shafer, Roy. "Content Analysis in the Rorschach Test," in Knight, *Op. cit.*, 213-217.

23. Shafer, Roy. *The Clinical Application of Psychological Tests*. New York: International University Press, 1948.

24. Stolz, R. & Couharp, F. "Clinical Judgements and the DAP," *J. Consult. Psychol.* (1961) 25, 43-45.

25. Zeligs, Meyer. "Acting in," *J. Amer. Psychiat. Assoc.* (1957) 5, 685-706.

For Product Safety Concerns and Information please contact our EU
representative GPSR@taylorandfrancis.com
Taylor & Francis Verlag GmbH, Kaufingerstraße 24, 80331 München, Germany

www.ingramcontent.com/pod-product-compliance
Ingram Content Group UK Ltd.
Pitfield, Milton Keynes, MK11 3LW, UK
UKHW022115190926
475702UK00013B/1450
* 9 7 8 0 2 0 2 3 6 3 2 1 9 *